W9-BSD-053

# THE
# MICHELIN
## GUIDE

## SAN FRANCISCO
### BAY AREA & WINE COUNTRY

**Michelin Travel Partner**
Société par actions simplifiées au capital de 11 288 880 EUR
27 Cours de l'Ile Seguin - 92100 Boulogne Billancourt (France)
R.C.S. Nanterre 433 677 721

© **Michelin, Propriétaires-Éditeurs**

Dépôt légal septembre 2016

Printed in Canada - septembre 2016
Printed on paper from sustainably managed forests

Impression et Finition : Transcontinental (Canada)

# Dear Reader

*I*t's been an exciting year for the entire team at the MICHELIN guides in North America, and it is with great pride that we present you with our 2017 edition to San Francisco, Bay Area & Wine Country. Over the past year our inspectors have extended their reach to include a variety of establishments and multiplied their anonymous visits to restaurants in our selection in order to accurately reflect the rich culinary diversity this great city has to offer.

As part of the Guide's highly confidential and meticulous evaluation process, our inspectors have methodically eaten their way through the entire city, Bay Area, and Wine Country with a mission to marshal the finest in each category for your enjoyment. While they are expertly trained professionals in the food industry, the Guides remain consumer-driven and provide comprehensive choices to accommodate your every comfort, taste, and budget. By dining and drinking as "everyday" customers, they are able to experience and evaluate the same level of service and cuisine as any other guest. This past year has seen some unique advancements in San Francisco's dining scene. Some of these can be found in each neighborhood introduction, complete with photography depicting our favored choices.

Our company's founders, Édouard and André Michelin, published the first MICHELIN guide in 1900, to provide motorists with useful information about where they could service and repair their cars as well as find a good quality meal. In 1926, the star-rating system was introduced, whereby outstanding establishments are awarded for excellence in cuisine. Over the decades we have made many new enhancements to the Guide, and the local team here in San Francisco eagerly carries on these traditions.

As we take consumer feedback seriously, please contact us at: michelin.guides@michelin.com. You may also follow our Inspectors on Twitter (@MichelinGuideSF) and Instagram (@michelininspectors) as they chow their way around town. We thank you for your patronage and truly hope that the MICHELIN guide will remain your preferred reference to San Francisco's restaurants.

# Contents

Dear Reader                                    3
The MICHELIN Guide                             6
How to Use This Guide                          8

## ● Where to **Eat**                                   10

### San Francisco                                  12

▶ **Castro**                                        14
Cole Valley • Haight-Ashbury • Noe Valley

▶ **Civic Center**                                  22
Hayes Valley • Lower Haight • Tenderloin

▶ **Financial District**                            42
Embarcadero • Union Square

▶ **Marina**                                        58
Japantown • Pacific Heights • Presidio

▶ **Mission**                                       74
Bernal Heights • Potrero Hill

▶ **Nob Hill**                                      98
Chinatown • Russian Hill

▶ **North Beach**                                  116
Fisherman's Wharf • Telegraph Hill

▶ **Richmond & Sunset**                            130

▶ **SoMa**                                         144

Contents

| East Bay | 170 |
| Marin | 210 |
| Peninsula | 232 |
| South Bay | 270 |
| Wine Country | 306 |
| ▶ Napa Valley | 306 |
| ▷ Sonoma County | 340 |

## Indexes — 374

| Alphabetical List of Restaurants | 376 |
| Restaurants by Cuisine | 384 |
| Cuisines by Neighborhood | 392 |
| Starred Restaurants | 402 |
| Bib Gourmand | 405 |
| Under $25 | 406 |
| BART map | 414 |

# The MICHELIN Guide

*"This volume was created at the turn of the century and will last at least as long."*

This foreword to the very first edition of the MICHELIN guide, written in 1900, has become famous over the years and the Guide has lived up to the prediction. It is read across the world and the key to its popularity is the consistency in its commitment to its readers, which is based on the following assurances.

### → Anonymous Inspections

Our inspectors make anonymous visits to restaurants to gauge the quality of cuisine offered to the everyday customer. They pay their own bill and make no indication of their presence. These visits are supplemented by comprehensive monitoring of information—our readers' comments are one valuable source, and are always taken into consideration.

### → Independence

Our choice of establishments is a completely independent one, made for the benefit of our readers alone. Decisions are discussed by the inspectors and editor, with the most important considered at the global level. Inclusion in the Guide is always free of charge.

### → The Selection

The Guide offers a selection of the best restaurants in each category of comfort and price. A recommendation in the Guides is an honor in itself, and defines the establishment among the "best of the best."

## → Annual Updates

All practical information, the classifications, and awards, are revised and updated every year to ensure the most reliable information possible.

## → Consistency & Classifications

The standards and criteria for the classifications are the same in all countries covered by the Michelin Guides. Our system is used worldwide and easy to apply when selecting a restaurant.

## → The Classifications

We classify our restaurants using  to indicate the level of comfort. A symbol in red suggests a particularly charming spot with unique décor or ambience. The ✿✿✿-✿ specifically designates an award for cuisine. They do not relate to a chef or establishment and are unique from the classification.

## → Our Aim

As part of Michelin's ongoing commitment to improving travel and mobility, we do everything possible to make vacations and eating out a pleasure.

# How to Use This Guide

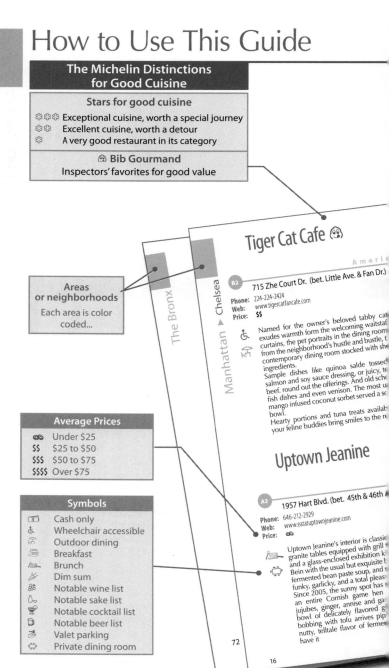

**The Michelin Distinctions
for Good Cuisine**

**Stars for good cuisine**

❀❀❀ Exceptional cuisine, worth a special journey
❀❀ Excellent cuisine, worth a detour
❀ A very good restaurant in its category

🅑 **Bib Gourmand**
Inspectors' favorites for good value

**Areas
or neighborhoods**
Each area is color
coded...

## Average Prices

| ✇ | Under $25 |
|---|---|
| $$ | $25 to $50 |
| $$$ | $50 to $75 |
| $$$$ | Over $75 |

## Symbols

| ▣ | Cash only |
|---|---|
| ⅁ | Wheelchair accessible |
| ⌖ | Outdoor dining |
| ▤ | Breakfast |
| ▥ | Brunch |
| ✗ | Dim sum |
| ஐ | Notable wine list |
| ᷣ | Notable sake list |
| ▽ | Notable cocktail list |
| ▭ | Notable beer list |
| ▨ | Valet parking |
| ✤ | Private dining room |

The Bronx

Manhattan ▶ Chelsea

## Tiger Cat Cafe 🅑

Ameri

**B2** 715 Zhe Court Dr. (bet. Little Ave. & Fan Dr.)

Phone: 224-224-2424
Web: www.tigercatfancafe.com
Price: $$

Named for the owner's beloved tabby cat
exudes warmth form the welcoming waitstaf
curtains, the pet portraits in the dining room
from the neighborhood's hustle and bustle, t
contemporary dining room stocked with she
ingredients.
Sample dishes like quinoa salde tossed
salmon and soy sauce dressing, or juicy, te
beef. round out the offerings. And old scho
fish dishes and even venison. The most u
mango infused coconut sorbet served a so
bowl.
Hearty portions and tuna treats availab
your feline buddies bring smiles to the re

## Uptown Jeanine

**A2** 1957 Hart Blvd. (bet. 45th & 46th

Phone: 646-212-2929
Web: www.eatatuptownjeanine.com
Price: ✇

Uptown Jeanine's interior is classie
granite tables equipped with grill
and a glass-enclosed exhibition ki
Bein with the usual but exquisite b
fermented bean paste soup, and s
funky, garlicky, and a total pleas
Since 2005, the sunny spot has
an entire Cornish game hen
jujubes, ginger, annise and ga
bowl of delicately flavored g
bobbing with tofu arrives pip
nutty, telltale flavor of fermen
have it

72

16

## Restaurant Classifications by Comfort

### More pleasant if in red

| | |
|---|---|
| X | Comfortable |
| XX | Quite comfortable |
| XxX | Very comfortable |
| XxxX | Top class comfortable |
| XxXxX | Luxury in the traditional style |
| ▥ | Small plates |

**Map Coordinates**

# Sonya's Palace ✿

Italian    XxxX

**A4**

**100 Reuther Pl. (at 30th St.)**

Dinner Mon – Sat

Subway: 23rd St (Eighth Ave.)
Phone: 917-222-1155
Web: www.sonyasfabulouspalace.com
Price: $$$$

Home cooked Italian never tasted so good than in this pretentious palace. The decor claims no big name designers, and while the Murano glass light fixtures are chic and the velveteen-covered chairs are comfortable, this isn't a restaurant where millions of dollars were spent on the interior.

Instead, food is the focus here. THe restaurant's name may not be Italian, but it nonetheless serves some of the best pasta in the city, made fresh in-house. Dishes follow the seasons, thus ravioli maybe stuffed with fresh ricotta and herbs in summer, and pumpkin in fall. Most everyting is liberally dusted with Parmigiano Reggiano, a favorite ingredient of the chef. Start meals with an immaculately fresh caprese salad, then sample a crisp pie from the Neapolitan wood-burning pizza oven. One bite of her lasagna, rich with creamy ricotta and hearty Bolognese, will have you cheering "Mamma mia," while oversized portions have some crying "basta!"

For Dessert, you'll have to deliberate between the likes of creamy tiramisu, ricotta cheesecake, and the homemade geltao. One thing's for sure: you'll never miss your nonna's cooking when eat at Sonya's..

17

Manhattan ▶ Chelsea

San Francisco ▶ Nob Hill

▥▥

Lunch daily

ntly

cafe
cafe
spite
asts a
erican

cured
prime
ocktail,
ere is a
shaped

ome for

ean    X

Lunch Tue – Sun
Dinner nightly

cted, thanks to
itilation hoods,
d in the back.
pickled turnips,
d house kimchi,

yetang, featuring
glutinous rice,
an earthenware
. A cloudy soup
asting that sharep,
urd, and seems to

ever,
staff
ing
dly

he
m

107

San Francisco _____ 12
East Bay _____ 170
Marin _____ 210
Peninsula _____ 232
South Bay _____ 270
Wine Country _____ 306

Where to Eat

# San Francisco

# Castro

The Castro, once a cluster of farmland, is today a pulsating community punctuated by chic boutiques, hopping bars, and handsomely restored Victorians. In fact, it's a perpetual party here, with everybody waiting to sample the area's range of shabby to sleek bars and dance clubs that spin tunes from multi-platinum pop icons. To feed its buzzing population of gym bunnies, leather daddies, and out-of-towners on tour to this mecca, the Castro teems with cool cafeterias. Start your day right at **Kitchen Story**, where the mascarpone-stuffed, deep-fried French toast has a following as large as the district's diversity. Then, stop in at **Thorough Bread & Pastry** if only to watch their

bakers craft the best almond croissant in town. Linger at **Café Flore**, whose quaint patio is more evocative of its Parisian namesake than the simple continental fare. And primo for a quick lunch, the original **Rosamunde Sausage Grill** serves a variety of sandwiches like those stuffed with links of wild boar, cheddar brat, and chicken habanero. Counter seats are limited, so grab your sausage and head next door to enjoy it with a pint at **Toronado**. While gourmands may prefer the likes of **La Mediterranee** for worthwhile cuisine, word on the street is that the best flavors here are served on the run. In fact, look no further than the kitschy kiosk **Hot Cookie** for that ideal bit of sweet.

## COLE VALLEY

Neighboring Cole Valley may be small in size, but flaunts huge personality. Cradling a mix of yuppies and families, this snoot-free quarter also embraces global flavors as seen in purveyors like **Say Cheese**, filled with quality international varieties. On Monday nights, dog-lovers treat the whole family to dinner at **Zazie**. Equally fun is a visit to **Val de Cole**, a wine shop offering value table wines to go with a delish dinner. The back garden patio at quaint **Cafe Reverie** is a stroller-friendly

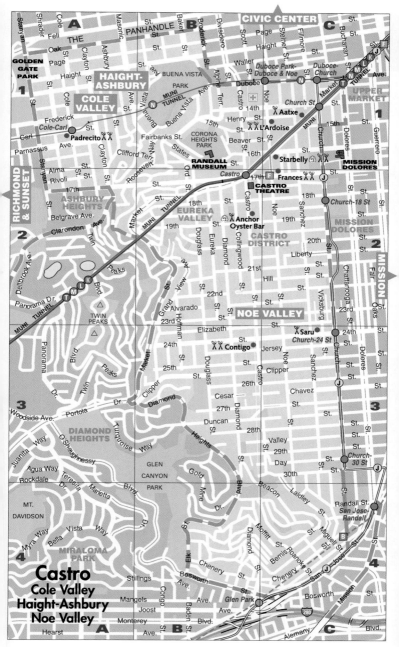

Castro
Cole Valley
Haight-Ashbury
Noe Valley

favorite, **Parada 22** for authentic *pernil asado*; or **Cha Cha Cha**, a groovy tapas bar flowing with fresh-fruit sangria. Nurse that hangover with greasy hash browns and hotcakes at **Pork Store Cafe**, or head to **Haight Street Market** for a ready-made gourmet feast. On game night, kick back with a pint and plate of wings at old-school **Kezar Pub**.

## NOE VALLEY

Noe Valley is known for its specialty shops, and Italian emporium **Pasta Gina** sells everything you might need for a night in with *nonna*. **Noe Valley Bakery** bakes the best bread around, after which a pour of coffee from **Castro Coffee Company** is a must. Imported chocolates are front and center at **Chocolate Covered**, while **Marcello's** is *the* hub for fast, fab pizza. Keeping pace with this sense of "spirit," **Swirl on Castro** is a sleek space that is big on boutique wines. But, if booze doesn't fit your mood, then head for a soothing brew at **Spike's Coffees & Teas**, specializing in artisan loose-leaf teas.

spot for a snack, whereas the 1930's throwback **Ice Cream Bar** with a soda fountain and lunch counter is mobbed by hipsters. Counter-culturalists have long sought haven in the hippiefied Haight-Ashbury where, despite the onslaught of retail chains, smoke shops and record stores still dominate the landscape. And yet, **IndoVino** continues to thrive as a favored wine bar among locals and visitors for its tasty Italian small plates and an interesting selection of—you guessed it—*vino*. The Valley's aversion to fine dining and adoration for laid-back spots is further evident in lines that snake out the door of Puerto Rican

# Aatxe

Spanish ✗

**2174 Market St. (bet. 14th & 15th Sts.)**

**Phone:** 415-471-2977
**Web:** www.aatxesf.com
**Price:** $$

Dinner nightly

The name is pronounced "ahh-chay" and the food is pronounced "delicious" at this Spanish charmer, where *pintxos* like *boquerones* with green olive, smoked salmon deviled eggs, and chanterelle *croquetas* taste straight out of San Sebastián. Keep it classic with shrimp *al ajillo*, bathed in sizzling garlic-chili oil, or try the adventurous "Spanish fried rice," a take on paella packed with smoky chorizo, tender cuttlefish, and nuggets of tortilla Española.
Set in the historic Swedish-American Hall, the small, modern art-packed space has an open kitchen and a thumping, clubby vibe—it's not the place for quiet conversation. But thanks to the well-curated menu of gin and tonics (a Spanish favorite), it's ideal for letting loose and having fun.

# Anchor Oyster Bar 😳

Seafood ✗

**579 Castro St. (bet. 18th & 19th Sts.)**

**Phone:** 415-431-3990
**Web:** www.anchoroysterbar.com
**Price:** $$

Lunch Mon – Sat
Dinner nightly

Landlubbers seeking a taste of the sea can be found pulling up a stool at this Castro institution, where waves of waiting diners spill out the doors. This tiny, minimally adorned space filled with old-fashioned charm is better for twosomes than groups. While the menu may be petite, it's full of fresh fare like a light and flavorful Dungeness crab "burger" on a sesame bun; Caesar salad combining sweet prawns and tangy anchovy dressing; or a cup of creamy Boston clam chowder loaded with clams and potatoes. As the name portends, raw oysters are a specialty, so briny that the accompanying mignonette may not be necessary. And of course, the cioppino is unmissable as this signature item turns deadly when paired with delicious and buttery garlic bread.

# Contigo

Spanish ✗✗

**B3**

1320 Castro St. (bet. 24th & Jersey Sts.)

**Phone:** 415-285-0250                    Dinner Tue – Sun
**Web:** www.contigosf.com
**Price:** $$

Contigo continues to flourish as a meeting spot among Noe Valley residents, and you'll want to bring some of your favorite people along to linger in this Iberian charmer's warm and bustling dining room. Sustainability is a watchword here: the design incorporates recycled materials and each dish reflects the season's best ingredients.

Although not as inspired as it once was, the food is still consistently good, and tempts with caramelized *coca* (flatbread) with garlicky *txistorra*, pickled shallots, figs, and Manchego. Simple yet tasty offerings go on to feature slices of levain topped with smashed peas and roasted porcinis. Finally, the pork-lamb-*jamón* meatballs in a tomato-sherry sauce are among the best *albondigas* you'll find in town.

# Frances

Californian ✗✗

**C2**

3870 17th St. (at Pond St.)

**Phone:** 415-621-3870                    Dinner nightly
**Web:** www.frances-sf.com
**Price:** $$

This tiny, intensely personal restaurant from Chef/owner Melissa Perello has been a neighborhood hit from the get-go. Chic, cozy, and perpetually packed, it's as perfect for a low-key date night as it is for dinner with the kids. And while reservations are a nigh-impossible score, the gracious staff saves ten counter seats for walk-ins—and serves every diner with equal aplomb.

Perello eschews trendy powders and foams for hearty, seasonal fare, like bacon beignets with maple-chive crème fraîche, vibrant spinach and green garlic soup with black pepper cookies, and pan-seared wild trout with sunchokes and spiced yogurt. An array of exquisite desserts, like buttermilk panna cotta with strawberries, offers a fresh, light conclusion.

19

# L'Ardoise

**C1**

### 151 Noe St. (at Henry St.)

**Phone:** 415-437-2600

**Web:** www.ardoisesf.com

**Price:** $$

Dinner Tue – Sat

Local couples do date night in high Parisian style at this long-running Duboce Triangle bistro, where a largely French staff serves up classics like coq au vin and steak frites. The seafood *cassolette* brings together plump prawns, huge mussels, and flaky fish over a bed of mashed potatoes, then swaths them in a velvety lobster bisque reduction. A floating island of caramelized meringue is especially indulgent when served in a pool of crème anglaise with strawberries and caramel sauce.

Set on a charming, tree-lined block, L'Ardoise's secret weapon is its softly lit back area, whose rich burgundy walls draw in diners. Given the compact space and subdued ambience, save this one for a tête-à-tête, not a big group.

# Padrecito

**A1**

### 901 Cole St. (at Carl St.)

**Phone:** 415-742-5505

**Web:** www.padrecitosf.com

**Price:** $$

Lunch Fri – Sun
Dinner nightly

Like its sib Mamacita, this easygoing cantina serves modern Cal-Mex food crafted with excellent, locally sourced ingredients. Padrecito bears a bohemian, south-of-the-border spirit with a buzzy cocktail bar that pours a remarkable list of tequilas. Its dining room is rife with reclaimed wood, but climb a few colorful steps to arrive in the lovely mezzanine decked in chandeliers glinting over the main room.

Adept, smiling servers whirl around diners cradling such specials as *sopa Azteca*, a purée of ancho chilies and tomato bobbing with tender *queso* Oaxaca and avocado; or grilled Arctic char tacos sauced with crimson-red achiote and crowned with mango-jicama slaw. Warm, sugary churros with mascarpone-coffee *crema* offer *mucho* fulfillment.

# Saru

Japanese ✗

**C3**

3856 24th St. (bet. Sanchez & Vicksburg Sts.)

**Phone:** 415-400-4510
**Web:** www.akaisarusf.com
**Price:** $$

Lunch & dinner Tue – Sun

Hilly, idyllic Noe Valley is the perfect setting for this little jewel of a sushi restaurant, whose L-shaped counter and handful of tables are always full. The menu is thoroughly Japanese, with a few quirky California touches—think grilled shishito peppers tossed with ribbons of crunchy daikon in a ponzu dressing.

Be sure to start with the perfectly sized tasting spoons, two tiny helpings of rotating specials like tuna tartare with *yuzu kosho* or monkfish liver with grated radish and scallions. Though rolls are available, regulars opt for the excellent nigiri, which might include marinated wild sardines, soy-kissed *madai*, and creamy uni. If you'd like the chefs to choose, several omakase (including an all-salmon variation) are also on offer.

# Starbelly 🙂

Californian ✗✗

**C1**

3583 16th St. (at Market St.)

**Phone:** 415-252-7500
**Web:** www.starbellysf.com
**Price:** $$

Lunch & dinner daily

The simplest things are often the best, as a meal at Starbelly deliciously proves. Whether you're twirling a forkful of garlicky tomato spaghetti with jalapeños and house-made bacon, or squeezing a lime wedge over exquisite cornmeal-crusted fish tacos with spicy cabbage slaw, you're sure to savor something beautifully made, seasonal, and unfussy. Even an old-school sticky toffee cake is elevated with fresh Medjool dates and tangy mascarpone.

A nexus of the Castro social scene, the cheerful, wood-paneled space is always full of locals hopping from table to table to greet their friends, and the back patio (heated and sheltered when it's foggy) is an appealing refuge. Be sure to make reservations: this is a local favorite, and for good reason.

# Civic Center

## HAYES VALLEY · LOWER HAIGHT · TENDERLOIN

Anchoring this old, new, and now fashionable district is the gilded beaux arts-style dome of City Hall, whose architectural splendor gleams along the main artery of the Civic Center. Following in these footsteps, refined details grace the neighborhood's prized cultural institutions like the War Memorial & Performing Arts Center, as well as the Asian Art Museum. On Wednesdays and Sundays, SF's oldest market, **Heart of the City**,

ginger and Buddha's hand. Ground zero for California's marriage equality movement and countless political protests, City Hall's plaza is also home to galas like LovEvolution; the SF Symphony's biennial Black & White Ball; as well as the annual St. Patrick's Day parade and festival.

Neighboring Tenderloin successfully alleviates this region's now-defunct repute as a

erupts in full form on the vast promenade outside City Hall. This independent and farmer-operated arcade is a hit among locals thanks to an extensive offering of high-quality, locally sourced, and attractively priced produce—not to mention rare Asian ingredients like young

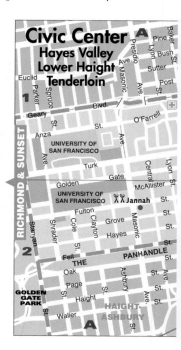

"food desert." Similar, in some ways, to Manhattan's Meatpacking District and home to a vast Asian—particularly Vietnamese—population, this once tough but now trendy "underbelly" boasts an incredible array of authentic ethnic eateries. Gone are those gangs of organized crime, and in place Larkin Street (also known as "**Little Saigon**") is crowded with mom-and-pop shops like **Saigon Sandwich**—leading the way with spicy *báhn mì* made from fresh, crusty baguettes for only $3.75 a pop. Nearby, **Turtle Tower** has amassed quite a patronage (celebrity chefs included) for fragrant *pho ga*; while romantic little **Bodega Bistro** is best known for bold aromas, French flavors, and more *pho*. Score points

among family and friends by treating them to an authentic and elaborate Vietnamese spread at the **Four Seasons Restaurant**. After indulging in a shining plate of their garlicky noodles, savor an equally excellent selection of classic cocktails reinterpreted

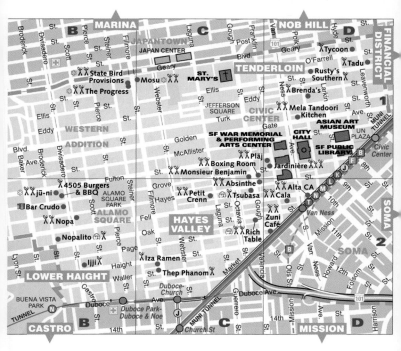

macarons served in a French-style setting. Carnivores delight in **Fatted Calf Charcuterie** where fresh, smoked and cured meats abound in loaded display cases. Here the cheese selection is solid too, so do all your stocking up, pre-picnic. Then, sate all these salty eats with a quenching sip from **True Sake**, a super-cool and all-sake business; just as caffeine junkies get their daily dose of **Blue Bottle** straight from the kiosk on Linden Street. Finish with a tour of Europe at **Miette**, an impossibly charming confiserie jammed with rare chocolates, salted licorice, taffy, and gelées; or **Christopher Elbow Artisanal Chocolate** for a smidge of bliss.

at **Bourbon & Branch**—a sultry hideaway and former speakeasy. For a more sober and substantial meal, local suits head to **Elmira Rosticceria** for a range of Italian-inspired eats—take advantage of their flourishing take-out business during the lunch rush. Come nightfall, the Tenderloin's muddle of strip clubs and bars becomes a hot hub for a decadent nightlife. And boasting an impressive selection of craft libations, **Tradition** is a hip venue housed on Jones Street that redefines the hand-crafted American cocktail experience by serving traditional drinks as well as updated versions in a vintage speakeasy setting.

West of the Civic Center, Hayes Valley is undeniably polished, with a coterie of designer boutiques set amid a medley of sleek retreats. Some residents find themselves smitten by **Chantal Guillon**, which spotlights exquisitely flavored

## LOWER HAIGHT

Steps to the west, the Lower Haight attracts sporty troupes and hipster groups for sake-infused cocktails at **Noc Noc**, followed by fantastic live tunes at The Independent, a standing room-only music venue. Some dress to impress the über-cool crowd at **Maven**, where inventive cocktails, tasty bites, and groovy tunes guarantee a great night out. Speaking of beats, the Fillmore Jazz District continues to seduce (and save) music lovers today. Settled by African-American GI's at the end of World War II, the Lower Haight hummed with jazz greats like Billie Holiday and Miles Davis. With the attempted resurgence of the jazz district, the Fillmore today goes on to resound with music from rock icons like Jimi Hendrix and The Dead. Of course, the annual Fillmore Jazz Festival is a must-see celebration of musical magnificence.

# Absinthe

Mediterranean ✗✗

**C2**

### 398 Hayes St. (at Gough St.)

**Phone:** 415-551-1590  
**Web:** www.absinthe.com  
**Price:** $$$

Lunch & dinner daily

The original colonist of Hayes Valley's now-bustling restaurant row, this "green fairy" still has plenty of sparkle, thanks to its timeless brasserie atmosphere and classic French and Mediterranean-inspired menu. Even a lowly chicken breast gets the magic treatment here, with crunchy skin, perfectly wilted lacinato kale, and swirls of luscious Bourbon-yam purée. The same goes for a little gem lettuce salad with fine herbs dressed in a red wine-shallot vinaigrette.

Perched between formal and casual, the restaurant draws relaxed alfresco lunchers with dogs by day and stylish symphony or opera patrons by night. In either incarnation, it's a lovely place for a cocktail—a few may earn you a wink from those fairies, flitting across the dining room mural.

# Alta CA

Californian ✗✗

**D2**

### 1420 Market St. (bet. Fell St. & Van Ness Ave.)

**Phone:** 415-590-2585  
**Web:** www.altaca.co  
**Price:** $$

Lunch Mon – Fri  
Dinner nightly

Though this hip techie gathering place is relaxed at lunch—it wouldn't be uncommon to see diners pecking away at their laptops—it's the place to be after work. There, in the shadow of the Twitter building across the street and beneath a massive floor-to-ceiling shelf loaded with bottles, sharply attired CEOs and hoodied engineers congregate for cocktails at the triangular bar.

The Eastern European-influenced menu kicks off with drinking snacks like wispy, savory beef tendon puffs, then moves into hearty plates like pierogies, beef stroganoff, and house-cured pastrami stuffed inside soft, chewy bialys. And when it comes to dessert, even the most plugged-in programmers will put away their iPhones for a bite of the creamy lemon and poppy seed sundae.

# Bar Crudo

Seafood

B2

**655 Divisadero St. (bet. Grove & Hayes Sts.)**

**Phone:** 415-409-0679
**Web:** www.barcrudo.com
**Price:** $$

Dinner Tue – Sun

Seafood, and plenty of it, is the specialty at this Divisadero hot spot. As the name suggests, their crudo is supreme: whether it's Arctic char with horseradish crème fraîche, wasabi tobiko, and dill; or perhaps raw scallop with sweet corn purée, tarragon oil, and popped sorghum—the combinations are fresh and delicious. Platters of shellfish are available, and there are a few hot dishes like head-on Louisiana prawns in a lobster broth, served beside a baby fennel-pea shoot salad.

This small and popular restaurant is often standing room-only, with just a handful of tables; most guests pack in at or around the bar. Grab a glass of wine or a beer, peek into the open kitchen, and be sure to check out the futuristic mermaid art on the walls.

# Boxing Room

Southern

C1

**399 Grove St. (at Gough St.)**

**Phone:** 415-430-6590
**Web:** www.boxingroom.com
**Price:** $$

Lunch & dinner daily

A trip to the real-life Big Easy may be short on veggies (unless fried okra counts), but northern California balances the Cajun and Creole indulgences on offer at this lively restaurant, leading to dishes like a spicy-sweet fig and arugula salad with spiced pecans and pan-seared goat cheese. Casual and sleek, it draws business types for lunch and happy hour, when they cluster around the oyster bar with beers and boiled peanuts.

All the classics can be found here, including gumbo, fried alligator, and a perfect jambalaya studded with spicy andouille and tender roasted duck. The simple and high-ceilinged dining room encourages lingering—as does the airy angel-food "strawberry shortcake" with lemon verbena ice cream and tangy whipped yogurt.

# Brenda's

**D1**

### 652 Polk St. (at Eddy St.)

**Phone:** 415-345-8100

**Web:** www.frenchsoulfood.com

**Price:** $$

Lunch daily
Dinner Wed – Sat

Big portions and even bigger flavors are the draw at this taste of New Orleans, helmed by Louisiana-bred Chef/owner Brenda Buenviaje. Chicken étouffée offers a smoky, dark roux packed with vegetables, while a flawless *muffuletta* is packed with savory meat, provolone, and spicy olive salad (it's great with an ice-cold Abita beer). Sweet and salty golden beignets, filled with cheesy crawfish or molten Ghirardelli chocolate, could be a meal on their own.

The Tenderloin address is rough around the edges, but Brenda's interior is quite lovely, with a light-filled dining room, bright murals, and high ceilings. Count on a wait here now that the secret is out, particularly at lunch and brunch. Or, check out the equally delicious Divisadero sequel, Brenda's Meat & Three.

# Cala

**D2**

### 149 Fell St. (bet. Franklin St. & Van Ness Ave.)

**Phone:** 415-660-7701

**Web:** www.calarestaurant.com

**Price:** $$$

Lunch Sat – Sun
Dinner Mon – Sat

A Mexico City superstar with the seafood-centric Contramar, Gabriela Cámara has brought her magic touch to this Civic Center hottie, where she serves similar food. Nothing is lost in translation: filleted black cod with red chile adobo is silky and smoky after a wood grilling in collard leaves, while Cámara's famed tuna tostadas get a Bay Area sustainability update with ocean trout. And you won't want to miss the griddled black-bean *sopes*, which seem simple but sing with flavor.

Cala's minimalist aesthetic matches that of Contramar, with vaulted, skylight-dotted ceilings, a planter box full of climbing vines, and lots of light wood for a rustic-urban feel. Service can be spotty, but for a flavorful, unfussy meal, it's quickly become a hot ticket.

# 4505 Burgers & BBQ

Barbecue ✗

**B2**

### 705 Divisadero St. (bet. Fulton & Grove Sts.)

**Phone:** 415-231-6993
**Web:** www.4505meats.com
**Price:** ⊜

Lunch & dinner daily

With lines out the door and the scent of wood smoke heavy in the air, one thing is clear: this Civic Center barbecue spot is smokin' hot. And with no service or ambience to speak of (diners order at the counter, claim a spot at one of the picnic tables arranged in the parking lot, and then dig in), the focus is firmly on the food.

Chef and butcher Ryan Farr offers succulent bites by the plate or pound. Select a trio and revel in a meaty heap of pork ribs, super moist pulled chicken, and the Bay Area's best brisket accompanied by a Parker House roll, pickles, and sliced onion. Sides like the *frankaroni* (a mac and cheese fritter studded with hot dog) are average. Follow the crowd and pair your platter with 4505's "best damn grass-fed cheeseburger."

# Ijji

Japanese ✗

**B2**

### 252 Divisadero St. (bet. Haight & Page Sts.)

**Phone:** 415-658-7388
**Web:** www.ijjisf.com
**Price:** $$$

Dinner nightly

Seeking top-notch nigiri that doesn't break the bank? Head to this intimate Divisadero newcomer, which boasts just 17 seats—10 at tables, where items are served à la carte, and seven more at an omakase-centric sushi bar. Needless to say, reservations are a must.

While Ijji's nigiri aren't quite as dazzling as some of the city's starred spots, the silky, soy-brushed kanpachi; delicate firefly squid with white miso; and decadent toro are each an outstanding value for the restaurant's mid-range price point. The limited menu also features a few cooked dishes, like slivers of meaty king trumpet mushrooms in a nutty sesame paste. Just don't expect to socialize with the chefs: laser-focused on making sure your fish is perfect, they tend to keep mum.

29

# Iza Ramen

**C2**

Japanese ✗

**237 Fillmore St. (bet. Haight & Laussat Sts.)**

**Phone:** 415-926-8173
**Web:** www.izaramen.com
**Price:** ⊜◎

Lunch Fri – Sun
Dinner Wed – Mon

The Bay Area ramen renaissance is in full swing, and this Lower Haighter is among the best of the entries. Its broth is intense and delicious, blending classic *tonkotsu* pork stock with a hint of fish stock for lots of umami-rich flavor. Toss in handfuls of springy noodles, slices of juicy pork, and a single slow-cooked egg, and it's a big dose of comfort in a bowl.

Unlike holes-in-the-wall where waits for something slurp-worthy can wear on for an hour or more, Iza is big, spacious and bright, with a charcoal and teal color scheme, distressed wood benches, and rosewood tabletops. Attentive servers present every table with a beautiful iron pot of green tea—and if you play your cards right, you might score a scoop of blood-orange sorbet for dessert.

# Jannah

**A2**

Middle Eastern ✗✗

**1775 Fulton St. (bet. Central & Masonic Aves.)**

**Phone:** 415-567-4400
**Web:** www.yayacuisine.com
**Price:** $$

Lunch & dinner Tue – Sun

The name of Yahya Salih's lovely Middle Eastern restaurant translates to "heaven," a concept echoed by its blue walls and ceiling, adorned with puffy white cloud paintings and glowing chandeliers. From the large front bar to the back patio, it's an airy and inviting choice for groups or families.

Paradise extends to the plate, where seasonal California ingredients are highlighted in Kurdish and Iraqi specialties like grilled, mint-marinated lamb kabobs with outstanding accompaniments: creamy hummus, ultra-fresh tabbouleh, and crisp *lavash*. But diners veer towards more unique dishes like the *perdaplow*, a richly flavorful, *basteeya*-like phyllo pastry enclosing tender shredded chicken, fragrant cardamom, and sweet golden raisins.

# Jardinière

 Californian ✗✗✗

**D1**

### 300 Grove St. (at Franklin St.)

**Phone:** 415-861-5555
**Web:** www.jardiniere.com
**Price:** $$$

Dinner nightly

For a memorable night on the town, don your best dress, find a hand to hold, and head to this longtime favorite—tinged with a sense of bygone romance. Stop off at the circular bar and join the well-heeled couples sipping cocktails pre- or post-opera. Prime seats on the upstairs balcony overlook the bustling lower level, and stunning arched windows show off views of the street. Approachable, seasonal dishes abound on Jardinière's menu, from tender *tajarin* pasta with morel mushrooms and butter to a Mediterranean-inspired duo of lamb belly and shoulder with fresh fava beans and smoked yogurt sauce.

Indecisive sweet tooths will thrill to the *bonne bouche*, an array of candies, cookies, small cakes, and profiteroles that makes a striking conclusion.

# Mela Tandoori Kitchen

Indian ✗✗

**D1**

### 536 Golden Gate Ave. (bet. Polk St. & Van Ness Ave.)

**Phone:** 415-447-4041
**Web:** N/A
**Price:** $$

Lunch Mon – Fri
Dinner Mon – Sat

If "*mela*" means "fair" in Hindi, then Tandoori Kitchen is aptly named. As fun and lively as a carnival, this welcoming spot sports brightly striped walls and colorful splashes of paint set aglow by stylish pendant lights. Its menu displays a vast litany of eats, and obliging servers are happy to lend a hand with useful recommendations.

The lunch menu is a hit among office workers for hot, crispy samosas with sweet tamarind chutney, or fiery *tandoori* wings baked until smoky and juicy. The area takes a bit of a dive at sunset, but that doesn't curb this kitchen's appeal. Families keep coming to devour huge portions of *aloo gobi* in an onion-and-tomato masala along with intensely spicy lamb *vindaloo*—and inevitably leave toting leftovers.

# jū-ni ✿

Japanese ✗✗

**B2**

### 1335 Fulton St. (bet. Broderick & Divisadero Sts.)

**Phone:** 415-655-9924
**Web:** www.junisf.com
**Price:** $$$$

Dinner Mon – Sat

"Ju-ni" is Japanese for "twelve," which also happens to be the number of seats in this petite, omakase-only spot just off the busy Divisadero corridor. Its segmented, L-shaped sushi bar ensures personalized attention from the trio of chefs, often led by Chef/owner Geoffrey Lee. They're a young, lively crew, and they've designed this space with a crowd of similarly young, moneyed professionals in mind. Note the spotlights above the counter, placed for perfect Instagram snaps of dishes, and the thoroughly curated sake menu.

A meal may begin with a tasting of seasonal vegetables—think tomatoes over edamame hummus—before proceeding to an array of nigiri, painstakingly sourced straight from Tokyo's own Tsukiji fish market and delicately draped over well-seasoned pillows of rice. Standouts include *sakura masu* with a salt-cured cherry blossom leaf, buttery Hokkaido scallops, and the signature *ikura*—cured in soy, sake and honey and finished with a grating of velvety frozen monkfish liver.

Decadent supplements, like torched A5 Wagyu beef and luscious uni, can be added along the way. But the meal finishes with a surprisingly gentle sendoff: sweet, tender mochi dabbed with adzuki bean paste.

# Monsieur Benjamin

French  ✗✗

**C1**

### 451 Gough St. (at Ivy St.)

**Phone:** 415-403-2233
**Web:** www.monsieurbenjamin.com
**Price:** $$$

Lunch Sat – Sun
Dinner nightly

Chef Corey Lee's take on timeless bistro cuisine is as sleek and striking as the space it's served in. Fit for the cover of a magazine, this black-and-white dining room's minimalist, yet intimate décor is trumped only by its pièce de résistance: an exhibition kitchen where you'll find the meticulous brigade of cooks hard at work, producing impressively authentic French food.

Begin with the *pâté de Campagne*, enhanced with liver and shallots and presented with strong mustard, cornichons, and country bread. The Arctic char amandine is excellent, dressed with fragrant *beurre noisette* and served over a bed of crispy haricot verts and sunchoke. For a sweet and fruity finish, purists will delight in the dessert menu's *crêpe façon gâteau*.

# Nopa

Californian  ✗✗

**B2**

### 560 Divisadero St. (at Hayes St.)

**Phone:** 415-864-8643
**Web:** www.nopasf.com
**Price:** $$

Lunch Sat – Sun
Dinner nightly

Before you're able to enjoy a single forkful at this Bay Area sensation, you'll have to secure a table—and that takes some serious effort. Reservations are snapped up at lightning speed, and hopeful walk-ins must line up prior to the start of service to add their name to the list.

The good news? Your efforts will be well rewarded. Inside, an open kitchen, soaring ceilings, and hordes of ravenous sophisticates produce a cacophonous setting in which to relish Nopa's wonderful, organic, wood-fired cuisine. Dig into a bruschetta of grilled *levain* spread with smashed avocado, pickled jalapeños, lemon-dressed arugula, and shaved *mezzo secco*, or go for the roasted King salmon fillet over creamed corn, smoky maitakes, crisp green beans, and sweet tomato confit.

# Mosu ✿

**1552 Fillmore St. (bet. Ellis St. & Geary Blvd.)**

**Phone:** 415-735-7303
**Web:** www.mosusf.com
**Price:** $$$$

Dinner Tue – Sat

At first glance, Mosu can seem like a stark, unadorned space with only a handful of softly spot-lit tables amid white walls and dark wood furnishings. However, the serious crowd and highly trained, well-versed service staff are clear indicators of their very accomplished cuisine. There is no question that this is a place where guests are focused exclusively on the food.

Chef/owner Sung Anh's signature tasting menu is served as a progression of contemporary Asian dishes, with strong focus on Korea and Japan. The kitchen's skill and talent ensures that ingredients and flavors remain pure; nothing is fussy or contrived.

A series of small bites set the tone of the meal, with extraordinary highlights such as a brunoise of Wagyu beef that is barely "kissed with coal" and served over a crisp rice chip drizzled with chili sauce, sesame oil, and a sprinkle of powdered Wagyu fat that melts on the tongue. House-made sesame tofu is intensely creamy, soft, and downright delicious when paired with green apple and sturgeon caviar in a pool of an umami-rich bonito-soy sauce. Desserts include toasted rice ice cream with torn black sesame sponge cake and delightful Grand Marnier crème anglaise.

# Nopalito

Mexican 🍴

**B2**

### 306 Broderick St. (bet. Fell & Oak Sts.)

**Phone:** 415-437-0303
**Web:** www.nopalitosf.com
**Price:** $$

Lunch & dinner daily

Whether they're digging into a refreshing *ensalada de nopales* or sharing a platter of blue-corn tacos stuffed with spicy-smoky marinated fish, local couples and families adore this sustainable Mexican spot. Sister to Cal-cuisine icon Nopa, Nopalito is so beloved that an equally good and popular Inner Sunset location is also thriving.

The small, cheerful space with reclaimed wood and bright green accents doesn't take reservations; call ahead to get on the list, or try takeout. Once seated, friendly servers will guide the way with house-made *horchata* for the kids and an extensive tequila selection for grown-ups. Both groups will certainly agree on a sweet finish: the excellent vanilla bean flan topped with orange-caramel and orange supremes is unbeatable.

# Petit Crenn

French 🍴🍴

**C2**

### 609 Hayes St. (bet. Buchanan & Laguna Sts.)

**Phone:** 415-864-1744
**Web:** www.petitcrenn.com
**Price:** $$$$

Lunch & dinner Tue – Sun

Dominique Crenn may have built her reputation on the intricate, complex dishes at Atelier Crenn, but this sequel takes a more rustic direction. Housed on the ground floor of a Hayes Valley Victorian, the dining room is chic and comfortable, with throw-pillow-lined benches and light fixtures made from nautical rope.

The dinner menu, a five-course prix fixe served family-style, offers a taste of Crenn's youth in Brittany. Begin with delicate mussels *marinière* swimming in a creamy, briny broth that begs to be lapped up with crusty artisan bread, while whole wood-roasted trout, filleted tableside, is paired with a rich cauliflower gratin and caramelized carrots with yogurt and sumac. Far Breton, a traditional Armagnac-soaked apple cake, closes out the meal.

35

# Pläj

**D1**

Scandinavian ✗✗

**333 Fulton St. (bet. Franklin & Gough Sts.)**

**Phone:** 415-294-8925
**Web:** www.plajrestaurant.com
**Price:** $$

Dinner nightly

NorCal is short on the Scandinavian-inspired fare that's all the rage right now, so it's no wonder Bay Area foodies flock to this upscale spot. Steps from the opera, symphony, and ballet, Pläj has caught on like wildfire with the pre-theater crowd, who congregate at the linen-topped tables and cozy bar for a taste of Californian cuisine mingled with Nordic flair.

Swedish-born Chef/owner Roberth Sundell offers smart riffs on classic dishes, from a tender duo of potato dumplings accented with brown butter, caramelized onions, and bacon to deep-red seared elk medallions set in a woodsy juniper jus and accented by tart lingonberries. For dessert, a parfait-like take on princess cake, with layers of raspberry, sponge cake, and marzipan, is worthy of royalty.

# Rich Table

Contemporary ✗✗

**C2**

**199 Gough St. (at Oak St.)**

**Phone:** 415-355-9085
**Web:** www.richtablesf.com
**Price:** $$

Dinner nightly

Its rustic-chic décor, highlighting reclaimed and raw wood, gives Rich Table a farmhouse feel, and the crowds that pack it are equally stylish. Reserve early or expect a long wait, as there's serious competition for seats that quickly fill with young professionals. Adept servers time meals carefully to ensure that pre-theater dinners won't run late.

The contemporary American food from Chef/owners Evan and Sarah Rich is highly engaging with menu mainstays like crispy sardine chips and porcini-dusted doughnuts set alongside a warm raclette dip. Sample thin tajarin pasta in creamed kale sauce with crisp threads of fried onion and sorrel chiffonade. Pink-fleshed and beautifully pan-seared Mt. Lassen trout is simple, hearty and really delicious.

# The Progress ✿

Californian ✗✗

**B1**

## 1525 Fillmore St. (bet. Geary Blvd. & O'Farrell St.)

**Phone:** 415-673-1294                          Dinner nightly
**Web:** www.theprogress-sf.com
**Price:** $$$

This is the rare restaurant that guarantees its diners will never be bored, thanks to the sophisticated energy that flows directly from a notably ambitious kitchen.

Service is friendly and attentive. Sure, they may make an error in describing a dish, but they do it with panache. The gorgeous space has that Nordic look that California so loves, with plenty of bare wood, skylights, and an affluent crowd appearing informal in their Patagonias.

Be sure to try one of their clever cocktails, like the savory and refreshing house martini, finished with a droplet of rosemary oil.

The reasonably priced prix fixe begins with snacks and moves on to family-style dining. Sunchokes are at the center of an exceptionally good combination of crisp roti, buttermilk-sunchoke-ranch dressing, thin slices of turnip, radish, artisanal cheese, and Burgundy truffle. Slow-cooked rabbit is enriched with dark jus and smoked prune romesco. When they hit their mark, food like this transcends its ingredients and technique to result in something genius. When they occasionally miss it, you feel like you've eaten a plate of weird vitamins. Desserts like "deluxe" vanilla ice cream are far more decadent than they sound.

# Rusty's Southern

**D1**

**750 Ellis St. (bet. Larkin & Polk Sts.)**

**Phone:** 415-638-6974
**Web:** www.rustyssf.com
**Price:** $$

Lunch Thu – Sun
Dinner Tue – Sat

In the hard-charging techie wilds of San Francisco, homesick transplants can find Southern comfort at this Tenderloin charmer, which eschews fine-dining frills for rib-sticking simplicity. Its environs are a bit sketchy after dark, but that doesn't deter the young and stylish crowds, who swill craft beers at the front bar and congregate in groups in the casual, wood-accented dining room.

Rustic and homey treats arrive in abundant portions: tangy, smoky Brunswick stew is loaded with pork, chicken, collards, lima beans and tomatoes, while expertly brined fried chicken is encased in a crunchy, golden-brown breading. For a snack, the fluffy fried hush puppies come equipped with a decadent pimento-ranch dipping sauce, and pair nicely with an icy sweet tea.

# Tadu

**D1**

**484 Ellis St. (bet. Jones & Leavenworth Sts.)**

**Phone:** 415-409-6649
**Web:** www.taduethiopiankitchen.com
**Price:** 🍳

Lunch & dinner daily

Strength in numbers is the way to go when planning a visit to this charming Ethiopian newcomer: its neighborhood is one in which you won't want to walk alone, and besides, you'll need all the help you can get to tackle the hearty portions, all served family-style here. Despite its bleak environs, Tadu's cheerful décor and friendly, engaging staff make for a very warm welcome.

Rev up your palate with the spicy, golden-brown *sambussas*, filled with earthy lentils and caramelized onions. Then go full-throttle with the *kitfo*, a zippy mixture of ground beef, onion, jalapeño, and Ethiopian spices. There's plenty of fluffy, slightly sour *injera* to mellow the burn: you can even enjoy it cooked with spices and vegetables in the delightful *firfir*.

# State Bird Provisions ✿

American ✗✗

## 1529 Fillmore St. (bet. Geary Blvd. & O'Farrell St.)

**Phone:** 415-795-1272                              Dinner nightly
**Web:** www.statebirdsf.com
**Price:** $$

Welcome to the dining evolution, where streams of plates are passed between guests in dim sum-style, and the supremely seasonal California cooking is always very good, even vibrant and unexpected. You may not understand all of what you ordered, but prices are reasonable so pile on a few extra items and try everything that comes your way. No one leaves here hungry.

Servers circulate through the room with platters or push carts brimming with creative and utterly unique cooking. Highlights include a Vietnamese salad of deep-fried pork belly with plum, mint, basil, and cilantro in lime-fish sauce vinaigrette. Heartier but wow-inducing bites of crisp pan-fried ravioli stuffed with guinea hen and bathed in rich broth will have you wishing for a larger portion. Other exquisite creations include shaved hearts of palm with yuba ribbons, Lacinato kale, Asian pear, sesame seeds, and more served in a generous pool of tahini and chili oil for a wonderful spicy-creamy contrast.

Be forewarned: getting a reservation here is the ultimate challenge and walk-in spots require lining up around 4:30 P.M. Best to avoid nights when large parties are booked—this may negatively impact your experience.

# Thep Phanom

Thai ✗

**C2**

### 400 Waller St. (at Fillmore St.)

**Phone:** 415-431-2526
**Web:** www.thepphanom.com
**Price:** $$

Lunch Sat – Sun
Dinner nightly

A good Thai spot is as essential to a SF neighborhood as air to breath, and Lower Haighters have long pledged their allegiance to Thep Phanom's interpretation of the sweet and spicy cuisine. Whether they crave sinfully crisp, golden-brown chicken wings with sweet-chili dipping sauce or a range of healthy vegetarian options, they've yet to be disappointed.

Tucked just off bustling Haight and Fillmore, the location is no friend to drivers (prepare to circle), but once inside, it's dimly lit and low-key, ideal for a quiet date night or even solo dining. Spice levels are adjustable—and hot means hot—for all the dishes, ranging from creamy red pumpkin curry to "Thaitanic" tofu, eggplant, and string beans in a lemongrass-ginger- and Thai basil-sauce.

# Tsubasa 😊

Japanese ✗

**C2**

### 429 Gough St. (bet. Hayes & Ivy Sts.)

**Phone:** 415-551-9688
**Web:** N/A
**Price:** $$

Lunch Tue – Sat
Dinner Tue – Sun

Amidst the pricey boutiques and top-dollar restaurants of Hayes Valley, a good deal can be hard to come by. However, Tsubasa is a delightful exception, offering well-made nigiri, sashimi, and maki at a price point that belies the high quality of its fish.

The sleek dining room offers table seating, but the best seats in the house are at the sushi bar, where you'll be presented with generously portioned nigiri that range from cleanly flavored turbot to intense, vinegar-kissed *saba* (mackerel). There are also more elaborate maki, like a salmon and avocado roll topped with raw scallops and miso sauce. But the deepest pleasures are simple ones: excellent miso soup, a tuna roll with beautifully seasoned rice, and rich, custardy *tamago*.

# Tycoon

Thai 🍴

**D1**

### 620 O'Farrell St. (bet. Hyde & Leavenworth Sts.)

**Phone:** 415-796-3391
**Web:** N/A
**Price:** 🍽

Lunch & dinner daily

Its location in the gritty Tenderloin doesn't offer much in terms of ambience, but this Thai spot makes up for it with flavorful, fragrant cooking that's a cut above the standard pad Thai racket. You'll swoon for the utterly perfect *sai ua*, juicy, smoky pork sausages bursting with the aromas of makrut lime, lemongrass, and chili, and the delectable *pad ped*, a spicy coconut milk curry loaded with piquant green peppercorns, tender tofu, eggplant, and bell pepper.

For true culinary adventurers, there's a small selection of Laotian dishes, like *pad mee lao*, thin rice noodles with chicken, fresh mint, and a splash of earthy black bean sauce. Also notable is the unusual and authentic drink selection, which includes vibrant *pandan* and chrysanthemum juices.

# Zuni Café

Mediterranean 🍴🍴

**D2**

### 1658 Market St. (bet. Franklin & Gough Sts.)

**Phone:** 415-552-2522
**Web:** www.zunicafe.com
**Price:** $$

Lunch & dinner Tue – Sun

Almost forty years young and still thriving as if it were newborn, locals and visitors remain drawn to this SF institution. Famous for its laid-back California vibe and great, locally sourced eats, this iconic space embraces its unique shape, and is styled with bold artwork-covered walls, a copper bar counter, and wood-burning oven sending out delightful pizzas and filling the room with mouthwatering aromas.

Given its ace location, Zuni makes for a divine lunch destination—and proof is in the many business folk, trendy ladies-who-lunch, and tourists that fill its tables midday. Menu treasures include sliced persimmon scattered with shaved Jerusalem artichoke and baby arugula leaves, tailed by toothsome artisanal rigatoni clutching fragrant lamb sugo.

# Financial District

## EMBARCADERO · UNION SQUARE

Booming with high-rises and large-scale companies, the Financial District is world-renowned. While the city itself is reputed for its easygoing vibe and cool 'tude, the financial sector is ever-bustling with the prominence of Fortune 500 companies, multi-national corporations, major banks, and law firms. Settled along the west of the waterfront, expect to see streetcars, pedestrians, and wildly tattooed bicycle messengers on weekdays clogging the routes of the triangle bounded by Kearny, Jackson, and Market streets. Come noon, lines snake out the doors of better grab-and-go sandwich shops and salad spots.

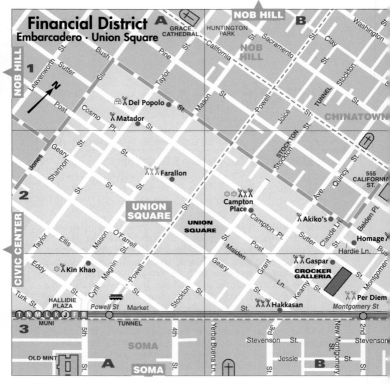

Of course, there is always a steady stream of expense-account clients who continuously patronize this neighborhood's host of fine-dining establishments; whereas along Market Street, casual cafés and chain restaurants keep the focus on families, tourists, and shoppers alike.

## EMBARCARDERO

Despite all that this area has to offer, its greatest culinary treasures lies within the famed **Ferry Building**. This 1898 steel-reinforced sandstone structure is easily recognized by its 244-foot clock tower that rises up from Market Street and way above

the waterfront promenade—**The Embarcadero**. It is among the few survivors of the 1906 earthquake and fire that destroyed most of this neighborhood. Thanks to a 2004 renovation, the soaring interior arcade makes a stunning showcase for regional products, artisanal foods, rare Chinese teas, and everything in between. Popularly referred to as the **Ferry Building Marketplace**, every diligent foodie is destined here for the likes of Chef Amaryll Schwertner's breakfast specialties at the beloved **Boulettes Larder**, where guests literally sit in the kitchen as their spread is prepared—multigrain griddle cakes with ricotta and seasonal

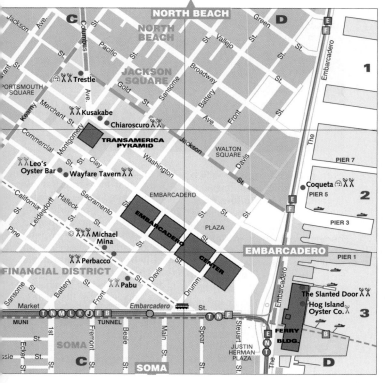

fruit are a favorite for fitting reason. This emporium also pays homage to the surrounding food community by highlighting small producers. Two of the most popular among them are **Cowgirl Creamery**'s farmstead cheeses, and Berkeley's **Acme Bread Company**—whose organic breads are a sight (and smell) to behold! Following this philosophy, find numerous organic and exotic mushrooms, medicinal herbs, and themed products at **Far West Fungi**. Here, patient enthusiasts can

includes an impressive array of olive oil-based products. While such world-class food shopping may whet the appetite of many, more immediate cravings can be satisfied at the Building's more casual dining delights like **DELICA**, popular for beautifully prepared Japanese fusion food, from signature sushi rolls to savory croquettes. Join the corporate lunch rush seated at picnic tables in **Mijita** (run by Traci Des Jardins of **Jardinère** fame) to sample such treats as *queso fundido* or Baja-style

even purchase logs on which to grow their own harvest. Legendary **Frog Hollow Farm** is also stationed nearby, offering pristine seasonal fruit alongside homemade chutneys, marmalade and fresh-baked pastries. Known for their Parisian-style chocolates and caramels, **Recchiuti Confections** has elevated their craft to an art form that can only be described as sublime.

And, completing this gourmet trend are gleaming bottles of **McEvoy Ranch Olive Oil** from their Petaluma ranch that also

fish tacos. Alternatively, claim a patio seat at **MarketBar** for market-inspired salads, flatbreads and American brasserie fare. While this is a great spot to sit and take in the view, the most decadent takeout option is still **Boccalone Salumeria** for their comprehensive charcuterie. Whether purchasing these salty eats by the platter, pound, or layered in a single-serving "cone," prepare for an unapologetically carnivorous treat. On Tuesday, Thursday, and Saturday mornings, high-minded chefs share laughs with the

locals at **Ferry Plaza Farmer's Market**, dealing in everything from organic produce and baked goods to fresh pastas and tons more. On market days, open-air stands and tents line the picturesque sidewalk in front of the Ferry Building and rear plaza overlooking the bay.

Tourists and unwearied locals are sure to enjoy some visual stimulation at The Bay Lights—an undulating light installation by artist Leo Villareal—illuminating the west span of the Bay Bridge. **The Embarcadero** boasts the best view of this beautiful piece. Meanwhile, groups of suits know to head to the **Embarcadero Center** (spanning five blocks and boasting reduced parking rates on weekends) to get their midday shopping fix in the sprawling three-story indoor mall, or to grab a quick lunch at one of the

thirty-some eateries ranging from mini-chains to noodle shops. A speck of sweet from **See's Candies** or caffeine from **Peet's** makes for an ideal finale.

## UNION SQUARE

Upscale department stores like Barneys, Neiman Marcus, and Saks Fifth Avenue preside over Union Square, where foodies gather for a gourmet experience and fashionistas flock to the plethora of designer shops. And, just as noodle lovers form a queue outside **KATANA-YA** for their steaming bowls of slurp-worthy ramen, shopaholics and local bargain hunters alike pop into **Tout Sweet Patisserie** (housed inside Macy's) for a pick-me-up in the form of pastries, candies, and macarons. Take home a few extra goodies, if only to appreciate their beautiful packaging.

# Akiko's

Japanese ✗

**B2**

**431 Bush St. (bet. Grant & Kearny Sts.)**

**Phone:** 415-397-3218
**Web:** www.akikosrestaurant.com
**Price:** $$$

Lunch Mon – Fri
Dinner Mon – Sat

Akiko's is hard to find. In addition to sharing a name with a lesser nearby sushi bar, it's hidden just off an alleyway and has no sign. The cool clientele is probably happy to avoid any more competition for the mere handful of tables and seats at the small sushi bar.

Arrive at dinner, sit at the counter, toss aside that à la carte menu, and opt for an omakase feast created by the very talented chefs. Expect them to take liberties and leave tradition behind; yet the quality remains high with pristine nigiri featuring fluke, scallop, or geoduck clam minimally garnished and perched atop rice with a touch of nutty red rice vinegar. Bookend the meal with rich tuna poke with sesame, or a lightly torched slice of A5 Wagyu beef with black truffle shavings.

# Chiaroscuro

Italian ✗✗

**C1**

**550 Washington St. (bet. Montgomery & Sansome Sts.)**

**Phone:** 415-362-6012
**Web:** www.chiaroscurosf.com
**Price:** $$

Lunch Mon – Fri
Dinner Mon – Sat

An upscale retreat for well-heeled FiDi deal-doers, Chiaroscuro brims with a lunchtime crowd tucking into memorable pastas. One such standout is the delicate house-made *tagliolini* with julienned winter vegetables and a light, truffle-scented sauce enriched with *Parmigiano*. If you can't choose a single dish, opt for the popular "trilogia" of three daily delights, then follow it with *pollo ai peperoni*, a delicious chicken roulade stuffed with roasted bell pepper and served over crisp vegetables.

While its food is classically Roman, Chiaroscuro's décor is modern, sleek, and chic, with pillow-topped concrete banquettes and modern glass-and-metal chandeliers. For a quieter meal, come at dinner, when the crowds dissipate and the menu goes prix-fixe.

# Campton Place ✿ ✿

**B2**

Indian ✖✖✖

### 340 Stockton St. (bet. Post & Sutter Sts.)

**Phone:** 415-955-5555
**Web:** www.camptonplacesf.com
**Price:** $$$$

Lunch & dinner daily

With its sleek booths, wall-to-wall windows, plush carpeting, and pristinely robed tables, this elegant oasis in the Taj Hotel is as formal and traditional as one would expect. An odd mix of gourmands and hotel guests keep the vibe desultory inside, but by greeting each diner as they enter, the staff maintains a sense of refinery that is true to this contemporary Cal-Indian menu.

The full talent of this kitchen is showcased at dinner. Courses, which arrive on charcoal-glazed ceramics, allude to Indian spices but honor outstanding skill and taste over drama or novelty. Lighter dishes cover all bases of flavor and texture as witnessed in a modern expression of *chaat* (carrots, peas, and tamarind tossed in "whey shorva" dotted with chutney); or spicy, pan-fried potato-corn *tikkis* lodged atop a bright salad of plum brunoise and cilantro. Dollops of tangy lime curd expertly complete this sublime, seasonal plate, while charred potatoes and leeks accentuate a decadent butter-poached Maine lobster.

Just as slow-cooked meat dishes have an elegant undertone of *garam masala*, for dessert, *tandoori* strawberries with lemon ice cream may under-promise on paper but will over-deliver on taste and flavor.

# Coqueta

**Spanish** ✗✗

**D2**

### Pier 5 (at The Embarcadero)

**Phone:** 415-704-8866
**Web:** www.coquetasf.com
**Price:** $$

Lunch Tue – Sun
Dinner nightly

  ♿

A tasty little morsel of a space serving up mouthwatering tapas, Michael Chiarello's Pier 5 destination offers shimmering views of the bay from its rustic dining room, equipped with rough-hewn wooden tables, cowhide rugs, and a big, theatrical open kitchen and bar. There's a bit more room on the tented outdoor patio, but if your heart is set on a table, book early.

Its name is Spanish for "flirt," and Coqueta's alluring menu has caused more than one enraptured diner to over-order. Some fine options: crunchy-creamy chicken and pea *croquetas*, mini sandwiches of smoked salmon with *queso fresco* and truffle honey, and wood-grilled octopus with tender fingerling potatoes. Complete the experience with the Asturian apple pie with Cabrales blue cheese ice cream.

# Del Popolo

**Pizza** ✗

**A1**

### 855 Bush St. (bet. Mason & Taylor Sts.)

**Phone:** 415-589-7940
**Web:** www.delpopolosf.com
**Price:** $$

Dinner Tue – Sun

  ♿

If you've got eyes for killer pies, you'll want to make a beeline to this chic and simple Italian hot spot. The open space is centered around a big, blazing oven, and crowds arrive early to score every last no-reservations seat. (The host is happy to text when yours is ready.)

Del Popolo may have gotten its start as a food truck, but one bite of the wood-fired pizza and its clear how it earned its address. Chewy, blistered, and caramelized, the crusts arrive laden with toppings both traditional (mozzarella, tomato sauce, house-made sausage) and California cool (roasted winter squash, mascarpone, spring onions). Don't sleep on the antipasti, either—a smoked, cumin-infused sweet potato with pecan salsa verde and a poached egg is dizzyingly delicious.

# Farallon

**A2**

Seafood XXX

## 450 Post St. (bet. Mason & Powell Sts.)

**Phone:** 415-956-6969  Dinner nightly
**Web:** www.farallonrestaurant.com
**Price:** $$$

Union Square's lauded seafood respite is an aquatic-themed fantasy at every turn. Dive in and enjoy an extravagant platter of *fruits de mer* while admiring their thematic, custom-made chandeliers and bar stools in The Jellyfish Lounge. Also known as the Jelly Bar, it's a San Francisco institution unto itself. Then head to the Pool Room (it once served as the pool room of the Elks Club) to dine on the kitchen's coastal cooking amid sparkling mosaics and a vaulted ceiling.

A raw first course unearths yellowtail sashimi adorned with garlicky aïoli, finely chopped piquillo peppers, and dollops of basil chantilly. Following that is an entrée of crisp-skinned grilled salmon, accompanied by torn croutons, heirloom tomatoes, red onions, and balsamic vinegar.

# Gaspar

**B3**

French XX

## 185 Sutter St. (bet. Kearny & Montgomery Sts.)

**Phone:** 415-576-8800  Lunch Mon – Fri
**Web:** www.gasparbrasserie.com  Dinner nightly
**Price:** $$

In a sea of faux-rustic restaurant décor, this *bijou* stands out for its sexy, intimate vibe, complete with dark-tufted banquettes, soft lighting, and an intimate downstairs bar. It's the kind of place where you'll see FiDi brokers rehash deals over pre-dinner cocktails, before being joined by their well-dressed dates for a swanky dinner party upstairs.

The menu of French brasserie favorites is prepared with skill, from grand plateaux of *fruits de mer* to a perfectly cooked flatiron steak with well-seasoned pommes frites and red wine bordelaise. Don't miss the outstanding *Paris-Brest*, golden-hued pastry filled with creamy rose mascarpone and juicy raspberries. Or if you'd rather skip sweets, opt for their well-curated cheese plate.

# Hakkasan

Chinese XXX

**B3**

**1 Kearny St. (at Market St.)**

| | |
|---|---|
| **Phone:** | 415-829-8148 |
| **Web:** | www.hakkasan.com |
| **Price:** | $$$$ |

Lunch & dinner Mon – Sat

An eclectic crowd of business people, cocktailing hipsters, and fashionable Chinese tourists descend on the SF outpost of this upscale international chain. Housed on the second floor of the historic One Kearny building, the dining room's luxe design features carved wood screens, embroidered white leather, and a striking, V-shaped bar—it's a scene worth dressing up for.

Sample Hakkasan's mouthwatering Cantonese eats, however, and you'll see that its appeal transcends the décor. The menu's extensive array of artfully plated treats includes hits like braised chicken dressed with soy sauce, toasted sesame oil, ginger, and scallions. The French green beans, stir-fried with minced pork, dried shrimp, and an umami-packed sauce, are just as magical.

# Hog Island Oyster Co.

Seafood X

**D3**

**1 Ferry Building (at The Embarcadero)**

| | |
|---|---|
| **Phone:** | 415-391-7117 |
| **Web:** | www.hogislandoysters.com |
| **Price:** | $$$ |

Lunch & dinner daily

Can't make the trip to Marin to shuck oysters on Hog Island's docks? They'll bring Tomales Bay's finest to you at this buzzing cityside outpost in the Ferry Building, which draws long lines of both tourists and locals for platters of some of the sweetest, freshest bivalves on the West Coast. You'll receive all the accompaniments—lemon, Tabasco, mignonette—but they're good enough to slurp solo.

Once you've had your fill, be sure to sample the other aquatic offerings: Peruvian-style crudo with silky sea bass; a hefty bowl of cioppino loaded with prawns, clams, mussels, and squid; and the exceptional Manila clam chowder, a bestseller for good reason. Throw in the expansive Bay views from the patio and dining room, and those lines come as no surprise.

# Homage

B2

Californian ✗

### 88 Hardie Pl. (off Kearny St.)

**Phone:** 415-800-8741     Lunch Mon – Fri
**Web:** www.homage-sf.com
**Price:** ⊛

Homage is a recent addition to an already stacked deck of daytime options for FiDi workers, but it's managed to stand out thanks to spankingly fresh farm-sourced ingredients—including an array of breads and pastries made with fresh-ground flour, like the decadent honey-cashew-lime sticky bun with buttermilk icing.

You'll order via counter service, but the food is sit-down quality. Even taken to-go, a salad of treviso, kale, and little gems with tangy crème fraîche vinaigrette. or a tartine of applewood-smoked chicken with crumbled feta, kumquats, and escarole is the opposite of a sad desk lunch. Got a full hour to relax and unwind? The rustic-chic, wood-accented space makes for a pleasant escape from cubicle life, and the staff is extra-friendly.

# Kusakabe

C1

Japanese ✗✗

### 584 Washington St. (bet. Montgomery & Sansome Sts.)

**Phone:** 415-757-0155     Dinner Tue – Sun
**Web:** www.kusakabe-sf.com
**Price:** $$$$

Serene with warm wood and clean lines, distinctive creativity is the motto of this sushi-focused operation. Inside, a stunning counter crafted from a piece of live-edge elm, oyster-hued leather chairs and a ceiling of wood slats complete the Japan-chic look.

While the preparation of their nightly omakase tasting might seem like a production line, by employing myriad cooking techniques, the kitchen ensures that every bite is memorable. Begin with warm kelp tea, before embarking on a sashimi parade of bluefin slices served with a yuzu-onion-sesame sauce. A soup course may feature fresh crabmeat in a delicate *tai* broth; and finally, a top rendition of sushi yields *shima aji* with daikon and *ayu* that is torched just enough to blister the skin.

# Kin Khao ❀

Thai ✗

**A3**

## 55 Cyril Magnin St. (entrance at Ellis & Mason Sts.)

**Phone:** 415-362-7456
**Web:** www.kinkhao.com
**Price:** $$

Lunch & dinner daily

Tucked into an alcove of the unprepossessing Parc 55 hotel, this restaurant won't win any awards in the décor department—it's spare and casual, with tables set with chopstick canisters and bowls of chili oil. But when it comes to delivering authentically layered, fiery Thai flavor with a produce-driven northern California flair, it has no equal.

Kin Khao reconcepts dishes from across Thailand to take advantage of the market's bounty, from a rich and creamy *hor mok* curry mousse starring locally sourced wild mushrooms to an unexpected take on *nam tok*, with meaty scarlet runner beans dressed in a tantalizing mixture of lime juice, chilies, caramelized shallots, rice powder, and herbs. More traditional options include classic Chiang Mai-style *khao soi*, a flavorful curry-soup with chicken, egg noodles and pickled mustard greens, and a Thai-Chinese mashup of flat rice noodles stir-fried with locally made tofu and XO sauce.

Needless to say, those avoiding spicy food or craving plain old pad Thai should look elsewhere. But if you're a straight-outta-Bangkok diehard, grab a cocktail, get a friendly server to guide you to the latest and greatest, and strap in for a wild—and delicious—ride.

# Leo's Oyster Bar

Seafood ✕✕

**C2**

568 Sacramento St. (bet. Leidesdorff & Montgomery Sts.)

**Phone:** 415-872-9982
**Web:** www.leossf.com
**Price:** $$$

Lunch Mon – Fri
Dinner Mon – Sat

The glamour of the past and the prices of the future collide at this tony '50s-inspired seafood spot, which offers an enchanting trip to a bygone era of Hollywood luxury— provided you're ready to spend like a movie star. Gold-framed mirrors, a rose onyx bar, and vintage light fixtures give the petite space an elegant, feminine vibe, which pairs nicely with the well-heeled ladies who flock here for an after-work cocktail.

Settle in with a mai tai or flute of champagne and prepare for an aquatic extravaganza. In addition to the requisite raw oysters, the chilled shrimp cocktail and delicate crab and lobster cake are worth savoring. Seeking a heartier meal? Silky pan-seared salmon with caramelized fennel and lemon-caper sauce is worth a deeper dive.

# Matador

Mexican ✕

**A1**

679 Sutter St. (bet. Mason & Taylor Sts.)

**Phone:** 415-923-8146
**Web:** www.matadorsf.com
**Price:** $$

Lunch & dinner daily

You might be tempted to dismiss this stylish retreat as just another tequila bar, but in addition to its huge tequila and mezcal selection and noteworthy cocktail program, Matador has taken the charge on offering delicious food. Griddled sopes come laden with smoky beef barbacoa, pinto beans, *pico de gallo*, and *crema*, while the seared ahi tuna tacos in a soy-chipotle reduction are a crowd favorite. Even the house-made flan gets a fun twist with the addition of guava.

The U-shaped bar draws a boisterous post-work crowd in the evening, when FiDi business types come to blow off steam with pitchers of margaritas as Spanish films screen overhead. But, it's not always bumping: those seeking a quieter meal should come for the under-the-radar lunch service.

# Michael Mina ✿

Contemporary 𝖄𝖄𝖄

**C2**

### 252 California St. (bet. Battery & Front Sts.)

**Phone:** 415-397-9222
**Web:** www.michaelmina.net
**Price:** $$$$

Lunch Mon – Fri
Dinner nightly

Dinner and drinks come with a side of deal-making at this nerve center for the Financial District's power players, where businesspeople come to woo clients with fine food and wine. It's the jewel in the crown of its prolific namesake chef/owner, who has many other restaurants around the city and country, but few quite this luxurious. From its high ceilings and cushiony banquettes to a huge and highly polished staff, this is an oasis for the corporate crowd.

The three-course, prix fixe menu has returned its focus to Mina's signature "trios" of dishes served on oversized platters, highlighting one ingredient prepared in different ways or three similar ingredients. A trio of *kataifi*-crusted blue prawns might arrive atop creamy yogurt with mint and grape, avocado purée with nectarine, and tomato confiture with basil and finger lime; while wild striped bass is served with fig and pistachio, corn and shishito pepper, as well as heirloom tomato with red miso.

For those looking to go all out, there's also a tasting menu option, complete with thoughtful wine pairings. If you'd rather not bring out the big guns, Mina offers a few of his signature dishes, such as ahi tuna tartare, à la carte.

# Pabu

**C3**

Japanese ✖✖

### 101 California St. (at Front St.)

**Phone:** 415-668-7228  
**Web:** www.pabuizakaya.com  
**Price:** $$$

Lunch Mon – Fri  
Dinner nightly

Michael Mina and Ken Tominaga have gone big with their Japanese offspring and baby boy is quite a looker. Encompassing a stunning, high-ceilinged bar, gleaming sushi counter, several dining rooms, and a casual ramen joint (The Ramen Bar, next door), Pabu is enormous in space but serene in atmosphere. The warm service is highly personal.

If you can fork over the requisite gobs of cash, the massive menu will accommodate seemingly any Japanese craving—from whole grilled squid and *izakaya*-style skewers of smoky chicken tails or thick trumpet mushrooms, to a sweet, salty, and savory burdock salad. Sushi fans can opt for the omakase or stick to à la carte treats like a tender *kanpyo* squash roll. The top-notch sake and Japanese whisky lineup is worth exploring.

# Perbacco

**C3**

Italian ✖✖

### 230 California St. (bet. Battery & Front Sts.)

**Phone:** 415-955-0663  
**Web:** www.perbaccosf.com  
**Price:** $$

Lunch Mon – Fri  
Dinner Mon – Sat

Slick financial types flex their expense accounts at this longtime Northern Italian favorite, whose polished décor belies an extensive menu of house-made pastas and comfort fare like roast chicken and meatballs at lunch, with slightly more refined takes at dinner. Dishes are executed with care—from mortadella-stuffed, black truffle-topped quail to handmade pastas—though portions can be a little scant.

The space is larger inside than it looks, with plenty of booths and seats at the marble bar up front, and buzzy tables in the back with a view of the open-plan kitchen. Well-versed servers will encourage saving room for the end of the meal—as the cheese display, an impressive selection of grappas, and the inventive, delicious desserts are all highlights.

# Per Diem

**B3**

### 43 Sutter St. (bet. Montgomery & Sansome Sts.)

**Phone:** 415-989-0300
**Web:** www.perdiemsf.com
**Price:** $$

Lunch Mon – Fri
Dinner Mon – Sat

This aptly-named hot spot is a favorite among the well-heeled FiDi power players who fill its dramatic, bi-level space. Equal parts industrial loft and swanky Prohibition-era club, Per Diem is a vision of rich wood surfaces, dramatic pillars, exposed brick, and concrete. It's a sleek atmosphere for a sleek crowd—but the real draw here is the food.

The chef has taken the menu in a seasonally inspired direction that's at once refined and approachable. Of-the-moment delights include a salty, smoky flatbread topped with slices of roasted porcini and hon shimeji mushrooms, shaved prosciutto, and crescenza cheese. This may be tailed by an equally impressive spinach-ricotta ravioli with roasted squash, a soft-poached egg, and sprinkle of lemon gremolata.

# The Slanted Door

**D3**

### 1 Ferry Building (at The Embarcadero)

**Phone:** 415-861-8032
**Web:** www.slanteddoor.com
**Price:** $$

Lunch & dinner daily

Reservations are a challenge at this modern stunner with a killer view of the Bay Bridge, which has managed to stay atop tourists' hit lists even as its NorCal spin on Vietnamese food has steadily become more uninspired and corporate. It's an efficient, professional place, but with little warmth; the hospitality is hit-or-miss at best.

Steer clear of the overpraised cellophane noodles with crab or overpriced shaking beef, and stick to more solid offerings like *gau choy gow*, pan-fried dumplings with Gulf shrimp and vibrant garlic chives accompanied by a zippy soy and fish-sauce dip. Half-orders are encouraged, so take advantage by sampling more than one of the delectable vegetable sides, like crisp, spicy broccoli with pressed tofu.

# Trestle 😋

A m e r i c a n  ✕✕

**C1**

### 531 Jackson St. (at Columbus Ave.)

**Phone:** 415-772-0922
**Web:** www.trestlesf.com
**Price:** $$

Dinner nightly

In SF's dizzyingly expensive dining landscape, this little hot spot, which offers a three-course menu for $35, is an incredible steal—provided you're willing to sacrifice freedom of choice. The two options for each course change daily based on what's freshest: our repast featured creamy wild mushroom risotto, fork-tender short ribs with charred onions and romesco, and a milk chocolate devil's food pudding cake with Mission figs, but yours might be different.

As with any killer deal, there are caveats: reservations are necessary (and hard to score), and the noise level is through the roof. But the historic brick space is lots of fun, with cool, contemporary art and a namesake central trestle table. The fact that the price is right only adds to the allure.

# Wayfare Tavern

G a s t r o p u b  ✕✕

**C2**

### 558 Sacramento St. (bet. Montgomery & Sansome Sts.)

**Phone:** 415-772-9060
**Web:** www.wayfaretavern.com
**Price:** $$

Lunch & dinner daily

Though it feels like it's been around for decades, celebrity chef Tyler Florence's FiDi favorite is actually a toddler—at least in tavern years. Nonetheless, it's become a standby for business types doing deals or enjoying post-work cocktails. Complete with dark wood and leather furnishings, a private billiards room, and bustling bar, Wayfare Tavern has the air of a gastropub-turned-private club.

Hearty Americana with seasonal accents defines the menu, like a take on biscuits and gravy that integrates plump dayboat scallops and spicy chili oil. Buttermilk-brined fried chicken, grilled hanger steak, and baked macaroni and cheese are pure comfort, as is a decadent TCHO chocolate cream pie with salty caramel ganache and devil's food cake crumble.

# Marina

Following the havoc wreaked by the 1906 earthquake, San Francisco began reconstructing this sandy marshland by selling it to private developers. They, in turn, transformed the Marina into one of the most charming residential bubbles in town. Picture young families, tech wealth, and an affluent vibe straight out of a 21st century edition of The Yuppy Handbook, and you're in the Marina! Pacific Heights is considered the area's upper echelon—known for older family money and members who couldn't care less about being edgy. Here, bronzed residents can be found jogging with their dogs at Crissy Field, or sipping chocolate from the **Warming Hut**. Parents can be seen pushing Bugaboos in haute couture boutiques or vying for parking in German-engineered SUVs.

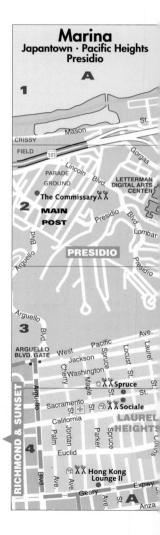

**Marina**
Japantown · Pacific Heights
Presidio

## CASUAL EATS

Marina girls as well as Pac Heights socialites are always on the go, and quick-bite cafés are their calling card. Find these denizens gathering at **Jane** for pastries and paninis to nibble along with sips from a range of excellent teas, coffees, and smoothies. **Cafe GoLo** brings to life a classic American coffeehouse replete with expected breakfast specials, salads, and sandwiches; and **The Tipsy Pig** is a welcoming gastropub boasting an impressive bevy of bites and brews. True burger buffs in the Marina seem to have an insatiable appetite for locally founded **Roam Artisan**

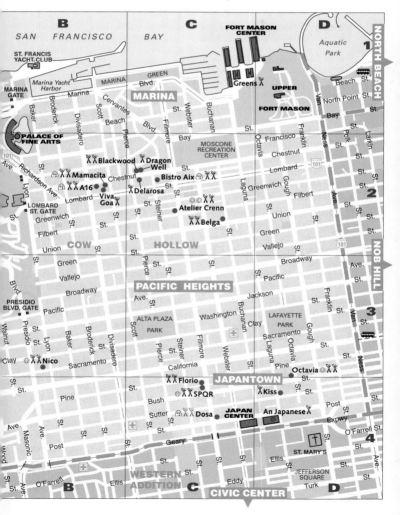

**Burgers**. Equally popular and sought-after are the contemporary, flavor-packed offerings at SoCal favorite, **Umami Burger**. In truth, quality cuisine has little to do with a Marina restaurant's success: the locals are unapologetically content to follow the buzz to the latest hot spot, where the clientele's beauty seems to be in direct proportion to its level of acclaim and popularity.

However, in the Presidio (home to Lucasfilm HQ) squads of tech geeks opt for convenience at nearby **Presidio Social Club**, cooking up tasty, regionally focused fare in a classic northern Californian setting. "**Off the Grid-Fort Mason**" is California's most coveted street food fair that gathers every Friday night and features a fantastic collection of vendors and food trucks—from **Curry Up Now** and the **Lobster Truck**, to **Johnny Doughnuts** and everything in between. Then again, food is mere sustenance to some, and simply a sponge for the champagne and chardonnay flowing at the district's numerous watering holes. The bar scene here is not only fun but also varied, with a playground for everyone. Oenophiles plan far in advance for the annual **ZAP**

**Zinfandel Festival** in the winter; while preppy college kids swap European semester stories at sleek wine spots like **Ottimista Restaurant & Bar** or **Nectar**. Couples on the other hand can find more romance by the fireplace at posh **MatrixFillmore**.

## JAPANTOWN

Evident in the plethora of restaurants, shopping malls, banks, and others businesses, the Asian community in the Marina is burgeoning. Thanks to the prominent Japanese population and abundant cultural events, **Japantown** is an exceptional and unique destination for tourists and locals alike. The **Northern California Cherry Blossom Festival** and **Nihonmachi Street Fair** bring to life every aspect of Asian-American heritage and living. Date-night is always memorable at the **Sundance Kabuki Cinema**, which happens to be equipped with two full bars. For a post-work snack, prepared meals, or even authentic imported ingredients, **Super Mira** is a market that offers a host of traditional eats. But for lunch on the run, grab excellent sushi, sashimi, or bento boxes at nearby **Nijiya Market**. Visitors and laid-back locals sojourn to **Daikoku by Shiki** (in the Kintetsu Mall) if only to admire their assortment of beautiful Japanese ceramics, cast iron teapots, sake sets, and glazed bowls. Just a couple blocks from Japantown is perhaps the best spice shop in the country. Featuring walls lined with stacks of jars, **Spice Ace** boasts of extensively curated spices, extracts, and salts, that can all be sampled before purchase.

# An Japanese

**D4**

### 22 Peace Plaza, Ste. 510 (bet. Buchanan & Laguna Sts.)

**Phone:** 415-292-4886
**Web:** www.sushiansf.com
**Price:** $$

Dinner Tue – Sat

With the retirement of Ino Sushi's longtime chef, this tucked-away space in Japantown has gotten a fresh moniker as well as a talented head chef (Kiyoshi Hayakawa). Along with his wife, the head server, and a second sushi chef, he provides a concise menu with a $30 à la carte minimum. And, serious sushi lovers can sample two nigiri-only menus or an all-out omakase with some cooked appetizers.

The nigiri are excellent, their gently seasoned rice draped with exceptionally pristine fish and for the finale, a buttery slice of seared Wagyu beef. Cooked dishes might include a vivid matsutake mushroom soup featuring an intense kelp broth.

Though the dress code is casual, the space is still small and very hushed, making for an intimate meal.

# A16 😳

**B2**

italian ✖✖

### 2355 Chestnut St. (bet. Divisadero & Scott Sts.)

**Phone:** 415-771-2216
**Web:** www.a16sf.com
**Price:** $$

Lunch Wed – Fri
Dinner nightly

An undying favorite of yuppies, families, and tourists alike, A16 is known for rustic Italian cooking and a vast selection of delicious, unusual wines from all over the boot. Dinner reservations are indispensable, especially if you want one of the prime counter seats facing the open kitchen and wood-burning pizza oven.

The menu's pies, pastas, and antipasti change with the season, so you could sample anything from a highly enjoyable *zuppa di ceci verde* flecked with green garbanzo beans and parsley, to perfectly al dente *cavatelli* tossed in a slow-cooking lamb sugo made extra hearty with the addition of plump barlotti beans. For dessert, look no further than the fig *crostata* with vanilla gelato, which tastes like the work of a particularly talented *nonna*.

# Atelier Crenn ✿ ✿

**C2**

### 3127 Fillmore St. (bet. Filbert & Pixley Sts.)

| | | |
|---|---|---|
| **Phone:** | 415-440-0460 | Dinner Tue – Sat |
| **Web:** | www.ateliercrenn.com | |
| **Price:** | **$$$$** | |

The refrain that echoes through this exquisite cuisine is *"poetic culinaria,"* and exactly what Chef Dominique Crenn means by that is redefined with each new course, from the lobes of Hokkaido uni beneath Persian cucumber "snow" to the granita hidden behind a sliding lid in a hollowed tree branch. Delicately balanced sauces to complement seafood inspire awe, while desserts can work hard to mystify. However, dining here is categorically unique and memorable.

This kitchen immediately proves its skill with an opening salvo of custard-like cauliflower bathed in a luxuriant sauce that combines beguiling technique with lots of cheese and butter. Chef Crenn's talent with seafood is otherworldly, especially the succulent lobster in a pool of tangy and citrusy fermented shiso broth, and raw scallops with pineapple water, finger lime, and fruity olive oil. A beautiful glazed Japanese bowl arrives with ribbons of interlacing squid and *lardo* finished tableside with *jamon Ibérico* broth.

Nothing is opulent or fussy, but formality and elegance is clear in every touch that resounds of the chef's poetic sensibility. The interior is neutral, minimalist, and as serene as the backlit reed canopy overhead, twinkling with light.

# Belga

Belgian

**2000 Union St. (at Buchanan St.)**

| | | |
|---|---|---|
| **Phone:** | 415-872-7350 | Lunch & dinner daily |
| **Web:** | www.belgasf.com | |
| **Price:** | **$$** | |

Belgian brews and bites are the cornerstones of this fresh recruit in the former Café des Amis, which has kept its brasserie look but pivoted from Paris to Brussels. All the classics are accounted for: well-salted frites with garlic aïoli; bowls of mussels; and of course, house-made sausages—try the combo board, which comes with andouille, *boudin noir*, *boudin blanc*, and *currywurst*, not to mention a generous bowl of spaetzle. Flatbreads and salads round things out.

The Euro-café vibe is fun with red banquettes, classic bistro chairs, and marble floors to complement the big beer selection (both European and domestic) and cocktails. Young Marinaites have, understandably, caught on quickly: the bar and dog-friendly patio are constantly abuzz.

# Bistro Aix 🙂

Mediterranean

**3340 Steiner St. (bet. Chestnut & Lombard Sts.)**

| | | |
|---|---|---|
| **Phone:** | 415-202-0100 | Dinner Mon – Sat |
| **Web:** | www.bistroaix.com | |
| **Price:** | **$$** | |

In the competitive Marina market, lovely Bistro Aix remains a charming and relatively affordable neighborhood option for thoughtfully made Southern French fare with a California touch. The dining room offers two distinct culinary experiences, beginning with seats in front at the convivial marble bar and small bistro tables. Beyond this, find the sunny bubble of the intimate back atrium, verdant with olive trees and flooded with natural light. A well-heeled crowd enlivens the space.

Dishes are simple and well executed, like roasted eggplant with toasted sesame seeds, gypsy peppers, and a topping of creamy burrata; or the excellently grilled sea scallops with earthy chanterelles and silky beurre blanc. Nicely chosen French wines complement each dish.

# Blackwood

**C2**

Fusion ✗✗

## 2150 Chestnut St. (bet. Pierce & Steiner Sts.)

**Phone:** 415-931-9663
**Web:** www.blackwoodsf.com
**Price:** $$

Lunch & dinner daily

For a hip, fusion-y take on Thai fare, Marina locals beeline to this stylish spot, which offers classic dishes like shredded mango salad with cilantro, scallions, and smoky tiger prawns, as well as more mod items such as grilled Wagyu flank steak massaged with a five-spice sauce, set atop ginger rice and garlicky long beans. Empanada-like samosas come stuffed with potato, caramelized onions, and carrots, accompanied by a light and refreshing cucumber-avocado salad.

The sleek interior features tufted banquettes and enormous mirrors, but the prime perch is their lovely front patio, with two fireside communal tables that face the hustle and bustle of Chestnut Street. Allow extra time for parking and expect a wait at weekend brunch—the most popular service.

# The Commissary

**A2**

Californian ✗✗

## 101 Montgomery St. (in the Presidio)

**Phone:** 415-561-3600
**Web:** www.thecommissarysf.com
**Price:** $$

Dinner Mon – Sat

Once an officer's mess for the soldiers of the Presidio, this historic space now offers more refined cooking, courtesy of superchef Traci Des Jardins. Inside, communal wood tables, a bustling chef's counter, and antique light fixtures honor the past while allowing for modern comfort. Dine alfresco on the big front porch, facing the former parade grounds, or grab cheese, wine, and charcuterie from the in-house shop.

The menu takes its cues from Spain, with richly seasoned chicken *basquaise* in a peppery tomato broth and *bacalao* salad strewn with fennel, olive, pomelo, and basil. *Jamón Ibérico*, gazpacho, and churros also make appearances.

For a double dose of Des Jardins, head to nearby Arguello, her Mexican concept in the Presidio Officer's Club.

# Delarosa

Italian ✗

**C2**

### 2175 Chestnut St. (bet. Pierce & Steiner Sts.)

**Phone:** 415-673-7100
**Web:** www.delarosasf.com
**Price:** $$

Lunch & dinner daily

People-watching aficionados will delight in this Marina favorite, where sidewalk tables afford a killer view of Chestnut Street's many stroller-pushing parents, awestruck tourists, and Pilates-toned socialites. Befitting the visual overload, bright orange is Delarosa's signature color, and can be seen in light fixtures hanging over the communal tables as well as eye-popping tiles in the kitchen.

Simple, rustic Italian food steals the show, like spicy-smoky thin-crust pizzas topped with salami, *coppa*, and chopped chilies, or a fresh, flavorful salad of young kale with a pecorino-Caesar dressing. The laid-back vibe extends to the signature dessert: a trio of puffy, sugar-dusted *bomboloni*, served warm with chocolate, raspberry, and mascarpone dipping sauces.

# Dosa

Indian ✗✗

**C4**

### 1700 Fillmore St. (at Post St.)

**Phone:** 415-441-3672
**Web:** www.dosasf.com
**Price:** $$

Lunch Wed – Sun
Dinner nightly

Grandeur and glamour infuse every inch of this stylish restaurant, whose soaring ceilings, colorful walls, and swanky demeanor complement the bold and fragrantly spiced food. As the name suggests, *dosas* are a highlight here, with crisp exteriors, spicy fillings, and excellent accompanying *sambar* and chutney. Warm servers will help translate street faves like *bhel puri* (a sweet-sour blend of puffed rice, crispy noodles, green mango, and chutney); or shake things up with *idli* fries, tailed by a Bengali gimlet with gin, curried nectar, and lime. Desserts are every bit as exotic as the rest of the menu, and may reveal *rasmalai*—patties of fresh cheese in sweet cream flavored with cardamom and rosewater.

Fans revel in the second, smaller location on Valencia Street.

# Dragon Well

**C2**

## 2142 Chestnut St. (bet. Pierce & Steiner Sts.)

**Phone:** 415-474-6888
**Web:** www.dragonwell.com
**Price:** ⌘

Lunch & dinner Wed – Mon

  Don't expect strict authenticity at this nearly two-decade-old Marina Chinese spot, which bypasses oil-heavy options for a lighter, fresher take prepared by skillful Cantonese chefs. Recommendations include the tea-smoked duck, which boasts a gentle, earthy flavor that's complemented by soft, sweet house-made buns; the minced chicken in lettuce cups; and the *chow fun*, with fresh rice noodles delivered daily from Chinatown.

Dragon Well's long, narrow space hasn't had much of an update since its 1998 debut, and it's almost obscured by the cluttered storefronts around it—which may explain why many customers opt for delivery. But should you stop in, expect a neighborly, friendly vibe, with diners of all ages enjoying their meals in delicious harmony.

# Florio

**C4**

## 1915 Fillmore St. (bet. Bush & Pine Sts.)

**Phone:** 415-775-4300
**Web:** www.floriosf.com
**Price:** $$

Dinner nightly

  After a day of shopping in the neighboring boutiques, locals head to Florio to nurse a glass of wine at the bar or to meet friends for a casual dinner. Complete with linen-topped tables, wood floors, and relaxed furnishings, it has the cozy, romantic vibe of an authentic bistro, and you're likely to see plenty of couples (sometimes in duos) out for a date night.

The approachable French-cum-Italian menu is full of hearty crowd-pleasers, like a salad of shaved summer squash with mint, pea tendrils, and dollops of creamy ricotta; or a juicy, deep-brown roast chicken laid over caramelized onions and blistered mild peppers. For a delicate finish, try the buttery almond tea cake, accompanied by sweet corn ice cream and tart blackberry verjus.

# Greens

Vegetarian 🍴

**C1**

### Building A, Fort Mason Center

**Phone:** 415-771-6222
**Web:** www.greensrestaurant.com
**Price:** $$

Lunch Tue – Sun
Dinner nightly

Annie Somerville's pioneering vegetarian restaurant has been around since 1979, but neither the menu nor the surroundings show Greens' age. Instead, fresh, energetic cuisine abounds, with a light touch and slight global inspiration. Brunch draws a big crowd, so be prepared to wait for those perfectly fried eggs over griddled potato cakes. Vegetarians and carnivores will rejoice after sampling the honest, colorful, down-to-earth seasonal entrées at dinner, followed by delightful desserts like a huckleberry upside down cake with a subtle kick from Meyer lemon.

Housed in historic Fort Mason, the warehouse-style space is rustic but refined, with sweeping views of the Golden Gate Bridge and sailboats on the Bay.

For a quick lunch, there's also a to-go counter.

# Hong Kong Lounge II 😊

Chinese 🍴🍴

**A4**

### 3300 Geary Blvd. (at Parker Ave.)

**Phone:** 415-668-8802
**Web:** www.hongkonglounge2.com
**Price:** $$

Lunch & dinner Wed – Mon

If the bland peach exterior of this restaurant doesn't entice you, trust that a juicy treasure lies beneath: some of the Bay's best dim sum offered at lunch. Skipping the carts for a made-to-order approach, the sizable menu groans with winners, including flaky, buttery baked pork buns, sautéed pea shoots delectably flavored with garlic, and one of the best egg custard tarts you're ever likely to taste—even if you've visited Hong Kong.

Throw in above-average tea options and a sizable vegetarian menu, and it's no wonder that this tiny gem draws legendary waits on weekend mornings. Just don't turn tail and head for the other Hong Kong Lounge further down Geary—despite their names, the two aren't affiliated, and the food isn't quite the same.

# Kiss

**D4**

Japanese ✗

### 1700 Laguna St. (at Sutter St.)

**Phone:** 415-474-2866
**Web:** www.kissseafood.com
**Price:** $$$

Dinner Wed – Sat

In a sea of trendy and flashy Japanese restaurants, this mom-and-pop standby sometimes gets drowned out—but one taste of its top-quality fish will have you hooked for life. Traditional nigiri, ranging from giant clam and halibut to bluefin tuna, arrives minimally dressed and served atop excellent rice. Appealing non-sushi options include a delicate *chawan mushi* filled with flaky white fish and buttery ginkgo berries, with an umami-rich dashi.

Adjacent to Japantown's Peace Plaza, tiny Kiss is easy to miss (look for the sign on the door), and reservations are recommended. Expect a quiet, sparse, and decorous atmosphere, with polite service from the husband-and-wife owners. The contemplative vibe encourages savoring each delicious morsel.

# Mamacita

**B2**

Mexican ✗✗

### 2317 Chestnut St. (bet. Divisadero & Scott Sts.)

**Phone:** 415-346-8494
**Web:** www.mamacitasf.com
**Price:** $$

Dinner nightly

An eclectic mix of young families, stylish hipsters, and see-and-be-seen Marinaites may pack its tables, but this hot ticket has more to offer than looks alone. The talented kitchen's creative takes on Mexican flavors are always on-point, from shrimp "al pastor" tacos with a sweet-spicy apple-mango salsa, to *molotes*, masa fritters oozing a delectable mixture of smoky ground beef and Monterey Jack cheese. Also try *esquites*, chile-inflected roasted corn with *cotija* and *crema*.

Mamacita's food is deeply flavorful, varied, and made for sharing (but you'll want to make a reservation if you bring a big group, because just about everyone has the same idea). Stuck with a wait? Head to the front bar for a tasty mezcal cocktail (or three) to help ease the sting.

# Nico ⚜

Contemporary XX

**B3**

### 3228 Sacramento St. (bet. Lyon St. & Presidio Ave.)

**Phone:** 415-359-1000
**Web:** www.nicosf.com
**Price:** $$$

Dinner Tue – Sat

Pacific Heights is a dreamy little pocket of San Francisco, with its colorful Victorians and sweeping views of the Bay. It's one of those magical places that linger in the memory, and now the area has yet another reason to remember it by: the lovely, urbane Nico—a relaxed and sophisticated French bistro with a distinctly Californian vibe.

The space houses only a 40-seat restaurant and a small bar area, but feels wonderfully expansive with its high ceilings, gleaming glass windows, seats overlooking Sacramento Street, and intimate tables with a view of the glass-enclosed kitchen in the back.

Diners at Nico experience a sophisticated five-course dinner, listed off a menu that notes only the main ingredients. Co-owners Nicolas and Andrea Delaroque are essentially asking you to play a trust game—and you should not hesitate to jump. Razor-thin slices of crispy artichoke arrive fanned over cool green herb jus and topped with delicious minced escargot; while a dish of wildly fresh peas finds perfect pairing in basil, peaches and sweet ricotta. Tender seared duck breast, duck confit roulade, and duck liver mousse are plated with *lentilles du Puy*, fresh cabbage, and roasted hedgehog mushrooms for an earthy finish.

# Octavia

**D3**

## 1701 Octavia St. (at Bush St.)

| | |
|---|---|
| **Phone:** | 415-408-7507 |
| **Web:** | www.octavia-sf.com |
| **Price:** | $$$ |

Dinner Tue – Sun

Chef/owner Melissa Perello may already be a local culinary personality at Frances, but her sequel, Octavia, shines even brighter from its home in the tony Lower Pacific Heights. Packed with a dynamic and diverse group of diners, the airy, open space feels minimalist and bistro-chic, from the white-tiled kitchen to those raw-wood benches lined with woolen pillows. Service is polite and efficient.

Chef Perello has a gift for elevating straightforward dishes through the use of superb ingredients and beautifully executed technique, beginning with a smoked trout fillet on a bed of cream cheese with green mustard seeds and steamed potatoes. Kale salad is deliciously crunchy and nicely matched with diced fennel, creamy avocado, salty aged parmesan, and breadcrumbs in a light vinaigrette. A petite filet of beef arrives tender and perfectly cooked to order, atop potatoes mashed with olive oil, grilled broccolini, and cabbage dressed in rapini pesto. Desserts are imaginative and masterful, so save room for their completely new take on profiteroles, soft and fresh, filled with poppy seed ice cream accented with tart rhubarb and kumquat.

Tables fill early, so be sure to reserve well in advance.

# Sociale

**A4**

Italian **XX**

### 3665 Sacramento St. (bet. Locust & Spruce Sts.)

**Phone:** 415-921-3200  Lunch Tue – Sat
**Web:** www.sfsociale.com  Dinner Mon – Sat
**Price:** $$

Italian in name but Californian in spirit, Sociale is a go-to for comfort fare that blends the best of both worlds. Creamy burrata is served over pumpkin purée and garnished with pepitas and pecans, while braised pork belly in a heady, robust sauce melts in the mouth. Dessert is a must; you'll be hard-pressed to find a table that can resist ordering the signature chocolate oblivion cake, a sinfully rich ganache accented with olive oil, sea salt, and amaretti cookie crumble. Located at the end of an alley with a heated patio, the vibe here is bistro-chic, with a hint of European flair accented by the warm, accommodating staff and the Italian and French chanteuses on the playlist. It's the kind of neighborhood gem that everyone wishes they had on their block.

# Viva Goa

**B2**

Indian **X**

### 2420 Lombard St. (bet. Divisadero & Scott Sts.)

**Phone:** 415-440-2600  Lunch & dinner daily
**Web:** www.vivagoaindiancuisine.com
**Price:** ☜☞

The Portuguese-influenced cuisine of Goa typically gets less play in the States than that of its northern neighbors. But Goan food takes center stage in this low-key dining room decked with burgundy booths. The kitchen is skilled at preparing delicious dishes like a spicy bronzed curry with prawns and coconut milk or *channa xacutti*, a creamy concoction of chickpeas, fresh coconut, onion, carrot, and poppy seeds.
The less adventurous will be pleased to find more familiar Indian items like crisp, golden-brown samosas filled with potato and peas, and chewy, smoky naan studded with garlic and fresh cilantro. Takeout and delivery are the core of the restaurant's dinner business, so those in search of a lively scene might prefer the crowd-drawing (and budget-friendly) lunch buffet.

# SPQR ❀

C4

### 1911 Fillmore St. (bet. Bush & Pine Sts.)

**Phone:** 415-771-7779
**Web:** www.spqrsf.com
**Price:** $$$

Lunch Sat – Sun
Dinner nightly

Pleasant and homey with excellent modern Italian cooking, there is little wonder why this destination is always bustling. Book in advance and assume that the dining counter reserved for walk-ins is already overflowing for the night. The space itself is narrow with tightly packed wood tables and furnishings; it would seem cramped were it not for the soaring ceiling, skylights, and open kitchen to brighten the mood. No matter where you look, the passion and enthusiasm for Italian specialties are palpable here—even contagious.

From *antipasti* to *dolce*, celebrated Chef Matthew Accarrino's extensive menu evolves with the seasons, yet remains as satisfying as it is impressive. Memorable and very creative pastas include supremely rich linguine in Alfredo sauce with abalone liver, grated *bottarga*, and the faintest hint of Meyer lemon. A *degustazione* of suckling pig arrives as six unique preparations, including medallions of succulent loin, slices of crisp-edged porchetta, and a cool pork terrine with pops of mustard seed.

Desserts feature the wonderfully sweet-tart flavors of thick and creamy maple panna cotta topped with wine-poached apple, a cloud of whipped cream, and cookie crumble.

# Spruce ✿

Californian ✕✕

**A4**

### 3640 Sacramento St. (bet. Locust & Spruce Sts.)

**Phone:** 415-931-5100
**Web:** www.sprucesf.com
**Price:** $$$

Lunch Mon – Fri
Dinner nightly

Set in one of San Francisco's snazziest neighborhoods, Spruce draws a regular crowd of wealthy retirees and corporate types by day. Evenings bring couples out for date night. The dining room, with its cathedral-style ceilings and skylight, is masculine yet modern—think studded leather chairs and splashes of charcoal and chocolate. A small front café serves coffee and pastries, while the marble bar lures happy-hour crowds for a cocktail or glass of wine from the extensive list.

Micro-seasonal and thoroughly Californian, Spruce spotlights cooking that's both simple and undeniably elegant. Rustic and homey starters may include hand-shaped ravioli filled with fresh ricotta and bathed in a broth of its tart whey, with fava leaf purée. A roulade of guinea hen stuffed with pork and duck sausage is exquisitely moist and juicy, and accompanied by thick fingers of nutty-sweet brown ale toast perfect for sopping up every last drop.

For dessert, a dense and decadent crème fraîche cheesecake is thick and creamy, with plenty of sweet vanilla flavor and a classic graham-cracker crust, and some added zing from juicy citrus segments and a quenelle of brilliantly tart Makrut lime ice cream.

# Mission

It's like the sun never goes down in the Mission—a bohemian paradise dotted with palm trees and doted on by scores of artists, activists, and a thriving Hispanic community. Here, urban life is illustrated through graffiti murals decorating the walls of funky galleries, thrift shops, and independent bookstores. Sidewalk stands burst with fresh plantains, nopales, and the juiciest limes this side of the border. Mission markets are known to be among the best in town and include **La Palma Mexicatessen** teeming with homemade *papusas*, chips, and fresh cheeses. **Lucca Ravioli** is loved for its legion of imported Italian goods; and the petite grocer, **Bi-Rite**, is big on prepared foods and flowers. Across the street, **Bi-Rite Creamery** is a cult favorite for ice cream. Moving on from markets to hip coffee haunts, **Ritual Coffee Roasters** is the leader of the pack. Join their fan base in single file outside the door, order a special roast from the barista, and find yourself in awe of this pleasing, very potent berry. Coffee connoisseurs also pay their respects at the original **Philz Coffee** for brews that cannot be beat.

## CLASSIC MEETS CUTTING-EDGE

The Mission is home to many contemporary hangouts, although those bargain *mercados* and dollar stores might suggest otherwise. **Dynamo Donuts** over on 24th Street is a dreamy retreat for these fried and sugary parcels of dough, complete with delectable flavors such as lemon-buttermilk and chocolate-star anise. **Walzwerk** charms with East German kitsch and is the go-to spot for traditional delights; while carb fiends know to stop by **The Sandwich Place** for freshly baked bread loaded with flavorful fillings. Here in the Mission, pizza reigns supreme and thin-crust lovers are happy to wait in line at **Pizzeria Delfina** for a wickedly good slice with crisped edges. A destination in its own right, **Tartine Bakery's** exceptional breads, pastries, and pressed sandwiches are arguably unmissable. However, to best experience this region's range of culinary talents, forgo the table and chairs and pull up at a curb on Linda Street, where a vigilant street food scene is brimming with a wealth of international eats.

## DAYTIME DELIGHTS

The city's hottest 'hood also offers a cool range of sweets. A banana split is downright retro-licious when served at the Formica counter of 90-year-old **St. Francis Fountain**, whose sundaes are made with Mitchell's Ice Cream, famous since 1953. Modish flavors like grasshopper pie and Kahlua mocha cream are in regular rotation at the newer **Humphrey Slocombe**; while **Mission Pie** is another local gem that tempts with a spectrum of pies—both sweet and savory. For more bold plates, **Plow** in Potrero Hill is a top breakfast and brunch hit. The space is small but insanely popular, so expect to wait a while before your first bite of lemon-ricotta pancake— there's even a menu for the little "plowers" who arrive by stroller. At lunch head to Peru by way of abuela-approved **Cholo Soy** for authentic, homemade, and always-affordable fare. **La Taqueria**'s carne asada burrito is possibly the most decadent around, but when it comes to tacos, it's a tossup on whether **El Gallo Giro** or **El Tonayense** takes the title for best truck in town.

## NIGHT BITES

The **Monk's Kettle** brags a beer list beyond par, with over 200 rotating craft brews on their carte. But, if cocktails are what you crave, then dash over to **Trick Dog** for tantalizing concoctions and creative small plates. Sate a late-night appetite at **Pig & Pie**, presenting an array of tasty eats including daily desserts, before dancing off these indulgences on Salsa Sunday at **El Rio**, the dive bar with a bustling back patio. Growling stomachs seem game to brave the harsh lighting at the many taquerias around, including **Cancún** for a veggie burrito or **El Farolito** for mind-blowing meats.

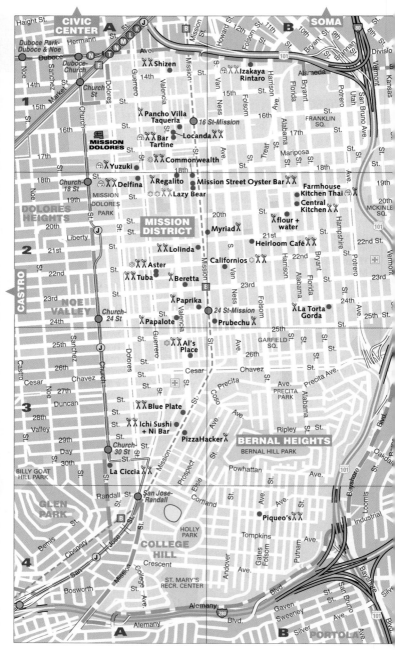

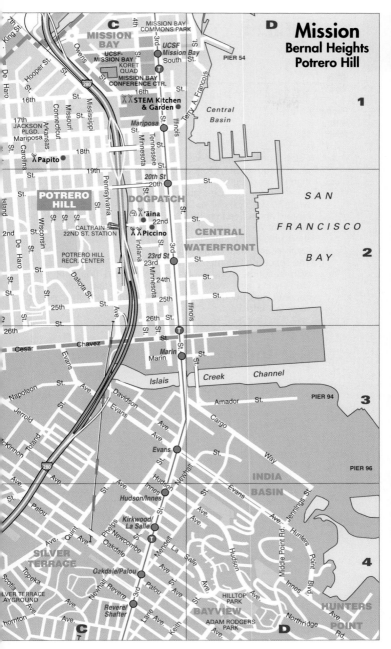

# Mission
## Bernal Heights
## Potrero Hill

**MISSION BAY**

MISSION BAY COMMONS PARK

4th St.

3rd St.

UCSF Mission Bay South St.

PIER 54

UCSF-MISSION BAY

KORET QUAD

MISSION BAY CONFERENCE CTR.

16th St.

STEM Kitchen & Garden

Central Basin

Owens St.

Hooper St.

De Haro St.

16th St.

Missouri St.

Mississippi St.

Minnesota St.

Tennessee St.

Illinois St.

Mariposa St.

17th St.

JACKSON PLGD.

Mariposa St.

Connecticut St.

Arkansas St.

Carolina St.

18th St.

Papito

19th St.

20th St.

20th St.

St.

SAN

**POTRERO HILL**

Pennsylvania St.

**DOGPATCH**

'āina

22nd

Piccino

CALTRAIN 22ND ST. STATION

Wisconsin St.

Island St.

De Haro St.

2nd St.

POTRERO HILL RECR. CENTER

Indiana St.

23rd St.

23rd St.

24th St.

FRANCISCO

CENTRAL WATERFRONT

BAY

3rd St.

Minnesota St.

Illinois St.

25th St.

25th St.

26th St.

26th St.

Dakota St.

Ave.

Cesar

Chavez St.

Marin St.

Marin

Evans St.

Napoleon St.

Jerrold St.

Islais

Creek

Channel

Amador St.

PIER 94

Davidson

Evans Ave.

Cargo Way

Evans Ave.

Evans St.

India St.

PIER 96

**INDIA BASIN**

Hudson

Innes

Newhall St.

Evans Ave.

Hudson/Innes

Kirkwood/La Salle

Phelps St.

Newcombe Ave.

Oakdale Ave.

Mendell St.

La Salle Ave.

Hudson Ave.

Jennings St.

Hunters Point Blvd.

Middle Point Rd.

Innes Ave.

**SILVER TERRACE**

Quint Ave.

Oakdale/Palou

Palou Ave.

Revere Ave.

Newhall St.

Revere Ave.

Shafter

HILLTOP PARK

**BAYVIEW**

ADAM RODGERS PARK

Keith St.

Lane St.

**HUNTERS POINT**

Northridge Rd.

Scotia

SILVER TERRACE PLAYGROUND

Topeka

Thornton

Ave.

77

# 'āina

**C2**

### 900 22nd St. (at Minnesota St.)

**Phone:** 415-814-3815
**Web:** www.ainasf.com
**Price:** $$

Lunch Wed – Sun

Catch some aloha vibes at this Hawaiian pop-up gone permanent in the Dogpatch, which imports many of its ingredients directly from the islands. The menu riffs on all the classics, from house-made "spam" *musubi* in lettuce-leaf wraps to warm, fluffy *malasada* doughnuts stuffed with guava custard and rolled in palm sugar. Larger appetites will love the decadent *loco moco*, made with slow-braised Korean-style short ribs, or the killer taro bread-French toast with coconut caramel and macadamia nuts.

The space isn't glamorous, but it's relaxed and comfortable, with beautiful wood tables, greenery, and floods of light. Don't miss the excellent low-ABV cocktails, either—the coconut milk punch with sweet vermouth and hibiscus-rose sugar is a knockout.

# Bar Tartine

**A1**

### 561 Valencia St. (bet. 16th & 17th Sts.)

**Phone:** 415-487-1600
**Web:** www.bartartine.com
**Price:** $$

Lunch Sat – Sun
Dinner nightly

A little bit Eastern European, a little bit Californian, and a whole lot of delicious, this is a fave among local gourmets. Now chef-owned (and with an impending name change), Bar Tartine's intensely satisfying menu continues to sate with everything from falafel-like sprouted lentil fritters with kefir and beet sauce, to roasted carrots with sumac yogurt and sunflower tahini. Wood-smoked, flash-fried potatoes, served with black garlic aïoli and an herb salad, are unmissable.

The hearty, homey vibe extends to the rustic dining room, with well-worn floors and simple wood furnishings, as well as the gracious staff, who makes diners feel right at home. Be sure to sample the tasting menu, which shows promise of great things to come, along with a house-made soda, tea, or cocktail.

# Al's Place ❀

Californian  ✗✗

**A3**

## 1499 Valencia St. (at 26th St.)

**Phone:** 415-416-6136
**Web:** www.alsplacesf.com
**Price:** $$

Dinner Wed – Sun

Fresh, seasonal vegetables and seafood headline this fantastic Mission District restaurant, where Chef Aaron London has managed to deftly recast proteins in a supporting role.

Straddling a sunny corner, Al's Place sports a bright blue façade and a kind of cheery, seaside, and retro-chic interior where tables are set with kitchen towel napkins and pendant lights glint against the natural light flooding into every corner. The service staff is friendly and attentive, but delightfully unfussy.

The restaurant's mix-and-match menu is easily shared, and dishes are light, incredibly flavorful and informal in all the right ways. Chef London combines thought-provoking flavors (think sunchoke and black lime) with ease, layering dimensions you didn't know existed. A soft and creamy plate of burrata finds its match in a coat of crunchy potato chips, and is plated with nutty potato skin mousse, grilled young asparagus, currant *soffritto*, and Miner's lettuce; while *tonnarelli* is paired with vibrant green garlic purée, citrusy bergamot and briny, grated *bottarga*. For dessert, don't miss the buttery Meyer lemon tart, studded with sweet strawberries and served with creamy lavender ice cream.

# Aster ⌘

Californian 🍴🍴

**A2**

## 1001 Guerrero St. (at 22nd St.)

**Phone:** 415-875-9810
**Web:** www.astersf.com
**Price:** $$$

Lunch Sat – Sun
Dinner nightly

These days, fine dining SF-style means hip soundtracks, spare spaces, and going to dinner in jeans, but Aster makes all of those trappings seem cool, never forced. Set in a quiet, residential corridor of the Mission, its caramel-colored banquettes, wood tabletops, and strands of LED lights add up to a studied, yet casual vibe. It's the kind of place where even the attentive, hospitable service manages to feel laid-back, but it's not just a den for hipsters, either—the older crowd is just as smitten.

Start with an aperitif as you peruse Chef Brett Cooper's elegant menu, which deftly interplays nutty, tangy, earthy, and salty elements in dishes like the soft-cooked farm egg, served atop crispy potatoes with a smoky bacon vinaigrette, crunchy puffed rice, and pearls of salmon roe. Steelhead trout arrives in a complex charred-allium bone broth, while deliriously rich pork head croquettes are balanced by a zippy arugula salad with blood orange *kosho*.

The lighter food makes it easy to save room for the excellent desserts, including a tart with layers of cookie crust, rich dark chocolate ganache, and white chocolate-parsnip ganache— plus a mist of vinegar for a hint of pleasant tanginess.

# Beretta

Italian ✗

**A2**

### 1199 Valencia St. (at 23rd St.)

**Phone:** 415-695-1199
**Web:** www.berettasf.com
**Price:** $$

Lunch Sat – Sun
Dinner nightly

A lively vibe, strong cocktail program, and late hours (until 1:00 A.M. nightly) ensure that the crowds have yet to abate at this longtime Mission hot spot. The menu is packed with flavorful Italian items and delicious antipasti, like rich and chunky eggplant *caponatina* with oozing burrata drizzled in excellent olive oil. Crisp thin crust pizzas are another highlight, with tangy sauce and cured meats like spicy salami and *coppa*.

A handful of booths offer a more private experience, while a large communal table serves the walk-in crowd. Whether you're spending an evening amid the glow of Edison bulbs and the clink of cocktail shakers or munching on a brunch-time pizza carbonara at a sunny outdoor table, you'll exit both sated and energized.

# Blue Plate

American ✗✗

**A3**

### 3218 Mission St. (bet. 29th & Valencia Sts.)

**Phone:** 415-282-6777
**Web:** www.blueplatesf.com
**Price:** $$

Dinner nightly

Wedged between the Mission and Bernal Heights, this casual and quirky charmer is constructed from reclaimed and repurposed materials all dripping with local art. This draws a relaxed crowd for comfort-food favorites. Dig into a vibrant heirloom-tomato salad with wedges of ripe peaches, sourdough, and creamy pecorino vinaigrette. Move on to slow-cooked pork belly with a smoked oyster-Thousand Island sauce and velvety soft-cooked egg.

The American menu shifts with the seasons, but a few dishes are constants, like the blue-plate meatloaf or fried chicken with cornbread. At nightfall, large groups and couples pack this long and narrow space to share slices of tangy key lime pie. Warm up from the winter chill at tables near the vibrant open kitchen.

# Californios ✿

Fusion 𝗫𝗫

**B2**

### 3115 22nd St. (bet. Capp St. & Van Ness Ave.)

**Phone:** 415-757-0994
**Web:** www.californiossf.com
**Price:** $$$$

Dinner Tue – Sat

In contrast to the bohemian posture of its neighborhood, this sterling debut by Chef Val M. Cantu is a luxurious oasis. A gleaming open kitchen and burnt caramel-hued banquettes pop against the dark lacquered walls, while sparkling chandeliers and shelves of cooking and design books further punctuate the upscale look of this intimate room. You'll feel as though you're dining in a chef's private atelier, complete with a polished, professional, and tight-knit staff that delivers truly impressive service.

While the feast set forth by Chef Cantu is inspired by Mexican flavors, it is modern Californian at its foundation. Produce plucked from nearby farms is transformed into stimulating bites to begin this tasting menu. Highlights from which have included delicious interpretations of *menudo* featuring fresh raw hamachi slices doused with a succulent tripe broth; and *esquites* that top a creamy sweet corn pudding with charred kernels and decadent Santa Barbara uni. Fourteen-day dry-aged Wagyu ribeye cap is grilled over the *binchotan* and served with charred onion, dabs of avocado purée, tomatillo salsa, as well as puffy, griddled sourdough tortillas.

And for dessert, if the sound of foie gras-and-coffee ice cream drizzled with *cajeta* seems crazy, just trust us—it's brilliant.

# Central Kitchen

Californian ✕✕

**B2**

### 3000 20th St. (at Florida St.)

**Phone:** 415-826-7004
**Web:** www.centralkitchensf.com
**Price:** $$$

Dinner Mon – Sat

A chic and sleek crowd of Mission foodies gathers at this trendy restaurant, nestled in a complex beside sister shop/deli Salumeria, cocktail bar Trick Dog, and coffee shop Sightglass. Wend your way to the central courtyard, with a trickling fountain and large glass doors leading into the main space, where a large open kitchen faces the simple wood tables.

Recent kitchen renovations resulted in a wood-burning hearth and expanded pasta program. Along the way, you might taste a mound of burrata surrounded by melon cubes, cucumber slices, and purslane tossed in a chili-herb vinaigrette. Gamey pork trotter agnolotti is balanced by lemon verbena; while hearth-roasted hen served in a black chili sauce and paired with chicken cracklings is nothing less than compelling.

# Delfina 😊

Italian ✕✕

**A2**

### 3621 18th St. (bet. Dolores & Guerrero Sts.)

**Phone:** 415-552-4055
**Web:** www.delfinasf.com
**Price:** $$

Dinner nightly

One of the city's greats for rustic Italian meals, Delfina is nestled on a block of gems for food lovers including Bi-Rite (and its creamery), Tartine Bakery, and sister spot Pizzeria Delfina. But even with this rarefied competition, Delfina books up well in advance and draws lines for its few walk-in seats.

The simple, yet lively dining room is attended to by a warm staff, and the bill of fare shifts with the seasons. Soul-satisfying dishes include house-made *fazzoletti* with garlicky basil pesto, tender potatoes, and crisp green beans, as well as a perfectly roasted half-chicken in a richly caramelized jus. For dessert, one spoonful of the creamy, delicate fig-leaf panna cotta, accented by macerated pluots, will have you floating home on a cloud.

# Commonwealth ❀

**A2**

### 2224 Mission St. (bet. 18th & 19th Sts.)

**Phone:** 415-355-1500
**Web:** www.commonwealthsf.com
**Price:** $$$

Dinner nightly

Commonwealth is a cool food-cum-tech haven, appropriately set in the heart of the Mission District. Inside, the dining room nails that Nordic-Cali sensibility, with sleek filament light bulbs, bare wood, and frosted glass that allows sunlight but shields guests from the bustling (read: gritty) surroundings. The hospitable team of servers shares that same informal style, making the counter the absolute best place to drink, dine, and chill with a few friends.

À la carte offerings are a welcome alternative to the fixed menu, and light portions encourage ordering four or more courses. The full tasting lets guests thoroughly explore the kitchen's adept contemporary cooking, but this meal may not be for everyone, as the chefs' creativity can be more eclectic than crowd-pleasing. Begin with small bites like house-made potato chips with malt vinegar foam and a jasmine tea cream accented with buttery nuts and crisp rice. Then transition into beautifully composed plates like artichoke toasts with black truffle cream or luscious sablefish with shrimp foam, coconut powder, and salt-roasted rutabaga.

For dessert, a lemon cake stuffed with pear purée is nicely enriched by burnt cinnamon ice cream.

# Farmhouse Kitchen Thai ☺

Thai 🍴

**B2**

### 710 Florida St. (bet. 19th & 20th Sts.)

**Phone:** 415-814-2920
**Web:** www.farmhousesf.com
**Price:** $$

Lunch & dinner daily

For authentic Thai flavors in a lively space, this Mission cutie is hard to beat—and has a dedicated following among the young techies and families who reside in the neighboring industrial lofts. Adorned with an accent wall covered in red and gold faucets and planter boxes full of Thai herbs, it's the kind of affordable weeknight spot that's designed for repeat business.

The array of classic dishes is prepared with quality ingredients, from the marinated flank steak rolled around crisp cucumber, cilantro and mint to the smoky coconut- and turmeric-marinated barbecue chicken with papaya salad and black sticky rice. A menu must: the herbal rice salad, a multi-dimensional blend of green mango, dried shrimp, chili, long beans, and much more.

# flour + water

Italian 🍴

**B2**

### 2401 Harrison St. (at 20th St.)

**Phone:** 415-826-7000
**Web:** www.flourandwater.com
**Price:** $$

Dinner nightly

As the name implies, two ingredients create a world of possibilities at this always-packed Mission hot spot. Neapolitan pizzas and handmade pastas (like al dente *garganelli* with whole-grain mustard and braised pork) will have you sighing after each bite, and a selection of more traditional mains (such as seared duck breast with chanterelles and pecorino-dusted charred Brussels sprouts) scores every bit as big as the noodles and pies.

Laid-back service, up-to-the-moment music, and a buzzy, effervescent vibe make flour + water the epitome of California cool.

Throw in a glass of their refined Italian wine, along with an alluring dessert like the salted caramel apple tart, and you can see why getting a table here is well worth the challenge.

# Heirloom Café

**Californian** ✗✗

2500 Folsom St. (at 21st St.)

**Phone:** 415-821-2500
**Web:** www.heirloom-sf.com
**Price:** $$

Dinner Mon – Sat

Though a nice selection of European vintages is a boon to this charming wine-centric bistro housed in a quiet corner of the Mission, the delicate and seasonal food keeps it bustling. Fresh and elegant Mediterranean-leaning dishes are pure expressions of California's bounty, especially the crunchy salad of Mutsu apples, Treviso, arugula, and toasted walnuts. Also try the crisp-skinned Hoffman chicken breast with roasted carrot hummus and salad of cucumber, avocado, onion, and feta. Simple desserts display a gentle touch. At the very least, indulge in a warm cookie, soft and golden brown, oozing with melting chocolate chips.

The dining room features communal tables, a marble counter with a close-up view of the open kitchen, warm candlelight, and even warmer service.

# Ichi Sushi + Ni Bar

**Japanese** ✗✗

3282 Mission St. (bet. 29th & Valencia Sts.)

**Phone:** 415-525-4750
**Web:** www.ichisushi.com
**Price:** $$$

Dinner Mon – Sat

Gone are the days when dining here was marred by the memory of how hard it was to score a table—this space down the street is much bigger than their previous spot. Relaxed and casual, with a big, fun mural on one wall, it's an über-busy smash among tech types and hipsters. Hit the central sushi bar for nigiri, or opt for *izakaya* dishes and sake (but no sushi) at adjacent Ni Bar.

The cognoscenti opt for the omakase, which might kick off with oysters garnished with yuzu juice and bits of caviar, followed by piping hot grilled skewers of tender and juicy miso-glazed pork. The nigiri pack punches of flavor from *yuzu kosho* or ponzu sauces and unique garnishes. The fish (maybe sea bream, Hokkaido scallops, ocean trout, or uni) are always fresh and delicious.

# Izakaya Rintaro 😊

Japanese ✗✗

**B1**

**82 14th St. (bet. Folsom & Trainor Sts.)**

**Phone:** 415-589-7022
**Web:** www.izakayarintaro.com
**Price:** $$

Dinner nightly

Delicate *izakaya* cuisine with a produce-centric NorCal sensibility awaits at this Japanese place, which transforms even the most humble dishes into art. Freshly made soft tofu is infused with fragrant bergamot peel, while meaty king trumpet mushrooms join classic chicken thighs and tender *tsukune* on the menu of smoky, caramelized charcoal-grilled skewers. The blancmange, infused with white sesame and topped with sweet black soybeans, is particularly unmissable. Housed in the former Chez Spencer, which was destroyed in a fire, Rintaro has kept its predecessor's gorgeous (and charred) arched ceiling beams, but added a delicate, wood-framed bar and booths. The result is a serene environment perfect for sharing and sampling the exquisite food.

# La Ciccia

Italian ✗✗

**A3**

**291 30th St. (at Church St.)**

**Phone:** 415-550-8114
**Web:** www.laciccia.com
**Price:** $$

Dinner Tue – Sun

Sardinian cuisine takes the spotlight at this family-run charmer, which draws a loyal crowd of Noe Valley regulars—particularly parents on a well-earned date night. The intimate, dark green dining room is always full, and nestled right up against the kitchen, from which the chef regularly pops out to greet guests in a blend of Italianenglish.

Start with the house-made bread and the home-cured *salumi* of the day (think citron-studded mortadella). The pasta *longa* with cured tuna heart slivers twirls fresh, delicious linguini with sea urchin and tomato, and an entrée of stewed goat is gamey but tender, served alongside braised cabbage, black olives, and fried capers. For a pleasant conclusion, cap it all off with the fluffy and airy ricotta-saffron cake.

# La Torta Gorda

B2

Mexican 🍴

**2833 24th St. (bet. Bryant & York Sts.)**

**Phone:** 415-642-9600
**Web:** www.latortagorda.net
**Price:** 🍜

Lunch & dinner daily

Those seeking a burrito respite along the 24th Street corridor would do well to head to this family-run diner, which serves some of the best *tortas* in town. Furnished with a retro diner counter, *fútbol* on the TV, and colorful décor, it's a place flooded with warmth and welcome, as its rotation of regulars attests.

The obvious move here is to go for a *torta*: the r*ajas con queso*, laden with peppers, Oaxaca cheese, refried beans, pickled jalapeños, and avocado, is lusciously melt-y and seriously good. But don't sleep on the specials from the owners' home district of Puebla, like the knockout *chile en nogada*, a poblano pepper stuffed with savory ground beef, nuts and raisins, and bathed in *crema* and pomegranate arils.

# Locanda

A1

Italian 🍴🍴

**557 Valencia St. (bet. 16th & 17th Sts.)**

**Phone:** 415-863-6800
**Web:** www.locandasf.com
**Price:** $$

Dinner nightly

This chic Roman-style *osteria* packs in the hipsters with a lively scene, killer cocktails, and inspired pastas, like radiatore tossed in tomato-lamb ragù with pecorino and hints of fresh mint. None of this is surprising, considering Locanda is from the team behind Mission favorite, Delfina. Classic chicken under a brick is characteristically on-point: smoky, tender, and served with a squeeze of lemon over nutty farro, Umbrian lentils, and red quinoa salad.

Reservations here are a tough ticket, but the attire and vibe are casual and welcoming (if noisy). Can't get a table? Seats at the bar, where the full menu is served, are a solid backup. Locanda's ultra-central address makes parking a challenge, so plan on using the valet or allotting extra time.

# Lazy Bear ✿ ✿

Contemporary 🍴

**A2**

### 3416 19th St. (bet. Mission & San Carlos Sts.)

**Phone:** 415-874-9921
**Web:** www.lazybearsf.com
**Price:** $$$$

Dinner Tue – Sat

Communal eating is the heart of this fine-dining dinner party. Lazy Bear may have its origins as an underground phenom, but today anyone can try to score a seat. That is, after jumping through a few virtual hoops: buy a ticket in advance and wait for an e-mail listing house rules to be followed in earnest. Rest assured this is all worth the effort.

The nightly tasting menu is dished out in a cool, bi-level warehouse and starts upstairs in the loft with aperitifs and snacks like Kumamoto oysters with apple-fennel mignonette. Then move downstairs to a dining room boasting two giant tree slabs as communal tables, each lined with 20 chairs. Diners are given a pencil and pamphlet informing them of the menu (with space for note-taking underneath) and are invited to enter the kitchen to chat with the talented cooks themselves. This leaves the young crowd dreamy-eyed with chef worship. The entire experience is more about the kitchen than the dining room, which isn't to everyone's taste.

Highlights include an elegant matsutake mushroom consommé with aromatic hints of redwood oil; and a decadent slice of deeply marbled Miyazaki ribeye, lightly seared and served with Asian pear and bone marrow-pumpkin pureé.

# Lolinda

**A2**

### 2518 Mission St. (bet. 21st & 22nd Sts.)

**Phone:** 415-550-6970  
**Web:** www.lolindasf.com  
**Price:** $$

Dinner nightly

Equal parts contemporary steakhouse and small plates spot, Argentine-inspired Lolinda is fun and sexy, loaded with twenty- and thirty-somethings gabbing over cocktails and sips of malbec. The soaring dining room with its wagon-wheel chandeliers and tufted-leather banquettes leads to a bustling second-floor mezzanine; whereas El Techo, a heated and more casual roof deck, offers sweeping views of the skyline. Sharing is encouraged and groups can be found divvying up plates of silky ono ceviche, flaky chicken empanadas, or sweet, caramelized pork belly.

Bull sculptures and murals remind diners that the chargrilled steak or crosscut beef short ribs with *chimichurri* are must-orders—tender and smoky, they'll transport you to Buenos Aires in a flash.

# Mission Street Oyster Bar

**A2**

### 2282 Mission St. (bet. 18th & 19th Sts.)

**Phone:** 415-621-6987  
**Web:** www.missionstreetoysterbarsf.com  
**Price:** $$

Lunch & dinner daily

Fans of the classic seafood dishes at the Castro's long-running Anchor Oyster Bar can skip the wait at this Mission retreat from its former chef. It's bigger, more modern, and a lot less charming than the mothership, but the menu is nearly identical. So, if you don't feel like waiting in line at itty-bitty Anchor, this is the place to go.

Anchor's cioppino is legendary, and the version here is also a must-order, piled high with clams, mussels, calamari, prawns, and flaky fish. The huge portion can easily serve two, especially with the accompanying cheesy garlic bread, ideal for dipping in the lip-smacking, tomato-kissed broth. If you still have any room, there are plenty of briny local oysters, seafood salads, Dungeness crab cakes, and more.

# Myriad

International ✗

**B2**

**2491 Mission St. (bet. 20th & 21st Sts.)**

| | | |
|---|---|---|
| **Phone:** | 415-525-4335 | Lunch & dinner daily |
| **Web:** | www.myriadsf.com | |
| **Price:** | **$$** | |

Not sure what to eat tonight? Bring your indecision and your appetite to this globe-trotting gastropub, which turns out skillfully prepared dishes from across cultures. Whether you're feeling like a dose of Moroccan (roasted lamb sandwich with tomato jam and feta), Mexican (*cochinita pibil*), French (farm toast with *fromage blanc* and roasted plums), Italian (ricotta *zeppole* with caramel sauce), or any combination of the above, there's a dish that's sure to satisfy. And, there's also a selection of beer and wine to match every delightful bite. Myriad sprawls over two long and narrow rooms, where hipster couples and families with kids trade bites of the shareable dishes. If you're paralyzed by choice, friendly servers are happy to lend a hand.

# Pancho Villa Taqueria

Mexican ✗

**A1**

**3071 16th St. (bet. Mission & Valencia Sts.)**

| | | |
|---|---|---|
| **Phone:** | 415-864-8840 | Lunch & dinner daily |
| **Web:** | www.sfpanchovilla.com | |
| **Price:** | ⊜ | |

Around the corner from the 16th and Mission BART stop, this long-running taqueria earns high marks from locals. Upon entering, take a moment to step back and examine the menu board; the vested attendants working the flat-tops and grills will be quizzing you on the beans, condiments, and choice of ten meats you desire. That line moves quickly, so be ready. After loading up your burrito, perhaps filled with thinly sliced steak and butterflied prawns, select an *agua fresca* from the glass barrels, and hit the salsa bar. It features award-winning varieties in every range of heat and sweet to complement their thin, ultra-crispy tortilla chips. Ambience is nil and tables can be hard to snag, but the reward is a fresh and flavorful taste of the Mission.

# Papalote

Mexican  🍴

**A2**

### 3409 24th St. (bet. Poplar & Valencia Sts.)

**Phone:** 415-970-8815
**Web:** www.papalote-sf.com
**Price:** 💰

Lunch & dinner daily

Head to this little standout for a lighter take on the gut-busting taqueria treats that define the Mission. Papalote manages to deliver the goods without the guilt, and the difference is clear in the outstanding fish tacos: corn tortillas piled with fresh, flaky white fish (sautéed in butter and garlic) along with sliced romaine and chopped tomato.

Unlike the competition, Papalote doesn't have a salsa bar, but it doesn't need one: its defining feature is its gobsmackingly good, house-made roasted tomato salsa, which you'll want to slather on dishes like the pitch-perfect breakfast burrito, stuffed with scrambled eggs, chorizo, cheese, and guacamole. The space and service are bare-bones, but with food this good, you won't care.

# Papito

Mexican  🍴

**C1**

### 317 Connecticut St. (at 18th St.)

**Phone:** 415-695-0147
**Web:** www.papitosf.com
**Price:** 💰

Lunch & dinner daily

It might be French-owned (neighboring bistro Chez Maman is a sibling), but Papito is 100% Mexican, as your first bite of the outstanding shrimp tacos, piled with spicy adobo and sweet mango salsa, will attest. An ear of caramelized, grilled corn slathered in spicy mayo, lime juice, and cotija cheese will transport you to the streets of D.F., while the smoky *coloradito* sauce that bathes tender chicken enchiladas will have you scraping your plate for more. Papito's flavors are big, but its space is no more than a shoebox, so be prepared to wait or take your order to-go. If you dine in, the vibrant look matches the energetic food, with bright walls and a bustling side bar. Note: Hayes Valley's Papito, once a satellite, now has different owners.

# Paprika

A2                                    Eastern European ✗
**3324 24th St. (bet. Bartlett & Mission Sts.)**

**Phone:** 415-375-1477                         Lunch Sat
**Web:** N/A                                  Dinner nightly
**Price:** ⊜⊜

Diners who set foot into Paprika, named for one of the most essential spices in Eastern European cooking, should prepare to feel as if they've been transported to Prague. It's a simple, no-frills, cash-only kind of place, but cheerful service, affordable fare, and a vast selection of European draft beers make for a relaxed, enjoyable atmosphere.

The small menu manages to cover all the bases, from tender, well-seasoned pork goulash packed with sweet tomatoes, caramelized onions, garlic, and zippy paprika, to a smoky, blistered Polish kielbasa over creamy mashed potatoes and paprika-infused gravy (you'll want some bread to soak up every last drop of this). Snag a table at one of the bay windows, then settle in to enjoy your meal with a stein of beer, of course.

# Piccino

C2                                            Italian ✗✗
**1001 Minnesota St. (at 22nd St.)**

**Phone:** 415-824-4224                      Lunch & dinner daily
**Web:** www.piccino.com
**Price:** $$

A progenitor of the increasingly hot Dogpatch restaurant scene, Piccino embodies the neighborhood's many flavors, drawing families with kids in tow, young tech types, gregarious retirees, and more. Its memorable yellow exterior houses a relaxed, artsy-urban interior with lots of wood and natural light, a perfect venue for unwinding with friends.

Everyone comes here for deliciously blistered pizzas like the *funghi*, with roasted mushroom duxelles, sautéed wild mushrooms, *stracchino*, and slivers of garlic. Though pizza is a focus, Piccino excels in appetizers like tender, skillfully prepared *polpette* in tomato sauce, and must-order desserts such as a delectable hazelnut-cocoa nib cake. Their adjacent coffee bar is an area favorite.

# Piqueo's

Peruvian XX

**B4**

### 830 Cortland Ave. (at Gates St.)

**Phone:** 415-282-8812          Dinner nightly
**Web:** www.piqueos.com
**Price:** $$

Gather your friends for a trip to Peru (with a layover in Bernal Heights) at Piqueo's, where the menu of flavor-packed small plates is built for sharing. From crispy yucca balls stuffed with cheese to tender pork adobo over mashed sweet potatoes, hearty palate-pleasers abound. Sauces are a house specialty; the tender beef empanada boasts a trio of garlicky *huacatay*, creamy *huancaina*, and spicy *rocoto*. And where else can you sample a quinoa-blueberry flan?

While not as glamorous as upscale sister La Costanera, Piqueo's has its own charm, thanks to a quaint atmosphere with wood floors and an open kitchen. It's a standby for Bernal families, who stroll over in the evenings to catch up with the friendly servers and dig into their favorite dishes.

# PizzaHacker

Pizza X

**A3**

### 3299 Mission St. (bet. 29th & Valencia Sts.)

**Phone:** 415-874-5585          Dinner Tue – Sun
**Web:** www.thepizzahacker.com
**Price:** $$

Wood-fired pizza, refreshing salads, cold beer: PizzaHacker may keep its programming simple, but the resulting product has no end of eager customers. Nicely blistered pies with topping combos like house-made Italian sausage, *sopressata*, and crimini mushrooms are the mainstays, but the Intermezzo salad, packed with beans, alfalfa sprouts, and tangy poppy-seed lemon dressing, has its devotees as well. Throw in a local brew or a simple glass of red, and you're good to go.

A young, tech-savvy crowd fills the Hacker's hall from the get-go, gathering at picnic tables under the long green chalkboard wall that doubles as the evening's menu. If you'd rather skip the boisterous scene, you can place a takeout order by text— they'll even text back with a pickup time.

# Prubechu

Chamorro 🍴

**B2**

2847 Mission St. (bet. 24th & 25th Sts.)

**Phone:** N/A
**Web:** N/A
**Price:** $$

Dinner Tue – Sat

Owned by two natives of Guam, Prubechu is the only Bay Area restaurant that serves the island's Chamorro cuisine. It's a shoebox-sized space without a full kitchen, but the intrepid staff manages to turn out utterly unique, utterly delicious meals like none you've ever had.

Diners can choose between a tasting menu offering intricate Chamorro interpretations, or a small selection of homey à la carte dishes. Either way, the results are thrilling, from a flavorful chicken sausage steamed with luscious coconut milk in a banana leaf, to umami-rich dried pork shoulder with nettle purée. The nutty, creamy toasted rice porridge with caramel soy and a tempura-battered soft-cooked egg is a standout, as is a gently sweet and caramelized banana donut.

# Regalito

Mexican 🍴

**A2**

3481 18th St. (at Valencia St.)

**Phone:** 415-503-0650
**Web:** www.sfregalito.com
**Price:** $$

Lunch Sat – Sun
Dinner Tue – Sun

*Regalito* is Spanish for "little gift," and those who dine here will surely understand the choice of name. Instead of relying on the bold, spicy approach of local taquerias, Regalito takes a milder, ingredient-focused path, infusing dishes like chicken enchiladas with new life via handmade corn tortillas, fresh roast chicken, and a delicate green chili sauce. Familiar Mexican favorites get an upgrade here, from the super-sweet, fresh corn on the cob *elote* with tangy chili-lime mayo and *cotija*, to a silky vanilla flan bobbing in a pool of caramel sauce.

The cheery, colorful space and friendly servers are welcoming, but the real charmers are the smiling cooks, who happily interact with diners in prime seats overlooking the open kitchen.

# Shizen

Vegan **✗✗**

**A1**

**370 14th St. (at Stevenson St.)**

**Phone:** 415-678-5767
**Web:** N/A
**Price:** $$

Dinner nightly

At first glance, this stylish *izakaya* and sushi bar could be another in a line of similar places that dot the San Francisco landscape, were it not for a major twist: everything on the menu is vegan. Purists and die-hard carnivores may scoff, but the food is exceptional, skillfully manipulating vegetables and starches to recreate seafood-centric Japanese favorites.

Spicy tuna gets a run for its money from the impressive spicy *tofuna* rolls, with chili-inflected minced tofu and cucumber crowned with creamy avocado and dusted in chili "tobiko." A yuba salad with miso dressing and tempura-battered shiitake mushrooms stuffed with faux-crab are equally compelling. Throw in a sleek, contemporary setting, and Shizen is a winner for eaters of all stripes.

# STEM Kitchen & Garden

Mediterranean **✗✗**

**C1**

**499 Illinois St. (bet. 16th & Mariposa Sts.)**

**Phone:** 415-915-1000
**Web:** www.stemkitchensf.com
**Price:** $$

Lunch Mon – Fri
Dinner Mon – Sat

Plenty of restaurants boast about their garden-fresh menus, but this Mission Bay hottie means business: most of its ingredients come straight from the raised garden beds on the rooftop patio, which also double as decorative elements. With its buzzing bocce courts and stunning fire-pit seating overlooking the Bay, it's already become a favorite among the staff at the nearby UCSF complexes.

Simple, delicious food is the order of the day. A salad of garden lettuces in Meyer lemon vinaigrette is delicate and bright, while a blistered pizza comes loaded with *broccoli de ciccio*, *guanciale*, and mozzarella. Piquant *berbere*-spiced chicken plays surprisingly well with a tangy kale Caesar, and the tart, creamy, unmissable Meyer lemon verrine is like spring in a glass.

Culinary Agents
Connecting the industry
Find the best jobs. Find the best people.
CulinaryAgents.com

Culinary Agents
Connecting the industry
Find the best jobs. Find the best people.
CulinaryAgents.com

# Tuba

**A2**

Turkish ✗✗

**1007 Guerrero St. (bet. 22nd & 23rd Sts.)**

**Phone:** 415-826-8822
**Web:** www.tubarestaurant.com
**Price:** $$

Dinner nightly

In a city where Turkish dishes are too often folded into in an unsatisfying "pan-Middle Eastern" menu, this bona fide charmer bursts with authentic flavor, as evidenced by its sizable clientele of handsome expats. Tuba's space is warm and welcoming, with crimson walls, soft, romantic lighting, and a friendly staff.

Start with a selection of meze like *sigara boregi* (thin phyllo-dough pastries filled with potatoes and peppery feta) and moist, fluffy falafel. Then dive into a smoky ground beef kebab with spicy chopped bell peppers and zesty spices. Desserts like the *künefe*, a mild white cheese wrapped in phyllo, soaked in syrup, and topped with pistachios, are worth saving room for, especially with a strong Turkish coffee or intensely flavored tea.

# Yuzuki 😊

**A1**

Japanese ✗

**598 Guerrero St. (at 18th St.)**

**Phone:** 415-556-9898
**Web:** www.yuzukisf.com
**Price:** $$

Lunch Sat – Sun
Dinner Wed – Sun

Formerly an *izakaya*, this elegant Japanese restaurant has changed chefs and focus, offering delicate Washoku-style fare (read: no sushi). A meal might begin with thin slices of lightly torched mackerel, artfully arranged on shiso leaves; then transition to tender Wagyu beef *tataki*, airy shredded vegetable and shrimp tempura, and a delicate sundae of azuki beans, mocha, and kelp gelée over vanilla ice cream.

With Tartine Bakery and other great gourmet spots sharing its block, there's no denying the fact that Yuzuki has a lot of competition. But with such an exquisite array of plates, not to mention outstanding organic sake and nutty buckwheat tea for sipping, it will transport you to Japan—provided you can snag a tough-to-get reservation.

# Nob Hill

Thanks in large part to its connection to the Gold Rush industry magnates, Nob Hill is San Francisco's most privileged neighborhood. Its many plush mansions, strategic location complete with breathtaking views of the Bay, and accessible cable car lines that chug up to the top, ensure that it remains home to the upper crust. Speaking of which, note the familiar tinkle from wind chimes and postcard-perfect brass rails checking tourists who dare to lean out and take in the sights. Despite the large scale devastation following the 1906 earthquake, this iconic part of town bordering the gorgeous Golden Gate Bridge and Alamo Square's "Painted Ladies" was able to retain its wealthy reputation thanks to an upswell of swanky hotels, door-manned buildings, and opulent dining rooms. Unsurprisingly, "Snob Hill" today continues to echo of mighty egos and wealthy families who can be seen making the rounds at **Big 4**, cradled within The Huntington Hotel. Named after the 1800s railroad titans, this stately hermitage is known for its antique memorabilia and nostalgic chicken potpie. A stop at **Swan Oyster Depot** for some of the finest seafood in town is a sure way to impress your out-of-town, tourist-trapped friends, but be prepared to wait up to several hours on busy days for one of their coveted few seats.

Cocktails and small plates ensure epic levels of enjoyment at the extravagant **Top of the Mark** restaurant, boasting a sleek, lounge-like vibe and panoramic vistas of the sun setting over the cityscape. Moving from day to night, a handful of food-centric saloons fortuitously sate the tastes of young professionals with pennies to spare. At the top is **Cheese Plus**, showcasing over 300 international varieties, artisan charcuterie, and of course, chocolate for added decadence. Just steps away, **The Jug Shop** is an old-time, reliable, and very personable destination among locals who can be seen lapping up micro-brew beers and global wines. For a total departure, kick back with a *mai tai* (purportedly invented at Oakland's Trader Vic's in 1944) at **Tonga Room & Hurricane Bar**—a tiki spot in the *très* chic

Fairmont, decked out with an indoor swimming pool that also functions as a floating stage.

## RUSSIAN HILL

Slightly downhill and north toward Polk Street, the vibe mellows on the approach to Russian Hill, named after a Russian cemetery that was unearthed up top. Chockablock with cute boutiques, dive bars, and casual eateries, this neighborhood's staircase-like streets are scattered with predominantly un-Russian groups and singles that seem more than willing to mingle. Good, affordable fare abounds here, at such popular haunts as **Caffé Sapore** serving breakfast specials, sandwiches, soups, and salads; as well as **Street** for fine, seasonal American cuisine. Tacky taqueria-turned-nighttime disco, **Nick's Crispy Tacos**, is a perennial favorite. The downright sinful and delicious chocolate

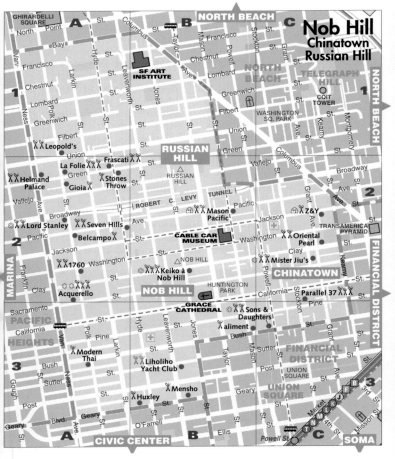

earthquake from **Swensen's Ice Cream**'s flagship parlor (in business since 1948) is undoubtedly the town's most treasured dessert. From flashy finds to tastefully decorated destinations, **Bacchus Wine Bar** is an elegant and ever-alluring Italian-style spot lauded for both its beautiful interiors and exceptional wine, beer and sake selections.

## CHINATOWN

Scattered with large parks—Huntington Park is perhaps the city's most coveted stretch of greenery—Nob Hill's scene begins to change as you venture east to the country's oldest **Chinatown**. Here, authentic markets, dim sum palaces, souvenir emporiums, banks, and other businesses, which employ scores of the immigrant community, spill down the eastern slope of the Hill in a wash of color and vibrant Chinese characters. Amid these steep streets find some of the city's most addictive and crave-worthy barbecue pork buns at old and almost antique dim sum houses where jam-packed dining is the name of the game. Even gastronomes flock here to scour the shelves at family-owned and operated **Wok Shop**, bursting with unique cookware, linens, tools, and all things Asian. Others may prefer to avoid the elbow-to-elbow experience and take home a slice of Chinatown by way of juicy dumplings, buns, and sweets from **Good Mong Kok Bakery**. Soldier on from this excellent and inexpensive take-out spot only to spin out a sugar-rush over creamy, oven-fresh custard tarts at **Golden Gate Bakery**; or prophetic little samples in the making at **Golden Gate Fortune Cookie Factory**. The amazing and very affordable **House of Nanking** is another rare (read: necessary) pleasure. Don't bother ordering from the menu—the owner will usually grab them from your hands and take over the ordering. But really, nobody is complaining. Finally, the **Mid-Autumn Moon Festival** brings friends and families together over mooncakes—a traditional pastry stuffed with egg yolk and lotus seed paste—and to reflect upon summer's bounty.

# Acquerello ✿ ✿

Italian XXX

**A2**

1722 Sacramento St. (bet. Polk St. & Van Ness Ave.)

**Phone:** 415-567-5432
**Web:** www.acquerello.com
**Price:** $$$$

Dinner Tue – Sat

With its air of old-world sophistication, Acquerello is the kind of establishment where one dresses for dinner, which is always an occasion. The room feels embellished yet comfortable, with vaulted wood-beamed ceilings, warm terra-cotta walls, and contemporary paintings. It seems to draw celebrants of a certain age who are happy to splurge on a white truffle-tasting menu.

Each prix-fixe promises expertise and finesse, with a carefully curated wine list to match. Count yourself lucky if your meal begins with their famed parmesan *budino* surrounded by black truffle "caviar." Pasta must not be missed, such as the very fine and vibrant tajarin with a tableside shaving of impossibly earthy white truffle. Venison medallions wrapped in crisped pancetta are served with beautiful simplicity alongside pear slices, onion jam, chanterelles, and butternut squash purée. Refreshing desserts include delicate almond milk-panna cotta covered with vin santo jelly and crowned by buttery crushed almonds, quince, and tufts of dehydrated Balsamic vinegar.

Save room for one of the best mignardises carts you will ever encounter, stocked with superlative house-made chocolates, macarons, *pâtes de fruits*, and caramels.

# aliment

**B3**

American ✗

**786 Bush St. (bet. Mason & Powell Sts.)**

**Phone:** 415-829-2737
**Web:** www.alimentsf.com
**Price:** $$

Dinner nightly

Named for the Latin term for nourishment, this chic and comforting retreat feeds the soul as well as the body. Cheery, upbeat service, a small but compelling wine list, and an eye-catching stainless steel and wood design make it a pleasant retreat from the heart of Union Square, located just blocks away.

The menu may be short, but it's saturated with flavor-packed, hearty options like a thick and succulent grilled pork chop with pink peppercorn, set over roasted fingerling potatoes and apple chutney; or seared diver scallops in green curry cream topped with crunchy quinoa. For dessert, the homemade custardy cheesecake, served on a delicately browned cookie-crumb base and coupled with chopped yuzu jelly and peel, is obligatory.

# Belcampo

**A2**

American ✗

**1998 Polk St. (at Pacific Ave.)**

**Phone:** 415-660-5573
**Web:** www.belcampomeatco.com
**Price:** $$

Lunch & dinner Tue – Sun

If dining in a butcher shop doesn't sound appealing, you haven't yet been to Belcampo. The space is downright elegant—all blue banquettes, rich paneled wood, and wide picture windows. Then imagine the local, organically raised meat, available to-go from a friendly butcher or cooked to perfection on your plate, which is bar none.

You'll taste the difference in the juicy, hand-chopped cheeseburger, swathed in melting cheddar and caramelized onions, and the tender smoked guinea hen with *chimichurri*. Herbivores will be pleased to know that meat isn't the only focus here (try the escarole-arugula salad, which gets bite from an almond-anchovy vinaigrette), and even the wine list is thoughtful. For dessert—an *alfajor* features crumbly cookies sandwiching dulce de leche.

# Frascati

**A2**

## 1901 Hyde St. (at Green St.)

**Phone:** 415-928-1406    Dinner nightly
**Web:** www.frascatisf.com
**Price:** $$

Forget circling for parking and hop on a cable car instead to reach this quaint Mediterranean standby, where you'll see more of the iconic vehicles pass by their large front windows. Inside, closely-spaced tables are ideal for an intimate meal, and local residents definitely know it, because reservations are always hard to come by.

Frascati's fare may not be the city's most innovative, but it is very satisfying, thanks to well-made classics like tender potato gnocchi with asparagus and peas in thyme-white truffle butter, or grilled duck breast in pomegranate sauce over hearts of palm and herb spaetzle. Split the luscious *pain perdu*, caramelized sponge cake soaked in citrusy crème anglaise, and let the friendly servers and soft lighting work their magic.

# Gioia

**A2**

## 2240 Polk St. (bet. Green & Vallejo Sts.)

**Phone:** 415-359-0971    Lunch & dinner Tue – Sun
**Web:** www.gioiapizzeria.com
**Price:** $$

With its large space and casual vibe, Gioia has become a Russian Hill standby, drawing families with kids, groups of friends, and even solo diners (there's lots of counter seating). The rustic décor features white subway-tile walls, an open kitchen, and wood and metal furniture. Be warned: the noise level can be a bit high for any intimate conversation.

The highlight here is pizza, with creatively topped pies like summer squash with pesto, burrata, and Calabrian chili, or sausage, broccoli, leeks, pecorino, and olives. They're pricey, but worth it. A selection of salads and antipasti make for great starters. Otherwise, opt for *rigatoncini* in a meaty pork ragù with fresh, creamy ricotta and more Calabrian chili.

A second location dwells in Berkeley.

# Helmand Palace

Afghan XX

**A2**

2424 Van Ness Ave. (bet. Green & Union Sts.)

**Phone:** 415-345-0072      Dinner nightly
**Web:** www.helmandpalacesf.com
**Price:** $$

A drab exterior and an awkward Van Ness address haven't always worked in Helmand Palace's favor, but the food-savvy know it's one of the Bay Area's best for Afghan cuisine. The well-appointed interior is worlds away from the busy thoroughfare's steady stream of traffic, with linen-draped tables, big blue-cushioned armchairs, and warm, inviting service.

Every meal here kicks off with a basket of fluffy flatbread, served with three irresistible dipping sauces. The *kaddo*, caramelized baby pumpkin and ground beef in a garlic-yogurt sauce, is a perennial favorite, as is the *chapendaz*, marinated beef tenderloin over a tomato-pepper purée, rice, and lentils. Vegetarians will find numerous dishes to enjoy, all of them just as flavorful as the carnivorous feast.

# Huxley

American X

**B3**

846 Geary St. (bet. Hyde & Larkin Sts.)

**Phone:** 415-800-8223      Lunch Sat – Sun
**Web:** www.huxleysf.com      Dinner Tue – Sat
**Price:** $$

Tattooed industry types can't get enough of this itsy-bitsy Tenderloin bistro, which serves as something of an oasis on an otherwise gritty block. The space has a vintage vibe, with brass art deco accents, etched mirrors, and lots of wood paneling, and even the '90s hip-hop soundtrack is a throwback.

Because of its small size, over half of Huxley's seating is at the counter, so take the hint and grab a front-row seat. There, you can watch the minuscule kitchen turn out quite the array of high-end comfort fare—from a simple, perfect salad of wild arugula with aged balsamic to a *plancha*-grilled fillet of Mt. Lassen trout with roasted sunchokes. The dry-aged "Hux Deluxe" burger is a big hit, particularly during the mega-popular weekend brunch.

# Keiko à Nob Hill ✻

Fusion **XxX**

### 1250 Jones St. (at Clay St.)

**Phone:** 415-829-7141
**Web:** www.keikoanobhill.com
**Price:** $$$$

Dinner Tue – Sun

Elegant, discreet, and romantic, Keiko à Nob Hill blends unique culinary style with traditional appeal. Cushioned banquettes wrap the square dining room, outfitted with subdued lighting, fabric-covered walls, and heavy brown trim, resulting in a space that is lovely (if of a certain age).

It is always best to be prompt: the formal service team is gracious but handles each night's single seating with precision, serving all guests at once. Arriving on time is crucial as this kitchen takes its work and its mission rather earnestly.

Chef Keiko Takahashi's nightly tasting menu is a twelve-course progression of French culinary technique with subtle hints of Japanese flavors. Her success is undeniable from the first taste of Japanese spiny lobster presented in a martini glass with lobster-tomato water foam and a chilled layer of fruity bell pepper mousse. Moist, fragrant, and remarkably delicious Cornish hen arrives tucked with razor-thin shavings of black truffle beneath its skin, complemented with parmesan foam, Ibérico ham-cream sauce, and asparagus. A simple parfait is an extraordinary finale that includes coffee *pâte de fruit*, marron, and bits of crunchy meringue atop Mont Blanc cream with grilled pears.

# La Folie

French

**A2**

**2316 Polk St. (bet. Green & Union Sts.)**

**Phone:** 415-776-5577
**Web:** www.lafolie.com
**Price:** $$$$

Dinner Tue – Sat

Few grandes dames of high-end French cuisine remain in the city, but this long-running spot from Chef/owner Roland Passot has held strong. With two formal dining rooms featuring starched tablecloths, polished servers, and a tall art deco wine case, it's a favorite among occasion-celebrating couples and the luxury-loving tourist crowd.

Diners can build their own three-to-five course prix-fixe, with classic dishes like a double bone-in lamb chop or a tower of crispy goat cheese, eggplant, and portobello mushroom. Thicker wallets can splurge on the chef's-choice tasting menu or the array of sumptuous supplements, like foie gras and butter-poached lobster. For dessert, chocolate lovers should be sure not to miss out on the velvety Valrhona mousse.

# Leopold's

Austrian XX

**A1**

**2400 Polk St. (at Union St.)**

**Phone:** 415-474-2000
**Web:** www.leopoldssf.com
**Price:** $$

Lunch Sat – Sun
Dinner nightly

The boisterous spirit of an Austrian *gasthaus* is alive and well in Russian Hill. All thanks are due to Leopold's, which draws a young crowd to its slice-of-Vienna dining room, adorned with wood booths and deer antlers, and attended to by cheerful female servers in dirndls. If dinner alone is your goal, go early; convivial groups lend the space a communal mien, but also get larger and louder as the night wears on and the boots of beer are drained.

The carte du jour is rife with well-executed classics like golden-brown pork wiener schnitzel with cucumber salad, vegetable strudel, and delectable raspberry Linzer torte. If you've got a group in tow, the *choucroute garni* platter, laden with pork ribs, sausage, potatoes, and sauerkraut, is a crowd-pleaser.

# Liholiho Yacht Club

B3

**871 Sutter St. (bet. Jones & Leavenworth Sts.)**

**Phone:** 415-440-5446
**Web:** www.liholihoyachtclub.com
**Price:** $$$

Dinner Mon – Sat

Hip professionals have dropped anchor at this buzzy Tendernob beauty, which draws lines even before it opens to sample Chef/owner Ravi Kapur's distinctly personal blend of Hawaiian, Californian, and South Asian flavors. The clean-lined space features a sunny yellow open kitchen and a big photo of Kapur's mother (circa 1975) that give it a touch of island flair.

His kitchen turns out items that are wide-ranging and flavorful—from duck hearts with pickled cherries and a five-spice glaze, to a quirky salad of tripe, marinated squid, cabbage and peanuts. Don't sleep on the house-made "spam" that enlivens fried rice with abalone mushrooms and uni; or the hearty country pork steak with coconut miso—all of which come in generous portions.

# Mason Pacific 😊

B2

**1358 Mason St. (at Pacific Ave.)**

**Phone:** 415-374-7185
**Web:** www.masonpacific.com
**Price:** $$

Dinner Tue – Sun

A devastating fire forced it to renovate and change chefs, but this Nob Hill gem has bounced back better than ever, and continues to draw an upscale crowd of couples seeking a cushy retreat. The space is divided into two parts: a front area furnished with a bar and high-tops as well as a second, more plush dining room appointed with tufted banquettes and soft lighting. Overall, this is a cozy and comfortable spot among the glamour set.

That designation also applies to the menu, with inventive creations like roasted potatoes in a sea urchin-egg yolk sauce; creamed summer corn with ribbons of squid and celery; as well as scallop crudo with avocado and citrus. Save space for the tangy lemon curd, topped with crumbles of buttery shortbread and toasted coconut.

# Lord Stanley

Californian ✗✗

**A2**

**2065 Polk St. (at Broadway)**

**Phone:** 415-872-5512
**Web:** www.lordstanleysf.com
**Price:** $$$

Dinner Tue – Sat

You'll feast like a very refined lord at this outstanding establishment, which, like its husband-and-wife chef/owners, is half Californian, half European. The West Coast vibe comes from the superlative local ingredients and airy, light-flooded contemporary space, while across-the-pond touches (both chefs trained in the UK) include house-made breads and confections as well as an intriguing wine list offering unusual Eastern European vintages.

Like its space, Lord Stanley's food is approachably refined, with stunning creations like a summer squash tart with almonds, summer squash, and herb aïoli. Silky black cod, pan-seared in butter and served in a spicy fava bean- and avocado-studded broth, is a showstopper. Even a seemingly simple dessert of grilled peaches with white Lillet sorbet and fruity olive oil gets an intriguing touch from slivers of Castelvetrano olives that add just the right amount of vibrancy.

In keeping with its San Franciscan ethos, Lord Stanley is a laid-back spot: the crowd of yupster couples often arrives on foot to the central Polk Street location, attired in casualwear. Be sure to quiz the attentive staff on the dishes—they'll happily explain each intricate layer.

# Mensho

Japanese 🍴

**B3**

672 Geary St. (bet. Jones & Leavenworth Sts.)

**Phone:** 415-800-8345
**Web:** www.mensho.tokyo
**Price:** 🥜

Dinner Tue – Sun

This little ramen shop is the first in the U.S. from the chef behind the highly popular Tokyo outposts, and its wait times are nothing short of epic—even in line-crazed San Francisco. No matter how early you arrive, snagging one of the 28 communal seats is at least a 30-minute affair that can easily run up to two hours. And the dicey Tendernob address means the line is often beset by aggressive panhandlers.

Only true aficionados can say if the ramen is worth it, but the *tori paitan* variety is one undeniably spectacular bowl, packed with springy, chewy noodles and outstanding duck *chashu* in a luxuriously creamy, umami-rich broth. Just know you'll be asked to slurp it down quickly: the hungry, huddled masses outside are anxious to take your seat.

# Modern Thai

Thai 🍴

**A3**

1247 Polk St. (at Bush St.)

**Phone:** 415-922-8424
**Web:** www.modernthaisf.com
**Price:** 🥜

Lunch & dinner daily

"Modern" is a bit of a misnomer, as this tropical Thai retreat actually feels like a step back in time with its whitewashed colonial façade, linen-topped tables, and rattan chairs. But the anachronism also applies to the portions (incredibly generous) and prices (incredibly reasonable), making it a favorite for nine-to-fivers seeking an affordable lunch break.

Sweet and spicy Thai flavors abound here, from warm salads of glass noodles and minced chicken with a fish sauce-lime vinaigrette to comforting noodle soups like the *khao soy*, with chicken and egg noodles in a rich coconut curry. And the MT sundae, a combo of coconut ice cream, sugar palm fruit, red beans, and jackfruit, is a refreshing dessert perfect for lunchtime dining.

# Mister Jiu's

Chinese ✗✗

**C2**

28 Waverly Pl. (bet. Clay & Sacramento Sts.)

**Phone:** 415-857-9688
**Web:** www.misterjius.com
**Price:** $$$

Dinner Tue – Sat

Chef/owner Brandon Jew has brought some of the sparkle back to Chinatown with this contemporary treasure, which puts a modern Californian spin on the Cantonese classics that once made the neighborhood a national dining destination. Impressively, the chef also makes all his Chinese pantry staples in-house, like the oyster sauce that coats a stir-fry of smoked tofu with long beans, tripe, and tendon; or *lap cheong* (Chinese sausage), which comes stuffed into roasted quail with sticky rice and jujube.

The menu is full of these clever touches, from the tomalley that adds depth to a rich Dungeness crab egg custard to the "tentacles" of fried fennel that echo the texture of salt-and-pepper squid.

Set in a longtime Chinese banquet hall, Mister Jiu's is bright and airy, with dramatic brass lotus chandeliers overhead. Food is served family-style, making it ideal for groups. But solo diners will also enjoy the sophisticated front bar, which serves up thoughtful, complex cocktails with Asian inflections like lemongrass milk and green tea.

Desserts are excellent, equally skillful and may incorporate black sesame, red bean, and osmanthus cream into preparations that will satisfy any sweet tooth.

111

# Oriental Pearl

**C2**

### 760 Clay St. (bet. Grant Ave. & Kearny St.)

**Phone:** 415-433-1817                          Lunch & dinner daily
**Web:** www.orientalpearlsf.com
**Price:** $$

Escape the cacophony of Chinatown at this calm upstairs retreat, where red ribbons hang in the light-filled windows and an attentive service staff offers some of the neighborhood's best service. Though the crowd is decidedly diverse with more than a few tourists mixed in, the food isn't overly Americanized and covers a range of regional specialties.

Commence your culinary tour of China with an order of barbecue spareribs, lacquered on the outside and exceptionally tender on the inside, or a piece or two of dim sum. Then dive into the Chiuchow-style marinated duck, a plateful of sweet-and-salty meat beneath crisp, golden-brown skin. The Singapore-style rice noodles, mixed with shrimp, pork, scallion, and yellow curry paste, are equally divine.

# Parallel 37

**C2**

### 600 Stockton St. (bet. California & Pine Sts.)

**Phone:** 415-773-6168                          Lunch & dinner daily
**Web:** www.parallel37sf.com
**Price:** $$$$

Housed in the posh Ritz-Carlton, Parallel 37 is a sleek and contemporary retreat. While the space, donning shades of brown and orange, is decidedly less grand than its surrounds, elegant details like leather chairs and banquettes, as well as a glass-enclosed wine cellar continue to lure a fetching crowd. If that's not enough, this kitchen's cuisine is as refined as its address. The staff is attentive yet laid-back and can be routinely found carrying around such intriguing offerings as seared octopus with garlic chips and green shiso sorbet; or butter-poached halibut served over Manila clam- and bacon-studded polenta.

If you leave without sampling dessert—perhaps the passion fruit mousse accompanied by a ginger-caramel sauce—well, you're missing out.

# Seven Hills

Italian ✗✗

**A2**

**1550 Hyde St. (at Pacific Ave.)**

| | | |
|---|---|---|
| **Phone:** | 415-775-1550 | Dinner nightly |
| **Web:** | www.sevenhillssf.com | |
| **Price:** | $$ | |

The dense sidewalk foliage, closely packed tables, and attentive service at this Russian Hill neighborhood hangout will transport you to Italy—that is, until you see the cable car rumbling its way up Hyde, and remember you're in San Francisco. The happy crowd of regulars wouldn't have it any other way.

They come to share bowls of house-made pasta, like a *tagliolini* mingled with asparagus and creamy buffalo ricotta (made fresh on-site). A thick grilled pork chop with gigante beans and charred Calçot onions sates heartier cravings, as do a few offal-centric dishes like rabbit tongues and roasted bone marrow. Finish with a creamy vanilla-blood orange panna cotta, or order a more superlative ricotta for dessert— this time drizzled with honey.

# 1760

Contemporary ✗✗

**A2**

**1760 Polk St. (at Washington St.)**

| | | |
|---|---|---|
| **Phone:** | 415-359-1212 | Lunch Sat – Sun |
| **Web:** | www.1760sf.com | Dinner nightly |
| **Price:** | $$$ | |

Fine dining with a bold Asian twist is the lure at this sleek spot, where the chef is fusing old-school bistro favorites (focaccia, lobster bisque) with island-inspired flavors. A quick scan of the menu will reveal palate-pleasers such as calamansi, ginger, coconut, and tamarind, resulting in tantalizing creations like succulent baby back ribs with hoisin barbecue sauce or ravioli stuffed with sweet corn purée and bathed in a lemongrass-infused red curry.

Owned by the team behind Acquerello, 1760 (named for its address) draws an older, upscale crowd to its gallery-like space. Generally speaking, the more refined your appetite, the greater the reward, as portions while tasty are petite and the recommended 2-3 plates per person may still not fill you up.

# Sons & Daughters ✧

C3

Contemporary ✗✗

**708 Bush St. (bet. Mason & Powell Sts.)**

**Phone:** 415-391-8311

Dinner Wed – Sun

**Web:** www.sonsanddaughterssf.com

**Price:** $$$$

Everyone at this inviting space is warmly professional, including the eager, well-paced staff. Add in the architecturally detailed dining room—a hybrid between your grandmother's home and a minimalist art gallery with its black-and-cream palette, leather banquettes, and vintage chandeliers—and you'll be counting down the days until your next visit.

Small but mighty, the kitchen turns out a seasonal, seven-course fixed menu that consistently pleases. A meal here might begin with candied limequat rind, briny sea beans, and light uni foam to flavor slices of sweet, silky scallops. Savory granola, served with roasted cauliflower and creamy sweetbreads, unites with trumpet mushrooms to form a perfect textural counterpoint to the smooth cauliflower soup poured tableside. And pork done three ways presents the loin dusted in pastrami spices; an exquisitely tender belly; and block of fried pork jowl set against pickled fennel and Satsuma segments.

Meyer lemon curd, sweet and tart with cranberry sauce, is a sublime dessert—but it's the intensely rich chocolate ganache, set over a bay leaf and chocolate cake crowned by pistachios, that showcases the technical prowess of this gifted kitchen.

# Stones Throw

Contemporary ✗

**A2**

### 1896 Hyde St. (bet. Green & Vallejo Sts.)

**Phone:** 415-796-2901
**Web:** www.stonesthrowsf.com
**Price:** $$

Lunch Sun
Dinner Tue – Sun

A good neighborhood restaurant should only be a stone's throw away, and this model has clearly hopscotched into Russian Hill's affections. Its terra-cotta floors, yellow walls, and chunky wood tables have a Mediterranean air, but the menu is more eclectically American, with a sizable beer and wine selection that makes the front bar great for a spur-of-the-moment drink and bite.

Clever takes on approachable dishes abound on the menu, from "toad in the hole" lasagna with a poached egg at dinner, to asparagus and duck confit hash at brunch. The creamy smoked salmon mousse, with bagel chips and crème fraîche, is rich and delicious. And pillowy doughnuts, topped with PB&J at dinner or pumpkin spice and pumpkin butter at brunch, are a delightful surprise.

# Z & Y

Chinese ✗

**C2**

### 655 Jackson St. (bet. Grant Ave. & Kearny St.)

**Phone:** 415-981-8988
**Web:** www.zandyrestaurant.com
**Price:** $$

Lunch & dinner daily

Some like it hot, and here they are in heaven. Be forewarned: timid palates should steer clear of the super-spicy Sichuan dishes that have made Z & Y a Chinatown smash hit. Nearly every dish is crowned with chilies, from the huge mound of dried peppers that rests atop tender, garlicky bites of fried chicken to the flaming chili oil anointing tender, flaky fish fillets in a star anise-tinged broth with Sichuan peppercorns aplenty.

The well-worn dining room may seem unremarkable and the service perfunctory, but the crowds are undeterred. Plan to wait among eager fans for a seat, then settle in for delicate pork-and-ginger wontons swimming in spicy peanut sauce and more chili oil. Allot time to navigate the challenging parking situation.

# North Beach

Relatively compact yet filled with cool restaurants, casual cafeterias, and a hopping nightlife, North Beach has that authentic Californian vibe that makes it just as much a local scene as a tourist mecca. Steps from the docks and nestled between bustling **Fisherman's Wharf** and the steep slopes of Russian and Telegraph Hills, this neighborhood owes its vibrant nature to the Italian immigrants who passed through these shores in the late 1800s. Many were fishermen from the Ligurian coast, and their seafood stew (cioppino) that they prepared and perfected on the boats evolved into a quintessential San Francisco trademark. Though Italian-Americans may no longer be in the majority here, classic *ristorantes*, pizzerias, and coffee shops attest to their idea of the good life. At the annual **North Beach Festival** held in mid-June,

a celebrity pizza toss, Assisi Animal Blessings, and Arte di Gesso also pay homage to this region's Italian roots. Foodies however can rest assured that dining here isn't all about lasagna-loving, red-sauce joints.

Brave the crowd of locals and visitors for some of the most fantastic fish and chips this side of the pond and fish tacos this side of the border, at **The Codmother Fish and Chips**. This veritable local favorite is essentially a small kiosk with a window to place your order and a handful of tables on the front patio. Clearly, it isn't about the dining experience here, and most people get their fish and chips to-go—perhaps for a stroll along the wharf?

## TELEGRAPH HILL

Cutting its angle through North Beach, Columbus Avenue is home to the neighborhood's most notable restaurants, bars, and lounges. Thanks to **Molinari's**, whose homemade salami has garnered a commendable following since 1896, whimsical, old-world Italian delicatessens are a regular fixture along these blocks. Pair their impressive range of imported meats and cheeses with some *vino* for a perfect picnic in nearby Washington Square Park.

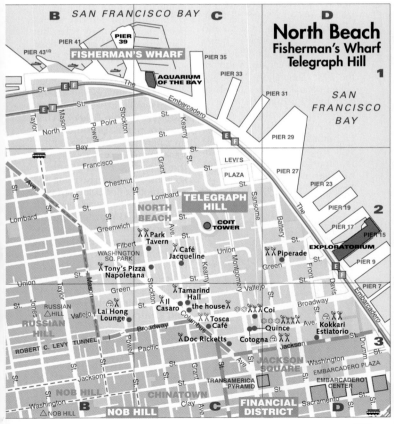

Preparing wood-fired pizzas with classic combinations since 1935, **Tommaso's Ristorante Italiano** is another citywide institution, situated on the southern end of North Beach. The décor and ambience may be a vestige from the past, but that hasn't prevented devoted locals from cramping its quarters. Fine-dining can also come with a throwback feel and **Bix** is a grand example. This bi-level arena with a balconied dining room, classic cocktails, and jazz club-ambience makes for date-night *extraordinaire*. Getting acquainted with North Beach is a never-ending but very telling experience. After all, these neighborhood venues were also home to a ragtag array of beret-wearing poets in the 1950s and remain a popular excursion for the Beat Generation. Those so-called beatniks—Allen Ginsberg and Jack Kerouac to name a few—were eventually driven out by busloads of tourists. Nonetheless, bohemian spirits still linger on here, at such landmarks as the City Lights bookstore and next door at **Vesuvio**, the quintessential boho bar.

## FEASTING IN FISHERMAN'S WHARF

**F**isherman's Wharf, that mile-long stretch of waterfront at the foot of Columbus Avenue, ranks as one of the city's most popular sites. There aren't many locals here and it teems with souvenir shops, street performers, and noisy rides. But you should go if only to feast on a sourdough bread bowl crammed with clam chowder, or fresh crabs cooked in huge steamers right on the street. Then, sample a bite of culinary history at **Boudin Bakery**. While this shop has bloomed into an operation complete with a museum and bakery tour, it stays true to its roots by crafting crusty sourdough every day, using the same mother first cultivated here in 1849 from local wild yeast. Not far behind, **Ghirardelli Square** preserves yet another taste of old San Francisco. This venerable chocolate company, founded by Domenico "Domingo" Ghirardelli in 1852, flaunts a host of delectable wares at the equally famous **Ghirardelli Ice Cream and Chocolate Manufactory**. When lingering here, don't forget to glimpse their original manufacturing equipment, while enjoying a creamy hot fudge sundae. On your way out, be sure to take away some sweet memories in the form of those chocolate squares.

# Café Jacqueline

French ✗

**C2**

1454 Grant Ave. (bet. Green & Union Sts.)

**Phone:** 415-981-5565
**Web:** N/A
**Price:** $$$$

Dinner Wed – Sun

You'll float away on a cloud at the first taste of Jacqueline Margulis' signature soufflés, light and fluffy masterworks that have kept her tables full for over 35 years. Since the chef makes each of her creations by hand, expect to spend three or so hours at the table—it's the perfect romantic escape for couples lingering over a bottle of wine.

To sate your appetite while you wait, a bowl of light carrot soup or a delicate cucumber salad in a champagne vinaigrette will do the trick. But the soufflés are the real draw, and keen diners plan on both a savory and a sweet course. For the former, a combination of flaky salmon, tender asparagus, and caramelized Gruyère is a delight. And the utterly perfect lemon soufflé will haunt any dessert lover's dreams.

# Carmel Pizza Company

Pizza ✗

**A1**

2826 Jones St. (bet. Beach & Jefferson Sts.)

**Phone:** 415-676-1185
**Web:** www.carmelpizzaco.com
**Price:** 🅐🅢

Lunch & dinner Thu – Tue

Don't let the touristy Fisherman's Wharf address keep you from visiting this ruby-red gem, which serves delicious wood-fired Neapolitan pies that belie its environs. (And in a bid to draw more patronage, the popular spot has covered and heated its rather special patio, a godsend on chilly afternoons.) With eight to ten daily pies to choose from, there's something for everyone. Bring the kids and go to town on the zesty Diavola, topped with spicy *salame*, minced pepperoncini, and crisp arugula, or try the classic Americana, a tasty mix of ham, onion, sausage, mushrooms, and black olives. And the crust? Oh, the crust: it's thin, chewy, and well salted, with blistered, perfectly caramelized edges. Why should out-of-towners get to have all the fun?

# Cotogna

Italian ✗✗

**C3**

490 Pacific Ave. (at Montgomery St.)

**Phone:** 415-775-8508
**Web:** www.cotognasf.com
**Price:** $$

Lunch & dinner daily

Though rustic compared to high-end sibling Quince, Michael and Lindsay Tusk's casual Italian offshoot would be elegant by any other standard. Stylish, bright, and a hot-ticket reservation, the space centers around an exhibition kitchen, from which crisp pizzas and hearty roasted meats emerge. The absolutely delicious menu highlights Chef Tusk's pristine pastas, like butternut squash *cappellacci* in caramelized brown butter drizzled in bitter cocoa reduction. Seasonal starters are equally pleasing, like kale and radicchio salad in tangy vinaigrette with hard-boiled farm egg and pecorino. A pretty wedge of the lime meringue tart with huckleberry compote is zippy, refreshing, and none-too-sweet.
The three-course prix-fixe offers an exceptional value.

# Doc Ricketts

American ✗

**C3**

124 Columbus Ave. (bet. Jackson St. & Pacific Ave.)

**Phone:** 415-649-6191
**Web:** www.docrickettssf.com
**Price:** $$

Lunch Mon – Fri
Dinner nightly

Nestled in a sea of spendy corporate hangouts and touristy Italian-American joints, Doc Ricketts is a welcome change of pace with its unique upstairs-downstairs vibe—the basement level is Doc's Lab, a comedy and music venue where the full menu is offered. The upstairs restaurant is simple and airy, with wood furnishings, wide windows, and engaging servers at the ready.
The American fare on the menu is unfussy and skillfully prepared, from butter-sautéed wild mushroom panzanella with chunks of torn sourdough and bacon-shallot vinaigrette, to a juicy, generously portioned half roast chicken, accompanied by toast slathered in chicken-liver mousse. Finish with a luscious chocolate *pot de crème*, topped with vanilla Chantilly and a chocolate cookie.

# Coi ✿✿

**C3**

## 373 Broadway (bet. Montgomery & Sansome Sts.)

**Phone:** 415-393-9000
**Web:** www.coirestaurant.com
**Price:** **$$$$**

Dinner Thu – Mon

While Daniel Patterson remains the owner of this tiny temple to fine-dining in North Beach, he's ceded control of the kitchen to new chef, Matthew Kirkley. The changeover has invigorated Coi's menu via a shift from Californian to classic French influences, with a particular focus on seafood. Kirkley's silky, slow-cooked turbot, "scaled" with discs of root vegetables, is nothing short of a revelation, as is a beautiful roulade of raw fluke with briny Osetra caviar, accented with the citrusy zest of *etrog*. And not all the delights are aquatic in nature: an engagingly earthy duo of squab with black truffle is perfectly rendered. The 10-12 course tasting nicely transitions into three light, delicate desserts, like cannoli with coconut cream or almond cake with amaretto mousse.

Despite a location just blocks from the seedy clubs of Broadway, the vibe inside Coi is hushed and Zen-like, thanks to low ceilings, soft lighting, and beautifully paced service.

While well-chosen wine pairings are available to match with the menu, diners should consider the restaurant's innovative tea pairing instead. Highlighting rare and aged teas, this is a truly thought-provoking journey that enhances the food.

# Gary Danko

Contemporary XXX

**A1**

## 800 North Point St. (at Hyde St.)

**Phone:** 415-749-2060
**Web:** www.garydanko.com
**Price:** $$$$

Dinner nightly

The elite meet to eat at this throwback favorite, which has been hosting the crème de la crème of the city (and its visitors) since the '90s. Set near Ghirardelli Square in Fisherman's Wharf, it features two lovely wood-paneled dining rooms and a small, bustling bar, all of them regularly full of hobnobbing business types and couples celebrating big occasions. With bursting flower arrangements, attentive servers, and well-dressed diners everywhere you look, it's hard not to be captivated.

The menu focuses on classic cuisine with some global twists; diners can create their own three, four, or five-course prix-fixe, or hand over the reins to the chef's tasting menu. Luxurious dishes include a luscious rock shrimp and Dungeness crab risotto, accented with butternut squash; branzino with fennel purée, olives, and a saffron-orange emulsion; as well as a perfectly cooked herb-crusted lamb loin, draped over date-studded farro and rainbow carrots.

While Danko may not be on the cutting edge of fine dining, its top-notch wine list and outstanding service make for the epitome of old-school luxury. Like the chocolate soufflé with vanilla bean crème anglaise that caps the meal, this is a classic for a reason.

# the house

**C3**

A s i a n

1230 Grant Ave. (bet. Columbus Ave. & Vallejo St.)

**Phone:** 415-986-8612
**Web:** www.thehse.com
**Price:** $$

Lunch Mon – Sat
Dinner nightly

  ♿

This perennially popular Asian bistro provides a welcome alternative to the Italian-heavy streets in North Beach. The décor is minimal with blonde wood tables, and there are always specials so listen closely to the efficient staff as they recite the bounties of the day. A versatile drinks list completes the enticing spread in addition to offering a happy reprieve to those who've endured a long wait for limited tables.

Dishes like delicately prepped scallops in saffron sauce, and crispy halibut tempura propped atop roasted cauliflower may vary by the day. But a playful, fusion element remains a steady feature in all items, including house specialties, of which warm wasabi noodles topped with flank steak or teriyaki-glazed salmon are perfect examples.

# Il Casaro

**C3**

P i z z a

348 Columbus Ave. (bet. Grant Ave. & Vallejo St.)

**Phone:** 415-677-9455
**Web:** www.ilcasarosf.com
**Price:** $$

Lunch & dinner daily

  ♿

In a sea of too-touristy Italian joints, Il Casaro is the rare North Beach spot that delivers the goods: Neapolitan-style pizza cooked to crispy perfection in a bright red wood-fired oven. Whether you opt for the classic Margherita or the zippy *diavola* (with spicy salami and Calabrian chiles), you're sure to achieve carbohydrate bliss. Throw in an antipasto or salad and a silky panna cotta with raspberry coulis, and you're all set—at an affordable price, to boot.

Il Casaro's space is simple but hip, with reclaimed wood, polished concrete floors, and utensils in empty San Marzano tomato cans. Don't expect more than cursory service, as the restaurant is always packed and doesn't take reservations: waits can run an hour or more at peak times.

# Kokkari Estiatorio

Greek ✕✕

**D3**

### 200 Jackson St. (at Front St.)

**Phone:** 415-981-0983
**Web:** www.kokkari.com
**Price:** $$

Lunch Mon – Fri
Dinner nightly

Zeus himself would be satisfied after a soul-warming meal at this Greek favorite, which serves up San Francisco chic with a side of old-world taverna hospitality. Translation? Once you're seated at the bar or settled near one of the roaring fireplaces, the thoughtful staff will cater to your every need.

Kokkari's sophisticated menu leans heavily on the wood grill and rotisserie, which produce smoky, juicy lamb souvlaki with warm pita and tangy chickpea salad; as well as charcoal-kissed, feta-stuffed calamari over fennel, oranges, and olive tapenade. Resist the urge to conquer the Olympus-sized portions: you'll want to sample the *galaktoboureko*, crispy phyllo rolls filled with creamy custard and topped with honey, figs, and crème fraîche ice cream.

# Lai Hong Lounge

Chinese ✕

**B3**

### 1416 Powell St. (bet. Broadway & Vallejo St.)

**Phone:** 415-397-2290
**Web:** www.LHKLounge.com
**Price:** $$

Lunch & dinner daily

This windowless dim sum lounge looks small from the outside, but there's room for over 100 diners inside its cherry-red dining room—with dozens more hopefuls lined up on the street outside. The largely Chinese crowd attests to the authenticity of the food, which ranges from steamed pork buns and taro dumplings to chicken feet with peanuts. (If you're hoping to skip out on the wait, go at dinner instead of lunch, or call for takeout.)

Smiling servers roll carts featuring no end of tasty options, so you'll have to make some hard choices. Favorites include gingery wonton soup, full of soft and savory little dumplings; enormous rice noodle rolls stuffed with ground beef and aromatic herbs, and crispy, golden pan-fried tofu with a silky interior.

# Park Tavern

**C2**

### 1652 Stockton St. (bet. Filbert & Union Sts.)

**Phone:** 415-989-7300
**Web:** www.parktavernsf.com
**Price:** $$$

Lunch Fri – Sun
Dinner nightly

North Beach favorite Park Tavern has a menu that spoils diners. Should you stick with the beloved Marlowe burger, or opt for a new plate like roasted sea bass with braised fennel and celeriac purée? The choices are plenty. Go another round with the time-honored Brussels sprout chips, or sample the newer lemon chips with burrata? Whatever you decide, you're unlikely to be disappointed.

Options also abound in terms of seating—the sidewalk tables, window seats, and marble-topped bar counter are equally appealing. In terms of drinking: the house-concocted cocktails, local beers, and varied global wines will each call your name. The good news is that a second visit will allow you to try more, provided you can snatch a table away from the other regulars.

# Piperade

**D2**

### 1015 Battery St. (bet. Green & Union Sts.)

**Phone:** 415-391-2555
**Web:** www.piperade.com
**Price:** $$

Lunch Mon – Fri
Dinner Mon – Sat

Basque Chef Gerald Hirigoyen blends the region's French and Spanish roots at this popular restaurant that's a favorite for business lunches. His roasted lamb gets a touch of Middle Eastern flavor thanks to merguez sausage and a sweet-smoky cumin-date relish, served with tender and caramelized roasted fennel bulb. A solidly Gallic apple galette is deliciously none-too-sweet, combining puff pastry, finely shaved apple slices, and decadant caramel sauce.

Located among historic warehouses in a commercial district, this charming dining room features wood floors, brick walls, and chandeliers made from empty wine bottles. Hold a confab at the eight-person round table, or enjoy a solo glass of wine on the covered front patio and while away a warm afternoon.

# Quince ✿ ✿ ✿

Italian ✗✗✗✗

C3

### 470 Pacific Ave. (bet. Montgomery & Sansome Sts.)

**Phone:** 415-775-8500

**Web:** www.quincerestaurant.com

**Price:** $$$$

Dinner Mon – Sat

An air of refinement touches this dining room—note the massive Murano chandelier, the stylish guests, and everything in between. No wonder this is where affluent tourists and locals alike come to celebrate their special occasions. From the moment the champagne cart arrives at your table to the last bite of the gueridon's mignardises, service is perfectly timed and attentive. The room is as lovely as ever, but has recently been tweaked to allow more space for private parties.

There was a time when Quince was home to traditional Italian cooking, but Chef Tusk's menu is increasingly contemporary. So while tortellini may sound familiar, this delicate pasta is a refined balance of the umami, earthy, and sweet flavors of red kuri squash, *colatura di alici*, and *lapsang souchong* black tea. *Lasagnette* is a masterpiece with dozens of layers of Swiss chard, guinea hen, and wild mushrooms. Crisp-skinned duck breast is beautifully roasted and impossibly tender, served in a pool of duck jus with turnips and black trumpets, alongside a pleasingly bitter *Tardivo* radicchio salad, topped with a skewer of duck offal. Desserts offer a smart and harmonious finale to your meal.

The wine list is wonderful, but pricey.

San Francisco ▶ North Beach

127

# Tamarind Hall

Thai ✗

**C3**

### 1268 Grant Ave. (at Vallejo St.)

**Phone:** 628-444-3158
**Web:** www.tamarindhall.com
**Price:** $$

Lunch & dinner daily

Though this address has been home to a Thai restaurant for many years, a recent change of ownership has led to a complete makeover—menu included. The freshly christened Tamarind Hall offers home-style cuisine in a laid-back atmosphere: think sweet, spicy, and pungent roasted duck *laab*, or smoky grilled chicken skewers with sticky rice and green papaya salad.

The restaurant's popular back bar serves Thai-inspired cocktails with accents like lemongrass, coconut, and of course, tamarind. They are best enjoyed alongside street-food-inspired bites like crunchy, fish-sauce-glazed chicken wings. The dining room features comfortable, high-backed chairs, wood tables, and framed Thai movie posters, creating a fun, relaxed setting for the flavorful food.

# Tony's Pizza Napoletana

Pizza ✗

**C2**

### 1570 Stockton St. (at Union St.)

**Phone:** 415-835-9888
**Web:** www.tonyspizzanapoletana.com
**Price:** $$

Lunch & dinner Wed – Mon

A veritable polymath of pizza, Tony Gemignani serves every variety imaginable at his North Beach institution, from wood-fired Neapolitan to gas-cooked New York to 1,000-degree coal-fired. Tucked into the ground floor of a quaint Victorian, the sparse décor directs focus to the 12 styles of pizza on offer. It's always crowded, so expect a wait—and don't bring a big group.

Pies and Italian-American dishes are as rich and complex as the space is simple, from the tangy, herbaceous tomato sauce lapping tender beef meatballs to the delicious interplay of soft quail eggs, smooth potato, and crisp *guanciale* atop a wood-fired pie. Can't wait? Gemignani also owns a quick-fix slice shop right next door, plus nearby Capo's, which focuses on Chicago-style pies.

# Tosca Café

**C3**

Italian ✖✖

242 Columbus Ave. (bet. Broadway & Pacific Ave.)

**Phone:** 415-986-9651
**Web:** www.toscacafesf.com
**Price:** $$$

Dinner nightly

This historic bar has been expertly revived under NYC stars, April Bloomfield and Ken Friedman, who spent millions to add a kitchen and make its old-school charm seem untouched. White-coated bartenders shake and stir behind the glorious carved wood bar, while diners feast in the cushy red leather booths. Tables are few, so expect a wait if you don't have a reservation.

The food is Italian-American with Bloomfield's signature meaty influences, like flavorful, gamey grilled lamb ribs that nearly fall off the bone. Pastas are strong, from creamy *gemelli cacio e pepe* to rich, spicy *bucatini all'Amatriciana*, but don't neglect their vegetables: a dish of tender cauliflower and potatoes in a rich taleggio sauce with crunchy breadcrumbs is a showstopper.

# Waxman's

**A1**

American ✖✖

900 North Point St. (bet. Larkin & Polk Sts.)

**Phone:** 415-636-9700
**Web:** www.waxmanssfo.com
**Price:** $$$

Dinner Tue – Sun

With this bright, airy restaurant set just steps from the waterfront in Ghirardelli Square, acclaimed NYC chef, Jonathan Waxman, has returned to his Bay Area roots, bringing his rustic American food with him. This hot spot's hearty cooking will appeal to the array of visitors who stream into the square each day, but this is no tourist trap—in fact, it's the perfect place to unwind from a hectic day of sightseeing, perhaps with a glass of pinot gris on the lovely patio.

On the menu, you'll find Waxman's famed roast chicken, with its crisply caramelized skin and zippy salsa verde as well as his signature golden-brown smashed potatoes. But don't miss the rotating offerings, either—from seared calamari salad to buttery strawberry crostata, everything's made with the season's best.

# Richmond & Sunset

Named after an Australian art dealer and his home (The Richmond House), quiet yet urban Richmond is hailed for the surf that washes right up to its historic Cliff House and Sutro Baths. Springtime adds to the area's beauty with Golden Gate Park's blushing cherry blossoms and whimsical topiaries—nevermind those bordering pastel row-houses in desperate need of a lick of paint. More than anywhere else in the city, this sequestered northwest enclave is ruled by a sense of Zen, and residents seem deeply impacted by it— from that incredibly stealthy sushi chef to über-cool Sunset surfer dudes. Given its multi-cultural immigrant community, Richmond's authentic cuisine options are both delicious and varied. Begin with an array of European specialty items at **Seakor Polish Delikatessen and Sausage Factory**, proffering an outstanding selection of smoked, cured meats, sausages, pickles, sauerkraut and more.

## NEW CHINATOWN

While Richmond does cradle some western spots, it is mostly renowned for steaming bowls of piping-hot *pho*, as thick as the marine layer itself. This area has earned the nickname "New Chinatown" for good reason; and plates of deliciously moist and juicy plates of *siu mai* are meant to be devoured at **Shanghai Dumpling King** or **Good Luck Dim Sum**. Speaking to this neighborhood's new nickname, **Wing Lee Bakery** is famed for its comprehensive selection of dim sum—both sweet and savory. And while you're at it, don't miss out on Frisco's finest roast duck, on display at **Wing Lee BBQ** next door. Those looking to replicate this Asian extravaganza at home should start with a perfect wok, stockpot, noodle bowl, and rice cooker among other stellar housewares and kitchen supplies available at **Kamei**. If that doesn't make you feel like

a kid in a candy store, Hong Kong–style delights (on offer even late at night) at **Kowloon Tong Dessert Café** will do a bang-up job. Clement Street, also an inviting exposition for the adventurous home cook and curious chef, features poky sidewalk markets where clusters of bananas sway from awnings and the spices and produce on display are as vibrant as the nearby **Japanese Tea Garden** in bloom. While the Bay Area mantra "eat local" may not be entirely pertinent here, a medley of global goodies abound and everything from tamarind and eel, to live fish and pork buns are available for less than a buck. There is a mom-and-pop joint for every corner and culture. In fact, this is *the* 'hood to source that 100-year-old egg or homemade kimchi by the pound. The décor in these divey shops is far from remarkable and at times downright seedy, but really, you're here for the food, which is undeniably authentic. Buses of Korean tourists routinely

pull up to **Han Il Kwan** for a taste of home. The space may be congested and service can be a disaster, but the kitchen's nostalgic cooking keeps the homesick coming back for more. Native-born aficionados can be found combing the wares at **First Korean Market**, poised on Geary Boulevard and packed with every prepared food and snack under the sun. Meanwhile, culture vultures gather for an intense Burmese feast at **B Star Bar**, after which a refreshing sip at **Aroma Tea Shop** is nothing if not obligatory. Their owners even encourage free tastings of exclusive custom blends of individually sourced teas from around the world.

## SUNSET

A dash more updated than bordering Richmond, Sunset—once a heap of sand dunes—retains a small-town vibe that's refined but still rough around the edges. Here, locals start their day with fresh-baked pastries at **Arizmendi Bakery** and then stroll around the corner for some much-needed caffeine at the **Beanery**. Asian appetites routinely frequent **Izakaya Sozai** for juicy *yakitori*, followed by cooling and fresh sashimi. Tourists taking in the sights at the de Young Museum or Academy of Sciences love to linger over lunch at **Wooly Pig Café**. Their namesake "Wooly Pig" sandwich, crafted from toasted challah and overflowing with pork belly, mizuna greens and pickled shallots, is guaranteed to knock your socks off. Yes, the space is tiny with only a

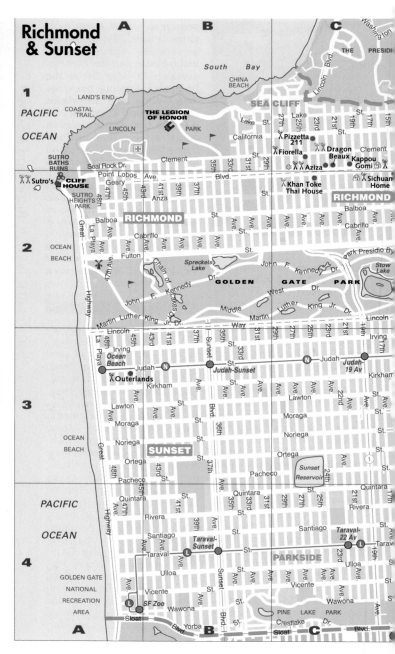

# Richmond & Sunset

**A**    **B**    **C**

Washington

South Bay

CHINA BEACH

THE PRESIDI

**1**

LAND'S END

COASTAL TRAIL

SEA CLIFF

PACIFIC OCEAN

LINCOLN

THE LEGION OF HONOR

PARK

Lincoln Blvd

Lake St.
27th
25th
23rd
21st
19th
17th
15th

California

St.

Pizzetta 211
Fiorella

Dragon Beaux
Clement

SUTRO BATHS RUINS

Seal Rock Dr.

Point Lobos

Clement

35th
33rd
31st
29th

Aziza

Kappou Gomi

Sutro's
CLIFF HOUSE

Geary
Ave.
Blvd.

Khan Toke Thai House

Sichuan Home

48th
45th
43rd
41st
39th
37th

Anza
St.

**RICHMOND**

SUTRO HEIGHTS PARK

Balboa
Ave.
Cabrillo
Ave.

**2**

OCEAN BEACH

La Playa
47th Ave.

Balboa
Cabrillo

Ave.

St.

**RICHMOND**

Ave.
St.
Ave.
Ave.
Ave.

Fulton

Chain of Lakes Dr.

Spreckels Lake

John F. Kennedy Dr.

Park Presidio By

Stow Lake

Great Highway

John F. Kennedy

**GOLDEN**   **GATE**   **PARK**

West
Dr.

Middle

Martin Luther King Jr. Dr.

Martin Luther King Jr. Dr.

Way

Martin

Luther

King Jr. Dr.

Lincoln

Lincoln

45th
43rd
41st
37th
35th
33rd
31st
29th
27th
25th
23rd
19th

**3**

Ocean Beach

La Playa
48th Ave.

Irving

Judah

N

Judah-Sunset

N

Judah

Irving
17th

Judah-19 Av

Kirkham

Outerlands

Kirkham

22nd

St.

Lawton
Ave.

Ave.
Ave.
Ave.

36th Blvd.
St.

Lawton

Ave.

St.

Moraga
St.

Moraga

OCEAN BEACH

Noriega
Ave.

43rd
St.
37th

Noriega

**SUNSET**

Ortega
St.

Pacheco

Ortega

Sunset Reservoir

Ave.
24th

St.

i

Pacheco

Quintara
St.

Quintara

27th
25th

21st
Ave.
17th

**4**

PACIFIC

OCEAN

Quintara
47th Ave.

Rivera

41st
39th
35th
33rd
31st
29th

Rivera

Great Highway

Santiago
Ave.
Ave.

Taraval-Sunset

St.

Santiago

Taraval-22 Av

Taraval

L

Taraval

Sunset Blvd.

**PARKSIDE**

23rd
19th

L

Taraval

GOLDEN GATE NATIONAL RECREATION AREA

Ulloa
Ave.

Vicente
St.

L

SF Zoo

Wawona
St.

Sloat

Ulloa

Vicente

Wawona

PINE LAKE PARK

Crestlake Dr.

Yorba

Sloat

Blvd.

Blvd.

**A**    **B**    **C**

smattering of tables, but with gorgeous Golden Gate Park just a block away, their offerings make for perfect picnic treats. Over on Noriega Street, the line lengthens out the door and down the sidewalk at **Cheung Hing**. If that isn't a sign that something special is going on here, sample their Chinese barbecue including whole roast duck, or take slices of tender-charred pork to-go. In fact, those leaving with bags of roasted meat can be assured of envious glares from the crowds waiting around. As the sun sets in the Sunset, savor dinner at **Pisces**, which flaunts dishes composed of local, seasonal, and nutritional ingredients. Reflecting the same philosophy, **Thanh Long** on Judah Street has gained a substantial local fan-base who seem unperturbed at the thought of waiting endlessly for their famous garlic noodles and whole-roasted Dungeness crab. Outer Sunset residents who are at the mercy of time may rest assured as **Noriega Produce** resides only steps around the corner, and is as immaculate as any farmer's market for sustainable, organic produce. Finally, no repast can be termed "regal" without a bit of sweet at **Holy Gelato!**—a quirky shop serving coffees, teas, and creamy gelatos in a wide range of flavors—maybe crème brûlée, goat cheese, and honey-lavender? Top off this sweet satisfaction at age-old, Asian kitsch fave, **Polly Ann Ice Cream**, with such inventive flavors as durian, jasmine tea or taro—and know that nothing but sweet dreams can follow.

# Aziza ❀

**C1**

### 5800 Geary Blvd. (at 22nd Ave.)

**Phone:** 415-752-2222  
**Web:** www.aziza-sf.com  
**Price:** $$$

Dinner Wed – Sun

Nestled in a corner of the Outer Richmond and along a street peppered with ethnic grocers, Aziza has been a fixture on the fine-dining scene for over a decade. In fact, this is one of those few upscale places where the chef is a local celebrity but is also nationally recognized for elevating Moroccan cuisine.

Following a recent design refresh, Mourad Lahlou's lovely Aziza is a charming retreat that continues to draw a loyal following. The result is exotic but accessible—a spot as perfectly appropriate for families with kids in tow as it is for a sultry rendezvous with your steady.

Chef/owner Lahlou loves to turn traditional Moroccan cooking on its head, (in fact, there's not a tagine in sight) infusing irresistible dishes with a palpable Californian sensibility. The outcome is quite incredible, with sweet and savory flavors tangling in harmony. It's hard to go wrong on this menu and you'll surely want to try a little bit of everything. But whatever you do, don't miss the kitchen's elegantly plated trio of dips. These may include silky cucumber yogurt and dill, smoky eggplant and a nutty piquillo pepper-almond dip. The perfectly seared lamb loin and belly is paired with creamy, green garlic-infused barley, grilled summer squash, and a flutter of fresh, peppery arugula.

# Burma Superstar

Burmese 🍴

**D1**

### 309 Clement St. (bet. 4th & 5th Aves.)

**Phone:** 415-387-2147
**Web:** www.burmasuperstar.com
**Price:** $$

Lunch & dinner daily

Like any celebrity, it's easy to recognize this unusual dark wood superstar from the eager crowds swarming like paparazzi. Everyone endures this no-reservations policy to Instagram their favorite Burmese dishes. See the iPhones poised over the famed rainbow and tea-leaf salads or *samusa* soup (also available as a lunchtime combo). Regulars stick to traditional items, marked by asterisks on the menu. Palate-tingling options include rice noodles with pickled daikon and tofu in a spicy tomato-garlic sauce, or pork and kabocha squash stewed in a gingery broth with coconut sticky rice. A creamy Thai iced tea is the perfect counterbalance to the spicy, boldly flavored fare.

Hipper digs, a cooler crowd, but updated favorites can be found at sib—Burma Love.

# Chapeau! 😊

French 🍴

**D1**

### 126 Clement St. (bet. 2nd & 3rd Aves.)

**Phone:** 415-750-9787
**Web:** N/A
**Price:** $$

Dinner nightly

For an oh-so-French experience on Asian food-centric Clement, denizens head to Philippe Gardelle's authentic bistro, where tightly spaced tables and paintings of the titular hats create a convivial atmosphere. Packed with regulars receiving *bisous* from the chef, Chapeau! is warm and generous, a vibe that's aided by its strong Gallic wine list.

Dishes are traditional with a bit of Californian flair, like fingerling potato chips in a friseé and duck confit salad or salted-caramel ice cream that tops the *pain perdu*. The cassoulet, wholesome with braised lamb, rich with smoky sausage, and earthy with white beans, is perfect for a foggy night in the Avenues. Come before 6:00 P.M. on weeknights for a $36.95 early bird prix fixe, or create your own from their many set menus.

# Dragon Beaux

**C1**

Chinese XX

**5700 Geary Blvd. (at 21st Ave.)**

**Phone:** 415-333-8899
**Web:** www.dragonbeaux.com
**Price:** $$

Lunch & dinner daily

This Richmond Chinese gem has a split personality that food fiends will adore: by day, it offers dim sum from the same owners as Daly City's acclaimed Koi Palace, while at night it segues into steaming hot pot offerings with top quality meats, seafood, and veggies for the picking. The dramatic, over-the-top space is lively in any light, thanks to its lit stone pillars, dark wood furnishings, and soaring ceilings.

Dim sum is the better quality meal here and seekers will have to take a number and wait (only parties of eight or more can reserve), but the rewards are numerous. Picture barbecue pork buns, crab roe-topped *siu mai*, or roasted pork belly with crackly skin. Egg custard tarts or sesame balls offer a sweet finish, and pair nicely with jasmine tea.

# Fiorella

**C1**

Italian X

**2339 Clement St. (bet. 24th & 25th Sts.)**

**Phone:** 415-340-3049
**Web:** www.fiorella-sf.com
**Price:** $$

Lunch Sat – Sun
Dinner nightly

In the foggy Outer Richmond, this casual neighborhood pizzeria has quickly become as hot as its wood-fired oven. Local families come in droves to share a pie or a plate of pasta in the vintage-chic dining room, where laid-back servers chat with patrons beneath funky wallpaper depicting a bevy of Bay Area landmarks and legendary locals.

The chewy, blistered crusts churned out of the kitchen are loaded with flavor, whether in a classic Margherita or salami pie with provolone and red chili. Throw in a seasonal salad, a pile of chicken wings tossed in a Calabrian chili-honey glaze, and a glass of Italian wine from the compact list. And be sure to save room for the delectable warm almond- and Meyer lemon-ricotta cake, which gets toasted to perfection alongside the pies in the oven.

# Kappou Gomi 😊

Japanese ✕

**C1**

5524 Geary Blvd. (bet. 19th & 20th Aves.)

**Phone:** 415-221-5353
**Web:** N/A
**Price:** $$

Dinner Tue – Sun

Sushi-seekers should take a pass, but those yearning for elegant, traditional Japanese food will find kindred spirits at this precious gem. The serene, ultra-minimalist dining room isn't fancy, with only a few shelves of ceramics as décor. But the older Japanese women in traditional garb who run the show are endlessly polite and attentive, so long as you're not raising a din—or requesting a spicy tuna roll.

The eight-page menu offers a head-spinning number of options arranged by ingredient, like umami-rich wilted mizuna salad with fava beans and bonito sauce, or pale green edamame tofu with fresh cherries, cherry blossom noodles, and a sour-salty cherry paste. The exquisitely moist and flaky black cod, grilled with a slightly sweet sake marinade, is revelatory.

# Khan Toke Thai House

Thai ✕

**C2**

5937 Geary Blvd. (bet. 23rd & 24th Aves.)

**Phone:** 415-668-6654
**Web:** www.khantokethai.com
**Price:** 🍜🍜

Lunch Tue – Sun
Dinner nightly

Don your best dinner socks for this traditional Thai restaurant, where diners are asked to remove their shoes before perching on low cushions at the intricately carved tables. Service is as slow as a glacier, making it more suited to casual dining than a business lunch. Still, Khan Toke is worth the wait.

Awaken the senses with a bowl of enticingly pungent and spicy-sour *tom yum* soup, loaded with tomato, onion, and sliced lemongrass, finished with fresh cilantro. Then dive into *gai ga prou*, a delicious stir-fry of chicken and bell peppers studded with sliced Thai chilies. Indeed, chili-lovers who order dishes "very spicy" will get what they want. There is no shortage of firepower in the bamboo shoots with chili sauce and excellent Panang curry.

# Kitchen Istanbul

**D1**

### 349 Clement St. (at 5th Ave.)

**Phone:** 415-753-9479

**Web:** www.kitchenistanbulsf.com

**Price:** $$

Lunch & dinner daily

This cheerful Inner Richmond spot has retained the chef, managing team, and décor of previous occupant Troya, but taken its menu in a more exclusively Turkish direction. The results—like a sublime lentil soup richly puréed and made slightly tart with lemon, or a juicy, perfectly grilled duo of lamb meatballs over basmati rice—will transport you to the Aegean sea.

A Mediterranean oasis surrounded by dozens of Chinese restaurants, Kitchen Istanbul is bright and well-lit, with red walls donning sleek black-and-white framed photos. The friendly staff is quick to recommend an unusual Turkish wine; if you're willing to put yourself in their hands, they're also happy to whip up a mini tasting menu of highlights, from creamy hummus to briny sardines.

# Lavash

**D3**

### 511 Irving St. (bet. 6th & 7th Aves.)

**Phone:** 415-664-5555

**Web:** www.lavashsf.com

**Price:** $$

Lunch & dinner Tue – Sun

You'll feel like you've dined in a Persian home after leaving family-run Lavash, which has become a neighborhood fixture thanks to warm service and sizable portions. Painted in hues of orange, gold, and rose, the casual and flower-filled space is inviting, and throughout a meal here, you'll see locals dropping in for takeout or just to chat.

Begin your feast with *sabzi panir*, a plate of fresh herbs, feta, cucumber, tomato, walnuts, and grapes that's perfect for ad hoc toppings on the cracker-like namesake bread. Then order up a skewer or two of tender and smoky ground beef and lamb *koobideh*, served over fluffy basmati rice. Finally, don't miss the crispy, sticky-sweet *baghlava*—it's available in traditional pistachio or as a chocolate "choclava."

# Orexi

**D4**

Greek ✗✗

### 243 W. Portal Ave. (bet. 14th Ave. & Vicente St.)

**Phone:** 415-664-6739
**Web:** www.orexisanfrancisco.com
**Price:** $$

Dinner Tue – Sun

Nestled away from the hustle and bustle in charming, village-like West Portal, Orexi offers a future-perfect twist on the classic Greek taverna. The long, narrow space, with its rustic wood beams, wood furnishings, and oversized mirrors, has a contemporary vibe that contrasts nicely with the homey food. The menu is full of light, yet satisfying dishes, like a Greek salad packed with crunchy cucumber, ripe tomato, and tangy feta. A juicy, well-seasoned lamb burger is topped with goat cheese, tomato, and crunchy red onion. Heartier fare includes moussaka, slow-braised lamb shank with orzo, and lamb chops among the options.

Be sure to sample the *kataifi*, a baklava-like phyllo pastry filled with chopped toasted almonds.

# Outerlands

**A3**

American ✗

### 4001 Judah St. (at 45th Ave.)

**Phone:** 415-661-6140
**Web:** www.outerlandssf.com
**Price:** $$

Lunch & dinner daily

For the residents of this Outer Sunset foggy beachside community, this hot spot is an ideal hangout. The salvaged wood-dominated décor is perfectly cozy, and all-day hours ensure crowds flock here for breakfast and Bloody Marys to start their day. A friendly staff, good, locally roasted coffee, and a nicely stocked bar with a fine listing of beers on tap encourages further lingering.

Stop in for fresh-baked pastries like coffee cake, scones, and glazed doughnuts; or dig into heartier fare like an open-faced sandwich topped with black eye pea purée, green tomato, and griddled ham slices. Once the sun sets over Ocean Beach, expect more ambitious cooking from the dinner menu, like smoked chicken with tomato panzanella and charred gem lettuce.

# Park Chow

**D2**

### 1240 9th Ave. (bet. Irving St. & Lincoln Way)

**Phone:** 415-665-9912                    Lunch & dinner daily
**Web:** www.chowfoodbar.com
**Price:** $$

Steps from the Golden Gate Park museums, Park Chow draws locals and tourists alike with its approachable and well-priced organic American comfort food. No matter the mood or time of day, something here will appeal. Options abound from kid-friendly mini-pizzas to lighter and healthier fare like a tangy beet and endive salad with creamy avocado and salty goat cheese. Find straightforward pleasure in the grilled free-range chicken BLT on a griddled bun with crisp fries. For dessert, don't miss the rustic ginger cake with pumpkin ice cream and caramel.

The homey space is full of appealing nooks, including a dog-friendly front patio and sunny roof deck. Remember to call ahead to get your name on the wait list (especially for weekend brunch).

# Pizzetta 211

**C1**

### 211 23rd Ave. (at California St.)

**Phone:** 415-379-9880                    Lunch & dinner Wed – Mon
**Web:** www.pizzetta211.com
**Price:** $$

This shoebox-sized pizzeria may reside in the far reaches of the Outer Richmond, but it's easily identifiable by the crowds hovering on the sidewalk to score a table. Once inside, you'll be greeted by *pizzaiolos* throwing pies in the tiny exhibition kitchen—ask for a counter seat to get a better view.

The thin, chewy, blistered *pizzettas* each serve one, making it easy to share several varieties. Weekly specials utilize ingredients like seasonal produce, house-made sausage, and fresh farm eggs, while standbys include a pie topped with wild arugula, creamy mascarpone, and San Marzano tomato sauce. Whatever you do, arrive early: once the kitchen's out of dough, they close for the day, and the omnipresent lines mean the goods never last too long.

# San Tung

Chinese ✗

**D3**

**1031 Irving St. (bet. 11th & 12th Aves.)**

| | |
|---|---|
| **Phone:** | 415-242-0828 |
| **Web:** | www.santungchineserestaurant.com |
| **Price:** | $$ |

Lunch & dinner Thu – Tue

If you don't know what to order, just repeat after us: dry-fried chicken wings. Tossed in a chili-flecked ginger glaze, they're the reason foodies flock to this tasty, Americanized Chinese spot, write their names on a whiteboard, endure a long wait on the sidewalk, and finally eat at a communal table with strangers. It's all part of the restaurant's ramshackle appeal (as are the ultra-affordable prices).

Even if poultry's not your thing, the menu's other offerings are well worth the effort it takes to eat here. Dry-fried prawns are tossed in a sweet-and-spicy chili-garlic sauce, and hot and salty twice-cooked pork is fried with a heap of bell peppers and dried red chilies. Tables turn fast, so don't plan to linger—but for a filling meal, this one's a winner.

# Sichuan Home ☺

Chinese ✗

**C2**

**5037 Geary Blvd. (bet. 14th & 15th Aves.)**

| | |
|---|---|
| **Phone:** | 415-221-3288 |
| **Web:** | N/A |
| **Price:** | $$ |

Lunch & dinner daily

One of the brightest offerings on Geary Boulevard, Sichuan Home lures diners far and wide. Its spotless dining room is a vision of varnished wood panels and mirrors, with plexiglass-topped tables for easy chili oil clean-up and menus that feature tempting photos of each item.

A sampling of the wide-ranging Sichuan cuisine should include tender, bone-in rabbit with scallions, peanuts, and a perfect dab of scorching hot peppercorns. Fish with pickled cabbage gets a delightfully restorative hit of bold flavors from mustard greens and fresh green chilies, and red chilies star in aromatic dry-fried string beans with minced pork. For dessert, rich and velvety mango pudding, topped with grapefruit sorbet and fresh pineapple, is a tropical treat.

# Sutro's

**Californian** ✗✗

**A2**

### 1090 Point Lobos Ave. (at Ocean Beach)

**Phone:** 415-386-3330
**Web:** www.cliffhouse.com
**Price:** $$$

Lunch & dinner daily

Set in the historic Cliff House, perched above the roaring Pacific, Sutro's would be worth a trip just for its commanding views of the rugged California coastline. But this SF landmark doesn't rest on its laurels; instead, it serves surprisingly good food. In season, Dungeness crab is unmissable here, whether in a terrifically colossal crab Louie with avocado mousse and hard-boiled eggs, or shatteringly crisp panko-crusted crab cakes over carrot hummus and lemon-tarragon aïoli. The tasty seafood-focused fare goes on to include mussels steamed in Anchor Steam beer and *harissa*; as well as a sautéed red trout sandwich with fennel, cucumber, and yogurt.

After your meal, stroll along the beach or visit the windswept ruins of the Sutro Baths next door.

# Trattoria da Vittorio

**Italian** ✗✗

**D4**

### 150 W. Portal Ave. (bet. 14th Ave. & Vicente St.)

**Phone:** 415-742-0300
**Web:** www.trattoriadavittorio.com
**Price:** $$

Lunch & dinner daily

*Mamma* knows best at this West Portal hot spot, with home cooking imported straight from the kitchen of the owner's Italian mother, Mamma Francesca. One bite of her lasagna, rich with creamy ricotta and hearty Bolognese, will have you cheering "Mamma mia," while oversized portions have some crying "basta!" A semi-open kitchen and cheerful staff add to the sense of homey hospitality. A kids' menu makes it an extra popular choice for families.

Start meals with an immaculately fresh caprese salad, then sample a crisp pie from the Neapolitan wood-burning pizza oven. Don't miss the outstanding tiramisu: ultra-creamy and not overly sweet, these layers of espresso-soaked cake with whipped mascarpone and shaved chocolate won't require coaxing to scrape clean.

# Wako ⁑

Japanese  ✗

**D1**

## 211 Clement St. (bet. 3rd & 4th Aves.)

**Phone:** 415-682-4875
**Web:** www.sushiwakosf.com
**Price:** $$$

Dinner Tue — Sun

Wako may blend right in with the sea of Asian restaurants on Clement Street, but don't let its nondescript exterior fool you—inside, you'll find some of the best sushi the Bay Area has to offer.

It's the kind of pristine omakase experience that connoisseurs as well as foodies crave, and unlike many others of its ilk its doors are still open to à la carte diners too. Just be sure to specify your seat when you make a (required) reservation as the omakase—and the service of the sushi chef—is only available at the counter. The dining room is a spare but serene space, composed of multi-hued wood surfaces and accented with fresh flowers.

Counter diners have their pick of an all-nigiri menu, or a cheaper option with a few non-sushi small plates. The latter might include a buttery sliver of poached monkfish liver, a creamy potato croquette dolloped with salmon roe, or a salad of crisp shaved apple and mizuna. But the real knockouts arrive on rice: squid with a touch of shiso and Meyer lemon zest; silky salmon with house-made *yuzu kosho*; custardy uni imported from Japan, wrapped in roasted seaweed; and to finish, a melt-in-your-mouth slice of gently seared A5 Wagyu beef.

# SoMa

Once the city's locus of industry, sprawling SoMa (short for South of Market) has entered a post-industrial era that's as diverse and energetic as San Francisco itself. From its sleek office towers and museums near Market, to the spare converted warehouses that house the city's hottest startups, SoMa teems with vitality, offering memorable experiences around every turn. Tourists may skip it for its lack of Victorians, but SoMa's culinary riches and cultural cachet are of a different, authentically urban kind—the neighborhood equivalent of a treasured flea-market find.

## FINE ARTS & EATS

Most visitors to SoMa tend to cluster in the artsy northeast corridor (bordering downtown) for trips to the Museum of Modern Art (now closed for renovations), Yerba Buena Center for the Arts, Contemporary Jewish Museum, and a profusion of other galleries and studios. For a pit stop, join the tech workers snagging a caffeinated "Gibraltar" from local coffee phenomenon, **Blue Bottle**, housed in the back of Mint Plaza (there is also a rotating schedule of food trucks that visit Mint Plaza). For a more serene setting, gaze into Yerba Buena Gardens with a cup of rare green tea and some spa cuisine at **Samovar Tea Lounge**.

In a city where everyone loves to eat, even the **Westfield San Francisco Centre** mall is a surprisingly strong dining destination, offering cream puffs, fresh fish, or even *bi bim bap* in its downstairs food court. And local chain **Buckhorn Grill**, in the Metreon Mall, is a sparkling treasure for deliciously marinated, wood-fired tri-tip. A hard day's shopping done, hit happy hour on Yerba Buena Lane with the yupsters fresh from their offices, indulging in a strong margarita at festive Mexican cantina, **Tropisueño**. But for a more sedate sip, make way to chic **Press Club**, which focuses on Californian wine and beer. In the midst of it all, the Moscone Center may draw conventioneers to overpriced hotel restaurants and clumsy chains, However, the savvier ones beeline to **ThirstyBear Brewing Company**, where classic Spanish tapas and organic brews come without the crowds or crazy prices. Then stroll over to the Rincon Center for a unique meal at **Amawele's South African Kitchen**, which has won the hearts of local office workers with unique eats like "bunny chow"—a curry-filled bread bowl.

## PLAY BALL

SoMa's southeast quarter has undergone a revival in the last decade, with baseball fans flooding AT&T Park to watch the Giants—perennial World Series contenders. The park's food options are equally luring and include craft beer, sushi, and Ghirardelli sundaes. Crabcake sandwiches at **Crazy Crab'z** have a fan club nearly as sizable as the team itself. Off the field, this corridor is dominated by the tech scene, which has transformed the area's former factories and warehouses into humming open-plan offices. An oasis of green amid the corporate environs, South Park is a lovely retreat, particularly with a burrito from cheerful taqueria **Mexico au Parc** in hand. Just outside the park, legions of young engineers in their matching company hoodies form long lines every lunchtime outside **HRD Coffee Shop**. It may look like a greasy spoon but serves tasty Korean-influenced fare like spicy pork and kimchi burritos. Hip graphic designers can be seen speeding their fixed-gear bikes towards Market to pick up desktop fuel from **The Sentinel**, where former Canteen Chef Dennis Leary offers house-roasted coffee in the mornings and excellent corned-beef sandwiches for lunch.

Silicon Valley commuters begin pouring out of the Caltrain station around 5:00 P.M., giving the area's nightlife

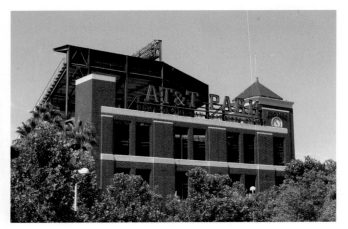

an extra shot in the arm. **21st Amendment**, a brewpub with hearty food and popular beers like Back in Black, is a favorite for a relaxed lunch; whereas Farmerbrown's **Little Skillet** might serve *the* best fried chicken and waffles in town. For those in need of an understated retreat, the 700-label selection at ripped-out-of-France wine bar, **Terroir**, will enchant natural-wine junkies.

SoMa's western half may be grittier, but it is still a must for those in search of great eats. After a closure and remodel, Vietnamese standby **Tú Lan** is once again drawing lines of customers for its killer imperial rolls, despite the drug-addled environs of its Sixth Street digs. Crowds also cluster at neighboring **Popsons**, where an impressive selection of juicy burgers and thick ice cream shakes are definitely worth the extra calories. Indeed, very little is same old-same old on this side of the city—whether it's the tattooed skateboarders practicing their moves, the omnipresent cranes constructing new condo towers, or the drag performers who entertain bachelorette parties over Asian-fusion food at bumping nightspot **AsiaSF**. Amidst the edgy bars, kitschy boutiques, and design start-ups of Folsom, **Citizen's Band** turns out seasonal "diner-inspired cuisine" like killer burgers on buns from next-door **Pinkie's Bakery**; while Ethiopian stews with spongy *injera* fuel a booming takeout business at **Moya**. Then feast on Thai curries at **Basil Canteen** in the original Jackson Brewery building. And finally, hit the 11th Street bars for hours of drinking and dancing, before soaking up all the evening's sins with a rich Nutella-banana triangle from late-night perma-cart, **Crêpes a Go Go**.

SoMa

NOB HILL

CHINATOWN

UNION SQUARE

TENDERLOIN

CIVIC CENTER

MARINA

MISSION

M.Y. China

The Cavalier

Hashiri

Volta

OLD MINT

54 Mint

MOSCONE CENTER WEST

Luce

Montesacro Pinseria-Enoteca

Tin Vietnamese

AQ

ASIAN ART MUSEUM

CITY HALL

SF PUBLIC LIBRARY

UN PLAZA

Civic Center

SF WAR MEMORIAL & PERFORMING ARTS CENTER

The Perennial

Van Ness

Una Pizza Napoletana

1601 Bar & Kitchen

Bar Agricole

Bellota

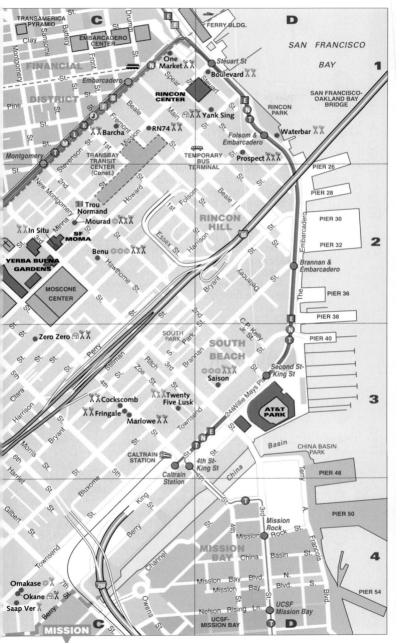

TRANSAMERICA PYRAMID
Clay
Sansome St.
Battery St.
Front St.
Davis St.
Drumm St.
EMBARCADERO CENTER
C
E
F
FERRY BLDG.
D
SAN FRANCISCO BAY
1
FINANCIAL
Pine St.
DISTRICT
Montgomery St.
Embarcadero
Steuart St.
One Market ✕✕
N
Boulevard ✕✕
Spear St.
RINCON CENTER
Main St.
Yank Sing ✕✕
Beale St.
Fremont St.
Barcha ✕
RN74 ✕✕
Stevenson St.
2nd St.
New Montgomery St.
TRANSBAY TRANSIT CENTER (Const.)
Howard St.
Mission St.
1st St.
Folsom St.
TEMPORARY BUS TERMINAL
Prospect ✕✕✕
Folsom & Embarcadero
E
N
T
RINCON PARK
Waterbar ✕✕
SAN FRANCISCO-OAKLAND BAY BRIDGE
Steuart St.
PIER 26
Trou Normand
Mourad ⊕✕✕✕
Minna St.
Natoma St.
In Situ ✕✕
3rd St.
SF MOMA
Benu ⊕⊕⊕✕✕✕
YERBA BUENA GARDENS
Hawthorne St.
Essex St.
Harrison St.
Bryant St.
RINCON HILL
80
Beale St.
Main St.
Spear St.
Embarcadero
PIER 28
PIER 30
PIER 32
Brannan & Embarcadero
2
MOSCONE CENTER
Zero Zero ⊕✕✕
Perry St.
5th St.
4th St.
Clara St.
Harrison St.
Bryant St.
Morris St.
Harriet St.
Gilbert St.
Cockscomb ✕✕
Fringale ✕✕
Marlowe ✕✕
Stillman St.
Zoe St.
Ritch St.
3rd St.
Brannan St.
SOUTH PARK
SOUTH BEACH
Saison ⊕⊕⊕✕✕✕
Twenty Five Lusk ✕✕✕
C.P. Kelly Jr. St.
Delancey St.
The Embarcadero
PIER 36
PIER 38
E
N
T
PIER 40
Second St-King St
AT&T PARK
24 Willie Mays Plz.
Townsend St.
King St.
2nd St.
E
N
T
Basin
CHINA BASIN PARK
PIER 48
3
CALTRAIN STATION
4th St-King St
Caltrain Station
Bluxome St.
King St.
Berry St.
5th St.
6th St.
Townsend St.
Channel
280
Owens St.
Berry St.
China Basin St.
4th St.
3rd St.
Terry A. François Blvd.
PIER 50
Mission Rock St.
Mission Rock
MISSION BAY
China Basin St.
N.
S.
Mission Bay Blvd.
Mission Bay Blvd.
Nelson Rising Ln.
UCSF-MISSION BAY
UCSF Mission Bay
T
PIER 54
4
Omakase ⊕✕
Okane ⊕✕
Saap Ver ✕
Berry St.
C
MISSION
D

149

# AQ

Contemporary ✗✗

**B3**

Contemporary ✗✗

### 1085 Mission St. (bet. 6th & 7th Sts.)

**Phone:** 415-341-9000
**Web:** www.aq-sf.com
**Price:** $$$

Lunch Sun
Dinner Tue – Sun

Like its once-sketchy, increasingly tech-centric SoMa corridor, this chic Californian restaurant is aiming for the stars—and even if it doesn't always succeed, it's certainly never a dull ride. Whether you opt for the four-course or tasting menu, you'll be wowed by flavor combos that are always intriguing and often breathtaking: think silky-sweet scallop crudo with white sesame and pineapple, earthy beets with snap peas and lavender ice cream, and black cod with clam butter.

AQ's hyperseasonal menus are gently accented by a quarterly décor shakeup; depending on the time of year, you'll find cherry blossoms or fall leaves accenting the sleek, neutral space. Be sure to come early to enjoy one of the exceptional cocktails at the front bar.

# Bar Agricole

**B4**

Californian ✗✗

### 355 11th St. (bet. Folsom & Harrison Sts.)

**Phone:** 415-355-9400
**Web:** www.baragricole.com
**Price:** $$

Dinner Mon – Sat

Cocktails and conversation are always a pleasure at Bar Agricole, which is known for having one of the city's best drink programs. Its narrow, industrial-modern dining room boasts soaring ceilings from which huge acrylic sculptures hang, while mod concrete booths line the side wall. An outdoor patio, with plant beds and a trickling fountain, is particularly popular on warm evenings.

The menu is thoroughly Californian and loaded with the season's best, showcased in dishes like a frisée, arugula, and radish salad with a *citronette* dressing; halibut *brandade* with asparagus; as well as roast pork leg and belly with Canario beans, greens, and horseradish. Buttermilk panna cotta with peaches and toasted oat streusel end things on a perfectly sweet note.

# Barcha

Mediterranean ✗✗

**C1**

28 Fremont St. (bet. Market & Mission Sts.)

**Phone:** 415-957-5463
**Web:** www.barcha-sf.com
**Price:** $$

Lunch Mon – Fri
Dinner Mon – Sat

Given its location at the base of the Salesforce building on Fremont, this exciting sequel to the Embarcadero's Sens could easily rest on its laurels. Instead, thanks to zippy and flavorful Mediterranean-accented cooking, it's become a new standard for the area's office types. Many items play on current standards, like a kale Caesar topped with delicately spiced duck *kefta*, or tangy sheep's milk cheese-potato croquettes drizzled with smoked paprika aïoli for added zing.

It helps that Barcha's got the looks to match its menu: walls of windows flood it with natural light, tufted caramel banquettes provide comfortable seating, and blue, aqua, and yellow tiles brighten everything up. For a nice business lunch that won't break the bank, it really hits the spot.

# Bellota

Spanish ✗✗

**B4**

888 Brannan St. (bet. 7th & 8th Sts.)

**Phone:** 415-430-6580
**Web:** www.bellotasf.com
**Price:** $$$

Dinner Mon – Sat

Iberian flavors and Cali-cool join forces at this SoMa Spanish stunner, where legs of the namesake *jamón ibérico de bellota* hang in a central glass case. They're flanked by a sumptuous exhibition kitchen framed in bronze and hand-painted tiles, as well as a glamorous U-shaped bar. Chic professionals (some of them from the neighboring offices of Airbnb) have already staked their claim for date night.

The menu adds seasonal touches to traditional Spanish tapas: picture yogurt-braised chicken *albóndigas* drizzled with pomegranate *agridulce*; or a fluffy *tortilla Española* with rainbow chard and chorizo crumbles. Paellas sized for 2-4 people are another popular option—try the Pluma, with Iberico pork shoulder, summer squash, and slivered squash blossoms.

# Benu ✿✿✿

**C2**

22 Hawthorne St. (bet. Folsom & Howard Sts.)

**Phone:** 415-685-4860
**Web:** www.benusf.com
**Price:** $$$$

Dinner Tue – Sat

Don't miss the street views directly into Benu's kitchen as you enter—the chefs here are preparing a series of masterpieces. The interior is awash in earthy colors and sleek banquettes, and the slate-gray dining room is serene, with clean lines drawing the eye across the meticulous design. Given the restaurant's high caliber, the staff is impressively warm and relaxed.

Chef Corey Lee's nightly tasting is a unique marriage of contemporary Asian influences, while Master Sommelier Yoon Ha oversees an exceptional beverage program. Each meal begins with a thrilling parade of bites like silky egg custard with faux "shark fin," slivers of Jinhua ham, and umami-rich black truffle. The main courses might include a delectable "thousand-year-old" quail egg atop bright ginger cream, followed by delicate *xiao long bao* filled with rich lobster and lobster coral. Then fork-tender beef braised in pear juice reaches a new height of excellence when paired with charred scallion purée and black trumpet mushrooms. The memory of the osmanthus gelée with almond cake and apricots will remain long after the last plate has been cleared.

Finally, sojourn to their pretty courtyard, to linger after this regal repast.

# Boulevard

Californian ✗✗

**D1**

## 1 Mission St. (at Steuart St.)

**Phone:** 415-543-6084

**Web:** www.boulevardrestaurant.com

**Price:** $$$

Lunch Mon – Fri

Dinner nightly

Housed in one of the city's most historic buildings, this Belle Époque stunner is still breathtaking after more than 20 years, with glamorous mosaic floors, colorful glass, and polished bronze at every turn. The Embarcadero-adjacent location offers lovely views of the Bay Bridge and the water, and business lunchers as well as evening romance-seekers adore its transporting vibe.

Chef/owner Nancy Oakes is known as a pioneer of Californian cooking, with comforting takes on standards like Dungeness crab with avocado and ruby-red grapefruit, burrata served with a side of shaved kale, and flaky halibut over a mashed potato cake. Sweets are notable: try the pear- and apple-studded winter symphony crisp or creamy butterscotch pudding with pecan granola for a bit of bliss.

# The Cavalier

Gastropub ✗✗

**B2**

## 360 Jessie St. (at 5th St.)

**Phone:** 415-321-6000

**Web:** www.thecavaliersf.com

**Price:** $$

Lunch & dinner daily

One of the city's high-profile hangouts, this is the third effort from the team behind Marlowe and Park Tavern. Everything here has a British bent, echoed in the hunting-lodge-gone-sophisticated décor with red-and-blue walls accented by taxidermied trophies and tufted banquettes. Across-the-pond classics have Californian twists like a deep-fried Scotch duck egg wrapped in truffled duck rillettes. The restaurant has quickly become a see-and-be-seen haunt of the tech oligarchy (complete with a private club). However, the food is comforting and homey as seen in a caramelized roast chicken set atop horseradish mash.

Though reservations are a must, its location in the Hotel Zetta means service runs from morning to night, giving diners plenty of options.

# Cockscomb

**C3**

### 564 4th St. (at Freelon St.)

**Phone:** 415-974-0700  
**Web:** www.cockscombsf.com  
**Price:** $$$

Lunch Mon – Fri  
Dinner Mon – Sat

Carnivores will thrill to the offerings at this favored spot from offal-loving *Top Chef Masters* champ Chris Cosentino. It doesn't shy away from aggressively rich fare like wood-grilled bruschetta topped with uni butter, sweet Dungeness crab, and buttery *lardo*, or smoky butterflied roast quail in a rich, salty tetrazzini gravy. Even veggie-centric celery Victor gets a meaty spin, its tangy vinaigrette accented by crisp chicken-skin *chicharrónes*.

Thanks to the hearty menu and location in a tech-centric corridor, Cockscomb draws a mostly male crowd that packs in for shellfish platters and intense, boozy cocktails named for SF landmarks. Laid-back, yet attentive service and a soaring, industrial space make it the very picture of a hot spot.

# 54 Mint

**B2**

### 16 Mint Plaza (at Jessie St.)

**Phone:** 415-543-5100  
**Web:** www.54mint.com  
**Price:** $$

Lunch Mon – Fri  
Dinner nightly

With its largely Italian waitstaff and clientele, a meal at 54 Mint is the next best thing to a plane ticket to Rome. A happy respite from the neighborhood's hustle and bustle, the space boasts a contemporary dining room stocked with shelves of Italian ingredients and a surprisingly tranquil front patio facing Mint Plaza.

The food is an authentic culinary journey through the Eternal City, with favorites like perfectly al dente *bucatini all'amatriciana*, twirled with smoked pancetta, sweet onion, tomato, and chili. The must-order *suppli*, fried balls of tomato risotto stuffed with smoked mozzarella, are best described as arancini on steroids. For dessert? The buttery, dark chocolate-flecked ricotta tart will leave you feeling *molto buono*.

# Fringale

French

**C3**

570 4th St. (bet. Brannan & Bryant Sts.)

**Phone:** 415-543-0573
**Web:** www.fringalesf.com
**Price:** $$

Lunch Tue – Fri
Dinner nightly

This tech-centric corner of SoMa has seen booms and busts aplenty since the restaurant's opening in 1991, but Fringale has held strong, with a loyal squad of regulars who come for a taste of its Basque-inflected French cooking. The timeless décor starring clean wood furnishings and soft lighting is ideal for a business lunch or date night.

Start with the tasty calamari *à la plancha*—its topping of briny black olives and sliced jalapeños clearly differentiates Fringale from its tired bistro competition. After the mostly French staff recommends a wine, dive into the juicy roasted chicken breast over fluffy Israeli couscous and crunchy fennel. Finish with a creamy, nutty hazelnut-and-roasted almond mousse cake, drizzled with rich dark chocolate, of course!

# In Situ

International

**C2**

151 Third St. (bet. Howard & Minna Sts.)

**Phone:** 415-941-6050
**Web:** insitu.sfmoma.org
**Price:** $$$$

Lunch & dinner daily

Housed in the renovated Museum of Modern Art, In Situ is an exhibition restaurant from Benu's Corey Lee. The menu showcases a revolving collection of dishes from iconic chefs and restaurants throughout the world. A meal here is a globe-trotting and time-traveling experience in culinary art, where a dish that originated in 1999 in Bangkok might be followed by one from 2005 in Copenhagen.

Items change every four months or so, spotlighting the work of longtime legends (Thomas Keller's seared duck breast with green lentils and red wine vinegar reduction) as well as new-guard talents (David Chang's rice cakes with Sichuan peppercorns and pork sausage). If you're looking to take your tastebuds on a trip without leaving SF, this is it.

155

# Hashiri ❀

Japanese 🍴🍴🍴

**B2**

### 4 Mint Plaza (at 5th St.)

**Phone:** 415-908-1919
**Web:** www.hashirisf.com
**Price:** $$$$

Dinner Tue – Sat

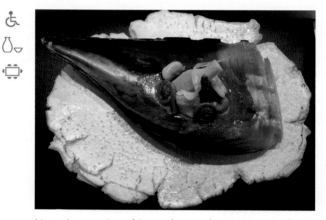

Upon its opening, this omakase-only Japanese newbie in Mint Plaza immediately became one of San Francisco's most expensive restaurants, but those who can afford the bill will be rewarded with a truly luxurious experience. Every detail of Hashiri has been finely crafted, from the hand-painted dishes and crystal sake glasses to the parting seasonal treat gifted to diners at the end of the meal. The dining room's elaborate digital video installation courts techies with money to burn—don't be surprised if you see a hoodie-clad millionaire or two seated next to you.

Exceptional kaiseki dishes showcase the best of the season, and have included stunningly tender pen shell clam with citrus-splashed fava beans and bamboo shoots; or lightly grilled, melt-in-your-mouth A5 Wagyu beef over celeriac purée and grilled ramps. They lead the way to a dozen outstanding nigiri, including buttery Spanish mackerel brushed with citrus, pungent *aji* with minced chives and ginger, silky *chutoro* and *otoro*, as well as uni imported straight from Hokkaido.

Sake connoisseurs will enjoy the exclusive selection of Dassai, milled to 23%, 39% or 50% of the original grain. For novices, the warm and welcoming staff will happily steer the way to the right selection.

# Luce ✿

Contemporary XXX

**B3**

888 Howard St. (at 5th St.)

**Phone:** 415-616-6566
**Web:** www.lucewinerestaurant.com
**Price:** $$$

Lunch & dinner daily

Know that the ambience is pleasant, the space is elegant, the service team is quick and polite, and the food is consistently excellent. Also, know that you probably won't have a hard time getting a reservation at this InterContinental Hotel restaurant—Luce is often inexplicably empty. Let its lack of popularity be your reminder to come here when looking for a little privacy—think date night.

Soaring ceilings, dark and dramatic spherical lights, a transparent wall of wine bordering the kitchen, and shiny cushioned banquettes give the dining room a sumptuous, airy feel that promises the high level of luxury echoed in the cuisine. This may be one of the city's more venerable mainstays, but a contemporary sensibility is clear throughout the décor and menu.

Luce serves breakfast, lunch, and brunch, but dinner is when the serious diner arrives for an entirely different experience. Highlights include a generous portion of perfectly white halibut poached in California olive oil and placed on a colorful bed of fresh shelling beans with artichoke and clams. Desserts may combine the wonderfully light flavors of sweet corn panna cotta with kernels of honey-caramel popped corn and huckleberry compote.

# Marlowe

C3

American ✗✗

### 500 Brannan St. (at 4th St.)

**Phone:** 415-777-1413
**Web:** www.marlowesf.com
**Price:** $$

Lunch & dinner daily

Despite a move to larger digs, the competition for a table or barstool at this American bistro in the heart of SoMa is still as hot as ever, making reservations a must. Like Raymond Chandler's gumshoe, Marlowe's dining room exudes a timeless, casual cool complete with a black-and-white color scheme, penny-tile floors, and vintage-inspired lighting.

Though it's best known for its (outstanding) burger, Marlowe handles the lighter side with equal aplomb. A little gem salad, packed with shaved heirloom carrots and radishes, is bright and citrusy, while the *poulet vert* or roasted chicken coated in garlicky, herbaceous herb pistou is wonderfully moist and juicy. Ready for more? Consider the chocolate cream pudding topped with cocoa nibs—for an earned indulgence.

# Montesacro Pinseria-Enoteca

B3

Pizza ✗

### 510 Stevenson St. (bet. 6th & 7th Sts.)

**Phone:** 415-795-3040
**Web:** www.montesacrosf.com
**Price:** ⊜

Lunch & dinner Mon – Sat

You'll need to sojourn into the edgy environs of Sixth Street to find this little enoteca, but rest assured: the food will reward your efforts. The focus is ultra-authentic Roman *pinsa* made with rice, soy and wheat flours and topped with everything from cheese to tender kale to *garum*, a fermented fish sauce that dates back to ancient Roman times. But you'll also find killer olive oil-marinated vegetables, briny olives, imported cheeses, and cured meats, all meant for enjoying with a glass (or three) of wine—Sardinian red, perhaps?

Cavernous and a little disheveled, this warm-hearted space is centered around a huge, 100-year-old brick oven that was found at the time of construction. It doesn't work (yet), but it is nonetheless, quite the looker.

# Mourad ✿

**C2**

140 New Montgomery St. (bet. Minna & Natoma Sts.)

**Phone:** 415-660-2500
**Web:** www.mouradsf.com
**Price:** $$$

Lunch Mon – Fri
Dinner nightly

San Francisco ▲ SoMa

This glamorous outpost at the base of the PacBell building introduces the unique soul of Chef/owner Mourad Lahlou's second restaurant—one that is a contemporary departure from Aziza. The area's food-obsessed techies flock to the boldly designed space, replete with soaring ceilings, glowing central columns, and a superb (suspended) wine cellar. The servers may not know the menu inside out, but a good sommelier and live music keep the crowds contented and lively.

Chef Lahlou is at his best when reinterpreting modern Moroccan cuisine with ingredients such as za'atar, harissa, and dates. Begin with the subtle and original combination of nicely charred octopus accented with an herbaceous oil, chili powder, and diced merguez, alongside an unctuous purée mixing chickpeas, citrus, and olives. Be sure to order the main courses in true Moroccan style, as shareable platters with plenty of sauces and sides. A remarkable take on lamb loin is cooked to perfection and intensely flavored with spiced black olives, surrounded by deliciously crunchy flatbreads.

Desserts embrace deconstruction and fusion, perhaps built on the powerful flavors of dark chocolate, jasmine cream, and ginger crumble.

# M.Y. China

Chinese   ✗✗

### 845 Market St. (bet. 4th & 5th Sts.)

**Phone:** 415-580-3001                  Lunch & dinner daily
**Web:** www.tastemychina.com
**Price:** $$

Need proof that Yan Can Cook? Just snag a table at the famed PBS chef's elegant restaurant. Housed under the dome of the Westfield San Francisco Centre shopping mall, M.Y. China is a dark, sultry space full of posh Chinese furniture, antiques, and dramatic lighting. Shopping-weary patrons fill the dining room, whereas chowhounds hit the exhibition counter to watch the staff masterfully hand-pull noodles and toss woks. The menu reads like an ode to regional Chinese cuisine, spanning chewy scissor-cut noodles with wild boar, fluffy *bao* stuffed with sweet and smoky barbecue pork, and, when it's in season, delectable pepper-dusted whole crab. Be sure to order strategically, as you'll want room for the flaky, buttery, creamy, and outright superb Macanese egg tarts.

# Okane

C4                                Japanese   ✗

### 669 Townsend St. (bet. 7th & 8th Sts.)

**Phone:** 415-865-9788                  Lunch Mon – Fri
**Web:** www.okanesf.com                  Dinner nightly
**Price:** $$

Can't afford to indulge in the exquisite sushi at Omakase? Consider heading to its next-door little sib, where the fish is still top-notch (it's all sourced from Japan) but the atmosphere is more laid-back. Okane draws lots of nearby Adobe and Zynga employees at lunch and big groups at dinner, all sharing bottles of sake and making the most of the small-plates menu. Sushi is, of course, a must: the nigiri is pristine and delicious, as are more Americanized rolls like the Harajuku (filled with shrimp tempura, avocado, and salmon and topped with tuna, eel sauce, and lotus root chips). But don't sleep on the non-sushi dishes—the cod marinated in sake lees is grilled to perfection, and broiled salmon aburi with avocado and ikura is delicious, too.

# Omakase ❀

**C4**

665 Townsend St. (bet. 7th & 8th Sts.)

Dinner Tue — Sun

**Phone:** 415-865-0633
**Web:** www.omakasesf.com
**Price:** $$$$

True, the vibe is friendly and the location is convenient for tech entrepreneurs, but superb Edomae sushi is the real reason why Omakase is always full. Do not forget to reserve.

The kimono-clad servers strain to place dishes in front of diners, who are usually packed in elbow-to-elbow at the tight L-shaped counter, but the chummy young professionals and gourmands don't seem to notice anything but the chefs.

Choose from two omakase menus; the more extensive (and expensive) one offers additional sashimi and nigiri courses. Begin with buttery ocean trout that has been steamed in sake and presented with a wedge of heirloom black tomato and herb salad in rice wine vinaigrette. Beautifully arranged sashimi features bluefin tuna with red-fleshed sea perch, garnished with strips of cured kombu, shiso leaf, wasabi, and a bit of chrysanthemum petal salad. Still, no dish can compare with the exquisite level of nigiri, which may showcase marinated *chutoro*, cedar-torched sea bream, Hokkaido uni with house-brined *ikura*, and a fluffy piece of lobster-infused *tamago*.

Extreme attention to detail is the hallmark of dining here, with customized portions of rice and wasabi adjustments for each guest's palate.

# One Market

Californian ✗✗

**C1**

1 Market St. (at Steuart St.)

**Phone:** 415-777-5577
**Web:** www.onemarket.com
**Price:** $$$

Lunch Mon – Fri
Dinner Mon – Sat

Located at the tail end of Market Street facing the Ferry Building, this perennial power-lunch spot draws crowds for its bright, bustling vibe, busy open kitchen, and attractive Bay views. Both the kitchen and the bow-tied waitstaff have made a science of getting the corporate crowd fed well and back to work in record time—just the way they like it.

One Market's contemporary Californian food is refreshing and seasonal, with options like potato pancakes garnished with cured salmon, pancetta vinaigrette, and a poached egg, or seared flounder over flavorful black-eyed peas with smoky bacon. Sweet tooths on a caloric budget will relish the miniature desserts (offered solo or as a trio), like a toffee-almond crunch cake coated in rich dark chocolate.

# The Perennial

Contemporary ✗✗

**A3**

59 9th St. (bet. Market & Mission Sts.)

**Phone:** 415-500-7788
**Web:** www.theperennialsf.com
**Price:** $$$

Dinner Mon – Sat

Quite possibly the world's most enviro-friendly restaurant, this hot spot is out to prove that sustainability can be delicious. Every ingredient is meticulously sourced, with much of the produce coming from the restaurant's own aquaponic farm in Oakland. From the modern dining room to the energy bill, the lowest possible carbon footprint is the goal.

Sure, but is it tasty? In a word, yes. From sustainable Kernza wheatgrass toasts topped with cauliflower to cheesy grain porridge thick with black trumpet mushrooms and artichoke hearts, there's a lot to savor (including hyper-homemade sodas and cocktails). And while the staff is happy to answer questions, they're not a drag—you won't get a seminar with your meal, unless you want one.

# Prospect

American 🗙🗙🗙

**D1**

### 300 Spear St. (at Folsom St.)

**Phone:** 415-247-7770
**Web:** www.prospectsf.com
**Price:** $$$

Lunch Sun
Dinner nightly

For a polished and contemporary experience that doesn't sacrifice approachability, FiDi denizens turn to Prospect, a crowd-pleaser for the full-pocketbook crowd. Set on the ground floor of a soaring high-rise, its airy space offers attractive, roomy tables, adept service, and a popular, well-stocked cocktail bar.

Simple, well-constructed American fare abounds, with menu mainstays like an heirloom tomato salad with creamy dollops of burrata and crisp, garlicky breadcrumbs; or a perfectly flaky Coho salmon fillet set over earthy black rice, sweet yellow corn, and caramelized summer squash. Dessert should not be missed: the butter brickle icebox cake with honey-glazed plums and toasted pecan butter crunch is a truly memorable treat.

# RN74

Californian 🗙🗙

**C1**

### 301 Mission St. (at Beale St.)

**Phone:** 415-543-7474
**Web:** www.rn74.com
**Price:** $$$

Lunch Mon – Fri
Dinner nightly

Named for Burgundy's most famous road, RN74 draws a crowd of suited corporate types who pack this high-ceilinged room for lunch. Come sunset, the lounge is equally busy for after-work drinks, but dinner is sedate. Burgundy is, of course, the house specialty here, and an array of high-end bottles is listed on a train station-style board, which clicks over as each one sells out.

The food is playful and globally inspired, from pastrami-style salmon tartare with warm brioche and creamy dill crème fraîche to a panzanella with arugula, cherry tomatoes, and pan-fried chicken breast. Each plate is artistically constructed, like the "peach mille feuille," which combines pretty dollops of vanilla cream and peach sorbet with peaches and shards of puff pastry.

# Saap Ver

Thai 🍴

**88 Division St. (bet. Townsend & King Sts.)**

**Phone:** 415-255-8188
**Web:** www.saapver.com
**Price:** $$

Lunch & dinner daily

A delightful all-Thai staff mans the floor at this lively Design District hangout, which specializes in Thai street food with an authentic flair. Casual and colorful, it's bedecked with posters for vintage Thai movies—some of which are projected in the dining room. Area tech workers crowd in at lunch, transitioning into neighborhood families in the evening.

While dedicated chili-hounds might be disappointed by the Americanized heat levels, Saap Ver's food is otherwise fresh and delicious, from top-notch pad Thai wrapped in a traditional egg crêpe to a spicy-tangy crisp rice salad with crumbles of Isaan sausage. It would be plain wrong to skip out on the excellent coconut ice cream sundae, served in a young coconut with the meat sliced out for easier access.

# 1601 Bar & Kitchen 😊

Sri Lankan 🍴🍴

**1601 Howard St. (at 12th St.)**

**Phone:** 415-552-1601
**Web:** www.1601sf.com
**Price:** $$

Dinner Tue – Sat

Sri Lankan flavors infuse the dishes at this quiet winner, which also employs Western ingredients to arrive at its very own delicious concoctions. For a more extensive exploration of this island nation's cuisine, go for the degustation menu. Or stick to such decidedly untraditional items as *lamprais*, which might stuff a classically French bacon-wrapped rabbit loin and eggplant curry into a banana leaf. Halibut "ceviche" is more like a flavored sashimi, with hints of coconut milk and serrano chilies.

This contemporary space with its wraparound windows and slate walls is a perfect showcase for the food. Dine solo at the bar with a bittersweet Dubonnet sangria, or come with friends to share food and wine—the polished staff makes either experience enjoyable.

# Saison ❀ ❀ ❀

Californian XXX

**D3**

178 Townsend St. (bet. 2nd & 3rd Sts.)

**Phone:** 415-828-7990                    Dinner Tue – Sat
**Web:** www.saisonsf.com
**Price:** $$$$

No expense has ever been spared in this massive wow-inducing space. There are enough shining copper pots to supply a village of restaurants in France; natural-edged wood tables and a minimalist backdrop conjure Scandinavia. There is also a refreshing breakdown of traditional barriers between the kitchen and dining areas, underscored by the chefs' visits to each table, personally presenting and describing dishes. While there are formal elements to the service, it is also natural and relaxed. An '80s soundtrack lightens the mood.

Chef Joshua Skenes uses extraordinary skill and detail to craft each item on his spontaneous menu—especially the seafood courses. Expect fermentation as well as the smoke of a wood-fired hearth to feature prominently throughout these wonderfully modern dishes. Meals may move from a purposeful pairing of briny caviar with a *chawan mushi*-style custard and smoky cube of hearth-toasted brioche, to a woodsy grilled root vegetable consommé with yuzu zest and butter-poached daikon. Pure flavors are paramount in the silky black cod grilled over embers and served in a tangy pool of cultured yogurt with makrut lime leaves.

Treat yourself to the exceptional wine pairing (and an Uber home).

# Tin Vietnamese

**B3**

937 Howard St. (bet. 5th & 6th Sts.)

**Phone:** 415-882-7188
**Web:** www.tinsf.com
**Price:** $$

Lunch & dinner Mon – Sat

The modern atmosphere at this downtowner might conjure thoughts of misguided fusion fare, but rest assured: when it comes to food, Tin is as traditional as it gets. Nonetheless, the dark wood walls, sleek glass pendant lights, and rich wood furnishings are a welcome change, making the spot a draw for groups residing far beyond its gritty, largely industrial neighborhood.

High-quality ingredients are the secret that sets this kitchen's cooking apart—from crunchy threads of banana blossom tossed with fried eel, shallots, peanuts, and herbs, to smoky soy-lemongrass pork shoulder atop rice noodles with a spicy lime-chili dipping sauce. Throw in some crunchy imperial rolls and garlicky, peppery wok-tossed shaking beef, and you'll have an affordable feast.

# Trou Normand

**C2**

140 New Montgomery St. (at Natoma St.)

**Phone:** 415-975-0876
**Web:** www.trounormandsf.com
**Price:** $$

Lunch & dinner daily

Named for the Norman tradition of drinking a glass of Calvados to revive the palate during a heavy meal, Bar Agricole's SoMa sequel shares its predecessor's skill with outstanding cocktails. They're perfect palate-cleansers for the expansive and delightful house charcuterie, like rich duck pâté with plum and Armagnac or garlicky *finocchiona* kissed with fennel seeds.

While their *salumi* and selection of spirits are huge draws, Trou Normand offers an all-day menu of shareable French- and Italian-leaning plates. Come for a croque madame with ramps and locally roasted coffee at brunch, sausage sandwiches with homemade sauerkraut at lunch, and pastas or roasted meats at dinner.

This large and glamorous space is a major hit among hipster tech types.

# Twenty Five Lusk

A m e r i c a n  XXX

C3

25 Lusk St. (bet. 3rd & 4th Sts.)

**Phone:** 415-495-5875
**Web:** www.25lusk.com
**Price:** $$$

Lunch Sun
Dinner nightly

Nestled in the center of SoMa's dynamic startup scene, this high-design stunner draws an equally high-powered crowd. They stream in at happy hour to catch up on the latest tech gossip in the swinging lounge, then head upstairs to wheel and deal in the refined dining room, which boasts an impressive glassed-in exhibition kitchen.

Lusk's food is American with contemporary touches, from the *togarashi* and carrot coulis that spikes a highbrow take on shrimp and grits, to the ginger vinaigrette that accents a summery salad of little gem lettuce and heirloom cucumbers. Dessert aficionados will thrill to the freedom from choice offered by the "sampling" trio, featuring creamy lime posset, spiced carrot cake, and a decadent salted-caramel brownie.

# Una Pizza Napoletana

P i z z a  X

A4

210 11th St. (at Howard St.)

**Phone:** 415-861-3444
**Web:** www.unapizza.com
**Price:** $$

Dinner Wed – Sat

In keeping with owner Anthony Mangieri's monastic devotion to the perfect pie, Una Pizza Napoletana is a spare space, housed in a chilly former garage on an industrial corner of SoMa. The vibe is completely casual yet alluring with crowds riveted by the altar—a tiled turquoise oven, where Mangieri stretches dough and deftly coaxes the crackling wood fire to produce his perfect pies. Their blistered and puffy crusts sport a delicious char as well as an addictively chewy texture thanks to tangy fermentation.

Waits are long, but the hassle is well worth it after one bite of the Filetti, slathered with creamy buffalo mozzarella and juicy cherry tomatoes. Mangieri is unquestionably a master of his craft, and his pies are a cut above local competition.

# Volta

**B2**

European 𝗫𝗫𝗫

868 Mission St. (bet. 4th & 5th Sts.)

**Phone:** 628-400-6200
**Web:** www.voltasf.com
**Price:** $$$

Dinner nightly

The menu at this *bijou* is equal parts classic French and old-school Swedish, thereby making it a definite departure from Perbacco and Barbacco—its Italian-inspired siblings. Less fusion than collaboration, this is the kind of place where a dish of five herring preparations (cured, pickled, in a beet-potato salad) sits side-by-side with pan-fried pig's head terrine over lentils and poached apples. And, desserts tend to be modern versions of traditional favorites—think deconstructed princess cake.

Located in the back of the Westfield Mall (with a separate entrance), Volta's contemporary space is already a hit with the expense-account crowd, who appreciate its white tablecloths, polished service, and convenience to the Moscone Center and downtown offices.

# Waterbar

**D1**

Seafood 𝗫𝗫

399 The Embarcadero (bet. Folsom & Harrison Sts.)

**Phone:** 415-284-9922
**Web:** www.waterbarsf.com
**Price:** $$$

Lunch & dinner daily

Stunning views of the Bay Bridge and people-watching along the promenade are chief draws at this Embarcadero favorite, designed for sipping wine on the lovely terrace and slurping oysters at the enormous raw bar. Though the polished, modern dining room can seem serious, warm and thoughtful service brings things back down to earth. Those tanks filled with ocean fish are photo-worthy.

Seafood-centric entrées make global use of the nearby waters' bounty by way of local Marin Miyagi and Point Reyes oysters. Try nicely cooked capellini twirled with slow-cooked egg, tomatoes, and thin slices of chorizo. An Americana-influenced dessert menu (think buttermilk panna cotta with poached pear and palmier) is the final touch in ensuring that Waterbar stays packed to the gills.

# Yank Sing

Chinese ✗✗

**D1**

### 101 Spear St. (bet. Howard & Mission Sts.)

**Phone:** 415-781-1111                                          Lunch daily
**Web:** www.yanksing.com
**Price:** $$

With a higher price tag than the average Chinatown joint, Yank Sing is arguably *the* place in town for dim sum. While peak hours entail a wait, one can be assured of quality and abundant variety from these rolling carts. The signature Peking duck with its lacquered skin and fluffy buns is a memorable treat, as are the equally sweet and salty *char siu bao*. Of course, dumplings here are the true highlight, from plump and fragrant pork *xiao long bao*, to paper-thin *har gao* concealing chunks of fresh, sweet shrimp. Don't see favorites like the flaky egg custard tarts? Just ask the cheerful staff, who'll radio the kitchen for help via headsets.

The upscale setting is cheaper by day, but the zigzagging carts can get hectic. Things calm down a bit at dinnertime.

# Zero Zero

Pizza ✗✗

**C3**

### 826 Folsom St. (bet. 4th & 5th Sts.)

**Phone:** 415-348-8800                                 Lunch & dinner daily
**Web:** www.zerozerosf.com
**Price:** $$

Zero Zero may be named for the superlative flour used in its blistered pies, but it is so much more than a pizzeria. While the Castro topped with oozing mozzarella and spicy *soppressata* is delicious, this casual spot offers far more than just a good slice. Absolute knockouts include a beautifully composed panzanella accompanied by basil pesto; while gnocchi tossed in a hearty pork belly ragù and decked with dollops of ricotta is light and bright, despite the indulgent ingredients.

A mix of families, hipsters, and business folk from the Moscone Center fill the warm, bi-level space. Group dining is ideal for sampling more of the menu, and the sizable bar will ensure that everyone's furnished with a terrific cocktail or pint of local draft root beer.

# East Bay

Asignature mash-up of wealthy families, senior bohemians, and college kids, Berkeley is extolled for its liberal politics and lush university campus. Snooty gourmands and reverential foodies consider it to be the Garden of Eden that sprouted American gastronomy's leading purist, Alice Waters. Her Chez Panisse Foundation continues to nurture the **Edible Schoolyard**, an organic garden-cum-kitchen classroom for students. Waters' also founded **Slow Food Nation**, the country's largest celebration of sustainable foods; and her influence can be tasted in numerous establishments serving Californian cuisine.

## GOURMET GHETTO

Budget-conscious Berkeleyites needn't look to restaurants alone for pristine, local, and organic food. Their very own **North Shattuck** corridor (also known as the "gourmet ghetto") gratifies with garden-fresh produce as well as takeout from **Grégoire** and **Le Petit Cochon**. This area is also home to aficionados who frequent co-ops like the **Cheese Board Collective**, **Cheese Board Pizza Collective**, and **Acme Bread Company** for first-rate produce and variety. **The Juice Bar Collective** keeps diet-conscious droves coming back for more; whereas meat addicts can't get enough of Chef Paul Bertolli's **Fra'Mani Salumi**, where

traditional Italian flavors mingle with creative techniques. Every Thursday, the **North Shattuck Organic Farmer's Market** draws cooking enthusiasts looking to expand their repertoire with a vast range of regionally sourced produce.

Meanwhile, hungover scholars can't imagine beginning a day without brunch at **La Note**, where the cinnamon-brioche *pain perdu* packs a walloping punch. Too rich? Test the spread at **Tomate Cafe**, churning out a wholesome Cuban breakfast followed by lunch on the pup-friendly patio. Cooks on a mission collect routinely at ingredient-driven **Berkeley Bowl**, a grocery store-farmer's market hybrid, to scan their offering of fresh produce, cooked items, and health foods. Named after a region in Southwest India, **Udupi Palace** is equally revolutionary in concept, with cooking that is wildly popular for that region's delicacies. Sample the likes of *dosas*, packed with spiced mashed potatoes and paired with spicy *sambar*, for an undoubtedly satisfying meal.

## OAKLAND

Located across the bridge from the city, Oakland may not exude the same culinary flamboyance. Nevertheless, this earnest and enterprising city has seen a resurgence of its own, thanks to an influx of businesses and residences. With panoramic views of the Bay, terrific restaurants, shops and a hopping nightlife, Jack London Square is not only a tourist draw but is equally revered by locals for sun-soaked docks and a **Sunday Farmers' and Artisan Market**. Routine-loving locals cherish mornings at **La Farine**, a European-style bakery, serving pastries, cakes, and buttery croissants. As noon sets in, downtown crowds nosh on po'boys from **Café 15**. But over in Temescal, **Bakesale Betty** caters to big appetites with bulky chicken sandwiches served atop ironing-board tables. Post-work revelry reaches epic status at **The Trappist**, pouring over 160 Belgian and other specialty beers. However, if dessert is the most divine way to end a day, then convene at **Fentons Creamery**, churning handmade ice creams for over 120 delicious years.

Similarly, **Lush Gelato** spotlights homegrown ingredients like Cowgirl Creamery Fromage Blanc or McEvoy Ranch Olive Oil in some of the city's most decadent flavors. **Tara's Organic Ice Cream** continues the craze with unique licks like beet-balsamic in compostable cups.

## HOME IS WHERE THE HEART IS

Down-home Mexican food fans get their fiesta on at taco trucks parked along International Blvd. But local joints like **Taqueria Sinaloa** remain the real deal for these treats. The Art & Soul Festival in August brings a buffet of world flavors; and **Chinatown Streetfest** adds to the lure with fragrant curries and barbecue. Bonus bites await at **Market Hall**, featuring seafood at **Hapuku Fish Shop**; specialty eats at **Pasta Shop**; and delicious blends from **Highwire Coffee Roasters**. Set between Oakland and Berkeley, Rockridge boasts of plethora of quaint boutiques and tasty eateries—namely **Oaktown Spice Shop** on Grand Avenue, showcasing excellent herbs and exotic spices, available in both small amounts and bulk bags.

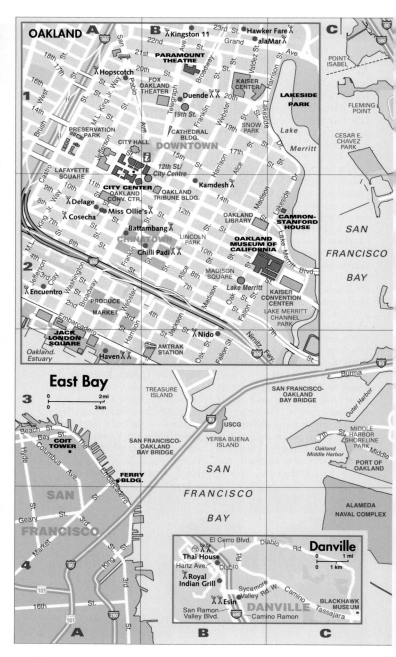

# OAKLAND

**A**    **B**    **C**

23rd St.

22nd St.

Kingston 11

Hawker Fare
alaMar

Grand Ave.

980

San Pablo

21st St.

18th St.

Broadway

Valdez St.

Harrison St.

POINT ISABEL

580

80

17th St.

20th St.

PARAMOUNT THEATRE

16th St.

Hopscotch

FOX OAKLAND THEATER

Telegraph Ave.

KAISER CENTER

FLEMING POINT

West St.

14th St.

Duende

20th

Webster St.

CESAR E. CHAVEZ PARK

M.L.K. King Jr. Way

Brush St.

19th St.

19th

Franklin St.

SNOW PARK

Lakeside Dr.

LAKESIDE PARK

Lake Merritt

**1**

PRESERVATION PARK

CATHEDRAL BLDG.

DOWNTOWN

17th St.

Alice St.

Castro St.

Jefferson St.

CITY HALL

15th St.

Madison St.

LAFAYETTE SQUARE

12th St/ City Centre

Kamdesh

CAMRON-STANFORD HOUSE

9th St.

10th

11th

CITY CENTER

OAKLAND TRIBUNE BLDG.

14th St.

Lakeside Dr.

SAN

8th St.

King Jr. Way

Delage

OAKLAND CONV. CTR.

12th St.

FRANCISCO

Cosecha

Miss Ollie's

OAKLAND LIBRARY

BAY

M.L.K.

6th St.

Battambang

CHINATOWN

LINCOLN PARK

OAKLAND MUSEUM OF CALIFORNIA

Lake Merritt Blvd.

**2**

4th

3rd

Clay St.

Chilli Padi

Franklin St.

10th St.

Encuentro

Washington St.

Broadway

Webster St.

8th St.

7th St.

MADISON SQUARE

Alice St.

Oak St.

Madison St.

Fallon St.

Lake Merritt

KAISER CONVENTION CENTER

2nd St.

PRODUCE MARKET

4th St.

LAKE MERRITT CHANNEL PARK

Embarcadero

Harrison St.

Jackson St.

Nido

Nimitz Fwy.

880

JACK LONDON SQUARE

AMTRAK STATION

Oak St.

Fallon St.

*Oakland Estuary*

Haven

---

# East Bay

**3**

0     2mi
0     3km

TREASURE ISLAND

SAN FRANCISCO-OAKLAND BAY BRIDGE

Burma

80

Beach St.

Bay St.

COIT TOWER

USCG

YERBA BUENA ISLAND

Outer Harbor

7th St.

MIDDLE HARBOR SHORELINE PARK

Columbus Ave.

SAN FRANCISCO-OAKLAND BAY BRIDGE

*Oakland Middle Harbor*

Middle

PORT OF OAKLAND

Hyde St.

The Embarcadero

FERRY BLDG.

SAN

ALAMEDA NAVAL COMPLEX

**SAN**

St.

Geary St.

3rd St.

FRANCISCO

**FRANCISCO**

Market St.

BAY

---

## Danville

0     1 mi
0     1 km

El Cerro Blvd.

Diablo Rd.

Thai House

Hartz Ave.

Diablo

**4**

Royal Indian Grill

Sycamore Valley Rd. W.

Camino Tassajara

80

King St.

101

16th St.

101

280

Esin

San Ramon Valley Blvd.

Camino Ramon

680

DANVILLE

BLACKHAWK MUSEUM

**A**    **B**    **C**

174

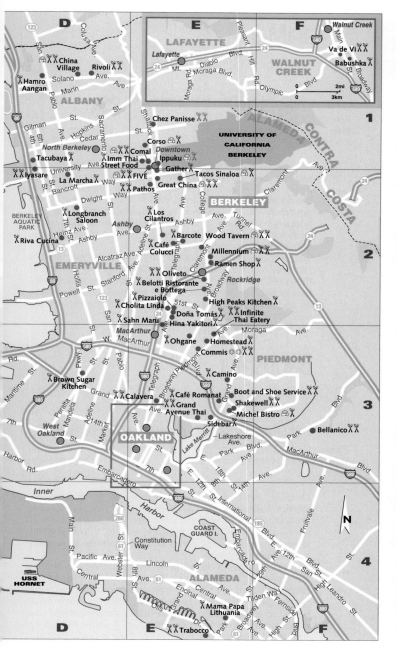

# alaMar

**B1**

### 100 Grand Ave., Ste. 111 (at Valdez St.), Oakland

**Phone:** 510-907-7555
**Web:** www.alamaroakland.com
**Price:** $$

Lunch Tue – Fri
Dinner Mon – Sat

While alaMar does a steady business serving sandwiches and salads to downtown Oakland office workers, the food-savvy prefer to dine here at night, when the menu flips to a memorable array of seafood dishes—many offered by the pound in low-country boil style. Golden-brown blue crab poppers boast a punchy anchovy-piquillo aïoli, while a boil of fresh local crawfish is studded with house-made sausage, corn on the cob, and spring garlic.

The space, with aqua-painted walls and rope elements, is tastefully nautical and designed to cater to guests' comfort as they peel apart dinner—there are towels on the tables and a special hand-washing sink. Bring a group to shoot the breeze as you work; then split some beignets with caramel-mocha sauce as a reward.

# Babushka

**F1**

### 1475 Newell Ave. (bet. Main St. & Maria Ln.), Walnut Creek

**Phone:** 925-210-0779
**Web:** www.babushkafood.com
**Price:** $$

Lunch Sat – Sun
Dinner Wed – Sun

Home to the best Russian food this side of Moscow, this Walnut Creek fixture has been a local favorite for two decades. Don't be misled by the deli of the same name in front—a door inside will transport you to a lovely white-tablecloth dining room, complete with charming servers and a full wine selection.

Rib-sticking classics are all perfectly executed here. Buttery and super-crispy chicken Kiev is made to order; thick borscht brims with rich beet flavor; beef stroganoff is an aromatic delight; and pork- and beef-stuffed *pelmeni* dance in an herbaceous broth. Keep your eye out for the refrigerated case of gorgeous, house-made desserts. But, if you're too full, be sure to take home a slice or two of their insanely delicious Napoleon sheet cake.

# Barcote

E2

Ethiopian 🍴

**6430 Telegraph Ave. (bet. Alcatraz Ave. & 65th St.), Oakland**

**Phone:** 510-923-6181
**Web:** www.barcote.com
**Price:** 💲💲

Lunch & dinner daily

The competition is stiff for a newcomer to Oakland's Ethiopian restaurant row, but thanks to a warm and welcoming team of chef/owners and a menu that excels in weaving together the spices and seasonings that give the cuisine its sparkle, Barcote stands out from the crowd. Whether you opt for a meaty plate of *kitfo* (spiced minced beef cooked in clarified butter); a sampler of vegetarian stews like spicy *misir wot* (lentils simmered in berbere sauce); or hearty *atakilt* (cabbage, potato, and carrot stew with turmeric); you'll be captivated by the layers of flavor.

The space is clean and simple, but friendly service and a tree-shaded front patio ensure that it's homey, not ho-hum. Don't come in a rush—this is a place to kick back and enjoy a leisurely meal.

# Battambang

A2

Cambodian 🍴

**850 Broadway (bet. 8th & 9th Sts.), Oakland**

**Phone:** 510-839-8815
**Web:** N/A
**Price:** 💲💲

Lunch Mon – Sat
Dinner nightly

Embrace the unknown at one of the Bay Area's very few Cambodian restaurants. Though the menu may be unfamiliar to Western palates, Battambang boasts warm, hands-on service that will make any diner feel at ease. Don't let its gaudy exterior deter you: the interior is pleasant and tastefully adorned.

The must-order here is the *amok trei*, a hard-to-find dish of catfish steamed in a fragrant banana leaf. Layered with red lemongrass sauce and coconut milk, it's utterly beguiling. Equally good is the spicy-sour *yihoeur char tumpaing*, a stir-fry of calamari and bamboo shoots with lemongrass and ground chili. Adventurous diners should also sample the omelet-like *num banchev*, an eggy rice-flour crêpe with chicken, prawns, sprouts, and a strong, funky fish sauce.

# Bellanico

Italian **XX**

F3

### 4238 Park Blvd. (at Wellington St.), Oakland

**Phone:** 510-336-1180  Lunch & dinner daily
**Web:** www.bellanico.net
**Price:** $$

Considering Bellanico is named for its owners' daughters, it's no surprise that this resto is a hit with families. The sibling of Potrero Hill's Aperto, it fills day and night with local couples (dining with or without their children), enjoying the cheery, persimmon-accented dining room, bustling open kitchen, and wall of windows overlooking Park Boulevard.

Kick off a meal with kid-friendly antipasti like Swiss chard-and-ricotta *malfatti* served in a browned butter sauce, seasoned with sage and sprinkled with nutty Grana Padano. Then dig into a delightfully tender pork chop served with roasted marble potatoes as well as a tangy red cabbage *agrodolce*. A square of the Laura Chenel goat cheese-cheesecake, crusted with pistachio, makes for a rather fine finale.

# Belotti Ristorante e Bottega

Italian **X**

E2

### 5403 College Ave. (bet. Kales & Manila Aves.), Oakland

**Phone:** 510-788-7890  Lunch & dinner Wed – Mon
**Web:** www.belottirb.com
**Price:** $$

Pasta aficionados will find *paradiso* in this petite restaurant and enoteca, set on a busy but bucolic stretch of Rockridge's main artery. Though it's still relatively new to the scene, it's already drawn a passel of regulars, who park at the bar to chat with the owner in Italian between bites.

Belotti dabbles in the traditional cuisine of *Piemonte* in such hearty dishes as *brasato*—braised beef with mushrooms served over polenta and finished with a *nebbiolo* reduction. House-made pastas are also a major draw, including heirloom grain *spaghettini* in a tomato sauce with creamy burrata. But more unexpected dishes excel as well: try the delicious butter lettuce salad with lemon and pine nuts, or the decadent *tortino*, a spinach flan with egg yolk and truffle.

# Boot and Shoe Service

Pizza ✖✖

**E3**

3308 Grand Ave. (bet. Lake Park Ave. & Mandana Blvd.), Oakland

**Phone:** 510-763-2668
**Web:** www.bootandshoeservice.com
**Price:** $$

Lunch & dinner Tue – Sun

Named for its former incarnation as a shoe-repair shop, this very accommodating Grand Avenue standby brings stellar pizzas and a totally relaxed vibe to its hungry neighborhood. The light, bright space suits every configuration, from the solo dining counter to gregarious communal tables and a semi-private room for large groups. Adept servers cater to the whims of hipsters and families alike.

Dig into blistered Californian pies like wild nettle and *ricotta salata*; or try bacon, Calabrian chili, and cream. Other menu offerings should also be explored, especially the chili-inflected heirloom bean ragù with a velvety soft-cooked egg, smoky from the wood-fired oven. Healthier options include a nutty farro salad with tender marinated beets and fresh herbs.

# Brown Sugar Kitchen

American ✖

**D3**

2534 Mandela Pkwy. (at 26th St.), Oakland

**Phone:** 510-839-7685
**Web:** www.brownsugarkitchen.com
**Price:** ⊜

Lunch Tue – Sun

Its industrial West Oakland location is far from any sort of restaurant row, but visitors to this soul-food palace (open for breakfast and lunch only) will find plenty of company—mostly ahead of them in line. Over the years, Chef/owner Tanya Holland has built a loyal following of families as well as foodies who arrive early to avoid those long waits for tender, flaky biscuits and signature buttermilk fried chicken with a cornmeal waffle. Others go for the juicy jerk chicken with a kick of heat, cooled by mashed yams and pineapple-red onion salsa. The earthy, well-seasoned black-eyed pea salad is another favorite—and fittingly so.

Casual and welcoming with a chill vibe and colorful look, BSK may be a crowd magnet, but it's earned the hype.

# Café Colucci

**E2**

### 6427 Telegraph Ave. (at 65th St.), Oakland

**Phone:** 510-601-7999          Lunch & dinner daily
**Web:** www.cafecolucci.com
**Price:** ⊜

On a stretch of Telegraph that's something of an Ethiopian restaurant row, Colucci stands out for its eye-catching décor, including a plant-laden terrace, fabric-draped ceiling, and selection of African art. As with all Ethiopian restaurants, bring clean hands and leave your fork at home: you'll be dining exclusively with *injera*, the spongy-sour bread that's traditional to the country.

The menu offers many appealing options to scoop, from mild *begue tibs* (lamb with onions, garlic, and rosemary), to spicy eggplant *wot* stewed in a piquant *berbere* sauce. Fried potato slices are great on their own, but extra tasty when paired with *assa tibs*, a whole baked fish. Save room for a buttery pistachio baklava and house-roasted Ethiopian coffee.

# Café Romanat

**E3**

### 462 Santa Clara Ave. (near Grand Ave.), Oakland

**Phone:** 510-444-1800          Lunch Sat – Sun
**Web:** www.caferomanat.com        Dinner Tue – Sun
**Price:** ⊜

In a stretch of Oakland that teems with Ethiopian restaurants, Romanat is a standout, thanks to deliciously spiced dishes served in generous portions. Locals (including some Ethiopian families) fill the small room, set with traditional low stools and woven tables and featuring colorful fabric curtains and artwork.

Order up an Ethiopian beer, honey wine, or a nutty ground flax or sesame seed juice to pair with the *sambussas*, triangular pastries stuffed with piquant, chile-flecked ground beef. All the combo platters, served on spongy, slightly sour *injera*, are perfect for sharing. And the veggie combo, with dishes like sautéed collard greens, lentils in smoky *berbere*, and split peas with turmeric and ginger, will delight any crowd.

# Calavera

Mexican

**E3**

2337 Broadway (bet. 23rd & 24th Sts.), Oakland

**Phone:** 510-338-3273
**Web:** www.calaveraoakland.com
**Price:** $$$

Lunch & dinner daily

For an interesting and upscale take on Mexican cuisine—complete with a carte of compelling cocktails—this Oakland outpost is the place to go. It's housed in an industrial brick building that sings with light and color, with a towering side bar slinging one of the Bay Area's best mezcal and tequila selections, and is eclectic at every turn.

The vibrant modernism extends into the cooking of course, which gleefully mashes up classics like guacamole with additions like *chapulines* (fried Oaxacan grasshoppers). Tuna ceviche gets an Asian twist (and umami boost) from Maggi, a popular soy-based condiment, and the "truffles" in the truffled rum old fashioned are actually *huitlacoche*. The young crowd is eating it up; and wise diners will reserve ahead.

# Camino

Californian

**E3**

3917 Grand Ave. (bet. Jean St. & Sunnyslope Ave.), Oakland

**Phone:** 510-547-5035
**Web:** www.caminorestaurant.com
**Price:** $$

Lunch Sat – Sun
Dinner Wed – Mon

With its look of a medieval refectory and that central wood-burning hearth, Camino can seem like a trip to the days of yore—but the cool crowd, fun cocktails, and innovative food are decidedly modern. Take a seat under wrought-iron chandeliers at one of the long, communal tables (one of them is cut from a single redwood tree!) and expect to make some new friends.

Chef-owner Russell Moore worked at Chez Panisse for many years, and his food is appropriately hyper-seasonal. An egg baked in the wood oven, its yolk still velvety, is nestled in leeks, herbs, and cream, while slices of char-grilled sourdough provide the base for a sandwich of juicy pancetta and rustic sauerkraut. Moist, sticky Lardy cake is also grilled, and topped with rich ricotta and honey.

# Chez Panisse

E1

Californian ✖✖

**1517 Shattuck Ave. (bet. Cedar & Vine Sts.), Berkeley**

**Phone:** 510-548-5525                          Dinner Mon – Sat
**Web:** www.chezpanisse.com
**Price:** $$$$

A legendary address with the foodie set, Alice Waters' Arts and Crafts bungalow continues to serve as the Bay Area's temple of California cuisine. Co-chef Amy Dencler, who cooks Monday-Wednesday, shares the kitchen with Cal Peternell, who in turn has the Thursday-Saturday shift. But the format in the dining room remains the same: one nightly fixed menu of four ever-rotating courses (three on Mondays).

What you'll get is a matter of chance, but be assured it will feature only peak-season produce—from the peas, asparagus, and black truffle in a bright spring risotto, to the sweet corn and crispy squash blossoms served with a summer preparation of pork loin. Seeking more freedom of choice? Head to the casual upstairs café, which serves meals á la carte.

# Chilli Padi

B2

Malaysian ✖✖

**366 8th St. (bet. Franklin & Webster Sts.), Oakland**

**Phone:** 510-891-8862                          Lunch & dinner daily
**Web:** N/A
**Price:** $$

Shake up your Oakland Chinatown routine with a trip to this contemporary spot, which blends Malaysian and Chinese flavors into an interesting menu that's jam-packed with flavor. Kick things off with the terrific Chilli Padi Sampler, which features tangy green papaya salad, moist chicken satay, samosas, tofu fritters, and a delicious Malaysian-style roti with warm curry dipping sauce.

From there, the mindful servers can recommend dishes like chili-soy chicken and vegetables served in a crisp taro nest, or classic *char kway teow*, flat rice noodles with shrimp, squid, and shrimp paste. With its dark wood floors and undulating fuchsia walls, the space is sleek and clean, which may explain why it has caught on with the largely local crowd.

# China Village

Chinese XX

**D1**

### 1335 Solano Ave. (at Ramona Ave.), Albany

**Phone:** 510-525-2285
**Web:** www.chinavillagealbany.com
**Price:** ⊜⊜

Lunch & dinner daily

It takes a village to feed a big group, and this laid-back spot is a favorite with families. A stylish recent renovation has added a sleek front bar, contemporary chandeliers, and dramatic Chinese art, but one look at the scorching-hot menu options—think spicy Sichuan frog and flaky sautéed fish with pickled chili peppers—confirms the authenticity factor.

Skip the Hunan, Mandarin, and Cantonese offerings in favor of the Sichuan specialties, like dry-fried, bone-in chicken laced with ground chili and numbing peppercorns. And be sure to order the five-spice hot and spicy pork shoulder. A house specialty, this mouthwatering dish is fork- (or chopstick) tender and rests atop a deliciously piquant chili-oil jus with baby bok choy, scallions, and garlic.

# Cholita Linda

Latin American 

**E2**

### 4923 Telegraph Ave. (bet. 48th & 51st Sts.), Oakland

**Phone:** 510-594-7610
**Web:** www.cholitalinda.com
**Price:** ⊜⊜

Lunch & dinner Mon – Sat

The old Bay Area saw of farm-to-table gets a tasty spin at this purveyor of Latin fare, which transformed from a megapopular farmer's market stand into a packed house of communal tables. Bright, colorfully decorated, and flooded with natural light, it's a casual space where diners order and pay at the counter, then sip drinks from glass Mason jars under the potted palms.

The outstanding Baja fish tacos are the source of Cholita Linda's reputation, but its dishes traverse Latin America, from a hearty Cubano to a plate of slow-braised, well-seasoned carnitas with black beans and fried plantains. With such reasonable prices, there's no excuse not to order a sweet, smooth mango *agua fresca* to wash down the tender, tangy *pollo al pastor* tacos.

# Comal 😊

Mexican ✕✕

**E1**

**2020 Shattuck Ave. (bet. Addison St. & University Ave.), Berkeley**

**Phone:** 510-926-6300                                      Dinner nightly
**Web:** www.comalberkeley.com
**Price:** $$

For bold, zesty Mexican food crafted with pristine ingredients, Berkeleyites throng this industrial-chic hot spot, where an excellent cocktail program and an extensive tequila and mezcal selection keep things buzzing. The large flat tortilla griddles for which it's named are on full display in the open kitchen, while a covered, heated back patio draws locals for year-round outdoor dining.

Comal's fryer-fresh warm tortilla chips, paired with perfect, creamy guacamole, are irresistible; summon an order as you peruse options like the refreshing white shrimp ceviche and earthy hen-of-the-woods mushroom quesadilla. Just make sure the smoky wood-grilled rock cod tacos, with creamy avocado aïoli and spicy cabbage slaw, are on your must-order list.

# Corso 😊

Italian ✕

**E1**

**1788 Shattuck Ave. (bet. Delaware & Francisco Sts.), Berkeley**

**Phone:** 510-704-8004                                      Dinner nightly
**Web:** www.corsoberkeley.com
**Price:** $$

A Tuscan follow-up from the couple behind nearby Rivoli, Corso is every bit the equal of its big sister, thanks to generous, Florentine-inspired dishes like a roasted squid panzanella with torn flatbread, buttery white beans, and bright dashes of lemon juice and chili oil. Pasta fiends will swoon for house-made tagliatelle in a meaty beef and pork sugo, while butter-roasted chicken boasts juicy meat, golden-brown skin as well as fresh peas and asparagus alongside.

Soul-warming in its hospitality, Corso is the kind of place where servers will bring complimentary pistachio biscotti simply because they're "so good when they're warm." It's no surprise that the tiny trattoria is a favorite among couples, so be sure to reserve in advance and come hungry.

# Commis ✿ ✿

Contemporary ✗✗

### 3859 Piedmont Ave. (at Rio Vista Ave.), Oakland

**Phone:** 510-653-3902
**Web:** www.commisrestaurant.com
**Price:** $$$$

Dinner Wed – Sun

Chef/owner James Syhabout may be keeping busy outside of Commis at his other popular restaurants, but this sparse Oakland original is still turning out elegant and creatively complex seasonal dishes to a packed house every night.

Tucked into colorful, boutique-strewn Piedmont Avenue, this dining space is a long, clean, minimalist number with a smattering of tables up front; intimate banquette seating in the back; and a lively counter overlooking the humming kitchen. Soft hip-hop music and a vibrant service staff set the mood—cool and contemporary; relaxed but serious.

In the kitchen, Chef Syhabout pairs well-sourced, local ingredients with precise technique to create his sophisticated nightly tasting, which continues to be exciting even for jaded gourmands. Dinner might unveil a plate of silky scallops paired with tangy crème fraîche, poached asparagus, and charred lemon granité; warm, roasted abalone with artichoke heart, fried artichoke slivers, and chicken sabayon; or a chilled fava bean soup laced with tarragon-infused crème fraîche, green tomato gelée, and smoked trout roe. A perfectly poached halibut with spring pea "porridge" and ginger foam is another beautifully composed plate that reflects the kitchen's attention to detail.

# Cosecha

A2

Mexican 🍴

**907 Washington St. (at 9th St.), Oakland**

**Phone:** 510-452-5900                          Lunch & dinner Mon – Sat
**Web:** www.cosechacafe.com
**Price:** 🍤

Even the pickiest Mexican *abuela* would be hard-pressed to turn down a meal at Cosecha, where the heartwarming blue-plate specials are made from scratch daily. Handmade tortillas stuffed with roasted yams and creamy Oaxaca cheese, or flaky fish and smoky chipotle *crema* are a cut above typical taqueria fare, while the chicken *torta ahogada* nearly bursts with tender grilled meat, soft pinto beans, garlicky guacamole, and spicy *guajillo* chile.

Housed in Old Oakland's historic Swan's Marketplace, Cosecha draws a loyal crowd of business people at lunchtime and local residents in the evenings. They order at the counter, take a seat at the communal tables, and sip tangy, refreshing lime *aguas frescas* as they await the delicious creations in store.

# Delage

A2

Japanese 🍴

**536 9th St. (bet. Clay & Washington Sts.), Oakland**

**Phone:** 510-823-2050                          Dinner Tue – Sat
**Web:** www.delageoakland.com
**Price:** $$$

The word is already out about this tiny, omakase-only Japanese gem, located adjacent to Swan's Market in Old Oakland. It's a simple, casual space with a small counter and handful of tables, but it also provides a fine spotlight for a mixture of high-quality nigiri and kaiseki dishes.

Meals typically run about eight courses, with seasonal starters like a grilled apricot and *mizuna* salad; salmon sashimi adorned with a slice of Saturn peach; or garlic shoots enhancing seared Miyazaki beef.

Excellent nigiri, from tuna to mackerel to fluke, arrive at intervals alongside other captivating items, like seared duck breast with *moro* miso or scallops with shiso and *umeboshi*. The only downside is that reservations can be a challenge—so be sure to plan well ahead.

# Doña Tomás

Mexican 🍴

**E2**

5004 Telegraph Ave. (bet. 49th & 51st Sts.), Oakland

**Phone:** 510-450-0522
**Web:** www.donatomas.com
**Price:** $$

Lunch Sat – Sun
Dinner Tue – Sat

Californian ingredients and Mexican flavors combine to create magic at this Temescal neighborhood standby, where regulars pour in at happy hour to chat with their favorite bartenders, and families savor warm Oakland nights on the spacious patio. In fact, Doña (and Berkeley sibling Tacubaya) is enough of a draw that you'll regret not making reservations, particularly on weekends.

Hearty but never heavy, meals here commence with fresh-fried chips and appetizers like a butternut squash quesadilla packed with caramelized onions, corn, and poblano chile. Delightfully smoky *mole negro* stars in the shredded chicken enchiladas, served with braised kale and black beans. For dessert, a traditional *tres leches* is light as air—and heavy on flavor.

# Duende

Spanish 🍴🍴

**B1**

468 19th St. (bet. Broadway & Telegraph Ave.), Oakland

**Phone:** 510-893-0174
**Web:** www.duendeoakland.com
**Price:** $$$

Dinner Wed – Mon

Savor the flavors and sounds of Spain at this novel restaurant in developing Uptown Oakland, where Chef/owner Paul Canales turns out everything from *pintxos* to paella. The voluminous bi-level space set in the historic Floral Depot is packed with large windows, exposed brick, and colorful murals which contribute a fun vibe attracting groups of hip, urban types.

The food is authentic with seasonal accents and has included rabbit and lobster sausage with blistered Padrón peppers; and seafood-studded *arroz negro*, thick with rockfish, scallops, cherry tomatoes, and garlic aïoli. The crowd is loud and festive, especially when one of the rotating local musicians hits the stage for a set. Like the food and ambience, the music lends Duende a casual, warm energy.

# Encuentro

Vegetarian &#9903;

**A2**

### 550 2nd St. (at Clay St.), Oakland

**Phone:** 510-832-9463  
**Web:** www.encuentrooakland.com  
**Price:** $$

Dinner Tue – Sun

Encuentro sits prettily in an industrial-chic space fitted with large windows, lofty ceilings, and an easy-breezy front bar. Though it's minimal in a California-meets-Manhattan way, the kitchen promises maximum satisfaction via its haute (read: heavenly) take on vegan treats. Avocado bruschetta drizzled with olive oil and chili jam entices with a kick of spice, while baby kale and roasted veggies are enriched with toasted quinoa and a lemon-tahini dressing.

Here, each menu item is so carefully composed and appetizingly prepared (think of empanadas stuffed with pumpkin seed *picadillo* served atop pinto beans with cashew *crema*) that you won't miss the meat—which explains why the dining room is peppered with carnivores.

# Esin

**B4**

### 750 Camino Ramon (at Sycamore Valley Rd.), Danville

**Phone:** 925-314-0974  
**Web:** www.esinrestaurant.com  
**Price:** $$

Lunch & dinner daily

Good luck not eating dessert first at this Danville favorite, which can tempt the most hardline calorie-counter with the ever-changing array of house-made treats in the pastry case. From a perfect dark chocolate-espresso tart to a textbook lemon meringue pie, Esin is nirvana for sugar fiends—but that doesn't mean you should discount the savory options, ranging from an all-American pot roast with buttery mashed potatoes to a Mediterranean-inflected pasta with shrimp, mushrooms and peppers.

Thanks to its palatial size, wood-trimmed dining area, soft beige walls, and bright windows, the space offers plenty to accommodate both lunching business people and locals on date-night. For a more casual meal, try the owners' latest Revel Kitchen & Bar, located downtown.

# FIVE

American ✗✗

**E2**

### 2086 Allston Way (at Shattuck Ave.), Berkeley

**Phone:** 510-225-6055
**Web:** www.five-berkeley.com
**Price:** $$

Lunch & dinner daily

Right off Berkeley's main drag, this pre-cinema and pre-theater favorite in the historic Hotel Shattuck Plaza boasts a seriously impressive dining room, with airy high ceilings, dramatic pillars, and a gorgeous statement chandelier. Locals and hotel guests seem to be equally in love with its large front bar.

Fine dining it isn't, but FIVE has become a favorite for approachable American food—including items designed for Berkeley's sizable vegetarian crowd. A golden beet salad is a cornucopia of Californian ingredients, including fresh ricotta, tomato, and cucumber, while the juicy, delicious house-ground burger is accompanied by addictive parmesan fries. For dessert, persimmon sorbet gives a burst of freshness to dense, intense chocolate lava cake.

# Gather

Californian ✗

**E2**

### 2200 Oxford St. (at Allston Way), Berkeley

**Phone:** 510-809-0400
**Web:** www.gatherrestaurant.com
**Price:** $$

Lunch & dinner daily

With its heavily Californian bill of fare, repurposed décor, and Berkeley clientele, Gather is a must for hordes of wholesome foodies of all ages. The aptly named hit serves busy professors during the bustling lunch hour before welcoming a more relaxed evening crowd, who come to sip at the bar and sup *en plein air* on the patio.

Pescatarians will delight in thick-cut toast spread with albacore tuna rillettes and topped with pan-fried *broccoli de ciccio*, pickled radishes, and potatoes, while vegetarians will find it hard to resist a hefty portion of arugula salad tossed with goat cheese, almonds, pomegranate, and balsamic dressing. Be sure to try some dessert—specifically the luscious lime curd tart and its thick dollop of meringue. You won't be sorry.

# Grand Avenue Thai

Thai ✖✖

**384 Grand Ave. (bet. Perkins St. & Staten Ave.), Oakland**

**Phone:** 510-444-1507
**Web:** www.grandavethai.net
**Price:**

Lunch Mon – Fri
Dinner nightly

 

Thanks to its charming décor, friendly service, and flavorful cuisine, Grand Avenue Thai is a winning standout—just one block from picturesque Lake Merritt. The space is small with bright walls, fresh flowers, and colorful local artwork. Service is prompt even with a steady to-go business.

Be sure to try one of the house favorites like the sweet and fragrant coconut curry with chunks of pumpkin, eggplant, broccoli, and string beans. Summer rolls neatly wrap up fresh veggies and garlicky rice noodles for a dip in peanut-chili sauce, while the ever-popular pad Thai combines plump prawns stir-fried with egg, bean sprouts, scallions, and peanuts in a tasty tamarind-Thai fish sauce. Spice can be tame, but the kitchen is happy to indulge the fire fiends.

# Great China 😊

Chinese ✖✖

E2

**2190 Bancroft Way (at Fulton St.), Berkeley**

**Phone:** 510-843-7996
**Web:** www.greatchinaberkeley.com
**Price:** $$

Lunch & dinner Wed – Mon

Chic enough for the style-savvy, cheap enough for students, and authentic enough for local Chinese families, Great China is one of the few Berkeley restaurants everyone can (and does) agree on. Spicehounds should look elsewhere, as the food is somewhat mild, but the ingredients are higher quality than the average Chinese spot.

Kick things off with an aromatic bowl of hot and sour soup or an order of vegetarian egg rolls, then sample generously portioned favorites like the sweet-and-spicy *kung pao* chicken; the beautifully lacquered tea-smoked duck; or the beloved "double skin"—a platter of mung bean noodles tossed with pork, mushrooms, squid, and a soy-mustard dressing. Only larger parties can reserve, so be aware there may be lines at peak hours.

# Hamro Aangan

 **D1**

Nepali

856 San Pablo Ave. (bet. Solano & Washington Aves.), Albany

**Phone:** 510-524-2220
**Web:** www.hamroaangan.com
**Price:** ⊜⊜

Lunch & dinner Thu – Tue

Nepali restaurants have proliferated in the East Bay of late, but Hamro Aangan remains at the top of the heap thanks to its rustic, flavorful, generously portioned dishes. The handmade *momos* (steamed dumplings filled with spiced cabbage, carrot, and onion) are accompanied by a garlicky curry sauce, while the fluffy, layered chicken biryani is rich with caramelized onions and ground cardamom. Goat stew with tomato and an intensely-spiced gravy is another delicious option.

Located on busy San Pablo Avenue, Hamro is low-key, with red, rose, and copper décor and a beautiful mural from a local Nepali artist on the wall. It attracts a steady stream of regulars, particularly families, making it an excellent choice for a casual meal with kids in tow.

# Haven

 **A3**

Contemporary

44 Webster St. (at Jack London Sq.), Oakland

**Phone:** 510-663-4440
**Web:** www.havenoakland.com
**Price:** $$

Lunch Sat – Sun
Dinner nightly

Locals continue to rely on this delight (part of the Daniel Patterson Group) for good food and a sleek, industrial-chic setting in prime Jack London Square. With windows facing the Square and counter seats offering great views into the open kitchen, it's hard to pick a perch; in either case, kick things off with one of the intriguing barrel-aged cocktails. The food is contemporary and seasonal, with exquisite ingredients in dishes like roasted Monterey squid with smoked fingerling potatoes, chorizo, and green olives, or lamb roulade with warm lentils and roasted fennel. For dessert, cinnamon churros with caramelized peaches and nasturtium whipped cream are quite divine.

Haven now offers a fixed three- or four-course menu in the dining room as well as a limited à la carte at the bar.

# Hawker Fare

Asian ✗

**B1**

**2300 Webster St. (at 23rd St.), Oakland**

**Phone:** 510-832-8896
**Web:** www.hawkerfare.com
**Price:** 💶

Dinner nightly

Those hawker stalls across Southeast Asia may not qualify as trendy, but here in uptown Oakland, hipsters in oversized eyeglasses and skinny jeans clamor for humble and tasty (if toned-down) street food. Groups of hard-drinking twenty- and thirty-something's are everywhere at Hawker Fare, sharing plates, perusing the faux-graffiti on the walls, and bobbing their heads to the beat of their own soundtrack.

They come for well-made Thai like arugula salad with lotus root, jicama, and Chinese sausage; or spicy *gang dang* tofu curry with pumpkin over steamed rice. The Issan gin and tonic is flavored with makrut lime leaves, while desserts like a coconut pudding with banana jam and sesame delights.

A second location in SF's Mission is equally popular.

# High Peaks Kitchen

Indian ✗

**E2**

**5299 College Ave. (bet. Clifton St. & Manila Ave.), Oakland**

**Phone:** 510-450-0644
**Web:** www.hipeaks.com
**Price:** $$

Lunch & dinner Wed — Mon

The Himalayan-inspired name and Dalai Lama headshot might have you guessing correctly that this retreat is owned by Tibetans, but there's a twist: they were raised in India, and South Asian cooking is their specialty. The simple space, with its bright colors, small open kitchen, and inviting patio, is a cheerful setting for enjoying the delicious, affordable food.

A range of well-spiced dishes boast layers of aroma and flavor, from the whole cardamom, shredded ginger, and star anise in a fiery potato *vindaloo*, to the potent yellow curry in a stewed chicken *jalfrezi*. The clientele is largely Indian, a testament to the kitchen's authenticity, and they can be found filling up on potato-stuffed naan with toasted coriander and cumin as well as smoky, moist ground lamb kebabs with mint chutney.

# Hina Yakitori

Japanese ✕

**E2**

4828 Telegraph Ave. (bet. 48th & 49th Sts.), Oakland

**Phone:** 510-593-2152                    Dinner Wed – Sun
**Web:** www.hinayakitori.com
**Price:** $$

The thrill of the grill is evident at this Temescal *izakaya*, which specializes in *yakitori* cooked over the traditional charcoal *binchotan*. From meltingly tender chicken thighs and smoky King Trumpet mushrooms to luscious chicken *tsukune*, these are skewers at their best. And the assortment of small plates, like sweet corn and tofu salad and excellent fried chicken for instance, is also worthy.

Hina's petite space blends traditional Japanese wood accents with eye-catching yellow-and-black pop art. Given its small size and lack of reservations, though, big groups are best avoided. And whatever you do, be sure to arrive early: a limited number of whole chickens are broken down each night for the yakitori dishes, and once they're gone, they're gone.

# Homestead

American ✕

**E3**

4029 Piedmont Ave. (bet. 40th & 41st Sts.), Oakland

**Phone:** 510-420-6962                    Dinner Tue – Sun
**Web:** www.homesteadoakland.com
**Price:** $$

If it wasn't housed in a beautiful Julia Morgan-designed building, this farm-to-table jewel would be defined by the enticing smells that engulf you upon entrance. It's a rustic space, full of large windows peering onto Piedmont Avenue, and the jars of dry ingredients, pickling vegetables, and Julia Child cookbooks on the counter create an upscale country-kitchen vibe.

The menu focuses on the best and freshest of local produce, such as a panzanella with shaved carrot and crunchy asparagus. Braised octopus with Marcona almonds is light and fresh, allowing room for the star of the show: incredible wood-roasted pork, tender and moist, with potato gratin alongside. For a bright breakfast, look no further than the house-baked pastries and quiche.

# Hopscotch

American American ✗

**A1**

**1915 San Pablo Ave. (at 19th St.), Oakland**

**Phone:** 510-788-6217      Lunch & dinner daily
**Web:** www.hopscotchoakland.com
**Price:** $$

A stone's throw from the heart of transitioning (read: gentrifying) uptown Oakland, Hopscotch's Kickstarter buzz may have died down, but its small size means that reservations are still a must. Checkered floors and red-and-chrome chairs lend a retro diner vibe, but you'd be hard-pressed to find cocktails as intriguing as a Domino (combining Scotch, amaro, blackberry, and jalapeño) at some local greasy spoon. The winning American cooking boasts subtle Japanese influences like the kabocha pumpkin cake with fresh pomegranate seeds. In the same vein, a tangy and bright pomegranate-and-sunchoke salad offers a refreshing counterpoint to heartier options like the cheekily named "first base" burger, topped with sesame aïoli and griddled beef tongue.

# Imm Thai Street Food

Thai ✗

**E1**

**2068 University Ave. (bet. Milvia St. & Shattuck Ave.), Berkeley**

**Phone:** 510-898-1123      Lunch & dinner daily
**Web:** N/A
**Price:** ⊝

While you won't actually be eating on the street, this bitty Berkeley spot isn't much more than a sidewalk stand with a handful of tables and counter seats. But what Imm lacks in glitz it more than makes up for in its bold, intensely spiced Thai cooking.

Bring the gang for an insanely affordable spread: start with thin slices of kabocha squash, battered and deep-fried until tender and served with a sweet-sour dipping sauce, or a tangy green papaya salad with fresh shrimp and a spicy chili-lime vinaigrette. Creamy red coconut curry is loaded with zucchini, bell peppers, bamboo shoots, and cubes of fresh tofu. And, don't skip out before trying the *suki*, a Thai-style hot pot packed with beef, chicken, prawns, tofu, veggies, glass noodles, and plenty of herbs.

# Infinite Thai Eatery

Thai ✗✗

**E3**

### 4301 Piedmont Ave. (at John St.), Oakland

**Phone:** 510-817-4816
**Web:** www.infinitethai.com
**Price:** 🍴🍴

Lunch & dinner Tue – sun

Infinitely warm service is the hallmark of this engaging Thai restaurant, where the attentive owner checks in on each customer to ensure they're enjoying their meal (an easy task, as the food is fresh, fragrant, and prepared with top-notch ingredients). And if you like things spicy, don't worry, western palates aren't shortchanged here.

Kick things off with a classic *larb gai*, a cool salad of ground chicken mixed with lots of herbs and sliced shallots in a zippy lime dressing. Then turn up the temperature with the drunken rice noodles, packed with chicken and crisp vegetables in a fiery red chili-garlic sauce. If there's still room, opt for *moo yang*, grilled marinated pork boasting a rich smokiness and a tangy lime-chili dipping sauce.

# Ippuku

Japanese ✗

**E1**

### 2130 Center St. (bet. Oxford St. & Shattuck Ave.), Berkeley

**Phone:** 510-665-1969
**Web:** www.ippukuberkeley.com
**Price:** $$

Lunch Fri – Sat
Dinner nightly

Can't swing a ticket to Tokyo? Dinner at Ippuku is the next best thing. With its low Japanese-style tables, extensive woodwork, and enormous selection of sake and shochu, it feels like an authentic *izakaya* transplanted into a corner of downtown Berkeley. The low-profile entrance adds to the feeling you've lucked upon a special dining secret—assuming you don't stroll right past it, that is.

*Yakitori* are the big draw here, with smoky, salty chicken thighs, necks, hearts, and gizzards arriving fresh off the *binchotan*.

Other excellent small plates include *korokke*, or golden-brown Dungeness crab croquettes, crisp on the outside and with a creamy interior, or *yaki imo*, caramelized white sweet potato with a sweet-and-salty glaze.

# Iyasare

D2

Japanese ✗✗

## 1830 4th St. (bet. Hearst Ave. & Virginia St.), Berkeley

**Phone:** 510-845-8100          Lunch & dinner daily
**Web:** www.iyasare-berkeley.com
**Price:** $$$

Japanese techniques and Californian ingredients blend harmoniously at this charming Berkeley getaway, which flaunts a buzzing dining room and a delightful (heated) patio. Start the evening off right with an excellent (and reasonably-priced) local wine on tap or a selection from the well-edited sake list. Then, order a variety of their exquisite small plates for sharing.

Every dish is a carefully crafted delight for the senses. Baby kale and mustard greens might not sound very Japanese, but they blend beautifully in a salad with Fuji apple and a sesame-miso dressing. The superb hamachi crudo is dusted with a sprinkle of wasabi snow and lemon-tamari oil, while fresh Manila clams arrive in an aromatic broth of sake, bacon, potatoes, and earthy shiitakes.

# Kamdesh

B2

Afghan ✗

## 346 14th St. (at Webster St.), Oakland

**Phone:** 510-286-1900          Lunch & dinner daily
**Web:** N/A
**Price:** ⊜

In the sometimes-dodgy environs of downtown Oakland, Kamdesh's sunny-yellow façade is always a welcome sight for those in need of a hearty Afghan feast. Expect to find corporate groups at lunch, locals at dinner, and a takeout clientele all day long.

Kababs are all the rage here: perfectly seasoned, marinated, and charbroiled, they're absolutely tender and mouthwatering. While all choices are great, the ground beef *chapli* kabab patties mixed with tomato, onion, cilantro, and scallions are especially tasty piled over fluffy, cumin-tinged *pallow*. Other delicious items include tender *mantoo* stuffed with seasoned ground beef and onions and drizzled with tangy yogurt sauce; or the flavorful charbroiled chicken wrap in a chewy, Afghan-style naan.

# Kingston 11

Caribbean ✗

**B1**

**2270 Telegraph Ave. (bet. 23rd St. & Grand Ave.), Oakland**

**Phone:** 510-465-2558  Lunch Tue – Fri & Sun
**Web:** www.kingston11eats.com  Dinner Tue – Sat
**Price:** $$

Thanks to this lively Jamaican pop-up gone permanent, authentic island flavors have arrived in uptown Oakland. Its environs remain a bit dicey, but once inside, the smiling servers, boisterous crowds of families and friends, and reggae beats will transport you to the Caribbean—with a dose of California-chic from the modern interior design.

Boldly flavored fare includes tender, smoky jerk chicken with an intense and peppery spice rub, and a milder (but wildly delicious) curried goat stew with potato, carrots, and onion. Crisp and flaky salt-fish fritters are mouthwateringly delicious, and ideal for dunking in an herbaceous *chimichurri*. Skip the forgettable desserts and save your calories for a refreshing rum cocktail from the Fern Gully bar.

# La Marcha

Spanish ✗

**D2**

**2026 San Pablo Ave. (bet. Addison St. & University Ave.), Berkeley**

**Phone:** 510-269-7374  Dinner Tue – Sun
**Web:** www.lamarchaberkeley.com
**Price:** $$

This Spanish delight from the team behind acclaimed caterer Ñora Cocina Española does double duty as a mecca for both tapas and paella, offered in varieties from the traditional *mixta* (prawns, chicken, chorizo, garlic, peppers) to the inventive *"tres cerditos"* (three little pigs) featuring pork chorizo, shoulder, and belly. The classic tapas are also out in full force—from grilled head-on garlic shrimp and salt cod croquettes with nutty romesco, to *tortilla Española*.

Located on busy San Pablo Avenue, the lively space offers enticements for groups of all sizes: foursomes can make the most of the sizable paellas, while a duo of happy hours offer discounts on wine at the L-shaped bar and a selection of free tapas, perfect for solo diners or couples.

# Longbranch Saloon

**D2**

Gastropub ✗

2512 San Pablo Ave. (bet. Dwight Way & Parker St.), Berkeley

**Phone:** 510-984-0518      Dinner Tue – Sun
**Web:** www.longbranchberkeley.com
**Price:** $$

The wonders of whiskey are on full display at this relatively recent gastropub, which stocks a sizable selection of Bourbon, Scotch, and rye. If you're new to the brown elixir, never fear: well-chosen tasting flights will help you gain proficiency, and the laid-back crew of locals is engaging, never snobby.

The kitchen's signatures are worthy of the bar's spirits selection, which explains why the space fills quickly with a local crowd. Order up a cocktail and half-dozen Tomales Bay oysters with mignonette. Then tuck into the hearty bangers and mash featuring a juicy house-made white sausage and buttery potato purée. Lighter appetites will love the asparagus *sformato*, a custardy, savory pudding accompanied by a tangy fennel salad with pickled grapes.

# Los Cilantros

**E2**

Mexican ✗

3105 Shattuck Ave. (bet. Prince & Woolsey Sts.), Berkeley

**Phone:** 510-230-7350      Lunch & dinner Wed – Sun
**Web:** www.loscilantrosrestaurant.com
**Price:**

If there's no Mexican grandma in your life, Los Cilantros will show you what you've been missing: homey, authentic south-of-the-border fare. And if there is, it might just give her a run for her money. Whether you're biting into a crunchy tostada topped with chipotle chicken, black beans, sour cream, and avocado, or savoring rustic chicken enchiladas in a tangy green chile-tomatillo salsa, this is comfort food at its best.

Cute and simple, this Berkeley darling features tiled floors, pops of yellow and orange, and colorful paintings by Mexican artists. Settle in at one of the wooden tables and let the gracious staff make you feel right at home, or, if the weather's nice, grab a seat on the tiny front patio and catch some rays.

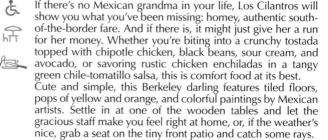

# Mama Papa Lithuania

E4

Eastern European

**1241 Park St. (bet. Encinal & San Antonio Aves.), Alameda**

**Phone:** 510-522-4100                  Lunch & dinner daily
**Web:** www.mamapapalithuania.com
**Price:** $$

Even highly avid diners may be unacquainted with Lithuanian food, but they won't be for long if this Alameda charmer—reputed to be the only one of its kind on the West Coast—is any indication. With exceptionally hospitable service and a cozy, brick-walled room full of rustic wooden tables, it's the next best thing to a home-cooked meal in Vilnius.

Lithuania's iconic dumpling dish, *cepelinai,* is a must for newbies: the potato dough, filled with pork, caramelized onion, and a little cinnamon, is rib-stickingly rich. Refresh your palate with a cooling summer borscht, creamy with beets and yogurt; then go for broke with the meaty, yet delicate stuffed cabbage. Try and leave room for dessert, as the sweet cherry dumplings with sour cream are to die for.


# Michel Bistro 😊

E3

French

**3343 Lakeshore Ave. (at Trestle Glen Rd.), Oakland**

**Phone:** 510-836-8737                     Lunch Sat – Sun
**Web:** www.michelbistro.com             Dinner Tue – Sun
**Price:** $$

A slice of France on a prime block of Lakeshore Avenue, this bistro boasts a heavily Gallic waitstaff and clientele chatting away in their native tongue. With its exposed brick, soaring ceilings, and cute accents like an excerpt from a Marcel Pagnol play inscribed on the wall, it's a simple but pleasant spot to enjoy a delicious, low-key meal.

The food is authentic, with some modern touches like the green almonds in a trout *amandine* with Lyonnaise-style potato salad, or the bison tartare with a quail egg. Brunch is a highlight with a gourmet eggs Benedict over artisan *levain* and butter-basted asparagus that steals the show.

At either meal, the vanilla crème brûlée is a rich treasure—too often jumbled on other menus, it's perfectly rendered here.

# Millennium

Vegan ✕✕

5912 College Ave. (bet. Chabot Rd. & Harwood Ave.), Oakland

**Phone:** 510-735-9459 Lunch Sun
**Web:** www.millenniumrestaurant.com Dinner nightly
**Price:** $$

After more than 20 years in San Francisco, this vegan paradise relocated to Oakland, where it's continuing to put out some of the most unique, delicious plant-based cuisine in the country. The rustic-chic new space is laid-back and unfussy, with lots of dark wood, a patio for alfresco dining, and a crowd of young families and professionals attended by welcoming servers.

While dedicated vegans are sure to swoon, even hardcore carnivores might reconsider the lifestyle after a dose of Chef/owner Eric Tucker's culinary creativity, showcased best on a five-course "Taste of Millennium" menu. Spicy *sopes* with a smoked eggplant *picadillo* and pumpkin seed cream are knockouts, as is the take on a Thai *larb* salad made with ripe red plums.

# Miss Ollie's

Caribbean ✕

901 Washington St. (bet. 9th & 10th Sts.), Oakland

**Phone:** 510-285-6188 Lunch & dinner Tue – Sat
**Web:** www.realmissolliesoakland.com
**Price:** $$

Even on the coldest (a.k.a. 50-degree) Oakland day, the soul-warming Caribbean cuisine at this little cutie will transport you to the islands. Barbados-born Chef/owner Sarah Kirnon named her restaurant after her grandmother, and it now serves up many of her childhood favorites, including plump, sweet grilled shrimp in a jerk marinade and some of the best fried chicken in town—with a flaky golden-brown crust.

Housed in the historic Swan's Market building in Old Oakland, Miss Ollie's has a particularly loyal crowd of lunchtime regulars, who sip tart ginger limeade as they liberally dose their food with the excellent Scotch bonnet hot sauce. With colorful Afro-Caribbean art on the walls and a welcoming staff, it's a rustic slice of Caribbean soul.

# Nido

Mexican ✗

**B3**

444 Oak St. (at 5th St.), Oakland

**Phone:** 510-444-6436
**Web:** www.nidooakland.com
**Price:** $$

Lunch Tue – Sun
Dinner Tue – Sat

The industrial area west of the I-880 freeway doesn't boast many good restaurants, but this hidden Mexican gem is an exception. Complete with hip reclaimed-wood décor and a local clientele of business people along with trendy foodies, it's definitely a cut above a taqueria in terms of quality and price, with fresher, lighter food in smaller—but by no means stingy—portions.

At lunch, a trio of tacos includes moist pork *adobado* with a sweet-and-spicy pineapple salsa, grilled chicken with *chamoy* glaze, and smoky beef *barbacoa* with caramelized onions. Dinner brings pozole with chicken and *chile negro*, and a grilled pork chop with braised greens and almond *mole*. With a truly relaxed vibe and home-cooked feel to the food, it's worth the extra effort to drop by.

# Ohgane

Korean ✗

**E3**

3915 Broadway (bet. 38th & 40th Sts.), Oakland

**Phone:** 510-594-8300
**Web:** www.ohgane.com
**Price:** $$

Lunch & dinner daily

Thanks to its delicious food, contemporary dining rooms, and the added bonus of a private parking lot, Ohgane still beats out Oakland's Korean competition. Ravenous diners particularly appreciate the all-you-can-eat menu, which starts with an assortment of banchan—16 small bites like spicy kimchi, glazed sweet yam, and sesame oil-bean sprouts.

Local families gather beneath the ventilation hoods for tabletop mesquite grilling, a specialty that reigns supreme on the dinner menu. Speaking of which, try the smoky, caramelized *bulgogi* with sesame oil-infused *japchae*. If you'd rather not grill, their fried chicken wings glazed in sweet, spicy and vibrant *gochujang* or those crisp vegetable pancakes with a fluffy, savory center are excellent cooked-for-you options.

# Oliveto

Italian Italian ✗✗

E2

**5655 College Ave. (at Shafter Ave.), Oakland**

**Phone:** 510-547-5356
**Web:** www.oliveto.com
**Price:** $$$

Lunch Mon – Fri
Dinner nightly

Its memorable location in a prime corner of Rockridge is only the first hint of Oliveto's good looks: diners enter through a delightful mini-market and café—selling everything from pasta to Maine lobster—before climbing the spiral staircase into this elegant dining room, where a huge wood-burning oven, linen-topped tables, and bunches of fresh flowers delight the eye.

Nothing about Oliveto screams "Italian," from the décor to the all-American staff; yet its menu is completely authentic. Crisp, pan-roasted chicken breast rests on juicy herbed barley and asparagus, while charred Brussels sprouts get a kick from sweet *saba* and chopped walnuts. Barbaresco and Barolo, perfect with the strong selection of pastas and roasted meats, dominate the wine list.

# Pathos

 Greek ✗✗

E2

**2430 Shattuck Ave. (bet. Channing Way & Haste St.), Berkeley**

**Phone:** 510-981-8339
**Web:** www.pathosrestaurant.com
**Price:** $$

Dinner Wed – Sun

Forget the flaming *saganaki* and cries of "Opa!"; Pathos is a sophisticated place that will dispel any tired conceptions of Greek food. You'll want to dress up and bring a date to match its stylish décor, all hammered copper bar, oversized framed windows, and patterned banquettes.

Most dishes come straight from the wood-fired oven, including a lighter take on moussaka, with nutmeg-infused Greek yogurt béchamel baked over ground beef and eggplant; or a roasted red bell pepper stuffed with ground beef and rice. The *htapodi*, tenderly grilled octopus over shaved red onion and fried capers, is another hit for its full, smoky flavor.

Turn to the friendly staff for help in selecting from among the many Greek wines, or try an ouzo or *metaxa* cocktail.

# Pizzaiolo

Pizza ✗

**E2**

**5008 Telegraph Ave. (bet. 49th & 51st Sts.), Oakland**

**Phone:** 510-652-4888                          Dinner Mon – Sat
**Web:** www.pizzaiolooakland.com
**Price:** $$

Lines are still a given at Temescal's long-running pizza palace, where eager patrons arrive before the doors even open to sample salads (try the arugula-frisée-apple combo), pastas, and seasonal plates like halibut with endive gratin. But few leave without ordering at least one pie, crisp from the wood-burning oven and topped with the finest of ingredients, like handcrafted sausage, caramelized rapini, and decadent panna.

The large dining room, with handsome plank floors and dark wood tables, centers around the exhibition kitchen, which is lined with bowls of pristine local produce. Couples and groups gather at tables or pack the polished wood bar. For a quieter experience, come at breakfast when the menu is rife with pastries, toast, and granola.

# Ramen Shop

Japanese ✗

**E2**

**5812 College Ave. (bet. Chabot Rd & Birch Ct.), Oakland**

**Phone:** 510-788-6370                          Dinner nightly
**Web:** www.ramenshop.com
**Price:** $$

The ramen is non-traditional and the staff non-Japanese at this hip Oakland noodle joint, but that doesn't keep an onslaught of young locals from flooding in for a Californian take on Japan's iconic dish. Chewy, springy noodles and fresh vegetables like maitake mushrooms and tomato confit fill each bowl, with a choice of rich, savory pork or veggie Meyer lemon broths.

With only three rotating ramens on the menu, appetizers actually make up most of the offering, and boy, they're killer—a shaved summer squash salad with creamy avocado and fried squash blossoms is to die for. The fun hipster vibe and delicious cocktails at the bar ensure this no-reservations spot fills up fast, so be sure to arrive early—or steel yourself for an inevitable wait.

# Riva Cucina

D2

Italian ✗

**D2**

800 Heinz Ave. (at 7th St.), Berkeley

**Phone:** 510-841-7482
**Web:** www.rivacucina.com
**Price:** $$

Lunch Tue – Fri
Dinner Tue – Sat

A labor of love from an Italian chef and his American wife, this Berkeley favorite overflows with families and their *bambini* (who get their own special menu). While he turns out the rustic, flavorful dishes of his youth in the kitchen, she attends to guests in the high-ceilinged, brick-walled dining room or on the flower-decked front patio.

Kick off a meal here with a fresh and vibrant panzanella packed with sweet heirloom tomatoes, diced cucumber, and shaved salty *ricotta salata*. Parsley-infused fettuccine is equally delightful, twirled with garlicky olive oil, mushrooms, and a dusting of truffled pecorino cheese. Finish with another study in delicious simplicity: the *torta della nonna*, with lemon cream and pine nuts in a cookie crust.

# Rivoli

Californian ✗✗

**D1**

1539 Solano Ave. (bet. Neilson St. & Peralta Ave.), Berkeley

**Phone:** 510-526-2542
**Web:** www.rivolirestaurant.com
**Price:** $$

Dinner nightly

Northern Californian cooking with a hint of regional Americana is the main draw at this lush charmer on the Albany-Berkeley border. It's popular with smartly dressed couples, who come here to savor items like an artfully presented arugula salad with winter citrus, Marcona almonds, and avocado, or a highbrow riff on gumbo with chicken confit and Andouille sausage perched atop Carolina rice. The excellent gâteau Basque, a caramelized wedge of creamy custard, is a must-order.

Set in an adorable cottage, Rivoli's dining room boasts enormous picture windows overlooking a lush "secret" garden blooming with tender fronds, camellias, and magnolia trees. Smartly serviced by an engaging waitstaff, the greenery is a nice contrast to the crisp, white-linen tables.

# Royal Indian Grill

Indian ✗

**B4**

**629 San Ramon Valley Blvd. (at Boone Ct.), Danville**

**Phone:** 925-743-1747                    Lunch & dinner daily
**Web:** www.royalindiangrill.net
**Price:** $$

Some of the East Bay's best Indian food can be found at this casual joint in a sprawling Danville strip mall, which is always packed with local families chatting, playing with kids, or catching Bollywood flicks on the overhead TVs. While it's not suited for those in a rush as service redefines slow, those who wait will be rewarded with fare worthy of royalty.

Many of the kitchen's best dishes pack a spicy punch like the hot, tangy lamb *vindaloo*, flavored with pungent ginger, cilantro, and onion; or the classic *aloo gobi*, a turmeric-based curry with cubed potatoes and florets of cauliflower. Ease the burn with some smoky, caramelized, and pillowy naan, before diving into superb chicken *kofta* stewed in a spice-laden, delicious cashew-tomato sauce.

# Sahn Maru

Korean ✗

**E2**

**4315 Telegraph Ave. (bet. 43rd & 44th Sts.), Oakland**

**Phone:** 510-653-3366                    Lunch & dinner Wed – Mon
**Web:** www.sahnmarukoreanbbq.com
**Price:** $$

As one of East Bay's top Korean restaurants, Sahn Maru's name (which translates as «top of the mountain») is perfectly fitting. Its casual vibe, large size, and friendly service make it a good choice for groups. Never mind the wainscoting and country-quaint chairs that juxtapose walls covered with pictures of Korean dishes—this is a place for authentic food.

Meals start with barley tea and tasty *banchan* like fiery daikon soup, kimchi, bean sprout salad in sesame oil, and fish cakes, alongside a bowl of delicately flavored kelp. Lunchtime might feature a deliciously unexpected combination of beef *bulgogi* stir-fried with *jap chae*. While the spot earns raves for Korean barbecue, the kitchen prepares it for you, as there are no tabletop grills.

# Shakewell

**3407 Lakeshore Ave. (bet. Longridge & Trestle Glen Rds.), Oakland**

**Phone:** 510-251-0329
**Web:** www.shakewelloakland.com
**Price:** $$

Lunch Wed – Sun
Dinner Tue – Sun

This trendy eatery, the brainchild of *Top Chef* alums Jen Biesty and Tim Nugent, was made for sipping and supping. Donning a bar up front and several dining nooks on either side of a central walkway, Shakewell keeps things Medi-chic with Moorish accents, reclaimed wood, and organic elements.

Service is particularly warm, and an even warmer teal-green wood-fired oven in the back turns out deliciously smoked items like crisp falafel topped with chorizo aïoli. A summer squash salad with heirloom tomatoes, fried bread, and feta offers an inspired blend of Greek and Tuscan flavors, and Bomba rice with braised fennel, *piperade*, chicken, and prawns is a fluffy take on paella. For a party in your mouth, finish with the caramel syrup-spiked flan Catalan.

# Sidebar

**542 Grand Ave. (bet. Euclid Ave. & MacArthur Blvd.), Oakland**

**Phone:** 510-452-9500
**Web:** www.sidebar-oaktown.com
**Price:** $$

Lunch Mon – Fri
Dinner Mon – Sat

A loyal crowd of regulars flocks to this lively Oakland gastropub, located right across Grand Avenue from Lake Merritt. Though it offers only a handful of tables, Sidebar makes eating at the spacious rectangular bar a delight, with attentive servers and a view of the action in the semi-open kitchen.

The cuisine is hearty and varied with starters like a chopped romaine salad with fennel salami and creamy garlic-herb dressing; braised chicken thighs with curried coconut-lime cream; and deviled eggs with smoky bacon and cheddar. The menu changes seasonally, and there are often daily specials, but there's no shame in sticking to the excellent Niman Ranch burger, with house-pickled onions and chipotle-Thousand Island dressing.

# Tacos Sinaloa

Mexican ✗

**E2**

**2384 Telegraph Ave. (bet. Channing Way & Durant Ave.), Berkeley**

| | |
|---|---|
| **Phone:** | 510-665-7895 |
| **Web:** | N/A |
| **Price:** | 🍲 |

Lunch & dinner daily

East Oakland's taco truck titans have finally put it in park with this outstanding Berkeley taqueria, which is quickly making its name as one of the best in the entire Bay Area. Sinaloa's logo is a smiling shrimp holding a taco, so your first choice may be the top-notch shrimp taco (full of plump, succulent, spice-rubbed shrimp), but there's more in store: smoky carnitas with fiery red chile salsa, tender roast chicken, and beautifully caramelized *al pastor*. For the adventurous eater, there's tripe, *suadero*, and pork stomach, too.

Like the truck, this operation is no-frills: pay at the counter, grab some plastic utensils, and seat yourself. But with food this good—and prices so low that even a penniless Cal student can afford to dine—who needs frills?

# Tacubaya

Mexican ✗

**D1**

**1788 4th St. (bet. Hearst Ave. & Virginia St.), Berkeley**

| | |
|---|---|
| **Phone:** | 510-525-5160 |
| **Web:** | www.tacubaya.net |
| **Price:** | 🍲 |

Lunch & dinner daily

Megapopular Oakland Mexican restaurant Doña Tomas is reincarnated in taqueria form at this Berkeley shopping complex, where families grab a bite before or after errands. A line of people extends out the door from morning until night, ordering tangy limeade at the counter and claiming seats in the festive pink-and-orange dining room or on the sunny front patio.

The crowds come for *chilaquiles* and churros at breakfast, then transition into flavorful chorizo-and-potato *sopes* with black bean purée at lunch. Moist, well-seasoned beef enchiladas are doused in a smoky, tangy *guajillo*-tomatillo sauce and covered with melted cheese. For a sweet finish, tamales filled with cranberry jam and drizzled with goat-milk caramel are both beguiling and unusual.

# Thai House

**B4**

Thai **XX**

254 Rose Ave. (bet. Diablo Rd. & Linda Mesa Ave.), Danville

**Phone:** 925-820-0635
**Web:** www.thaihousedanville.net
**Price:** $$

Lunch Mon – Fri
Dinner nightly

Many a warm evening has been spent on the garden patio of this fantastic Thai restaurant, where potted plants create a leafy retreat. Whether you're dining alfresco or tucked inside the tiny, colorful bungalow, you can be assured of a warm welcome and boldly flavorful food—a secret that's out with the locals, making this house a packed one from noon to night.

The consistently outstanding menu makes it hard to go wrong, but you can't miss with the creamy red pumpkin curry, full of tender scallops and prawns and perfectly balanced notes of sweet, spicy, salty, and sour. Other showstoppers may reveal *pad prig khing*, chicken in a spicy peanut-tamarind sauce, or the aromatic basil tofu, chockablock with fresh vegetables, chili, and garlic.

# Trabocco

**E4**

Italian **XX**

2213 South Shore Center (bet. Otis & Shoreline Drs.), Alameda

**Phone:** 510-521-1152
**Web:** www.trabocco.com
**Price:** $$$

Lunch & dinner daily

Big-city style and rustic Italian authenticity combine to create magic at this Alameda favorite, which is owned by a native of Abruzzo. Its location in a shopping center isn't the greatest, but the sleek and sophisticated dining room and spacious front patio are transporting enough that you won't mind. Also of assistance: killer cocktails starring Alameda craft distiller St. George Spirits.

The hearty food is a true taste of Italy, with lovingly hand-made dishes like *chitarrine* pasta swirled with a tender, tomato-flecked rabbit ragù. The massive wood-grilled pork chop is smoky, juicy, and accompanied by tender-crisp broccoli rabe. And for dessert, an airy *zabaglione*, delicately infused with a hint of Marsala, is served with fresh strawberries.

# Va de Vi

International ✕✕

F1

1511 Mt. Diablo Blvd. (bet. Locust & Main Sts.), Walnut Creek

**Phone:** 925-979-0100                          Lunch & dinner daily
**Web:** www.vadevi.com
**Price:** $$

"Va de vi" is a Catalan phrase that roughly means "It's all about wine." Here, you'll find no dissent from moneyed locals who gather to explore less common varietals in flights with such cheeky names as "New Faces, Different Places." The bucolic patio is an ace sipping destination, as is the L-shaped counter with a view of the open kitchen set amid polished woods.

Good wine demands good food, and the global menu offered here entices with ultra-fresh choices like tempura-battered squash blossoms filled with ricotta and sweet corn; or charred shrimp served atop a griddled Spanish rice cake. Asian influences abound, particularly in the duck *lumpia* coupled with green papaya-and-carrot salad. Add on a sweet staff and easy vibe—no wonder it's such a hit.

# Wood Tavern 😊

American ✕✕

E2

6317 College Ave. (bet. Alcatraz Ave. & 63rd St.), Oakland

**Phone:** 510-654-6607                          Lunch Mon – Sat
**Web:** www.woodtavern.net                       Dinner nightly
**Price:** $$

There's always a crowd at this lively neighborhood standby, where groups of friends, parents on date night, and hip couples congregate for drinks at the copper-topped bar. Flanked by organic groceries, indie bookstores, and antique shops, its surroundings reek of peace, weaving a pleasantly bohemian spell that captivates both regulars and newcomers alike.

Rustic American food with a hint of Italian flair dominates the menu, and the local Belfiore burrata—served atop diced pears, honey-cashew cream, and peppery arugula— is a surefire hit. Then pappardelle may arrive tangled in an intensely flavored veal ragù, enriched with spicy chili flakes and parmesan. For dessert, an apple-oatmeal crumble with sour cream ice cream is just the ticket.

# Marin

in farmstead cheeses alone, they have refined the process of artisan cheese-making, and ergo, garnered national respect along the way. Continue exploring these fromageries at **Point Reyes Farmstead Cheese Co.**, a popular destination among natives for the "Original Blue" and its famously lush and heady satisfaction. Thanks to such driven, enterprising cheese-makers (who live by terroir or taste of the earth), surrounding restaurants follow the European standard by offering cheese before or in lieu of a dessert course. After all this savory goodness, get your candy crush going at **Munchies of Sausalito**; or opt for a more creamy scoop at **Noci Gelato**.

Meandering Marin is located north of the Golden Gate Bridge and draped along breathtaking Highway 1. Coastal climates shower this county with abounding agricultural advantages, which in turn become abundantly apparent as you snake your way through its food oases, always filled with fresh, luscious seafood, slurpable oysters, and cold beer. Farm-to-table cuisine is de rigueur in this liberal-leaning and affluent county, boasting an avalanche of local food suppliers. One of the most celebrated purveyors is the quaint and rustic **Cowgirl Creamery**, whose "cowgirls" are charged with churning out delicious, distinctive, and hand-crafted cheeses. By specializing

If cheese and meat are a match made in heaven, then North Bay must be a thriving intermediary with its myriad ranches. At the crest is **Marin Sun Farms**, a glorified and dedicated butcher shop whose heart and soul lies

in the production of locally raised, natural-fed meats for fine restaurants, small-scale grocers, and everything in between. Championing local eating is **Mill Valley Market**, a can't-miss commitment among gourmands for top-quality foods, deli items, and other organic goods.

## STOP, SIP & SAVOR

To gratify those inevitable pangs of hunger after miles of scenic driving complete with ocean breezes, **The Pelican Inn** makes for an ideal retreat. Serving hearty English country cooking alongside a range of brews from their classic "bar," this nostalgic and ever-charming rest stop will leave you yearning for more. Continue your hiatus by strolling into **Spanish Table**, a shopper's paradise settled in Mill Valley, only to find foodies and locals alike reveling in unique Spanish cookbooks, cookware, specialty foods, and drool-worthy wines. Finally, peckish travelers with a sweet craving can also be found at **Three Twins Ice Cream** for their organically produced creamy goodness that promises to leave an everlasting impression.

Waters off the coast here provide divers with exceptional hunting ground, and restaurants throughout Marin count on supremely fresh oysters, briny clams, and meaty mussels. The difficulty in (legally) sourcing these large, savory mollusks makes red abalone a treasured species in area Asian establishments, though seafood does seem to be the accepted norm among restaurants in town. If fish doesn't float your boat, **Fred's Coffee Shop** in Sausalito is a no-frills find for fulfilling breakfast signatures like deep-fried French toast with a side of calorie-heavy, crazy-good caramelized 'Millionaire's bacon.' Carb addicts routinely pay their respects at **M.H. Bread & Butter**, said to be the best bakery around. Their crusty loaves make for fantastic sandwiches, but are equally divine just slathered with butter. If that's too tame for your tastes, enticing Puerto Rican flavors abound at **Sol Food**, settled in San Rafael. While this fertile county's natural ingredients are sold in countless farmers' markets, many other celebrations of food and wine continue to pop up throughout during the spring and summer months. Given its culinary chops and panoramic views, Marin is one of the most sought after stops for celebrities and visitors alike. True, some places can seem touristy. But, these chefs and restaurants are lauded for good reason, and know how to make the most of their choice homegrown produce and food purveyors.

# Arti

Indian ✗

**A1**

### 7282 Sir Francis Drake Blvd. (at Cintura Ave.), Lagunitas

**Phone:** 415-488-4700
**Web:** www.articafe.com
**Price:** ❧

Lunch & dinner daily

In sleepy Lagunitas, locals spice things up with a trip to this itty-bitty Indian favorite, where yellow walls and flowers liven the handful of tables. Set in a strip mall that also plays host to a hippie bookstore and yoga studio, this is a comforting den of peace and love for your palate, down to the fluffy basmati rice, creamy raita, and gluten-free naan (made with rice flour). Warm up a chilly night with hot and tangy lamb *vindaloo* mingling tender cubes of lamb with fork-tender potatoes; or go for the full comfort effect with creamy chicken korma. Finish with an order of *gulab jamun*, homemade cheese dumplings soaked in sweet syrup. If you're in for lunch, be sure to sample the Indian wraps, also available in whole-wheat and gluten-free versions.

# Arun

Thai ✗

**C1**

### 385 Bel Marin Keys Blvd. (near Hamilton Dr.), Novato

**Phone:** 415-883-8017
**Web:** www.arunnovato.com
**Price:** ❧

Lunch Tue – Fri
Dinner Tue – Sat

Don't be fooled by its location in an industrial park: this Thai restaurant is completely transporting, thanks to the small, well-tended garden in front, bubbling fountain, colorful walls, and dark wood tables. Dinner is more formal than lunch, but either service offers a calming air.

The standards are all present and accounted for: satays, curries (like a delicious, mildly spiced red curry with prawns, squash, and bell pepper), and heaps of fragrant jasmine rice. At dinner, Thai barbecue is king and unveils an appealing Islamic lamb dish. Vibrant in appearance and fresh in flavor, all items are strong, but the moneybag-like curry pouches are particularly memorable, thanks to their golden exterior, tie of leek at the top, and rich ground chicken filling.

# Baan

Thai ✗

B2

726 San Anselmo Ave. (bet. San Rafael & Tamalpais Aves.), San Anselmo

**Phone:** 415-457-9470                                    Lunch & dinner Tue – Sun
**Web:** www.baanthaimarin.com
**Price:** $$

Baan is Thai for "home" and this cozy space, full of warmth and laughter, will make you feel like you've found one—with better Thai food than your own, to boot. Local families regularly fill the bustling dining room, which features simple furnishings, cushioned banquettes, plenty of greenery, and authentic art on the walls.

Come for a quick lunch of tender pumpkin and plump prawns in a creamy, fiery red curry, or bring a crowd and share the spicy crying tiger salad, packed with grilled beef, red onion, tomatoes, and fresh herbs in a zippy lime dressing. Portions are absurdly generous, so plan on enjoying seconds of your moist green curry fried rice, spicy green beans, or charred yet tender *moo yang* (barbecue pork) for lunch the next day.

# Bar Bocce

Pizza ✗

A3

1250 Bridgeway (bet. Pine & Turney Sts.), Sausalito

**Phone:** 415-331-0555                                    Lunch & dinner daily
**Web:** www.barbocce.com
**Price:** $$

As chill a hangout spot as they come, Bar Bocce is seemingly designed to while away the hours with its pretty view of the water, namesake bocce courts, and roaring fire pit. Friendly and casual, it's a place where an afternoon glass of wine can easily fade into a multi-hour dinner, shared with a group of friends on the heated patio overlooking Sausalito's harbor.

Wood-fired sourdough pizzas, like a marble potato pie with fontina, bacon, and a fresh farm egg, are the heart of the menu, accented by antipasti such as shaved Brussels sprouts and pecorino salad or golden cod *brandade* fritters with a tangy citrus aïoli. Cheerful servers are always happy to recommend a bottle of *vino* (or three) to keep the festivities humming in the inviting little bungalow.

# Barrel House Tavern

Californian ✕✕

**A3**

### 660 Bridgeway (at Princess St.), Sausalito

**Phone:** 415-729-9593                                    Lunch & dinner daily
**Web:**   www.barrelhousetavern.com
**Price:** $$

The former San Francisco-Sausalito ferry terminal has found new life as this lovely Californian restaurant, which gets its name from its barrel-like arched wood ceiling. A front lounge with a crackling fireplace and well-stocked bar is popular with locals, while tourists can't resist the expansive dining room and back deck, which boasts spectacular views of the Bay.

The cocktail and wine offerings are strong, as is the house-made soda program, which produces intriguing, never-too-sweet combinations like yellow peach, basil, and ginger. These pair beautifully with meaty Dungeness crab sliders coupled with watermelon-jicama slaw; though they might be too tasty to keep around by the time grilled swordfish and pork belly with white beans hit the table.

# Buckeye Roadhouse

American ✕✕

**A2**

### 15 Shoreline Hwy. (off Hwy. 101), Mill Valley

**Phone:** 415-331-2600                                    Lunch & dinner daily
**Web:**   www.buckeyeroadhouse.com
**Price:** $$

This Marin hideout has welcomed generations of locals through its doors since 1937, even as its location on Highway 1 gave way to the more bustling 101. Enter the whitewashed craftsman building, and you'll be given your choice of dining in either the clubby bar or their grand dining room (complete with wood-paneled walls, red leather banquettes, and a tall fireplace).

The food here is classical but never dull, with a simple menu of salads, sandwiches, barbecue, and meat from the wood grill. A brunchtime meal of eggs Benedict boasts tender rosemary ham and rich potato croquettes, while plump asparagus ravioli with lemon olive oil stars in the evening. Finish up with a slice of pie—the famous s'mores version or a tart Key lime are both winners.

# Bungalow 44

B2

**American** ✕✕

**44 E. Blithedale Ave. (at Sunnyside Ave.), Mill Valley**

**Phone:** 415-381-2500
**Web:** www.bungalow44.com
**Price:** $$

Dinner nightly

Nestled amid the fancy stores of quaint Mill Valley, vibrant Bungalow 44 draws a varied crew to its casual, contemporary environs. It's always busy at the bustling bar and in the slightly more subdued dining room, so for some peace and quiet, retire to the tented outer room with its glowing fireplace. Some prefer the counter to soak up the sizzle from the open kitchen.

Playful American cuisine is their dictum, which shines through in tuna carpaccio—an homage to Italian antipasto—here starring tissue-thin slices of tuna served with citrusy *mizuna* and creamy mustard sauce. The whiff of cayenne from kickin' fried chicken is as tempting as the juicy meat—add the rich mashed potatoes. Local draft wines paired with pillowy-soft beignets make for a rewarding finish.

# Burmatown

C2

**Burmese** ✕

**60 Corte Madera Ave. (bet. Bahr Ln. & Redwood Ave.), Corte Madera**

**Phone:** 415-945-9096
**Web:** www.burmatown.com
**Price:** $$

Dinner Tue – Sun

Bypass the tired Asian-fusion offerings and head straight for the authentic Burmese dishes at this out-of-the-way cutie. A nutty, crunchy, and flavorful tea-leaf salad is the perfect answer to a hot summer day, while hearty potato-stuffed samosas and fresh, springy egg noodles tossed with barbecue pork and fried garlic chips will warm your soul in the cooler months.

Given the high quality of its food, it's no surprise that Burmatown is Corte Madera's most popular novel neighbor: it's big with local families from the surrounding residences, who pack every single table, attended to by warm servers. If you're willing to make a special trip to this charming bright-orange bungalow, the laid-back vibe will have you feeling right at home.

# Cafe Reyes

Pizza ✗

**A1**

### 11101 Shoreline Hwy. (at Mesa Rd.), Point Reyes Station

**Phone:** 415-663-9493      Lunch & dinner Wed – Sun
**Web:** N/A
**Price:** $$

This unassuming charmer in quaint Point Reyes Station is a perfect stop for day-trippers, who are sure to enjoy the many delicious dishes that emerge from its duo of wood-fired ovens. Pizza is the focus, with nine varieties ranging from a classic Margherita to more exotic combos of seasonal produce. But, there are also some delicious pies both savory (a spinach, egg, and cheese *tortino* with a salad of fresh greens) and sweet (a knockout berry version with a buttery crust). And every meal ends with a happy surprise—complimentary donut holes.

Given its cooking method, it's no surprise that Cafe Reyes is stacked high with wood, both against the walls and under the counter. The big, spacious, barn-like dining room is rustic and unfussy, perfect for groups.

# Copita

Mexican ✗✗

**A3**

### 739 Bridgeway (at Anchor St.), Sausalito

**Phone:** 415-331-7400      Lunch & dinner daily
**Web:** www.copitarestaurant.com
**Price:** $$

Set sail aboard the Sausalito ferry for dinner at this Mexican smash, just steps from the harbor's bobbing yachts. Colorful and casual, Copita's most coveted seats are on the sidewalk patio (complete with partial views of the water and the quaint downtown), but a spot at the exceptionally well-stocked tequila bar or in the brightly tiled dining room is no disappointment.

A light meal of tacos could include seared mahi mahi with pineapple *pico de gallo* and tomatillo salsa or tomato-accented chicken *tinga* with avocado and Mexican *crema*. Options abound for heartier appetites, like 24-hour carnitas and chicken *mole enchiladas*. And the lively surrounds are a hit with kids, who love sipping on the sweet house-made almond *horchata*.

**Marin**

# El Huarache Loco

**C2**

Mexican  ✗

1803 Larkspur Landing Cir. (off Sir Francis Drake Blvd.), Larkspur

**Phone:** 415-925-1403     Lunch & dinner daily
**Web:** www.huaracheloco.com
**Price:** 🞵🞵

In Mexico City, a *huarache* can be two things: a sandal, or a sandal-shaped disk of masa with delicious toppings—and talented native Chef/owner Veronica Salazar is definitely no cobbler. Though El Huarache Loco is housed in the tony Marin Country Mart, its crowd is largely Mexican, with many locals visiting this bright, airy counter-service spot for a taste of their homeland.

Served on beautiful hand-painted Mexican plates, these *huaraches* are unsurprisingly exceptional (try the version topped with nopales, tomato, onion, and *crema*). So, too, are regional specialties like *tlacoyito*, a cheese-stuffed blue corn masa cake layered with chicken *tinga*, onion, and cilantro, or *sopes* with tender potatoes and spicy chorizo.

# El Paseo

**B2**

American ✗✗

17 Throckmorton Ave. (at Blithedale Ave.), Mill Valley

**Phone:** 415-388-0741     Dinner nightly
**Web:** www.elpaseomillvalley.com
**Price:** $$$

"Rockstar chef" is a term that often gets tossed around, but it's all too true at this rustic charmer, co-owned by celebrity toque Tyler Florence and rocker Sammy Hagar. Hidden down an alley off the shopping arcade of Mill Valley, the space echoes old-world charm with rustic, wood-beamed ceilings and brick walls. Adding a dose of romance are cool high-backed leather chairs warmed by a fireplace.

Once seated, begin your meal with hot-from-the-oven popovers—a Tyler Florence signature. Then move on to a bowlful of tiny, tender clams in a garlicky saffron-wine broth with chili threads, chopped parsley, and toasted baguette slathered with aïoli. Finish with a surprisingly light and elegant cheesecake with the bright tang of Meyer lemon and compressed strawberries.

# Fish

A3

Seafood ✗

### 350 Harbor Dr. (off Bridgeway), Sausalito

**Phone:** 415-331-3474          Lunch & dinner daily
**Web:** www.331fish.com
**Price:** $$

Casual and family-friendly, this Sausalito seafood spot offers diners the choice of a bright and airy dining room with simple wood furnishings or an alfresco picnic table, both with great views of the harbor. If you dine outdoors, watch out for the local seagulls and crows, who are always ready to snag a snack from your plate (but provide great entertainment for the younger set).

The cooking is fresh and flavorful, from a Dungeness crab roll with butter and chives to crisp Anchor Steam-battered halibut served with house-made wedge fries and tartar sauce. Check the chalkboard for the latest specials, like mussels with chorizo and fennel or grilled Monterey sardines. After dining, visit the raw seafood counter for a selection of items to cook at home.

# Frantoio

A2

Italian ✗✗

### 152 Shoreline Hwy. (off Hwy. 101), Mill Valley

**Phone:** 415-289-5777          Dinner nightly
**Web:** www.frantoio.com
**Price:** $$

Named for the olive press used in oil production throughout Italy, Frantoio is distinguished by its own house-made olive oil, cold-pressed in a hefty granite contraption displayed just off the dining room. Bottled and sold on-site, this stellar product beams atop shavings of *prosciutto di Parma* with arugula and *mozzarella di bufala*. Pasta is noteworthy, especially the al dente *bucatini* swirled with San Marzano tomatoes, minced Calabrian chilies, and supremely rich Berkshire pork pancetta. Save room for decadent desserts, like a dark chocolatey tower of cake and mousse.

Though its proximity to Highway 101 and roadside hotels isn't ideal, an orange-and-charcoal color scheme and lofty ceilings ensure that the surrounds become a quickly fading memory.

# Insalata's

**Mediterranean** ✗✗

**B2**

### 120 Sir Francis Drake Blvd. (at Barber Ave.), San Anselmo

**Phone:** 415-457-7700       Lunch & dinner daily
**Web:** www.insalatas.com
**Price:** $$

San Anselmo restaurateur Chef Heidi Krahling honors her late father, Italo Insalata, at this crowd-pleasing Marin hangout. The *zucca*-orange stucco exterior alludes to the Mediterranean air within. Insalata's upscale setting is framed by lemon-yellow walls hung with grand depictions of nature's bounty setting the scene for the array of fresh and flavorful cuisine to come.

Sparked by Middle Eastern flavors, Insalata's specialties include velvety smooth potato-leek soup made brilliantly green from watercress purée. Also sample grilled lamb skewers drizzled with cumin-yogurt atop crunchy salad and flatbread. The takeout area in the back is stocked with salads, sides, and sandwiches made with house-baked bread. Boxed lunches are a fun, tasty convenience.

# Left Bank

**French** ✗✗

**B2**

### 507 Magnolia Ave. (at Ward St.), Larkspur

**Phone:** 415-927-3331       Lunch & dinner daily
**Web:** www.leftbank.com
**Price:** $$

The very picture of a neighborhood bistro, Left Bank's breezy ambience and oh-so-French fare have really hit home with Larkspur locals. Inside, a lovely stone hearth is surrounded by cheery yellow walls and vintage French posters, while the wraparound terrace outdoors is the place to dine on a lazy summer afternoon.

The kitchen does French classics to perfection, including a charcuterie board groaning with hefty portions of truffle-flecked chicken liver mousse, duck and pork rillettes, and country pâté. Tender rainbow trout Grenobloise arrives with grilled Provençal country bread, soaked in savory herb-and-garlic butter. Finish with fresh profiteroles, stuffed with vanilla ice cream and topped with rich, not-too-sweet dark chocolate sauce.

# Le Garage

French    🍴

**A3**

85 Liberty Ship Way, Ste. 109 (off Marinship Way), Sausalito

**Phone:** 415-332-5625
**Web:** www.legaragebistrosausalito.com
**Price:** $$

Lunch daily
Dinner Mon – Sat

Cultivated French technique meets bold California tastes at this petite canteen, which, as advertised, is housed in a former garage (complete with roll-up doors). Flavorful bouillabaisse packed with fresh *dorade*, plump scallops, and local shellfish; or a beet-and-apple salad with mandarinquats and goat cheese; or a tangy, buttery lemon tart are only some of the appealing menu options.

Le Garage's building was used to construct World War II battleships, but these days, it's more likely to house well-dressed sailors fresh off their yachts in the harbor, as well as lunching locals from the neighboring businesses. With coffee and croissants each morning, brunch on the weekends, and a thoughtful Cal-French wine list, it's a standby at any time of day.

# Marché aux Fleurs

Mediterranean    🍴🍴

**B2**

23 Ross Common (off Lagunitas Rd.), Ross

**Phone:** 415-925-9200
**Web:** www.marcheauxfleursrestaurant.com
**Price:** $$

Dinner Tue – Sat

Its dark wood dining room is charming, but Marché aux Fleurs truly comes alive on warm spring and summer evenings, when Marin residents flock to the picturesque hamlet of Ross to enjoy a meal on its front patio. Mediterranean-inspired eats with a California twist are what these patrons are after—imagine soft gnocchi with corn and chanterelles or squash blossom tempura with fresh ricotta and you will start to grasp the picture.

Local couples love it here, and though many are regulars, even first-timers receive a friendly welcome from the engaging staff. Groups are everywhere and their smiles all-knowing as they savor bacon-wrapped king salmon over sweet corn and green garbanzo succotash; or split bites of warm chocolate cake with vanilla bean ice cream.

223

# Marinitas

B2

✗✗

**218 Sir Francis Drake Blvd. (at Bank St.), San Anselmo**

**Phone:** 415-454-8900 Lunch & dinner daily
**Web:** www.marinitas.net
**Price:** $$

Latin comfort food is the draw at this cavernous space in the heart of downtown San Anselmo, where the welcome is warm and the salsas are hot. Outfitted with plenty of cute seating nooks and wood shelves filled with books and knick-knacks, it's quiet at lunchtime but can draw big crowds on weekends.

Order up a glass of something special from the extensive tequila selection, and you'll be primed to peruse the extensive menu, which offers everything from grilled cod tacos with super-spicy Tabasco *crema* to *garnachas*—thick and crispy masa cakes laden with plantains, duck confit, and mango-habanero sauce. Should you linger too long in Margaritaville, the friendly servers will be happy to point you in the right direction for soaking up any sins.

# Molina

B2

✗✗

**17 Madrona St. (bet. Lovell & Throckmorton Aves.), Mill Valley**

**Phone:** 415-383-4200 Dinner nightly
**Web:** www.molinarestaurant.com
**Price:** $$

Small and deeply personal, this Mill Valley destination is home to a team of talented chefs who simultaneously man the wood-fired oven and flip vinyl records that provide the soundtrack. Daily menus are printed alongside daily playlists. With a funky design full of wood and texture, it's almost like eating in the home of a friend—one with great taste in music who really knows his way around the kitchen.

The main carte showcases local wood-fired fare, like a fluffy frittata chockful of sweet Dungeness crab and earthy sunchokes garnished with chives and crème fraîche. Heartier dinners might feature hangar steak with green-garlic *chimichurri*. From the wine to the bread, everything is local, yet inventive and compelling: it's a gift both to and from the community.

# Nick's Cove

American ✗✗

**A1**

23240 Hwy. 1, Marshall

**Phone:** 415-663-1033
**Web:** www.nickscove.com
**Price:** $$

Lunch & dinner daily

It's hard not to fall for this sweet waterside retreat on the banks of Tomales Bay, which has served as a refuge for city-dwellers for decades. The vintage fuel pump outside is just for looks in this era of hybrid cars, and the updated interior has a lodge-like feel complete with vaulted ceilings, wood-paneled walls, a fireplace, and smattering of hunting trophies.

Unsurprisingly for northern California's oyster capital, the menu is heavy on seafood, from bivalves both raw and grilled to golden-brown Dungeness crab cakes. The white shrimp enchiladas with *salsa roja* and cilantro cream are soft and succulent. Longing for more even after you've finished your meal? Stay the night on their grounds in one of several cozy cottages with a wood-burning stove.

# Osteria Stellina

Italian ✗✗

**A1**

11285 Hwy. 1 (at 3rd St.), Point Reyes Station

**Phone:** 415-663-9988
**Web:** www.osteriastellina.com
**Price:** $$

Lunch & dinner daily

Its name is Italian for "little star," and this cutie spot does indeed shine in the heart of tiny Point Reyes Station, a one-horse clapboard town with little more than a filling station and a post office to its name. But the Wild West it's not: this frontier village is Marin-chic, and its saloon is a soothing retreat with soft sage walls, wide windows, and local produce on the menu.

You'll taste the difference in the pillowy house-made focaccia, the soothing chicken *brodo*, and the crisp salad of little gem lettuce with blue cheese, toasted walnuts, and honeycrisp apples. Organic, grass-fed beef stew is packed with spices and served over herbed polenta. Finish with a chocolate sponge cake with mocha mousse that's as unforgettable as the setting.

225

# Picco

**B2**

Italian XX

### 320 Magnolia Ave. (at King St.), Larkspur

**Phone:** 415-924-0300                                   Dinner nightly
**Web:** www.restaurantpicco.com
**Price:** $$

*Picco* is Italian for "summit," and this charming Larkspur hilltop home has long been a beacon among Marin County diners. Chef/owner Bruce Hill is a true local-food devotee: his Italian-influenced fare heaps on Marin ingredients like the fresh turnips that dot his silky-smooth duck *tortelli*, or the Meyer lemon yogurt and beets that sit atop a nourishing kale salad. The "Marin Mondays" menu is a particular steal.

The precise staff moves ably through the busy dining room, carrying bowls of creamy risotto made on the half-hour. With a high ceiling and exposed brick walls, the vibe is graceful but never fussy, making this the perfect setting for couples and groups of friends who congregate here.

Also check out Pizzeria Picco next door.

# Poggio ☺

**A3**

Italian XX

### 777 Bridgeway (at Bay St.), Sausalito

**Phone:** 415-332-7771                                 Lunch & dinner daily
**Web:** www.poggiotrattoria.com
**Price:** $$

You might forget you're not on the Adriatic coast midway through a meal at this Sausalito standby, where the Italian flavors are authentic and the views of yachts bobbing in the harbor add to the charm. Local regulars and tourists alike arrive early to snag one of the prime sidewalk seats overlooking the main drag; inside, the elegant dining room boasts a roaring pizza oven.

California-influenced appetizers like seared scallops with sunchoke purée and aromatic veal jus segue into comforting pastas—pappardelle tossed with braised pork ragout and *parmigiano*, anyone? Half-portions are available on every pasta and risotto, a bonus for those who want to save room for entrées like grilled yellowfin tuna with asparagus, green olives, and caramelized fennel.

# Prabh

Indian

**24 Sunnyside Ave. (at Parkwood St.), Mill Valley**

| | | |
|---|---|---|
| **Phone:** | 415-384-8241 | Lunch & dinner daily |
| **Web:** | www.prabhindiankitchen.com | |
| **Price:** | $$ | |

Located in a converted house and a welcome addition to Mill Valley's dining scene, this casual yet stylish Indian restaurant is a cut above the rest. South Asian art and sculpture, fresh flowers, and copper accents add splashes of color to the mahogany furnishings and granite tabletops, while the glass-enclosed front porch is a sunny spot to enjoy an easygoing lunch, kids included.

Bring a group and explore the menu family-style, as you won't want to miss the tender, well-spiced, and *garam masala*-redolent lamb *rogan josh* or the sizzling kebab of chicken tikka in its tangy, delectable yogurt marinade. Flaky samosas filled with a flavorful blend of potatoes, peas, caramelized onions, and served with a trio of tasty chutneys, are quite perfect.

# R'Noh Thai

Thai

**1000 Magnolia Ave. (bet. Frances & Murray Aves.), Larkspur**

| | | |
|---|---|---|
| **Phone:** | 415-925-0599 | Lunch Mon – Sat |
| **Web:** | www.rnohthai.com | Dinner nightly |
| **Price:** | ⊜⊗ | |

Generous portions and thoughtful preparations are the key ingredients at this Thai restaurant, which occupies a long wooden building overlooking a small creek. The interior is warm and inviting, with bright skylights, oil paintings of water lilies, and a fireplace crackling away.

R'Noh's popularity is most evident at lunch, when local business people drop in for the daily special of a light curry with salad and rice. Ginger chicken, packed with mushrooms and tender meat, is a more mild but still flavorful option. The menu expands slightly at dinner, offering delicious plates like a crispy shrimp roll filled with plump prawns. Highly attentive servers can recommend a wine from the short list, or try their supremely thirst-quenching homemade lemonade.

# Sir and Star

**Marin**

**A1**

Californian ✖✖

### 10000 Sir Francis Drake Blvd. (at Hwy. 1), Olema

**Phone:** 415-663-1034      Dinner Wed – Sun
**Web:** www.sirandstar.com
**Price:** $$

This quirky roadhouse in the historic Olema Inn is one-of-a-kind, from the displays of branches in the light-flooded dining room to the poetic menu descriptions ("Softly Smoked Halibut Plucked From Surrounding Seas"). But in the hands of Chef/owners and longtime Marin fixtures Daniel DeLong and Margaret Gradé, you can always expect a fine meal made with painstakingly sourced local ingredients.

Sip a glass of Marin-made mead by the fire; then head to the dining room, where you'll sample dishes like Point Reyes Toma cheese "fondue," golden beet soup, and fluffy cardamom sugar beignets with local honey and strawberries—all accompanied by excellent crusty bread.

Saturday nights are dedicated to a pricier prix-fixe menu, so be sure to plan accordingly.

# Sol Food

**C2**

Puerto Rican ✖

### 903 Lincoln Ave. (at 3rd St.), San Rafael

**Phone:** 415-451-4765      Lunch & dinner daily
**Web:** www.solfoodrestaurant.com
**Price:** $$

You won't be able to miss this Puerto Rican favorite, recognizable by its grasshopper-green exterior and overflowing crowds of festive diners. In fact, Sol Food's *comida criolla* is so popular that it's taken over the block: a sister bodega does a booming takeout business, while gift store Conchita sells wares from San Juan and beyond.

Sol Food's soul food is hearty and abundant, from tamale-like *pasteles* of mashed plantain and taro stuffed with garlicky pork to fragrant sautéed shrimp loaded with tomato, onion, and spices. Outstanding daily specials, from *arroz con pollo* to *pernil*, are also big draws. Wash it all down with a delicious mango iced tea, and don't skip the decadent pineapple bread pudding, soaked in warm, buttery mango sauce, for dessert.

# Sushi Ran

**Japanese** ✕✕

**A3**

**107 Caledonia St. (bet. Pine & Turney Sts.), Sausalito**

| | |
|---|---|
| Phone: | 415-332-3620 |
| Web: | www.sushiran.com |
| Price: | $$ |

Lunch Mon – Fri
Dinner nightly

Chefs have come and gone at this Sausalito staple, but its Zen-like atmosphere and exquisite selection of raw fish haven't changed for upwards of a decade—and that's just how the regulars like it. With its charming beachside-bungalow ambience, attentive staff, and thoughtfully curated sake selection, Sushi Ran is as dependable as a restaurant can get. Start off with a small bite like shrimp tempura over crisp veggies, *tobiko*, and asparagus, or a steamed red crab salad with seaweed, cucumber, and sweet soy dressing. Then move on to the main event: meticulously sourced, extraordinarily fresh *hamachi*, big-eye tuna, steamed blue prawns, and Santa Barbara uni. Whether you choose sashimi or nigiri, the talented chefs will steer you right.

# Thai Aroi-Dee

**Thai** ✕

**C2**

**1518 4th St. (bet. E & F Sts.), San Rafael**

| | |
|---|---|
| Phone: | 415-295-7464 |
| Web: | n/a |
| Price: | $$ |

Lunch & dinner daily

Marin isn't known for a preponderance of great Thai restaurants, but Aroi-Dee is so outstanding that it would be destination-worthy even for those who live outside the charming enclave. Though its San Rafael space may be small and sparse, the welcome is warm and the flavors are bold and exciting.

Americanized staples are available, but they're best skipped in favor of intense, authentic plates that aren't toned down for Western palates. Try the knockout duck *larb* with bright herbs, sharp sliced red onion, and smoky, rich meat, or salmon steamed in banana leaves with a fragrant, mousse-like coconut curry custard. If you like it hot, opt for the spicy spare ribs, stir-fried with house-made chili paste, young green peppercorns, and silky eggplant.

229

Marin

# The Western Room

**A1**

Californian

1 Old Rancheria Rd. (at Nicasio Valley Rd.), Nicasio

**Phone:** 415-662-2219　　　　　　　　　　Dinner Wed – Sun
**Web:** www.thewesternroomatrancho.com
**Price:** $$$

Ron Siegel has left San Francisco and the Marin County dining scene is on cloud nine. Tucked inside Rancho Nicasio, The Western Room is elegant and rustic, with pretty wood accents, paintings of rustic country scenes, and colorful wild flowers dotting the room.

Siegel's menu employs excellent local and seasonal ingredients, directly listing the farms, ranches, and producers they're sourcing from. In fact, the chef's years of fine dining experience take the farm-to-table experience to new heights—and the result is simply extraordinary. Rabbit liver is decadently layered with almond cake and hibiscus gastrique gelée; while tender ravioli is filled with velvety corn purée, and paired with wilted chard, baby squash, and shiitake mushrooms.

# Valenti & Co.

**B2**

Italian

337 San Anselmo Ave. (bet. Pine St. & Woodland Ave.), San Anselmo

**Phone:** 415-454-7800　　　　　　　　　　Dinner Tue – Sun
**Web:** www.valentico.com
**Price:** $$$

Guests leave both their hearts and their hunger behind after a meal at this utterly captivating spot in cozy San Anselmo, where the chef busily prepares each dish from scratch in the back as his bubbly wife hugs regulars and ushers them inside. Adding to the quaint trattoria feel, fragrant blooms from the window boxes release their delicate scents into the dining room.

The bill of fare is largely Italian, with a few fun twists: house-made fettuccine is twirled in a shrimp bisque and topped with plump, sweet Hawaiian prawns, and tiramisu becomes "crunchymisu" when puff pastry is subbed for ladyfingers. But even simpler dishes, like flaky, moist griddled Mt. Lassen trout with braised fennel, radicchio, and tangy lemon emulsion, are full of flavor.

230

# Village Sake 🐾

Japanese ✗

**B2**

### 19 Bolinas Rd. (bet. Broadway Blvd. & Mono Ave.), Fairfax

**Phone:** 415-521-5790                    Dinner Wed – Mon
**Web:** www.villagesake.com
**Price:** **$$**

No need to cross the bridge any longer for authentic Japanese—Village Sake is delivering the *izakaya* goods in the heart of quaint Fairfax. All the classic small plates are in full force: crisp and creamy *takoyaki* (octopus croquettes), *okonomiyaki*, *tataki* (here made with silky smoked hamachi), and coconut mochi cake, complete with cardamom gelato. If you must have sushi, there's a small selection of excellent nigiri, too—make sure to sample the *shima aji* and *kinmedai*. The look of the room suggests Tokyo, with closely spaced tables, an array of wood accents (including a live-edge wood counter), as well as a friendly staff, many of them Japanese natives. It's a popular spot that doesn't take reservations, so expect long lines, especially on weekends.

Remember, stars
(✿✿✿...✿) are awarded
for cuisine only! Elements
such as service and décor
are not a factor.

# Peninsula

# Peninsula

## A COLLISION OF CULTURES

Situated to the south of the city, the San Francisco Peninsula separates the Bay from the expansive Pacific Ocean. While it may not be known across the globe for stellar chefs and pioneering Californian cooking, the Peninsula boasts an incredibly diverse and rich Asian culture. Local eateries and numerous markets reflect this region's melting-pot and continue to draw residents for authentic international cuisines. Those in need of a taste from the Far East should join Korean natives at **Kukje Super Market** as they scoop up fresh seafood, rolls of *gimbap*, and a host of other prepared delicacies. Alternatively, one may practice the art of chopstick wielding at one of the many Japanese sushi bars, ramen houses and *izakayas*. Filipino foodies tickle their fancy with an impressive selection of traditional breads and pastries at **Valerio's Tropical Bake Shop** in Daly City. Fittingly set in a Filipino-dominated quarter referred to as **"Little Manila,"** Valerio's is famously revered as *the* best bakery around.

Beyond the Far East, sugar junkies of the Western variety savor classic Danish pastries at Burlingame's **Copenhagen Bakery**, also applauded for creamy special occasion cakes. Over in San Mateo, Italians can't miss a stop

at **pasta pasta** for freshly made shapes, homemade sauces, and salads that are both fulfilling and easy to put together at home. If your domestic skills leave much to be desired, charming **La Biscotteria** has premium, hand-crafted Italian pastries and cookies on hand, including cannoli, *amaretti*, *sfogliatelle* and biscotti in an assortment of flavors. This precious gem in Redwood City also sells beautiful hand-painted Deruta ceramics that are imported directly from Umbria.

The Peninsula is also known for its large Mexican-American population. Their taste for home can be gratified at such authentic taquerias as **El Grullense** in Redwood City; **El Palenque** in San Mateo; and **Mexcal Taqueria** in Menlo Park. Just as **Gabriel & Daniel's Mexican Grill** in the Burlingame Golf Center clubhouse is an ideal place to unwind after playing a round out on the plush course, dive-y **Back A Yard** in Menlo Park is eternally beloved among foodies yearning for flavorful Caribbean cuisine. Pescetarians know that **Barbara's Fishtrap** in Princeton by the Sea is a sought-after "catch" for fish 'n chips by the harbor, whereas pig trumps fish at **Gorilla Barbeque**. Here, fat-frilled pork ribs are all the rage, especially when served out of an orange railroad car parked on Cabrillo Highway in Pacifica.

## SUMMER'S BOUNTY

In addition to harboring some of the Bay Area's most authentic Cantonese dens and dim sum houses, Millbrae is a lovely spot to raise one last toast to summer. In fact, **The Millbrae Art & Wine Festival** is a profusion of wicked fairground eats—from meltingly tender cheesesteaks and Cajun-style corndogs, to fennel-infused sausages and everything in between. Motivated home chefs head to **Draeger's Market** in San Mateo to pick up some wine and cheese for dinner, and perhaps even sign up for cooking classes in a range of basic to highly specialized subjects. Finally, when hanging out in this 'hood, be sure to revel in a riot of Japanese goods at **Suruki Market**.

Half Moon Bay is a coastal city big on sustainable produce; and in keeping with this philosophy, residents prepare for cozy evenings indoors by loading up on local fruits and vegetables from one of the many roadside stands on Route 92. Find them also scanning the bounty at **Coastside Farmer's Market**, which has been known to unveil such Pescadero treasures as Harley Farms goat cheese as well as organic eggs from **Early Bird Ranch**.

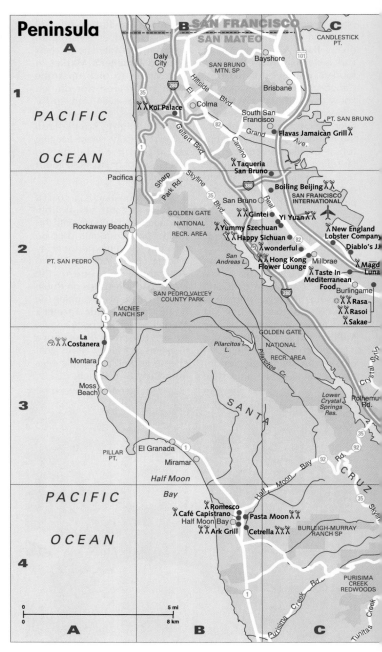

# Peninsula

**A**

**B** SAN FRANCISCO
SAN MATEO

**C**

CANDLESTICK PT.

PACIFIC

OCEAN

Daly City

San Bruno Mtn. SP

Bayshore

101

Brisbane

280

35

Hillside Blvd

El Camino

Koi Palace

Colma

South San Francisco

PT. SAN BRUNO

1

Gellert Blvd

Grand Ave.

Flavas Jamaican Grill

82

Pacifica

Sharp Park Rd.

Skyline Blvd

Taqueria San Bruno

380

Boiling Beijing

San Bruno

Real

SAN FRANCISCO INTERNATIONAL

Rockaway Beach

GOLDEN GATE NATIONAL RECR. AREA

35

Gintei

Yi Yuan

New England Lobster Company

PT. SAN PEDRO

Yummy Szechuan
Happy Sichuan

wonderful

Diablo's JJ

Magd Luna

2

San Andreas L.

82

Hong Kong Flower Lounge

Millbrae

Taste In Mediterranean Food

SAN PEDRO VALLEY COUNTY PARK

280

Burlingame

Rasa

MCNEE RANCH SP

Rasoi

Sakae

La Costanera

GOLDEN GATE

1

Montara

Pilarcitos L.

NATIONAL

RECR. AREA

Pilarcitos Cr.

Crystal Sgs

Moss Beach

3

S A N T A

Lower Crystal Springs Res.

Polhemu Rd.

35

PILLAR PT.

El Granada

1

92

92

Rd.

C R U Z

Miramar

Half Moon

Half Moon Bay

35

Skyline

PACIFIC

Bay

Romesco

Café Capistrano

Pasta Moon

OCEAN

Half Moon Bay

Cetrella

BURLEIGH-MURRAY RANCH SP

Ark Grill

4

PURISIMA CREEK REDWOODS

Purisima Creek Rd.

Tunitas Creek

0       5 mi
0       8 km

**A**

**B**

**C**

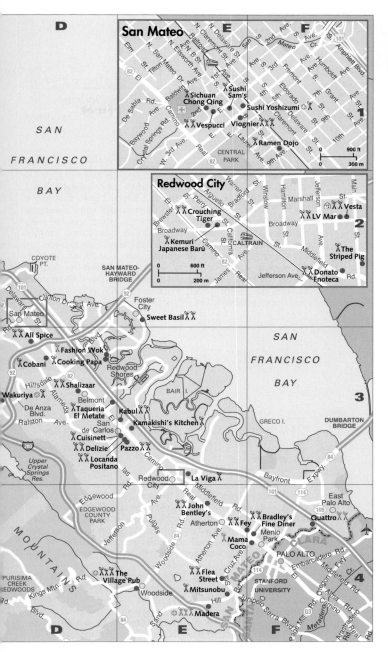

## San Mateo

Elm St.
N. Claremont St.
N. Ballroad
N. B St.
N. Delaware St.
N. San Mateo Dr.
N. El Camino Real
N. Ellsworth Ave.
De Sabla Rd.
Tilton Ave.
Baywood Ave.
Baldwin Ave.
Crystal Springs Rd.
W. 3rd Ave.
W. 2nd Ave.
1st Ave.
S. B St.
2nd Ave.
3rd Ave.
4th Ave.
5th Ave.
6th Ave.
7th Ave.
8th Ave.
9th Ave.
Delaware St.
Claremont St.
E. Laurel Ave.
S. Railroad Ave.
S. Claremont St.
N. 2nd Ave.
San Mateo Ave.
Fremont St.
Eldorado St.
10th Ave.
Humboldt St.
Amphlett Blvd.
Grant St.
101

**Sushi Sam's**
**Sichuan Chong Qing**
**Vespucci**
**Viognier**
**Sushi Yoshizumi**
**Ramen Dojo**

CENTRAL PARK
82

0    900 ft
0    300 m

## Redwood City

Warren St.
Brewster St.
Arguello St.
Bradford St.
Winslow St.
Hamilton St.
Marshall St.
Jefferson Ave.
Main St.
El Camino Real
Perry St.
Broadway
California St.
Broadway
Middlefield Rd.
James Ave.
Jefferson Ave.

**Crouching Tiger**
**Kemuri Japanese Barü**
**Vesta**
**LV Mar**
**The Striped Pig**
**Donato Enoteca**

CALTRAIN
82

0    600 ft
0    200 m

SAN FRANCISCO BAY

COYOTE PT.

SAN MATEO-HAYWARD BRIDGE

San Mateo
101
Delawards Rd.

Clinton Dr.  3rd Ave.
92
Foster City
**Sweet Basil**

**All Spice**

**Fashion Wok**
**Cobani**  **Cooking Papa**
Blvd.
Redwood Shores

Hillsdale
82
**Shalizaar**
**Wakuriya**
De Anza Blvd.
Belmont
Ralston Ave.
Alameda
280
**Taqueria El Metate**
San Carlos
**Cuisinett**
**Delizie**  **Pazzo**
**Locanda Positano**
**Kabul**
**Kamakishi's Kitchen**

BAIR I.

SAN FRANCISCO BAY

GRECO I.

DUMBARTON BRIDGE

84

Redwood City
**La Viga**
Camino

Bayfront
101
114
East Palo Alto
109

Upper Crystal Springs Res.

Edgewood Ave.
EDGEWOOD COUNTY PARK
Jefferson Ave.
Pulgas
Woodside Rd.
Atherton Ave.
84
**John Bentley's**
Atherton
**Fey**
**Bradley's Fine Diner**
Menlo Park
**Mama Coco**
**Quattro**
114
Middlefield Rd.
Embarcadero Rd.

PALO ALTO

SANTA CLARA

PURISIMA CREEK REDWOODS
MOUNTAINS
Kings Mtn. Rd.
**The Village Pub**
Woodside
**Flea Street**
**Mitsunobu**
Cruz Ave.
**Madera**
Hill
STANFORD UNIVERSITY
Junipero Serra Blvd.
SAN MATEO
Page Mill Rd.
Oregon Expwy.
Alma St.
Middlefield Rd.
El Camino Real
Arastradero Rd.
G3
84

237

# All Spice

International ✗✗

**D3**

1602 El Camino Real (bet. Barneson & Borel Aves.), San Mateo

**Phone:** 650-627-4303        Dinner nightly
**Web:** www.allspicerestaurant.com
**Price:** $$$

Set in a beautifully restored Victorian, All Spice feels like the most exquisite home in town. Each brightly colored room is set with fine linens, as large windows usher in light. It's a magical setting for a date, among a happy crowd that never seems too serious. Chef Sachin Chopra and wife, Shoshana Wolff, have created a "New American Exotic" cuisine with ingredients from around the globe. It may sound terribly conceptual, but fits the unique dining experience to a tee.

International tastes are on display with "*tandoori*" octopus set over a streak of earthy lentil purée with an Indian-spiced chickpea salad dressed in yogurt. Finish with tropical desserts like the spectacular coconut-*pandan* jellyroll cake, or cardamom *kulfi* with smooth dark chocolate.

# Ark Grill

Indian ✗✗

**B4**

724 Main St. (bet. Correas & Filbert St.), Half Moon Bay

**Phone:** 650-560-8152        Lunch & dinner Tue – Sun
**Web:** www.arkgrill.com
**Price:** $$

Like Indiana Jones' coveted treasure, this Ark can only be found by those in the know—and since it's off the main tourist drag in Half Moon Bay, the locals mostly have it to themselves. It's the kind of place where bringing a group (kids included) pays dividends, as you'll be able to sample more of the delicious North Indian fare, which boasts exceptionally high-quality ingredients.

Check out the Bollywood films projected on the wall as you savor crisp and flaky potato samosas; smoky and caramelized *tandoori* chicken; plump shrimp in a tangy, richly spiced *vindaloo*; and creamy *dal* fry starring yellow lentils and stewed tomatoes. Spice levels can be adjusted, but most dishes are mild—and fluffy naan is at hand to scoop up the curries.

# Boiling Beijing

Chinese
Chinese ✗✗

**C2**

649 San Mateo Ave. (bet. Angus & Kains Aves.), San Bruno

**Phone:** 650-952-3388

**Web:** www.boilingbeijing.net

**Price:** $$

Lunch & dinner daily

Those who love to gather around a steaming Chinese hot pot will bubble with excitement for this San Bruno treasure, which serves up its richly layered and delectable broths in beautiful enamel cloisonné pots bedecked with flowers and birds. On a frosty day (by Bay Area standards), Chinese families cluster around the sizable tabletops to sip and dip, twirling a variety of vegetables, meats, and fish in the simmering cauldrons.

Not in the mood for hot pot? Beijing's menu boils over into other Northern Chinese specialties, like smoky, fatty, twice-cooked pork, wok-fried and tossed with crisp bamboo shoots and chopped chilies. Another winner is the flaky, crispy fried pancake stuffed with ground beef, ginger, garlic, scallions, and a touch of sesame oil.

# Bradley's Fine Diner

American ✗✗

**F4**

1165 Merrill St. (at Oak Grove Ave.), Menlo Park

**Phone:** 650-494-4342

**Web:** www.bradleysfinediner.com

**Price:** $$$

Lunch & dinner Tue – Sun

Like a grown-up greasy spoon, this offspring from award-winning chef, Bradley Ogden, updates American favorites with quality ingredients and a dash of creativity. A delightful riff on Buffalo wings pairs crispy chunks of pork belly with a luscious Maytag blue cheese soufflé, while free-range chicken breast arrives moist and juicy, accompanied by a squash-centric panzanella. A piping-hot apple cobbler and killer butterscotch pudding are some of the stars on the dessert menu.

The sizable space has hip touches that appeal to the crowd of affluent Atherton locals, like a wood art piece embedded with chef's knives, a glowing neon sign, and wraparound porches for warm nights. For a classy yet unfussy night out, Bradley's is a fine choice indeed.

# Café Capistrano

Mexican ✗

**B4**

523 Church St. (at Miramontes St.), Half Moon Bay

**Phone:** 650-726-7699
**Web:** N/A
**Price:** 💰

Lunch & dinner daily

Chef/owner Arturo Mul grew up on the Yucatán peninsula, and the traditional Mayan dishes of his youth are now the backbone of this cute café in the heart of Half Moon Bay. Housed in an older home surrounded by gardens and a small side deck, the spot is warm, homey, and, to the delight of local families, off most tourists' radars.

Start with a Yucatecan appetizer plate of *salbutes* (fried tortillas topped with grilled chicken, pickled onion, and cabbage slaw) and empanadas. Then dig into the smoky pork enchiladas, crowned with cheese and garlicky red chili sauce, or the tender grilled chicken adobo. Be cautious with the house-made habanero sauce: its Mayan name, *xni-pec*, means "dog nose" and it'll have yours running if you exceed a few drops.

# Cetrella

Mediterranean ✗✗✗

**B4**

845 Main St. (at Monte Vista Ln.), Half Moon Bay

**Phone:** 650-726-4090
**Web:** www.cetrella.com
**Price:** $$$

Lunch Sun
Dinner Tue – Sun

What it lacks in million-dollar ocean views, Cetrella more than makes up for in charm. One of the most elegant and stylish restaurants along the coast, it's housed in a stunning Mediterranean-style villa with exposed trusses and skylights, a roaring central fireplace, and a humming exhibition kitchen. Throw in warm, welcoming service, and you'll never want to leave.

Seasonal Californian ingredients get a Mediterranean spin here, and nightly specials like a warm Brussels sprouts salad with wood-smoked salmon or roasted pork chop with porcini mushrooms, heirloom carrots, and smoked ham jus are transcendent. This is definitely a meal worth dressing up for, so be sure to swap your beachwear for something more sophisticated before setting foot inside.

# Cobani

Mediterranean ✗

**8 W. 25th Ave. (bet. El Camino Real & Flores St.), San Mateo**

**Phone:** 650-389-6861
**Web:** www.cobanigyro.com
**Price:** 🥜

Lunch & dinner daily

Just south of downtown San Mateo, this fast-casual Turkish spot is a favorite with the locals. Lunch hour brings a crowd—think nine-to-fivers and families with kids—and the modus operandi is simple: order at the counter, grab a number and utensils, and take a seat in the cheerful dining room, adorned with a colorful mural depicting a Turkish village.

The kitchen churns out a mix of Turkish, Mediterranean, and Middle Eastern items: you'll find an *adana* kebab—made of spicy, charbroiled minced lamb and beef—that's worthy of Istanbul. Then, look forward to shaved chicken gyros wrapped in lavash, followed by crispy falafel with baba ghanoush. And the skilled kitchen's take on *künefe*, a traditional dessert of mild white cheese broiled with syrupy pastry, is superlative.

# Cooking Papa

Chinese ✗

**949 Edgewater Blvd., Ste. A (at Beach Park Blvd.), Foster City**

**Phone:** 650-577-1830
**Web:** www.mycookingpapa.com
**Price:** 🥜

Lunch & dinner daily

Cantonese and Hong Kong-style dishes draw weekend crowds to the sleek and minimally adorned Cooking Papa, set back in a shopping center alongside one of the Foster City canals. Inside, find expats clustered around faux-granite tables armed with dark wood chairs and framed by a wall of windows running the length of the space. Every seat has a glorious water view.

The vast menu features all types of dishes, from simple, heart-warming rice noodle rolls with bitter melon and shredded chicken to crispy and intensely moist roasted duck served with a sweet chili sauce. Americanized standards have been known to disappoint, so it's best to follow the locals and think outside the box—subtle and satisfying pea sprouts sautéed with minced garlic come to mind.

# Crouching Tiger

Chinese ✗✗

**2644 Broadway St. (bet. El Camino Real & Perry St.), Redwood City**

**Phone:** 650-298-8881                    Lunch & dinner daily
**Web:** www.crouchingtigerrestaurant.com
**Price:** ⊜⊜

   ♿

The heat is on at Redwood City's palace of Sichuan fare, where spice-hounds come for a dose of the chili-packed Chongqing chicken, *mapo* tofu, and other regional specialties. Sure, there may be blander options, but steaming platters of green chili-topped, richly flavored cumin lamb or plump prawns and crisp sautéed vegetables in hot garlic sauce are enough to induce a love of spice.

Crouching Tiger's midday crowd can be its own fire-breathing dragon, with droves of local workers packing the tables for reasonably priced lunch specials with soup, salad, and rice. Large, round tables are great for big groups (kids too). The chic interior with its dark wood furnishings, art, and drum lanterns, is definitely a step up from the standard Chinese joint.

# Cuisinett

French ✗

**1105 San Carlos Ave. (bet. El Camino Real & Laurel St.), San Carlos**

**Phone:** 650-453-3390                              Lunch daily
**Web:** www.cuisinett.com                      Dinner Mon – Sat
**Price:** $$

   ♿
   🏠

French restaurants aren't often known for their chill vibe or affordability, but this counter-service charmer proves otherwise, with classic comfort foods like quiches, salads, and *plats* that are all available at down-to-earth prices. Diners customize with mix-and-match sauces like Dijon mustard or Cognac black pepper to pair with a steak and choice of sides. Families, kids, and those with pets in tow can be seen nibbling on refreshing *crevettes Basquaise* tossed with spicy paprika and sweet onions; or crispy skinned *poulet rôti* served in sauce *champignons* and accompanied by a delicately dressed *salade verte*. Note: there will be butter.

For that final bit of sweet, a creamy and luscious crème brûlée topped with a caramelized sugar shell is *très bien*.

# Delizie

Italian ✗✗

**E3**

**1107 San Carlos Ave. (bet. El Camino Real & Laurel St.), San Carlos**

**Phone:** 650-486-1539
**Web:** www.deliziesc.com
**Price:** $$

Lunch & dinner Mon – Sat

The name of this Southern Italian gem means "delicious," and its authentic fare delivers on the moniker. All credit goes to the owner, a native of Calabria who works hard to ensure that the welcome here is as warm and the house-made pastas as delectable as those of the Old Country.

Settle in under the twinkling chandeliers in the intimate space—nestled in the heart of San Carlos, just steps from the Caltrain station—then summon a plate of perfectly cooked pappardelle in a tomato-kissed wild boar ragù. Move on to an indulgently cheesy gratin of baked cauliflower (under its crisp breadcrumb topping lies a touch of cream sauce), before finishing with bittersweet cappuccino mousse, served over coffee sponge cake and crowned by a chocolate-coated coffee bean.

# Diablo's JJ

Mexican ✗

**C2**

**1302 Old Bayshore Hwy. (near Airport Blvd.), Burlingame**

**Phone:** 650-513-1706
**Web:** N/A
**Price:** ⊜⊘

Lunch & dinner Tue – Sun

It may be located in a blighted industrial area just south of the airport, but this hidden gem of a family-run taqueria could make you reconsider that flight to Mexico. Whether you're tucking into an oozing quesadilla stuffed with caramelized bell peppers and onions, supremely tender *al pastor* taco, or the house specialty—fiery *camarones del Diablo*—the menu is flavorful and fairly priced.

In addition to its excellent house-made salsas, Diablo's has yet another secret sauce: knockout customer service. The gracious staff loves to treat kids to free impromptu sweets, and repeat visitors are greeted like family. With food this sumptuous and staff this friendly, you'll find it easy to look past the parking-lot patio and picnic-table seating.

# Donato Enoteca

Italian

**F2**

**1041 Middlefield Rd. (bet. Jefferson Ave. & Main St.), Redwood City**

**Phone:** 650-701-1000
**Web:** www.donatoenoteca.com
**Price:** $$

Lunch & dinner daily

Set in Redwood City's sleek downtown, this Italian jewel draws lunching lawyers and civic workers from the nearby courthouses by day, and couples as well as families at dusk. The restaurant is spacious, with a patio boasting Sunbrellas and heat lamps, two dining rooms, and a large bar. Meanwhile, its rustic, wood-centric décor is glammed up with thick rugs and gilded mirrors.

An array of pastas, wood-fired pizzas, salads, and meat dishes will please diners of all stripes, whether they opt for the house-made *agnolotti del plin* in a tomato-onion ragù, or the roasted chicken in a buttery jus with green Bosana olives. Lingering in the laid-back environs is always encouraged, especially to savor the creamy melon semifreddo with candied almonds.

# Fashion Wok

Chinese

**D3**

**929A Edgewater Blvd. (near Shell Blvd.), Foster City**

**Phone:** 650-358-8820
**Web:** www.fashionwok.co
**Price:** 

Lunch & dinner daily

Chinese hot pot is usually a group activity, making it difficult for solo diners to partake. But this waterside spot does a solid for the singletons, serving up individually sized pots so packed with ingredients that only the most heroic appetite will be able to finish them. From the Sichuan high wok to the fisherman's kimchi wok, each bowl boasts no fewer than ten meats, seafoods, and vegetables.

The hearty food is manna to a hungry lunch crowd of young professionals, most of whom visit the lovely patio for an alfresco meal paired with a *boba* tea or juice. Families arrive at dinner, as do boaters, who tie right up to the dock outside. No matter when you come, allow plenty of time to dine: it's a popular spot, and waits are all but assured.

# Fey

Chinese XX

**E4**

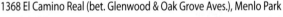

**1368 El Camino Real (bet. Glenwood & Oak Grove Aves.), Menlo Park**

**Phone:** 650-324-8888                    Lunch & dinner daily
**Web:** www.feyrestaurant.com
**Price:** $$

"Glitzy" isn't a word commonly used to describe Sichuan restaurants, but with its glamorous chandeliers and metallic wall art, Fey's interior is exactly that. The crowd follows suit, with Chinese investors conducting big negotiations alongside families dressed to the nines.

Though Westernized food is on offer, diners who order Sichuan dishes—like wok-fried Chongqing chicken buried under piles of dried chilies, or chili oil-drenched *mapo* tofu topped with ground pork—are rewarded with exceptional service and traditional spice. Ease the burn with hot black tea, then dive back into cold wheat noodles tossed with pork, cucumber, ground peanuts, and more chili oil, before heading to your car in the lot out back (an asset on this busy stretch of El Camino).

# Flavas Jamaican Grill

Jamaican X

**C1**

**314 Linden Ave. (at 4th Ln.), South San Francisco**

**Phone:** 650-244-9785                    Lunch & dinner Mon – Sat
**Web:** www.flavasjamaicangrill.com
**Price:** ⬜

South San Francisco has never been a restaurant hot spot, but this rookie could be a sign of things to come. The secret is already out among residents and Genentech employees, who fill the casual space for its good food, gracious service, and groovy reggae beats.

Flavas is decorated with basic furnishings and ocean-themed art, but its appeal is right there in the name. Authentic dishes brim with herbs, garlic, and Scotch Bonnet peppers, like the smoky and boldly spiced jerk chicken with caramelized fried plantains; or bready morsels of *ackee* cooked with salt cod and coupled with pickled cabbage and carrot. Make sure to keep an eye out for their intriguing daily specials, which may reveal jerk shrimp, snapper, and other island staples.

# Flea Street

**E4**

Californian ✗✗

**3607 Alameda de las Pulgas (at Avy Ave.), Menlo Park**

Phone: 650-854-1226
Web: www.cooleatz.com
Price: $$$

Dinner Tue – Sun

A pioneer in the locally sourced, sustainable movement, this intimate spot remains a die-hard darling with the older, moneyed Atherton crowd, who flood the space for special occasions and date nights. The petite dining rooms are quaint and homey, with linen-covered tabletops and flickering votive candles, and those alfresco sidewalk tables are hot tickets whenever the mercury rises.

Prepare to ponder "which came first?" with a dish of pasture-raised roast chicken over sautéed fiddlehead ferns, accompanied by a rich, soft-poached farm egg that enlivens its sherry jus. Moist, flaky house-smoked trout with horseradish crème fraîche begs to be scooped up by the accompanying waffle potato chips, and tangy lemon cake is a must for dessert.

# Gintei

**C2**

Japanese ✗✗

**235 El Camino Real (bet. Crystal Springs Rd. & San Felipe Ave.), San Bruno**

Phone: 650-636-4135
Web: www.gintei.co
Price: $$$

Lunch Tue – Fri
Dinner Tue – Sun

San Bruno's rep as a dining wasteland is due for a re-evaluation thanks to this sleek and stylish sushi spot, whose offerings can hang with the best in San Francisco. Bright and contemporary, with dramatic pressed-tin ceilings and a coveted eight-seat sushi counter, it's known as a reservations-required must for omakase enthusiasts, with deeply hospitable service.

Newbies to nigiri should make a beeline for the omakase, but the more experienced palate will revel in market specials like silky Hokkaido scallops, sweet and succulent live spot prawns (with the traditional deep-fried heads alongside), and firm yet tender octopus. Everything is minimally dressed—all the better to accentuate the fish's outstanding quality.

# Happy Sichuan

Chinese XX

C2

**1055 El Camino Real (at Meadow Glen Ave.), Millbrae**

**Phone:** 650-692-8858  
**Web:** N/A  
**Price:** $$

Lunch & dinner daily

The closure of several top Sichuan spots has saddened Peninsula diners in recent years, but Happy Sichuan is a worthy successor. Simply and minimally decorated, it won't win prizes for looks or surroundings (it's housed in a Millbrae strip mall), but servers are friendly and flavors appropriately bold.

Skip the milquetoast Americanized dishes and head straight for the menu's "Specialties" section, where you'll encounter the absolutely enormous hot pot—a flavorful, rich broth full of beef, chicken, lamb, and soft tofu. The magic chicken earns its name thanks to a crisp, chili-inflected coating, and the spicy cold wheat noodles with cucumber are a delight. With fiery fare this good and plentiful, you're sure to leave, well, happy.

# Hong Kong Flower Lounge

Chinese XX

C2

**51 Millbrae Ave. (at El Camino Real), Millbrae**

**Phone:** 650-692-6666  
**Web:** www.mayflower-seafood.com  
**Price:** $$

Lunch & dinner daily

Generations of dim sum diehards have patronized this palace of pork buns, where a small army of servers will throng you with carts from the moment you take your seat. They bear innumerable delights: rich barbecue pork belly with crispy skin, pan-fried pork-and-chive wontons steamed to order and doused in oyster sauce, delicate vegetable dumplings, and a best-in-class baked egg custard bun. Evenings are a bit more sedate, emphasizing Cantonese seafood straight from the on-site tanks.

As with all dim sum spots, the early bird gets the best selection (and avoids the non-negligible weekend waits). Thankfully, the super-central Millbrae location, towering over El Camino Real, boasts plenty of parking—and a machine-like staff that knows how to pack them in.

# John Bentley's

Peninsula

Contemporary XX

2915 El Camino Real (bet. Berkshire Ave. & Selby Ln.), Redwood City

**Phone:** 650-365-7777

**Web:** www.johnbentleys.com

**Price:** $$

Lunch Mon – Fri
Dinner Mon – Sat

A vine-covered trellis walkway leads to this stately spot, located on a quiet, somewhat hidden stretch of El Camino Real. Inside the quaint tavern, whose dark wood wainscoting and oil paintings recall an earlier era of power-lunching, business people and locals alike can be found savoring the contemporary American cooking.

The grilled watermelon Napoleon, layered with avocado, spicy jicama, and rich crab salad, is a favorite for lovers of lighter food, while those seeking richer sustenance should beeline for the sweetbreads in a rich, creamy veal sauce, accompanied by mashed potatoes and green beans. For dessert, a classic puff-pastry apple tart with a scoop of homemade ice cream—boasting a dried cherry surprise—hits the spot.

# Kabul

Afghan XX

135 El Camino Real (bet. F & Holly Sts.), San Carlos

**Phone:** 650-594-2840

**Web:** www.kabul-cuisine.com

**Price:** $$

Lunch Mon –Fri
Dinner nightly

Fans of Afghan cuisine flock from miles around to this homestyle spot in San Carlos, tucked away in a deceptively large space within a modest shopping plaza. Kabul's walls are festooned with deep red tapestries and other Afghan embroidery, and even on weekday nights it fills up with local families. There's even a semi-private side dining room for big groups.

The friendly staff is happy to suggest favorite dishes, from smoky chicken and lamb kabobs over spiced basmati rice to sweet, fork-tender sautéed pumpkin served with a garlicky yogurt sauce and fluffy flatbread. And though everything comes in generous portions, you'll want to save room for the *firnee*, a gently sweet milk pudding flavored with cardamom and rosewater and topped with pistachios.

# Kamakshi's Kitchen

Indian ✗

**E3**

601 Old County Rd. (at San Carlos Ave.), San Carlos

**Phone:** 650-401-6564
**Web:** www.kamakshiskitchen.com
**Price:** 🍴

Lunch Tue – Sun
Dinner Tue – Sat

Vegetarians will go gaga for this ultra-authentic South Indian restaurant, whose humble space facing the San Carlos Caltrain tracks turns out 100-percent meat-free food. Thankfully, butter chicken and biryani are nowhere in sight; instead, find explosively spicy dishes like chickpea batter-fried stuffed jalapeño fritters, dosas loaded with chili-flecked paneer, and savory *uttapams* that rule the day. All of these eats are sided by tasty coconut and toasted sesame chutneys.

Kamakshi's space and menu are both compact, with only a smattering of tables dotting the dining room and sidewalk. The no-frills hot spot has become a favorite with the workaday office crowd in the area, so expect a wait at peak lunch hours. For a quieter experience, stop by for dinner.

# Kemuri Japanese Barú

Asian ✗

**E2**

2616 Broadway (bet. El Camino Real & Perry St.), Redwood City

**Phone:** 650-257-7653
**Web:** www.kemuri-baru.com
**Price:** $$

Lunch Tue – Fri
Dinner Tue – Sun

You'll feel like you've strolled into a hip Tokyo nightspot when you enter Kemuri, which blends funky takes on *izakaya* dishes and a selection of Japanese-influenced craft beer and cocktails into a young, lively package. The spacious, industrial room—think bar shelves made of pipes and water spouts—is always abuzz with twenty-somethings who pack in at the communal wooden tables.

The menu is loaded with Japanese mashups that seem unusual but taste terrific, like a burger with "buns" made of griddled rice balls and stuffed with seared albacore, as well as a runny but perfectly tart sauce. Chilled poke udon, featuring marinated fish and sliced avocado, comes atop cold noodles complete with a barely poached egg, and even the crème brûlée is spiked with green tea.

# Koi Palace

Chinese  ✕✕

### 365 Gellert Blvd. (bet. Hickey & Serramonte Blvds.), Daly City

**Phone:** 650-992-9000                                   Lunch & dinner daily
**Web:** www.koipalace.com
**Price:** $$

Long regarded as one of the Bay Area's best spots for dim sum, Koi Palace continues to earn its serious waits (guaranteed on weekends, and common at weekday lunch). The dining room is a step up from its competition, with shallow koi ponds weaving between tables, high ceilings, and huge tables to accommodate the Chinese-American families celebrating big occasions.

They come to share plates of perfectly lacquered, smoky-salty roasted suckling pig or sticky rice noodle rolls encasing plump shrimp, sesame oil, and minced ginger. Not far behind, find lotus leaves stuffed with glutinous rice, dried scallop, and roast pork, as well as big pots of jasmine tea. Save room for desserts like the fluffy almond cream steamed buns and flaky, caramelized custard tarts.

# La Costanera 🍴

Peruvian  ✕✕

### 8150 Cabrillo Hwy. (bet. 1st & 2nd Sts.), Montara

**Phone:** 650-728-1600                                        Dinner Tue – Sun
**Web:** www.lacostanerarestaurant.com
**Price:** $$

Set atop one of the most beautiful perches in the entire Bay Area, this bungalow boasts a gorgeous patio and a dining room that's walled with windows.

While the panoramas are amazing—endless ocean, spectacular sunsets, and even frolicking dolphins if you're lucky—so are the boldly flavored plates produced by Chef Carlos Altamirano and his team. A *cebiche* tasting is the best way to experience Peru's national dish, while cool and creamy *causas*, perhaps topped with lobster and salmon roe, or garlicky *anticucho de camarones* hit with zesty *aji amarillo* and salsa verde are other treasures worth devouring.

Be sure to sample the creative cocktails. Alternatively, try a delicious and refreshing *chicha morada*, which is safer for the drive home.

# La Viga

Mexican ✗

**E3**

1772 Broadway (bet. Beech & Maple Sts.), Redwood City

**Phone:** 650-679-8141  Lunch & dinner Tue – Sun
**Web:** www.lavigarestaurant.com
**Price:** 💰

Named after Mexico City's massive seafood market, La Viga is a Redwood City favorite for oceanic fare with a Latin twist. Wedged between an industrial area and downtown, the basic but cheerful dining room draws both blue- and white-collar workers for heaping tacos—soft white corn tortillas stuffed with fried snapper fillet, cabbage, and chipotle *crema*; or crisp prawns with tomatillo-garlic sauce and *pico de gallo*. At the dinner hour, local residents stream in for the famed *camarones picantes*, a sizable mound of al dente *fideos* studded with plump prawns bathed in a spicy tomato sauce. With such fresh ingredients and bold flavors, the low prices and generous portions are particularly pleasing—be sure to allow room for a creamy, delicate flan to finish.

# Locanda Positano

Italian ✗✗

**E3**

617 Laurel St. (bet. Cherry St. & San Carlos Ave.), San Carlos

**Phone:** 650-591-5700  Lunch & dinner daily
**Web:** www.locanda-positano.com
**Price:** $$

Take a trip to the south of Italy by way of this casual Italian meal along the quaint San Carlos strip. Owned by a native and staffed mostly by Italians, this is a favorite among locals craving seasonal cuisine. The menu draws inspiration from the owner's mother, *mamma* Carmela, whose recipes have been known to draw a fan following. Start with the San Daniele pizza topped with tomato, mozzarella, arugula and prosciutto. Then, dive into gnocchi Sorrentina, served in a tangy sauce seasoned with garlic and oregano. Desserts don't disappoint either, especially *mamma's pastiera Napoletana*, a ricotta tart decked with powdered sugar and a single strawberry rose.

The sleek room with contemporary furnishings feels grown-up, but is far from low-key.

# LV Mar

 **F2**

Latin American ✗✗

2042 Broadway (bet. Jefferson Ave. & Main St.), Redwood City

**Phone:** 650-241-3111          Lunch & dinner daily
**Web:** www.chefmanuelmartinez.com
**Price:** $$

Located just a few blocks from its casual cousin La Viga, LV Mar is worlds away in terms of cuisine, offering sophisticated contemporary Latin American fare. The space is appropriately stylish, with slate floors, high ceilings, and paintings of ingredients on the walls. Business lunchers fill the tables by day, giving way to couples and families in the evening.

Local produce shines in dishes like the *pescado con pepitas*, a flaky sea bass fillet encrusted in pumpkin seeds and served over buttery *huitlacoche*-potato purée. The *gordita de pato* encases rich duck meat in a golden puff pastry with port and dried cherries, while caramelized Brussels sprouts boast a Manchego and *chile de arbol* vinaigrette. For the time-pressed, tortas are available at lunch.

# Magda Luna

**C2**

Mexican ✗

1199 Broadway, Ste. 2 (bet. Chula Vista & Laguna Aves.), Burlingame

**Phone:** 650-393-4207          Lunch & dinner Tue – Sun
**Web:** www.magdalunacafe.com
**Price:**

"Mexican food with a clean conscience" is on the menu at this Burlingame café, which prides itself on vegetable-heavy, oil-light dishes made with hormone-free, sustainably raised meats. Located on the main drag, this restaurant is full of color and authentic details like decorative murals of Dia de los Muertos-style skulls. A welcoming staff and special menu for *los niños* also make it an ideal choice for families.

Though healthy, the food here never skimps on flavor. Start with a cup of *pozole* stocked with shredded chicken, cabbage, and creamy avocado slices before delving into a crispy *sope* topped with *carnitas*, *salsa fresca*, and a drizzle of sour cream. Then enjoy the *huarache* with beans, carne asada, and cactus salad, or *enchiladas suizas*, which are at once filling and heartwarming.

# Madera ⁕

Contemporary 𝕏𝕏𝕏

**E4**

### 2825 Sand Hill Rd. (at I-280), Menlo Park

| | | |
|---|---|---|
| **Phone:** | 650-561-1540 | Lunch & dinner daily |
| **Web:** | www.maderasandhill.com | |
| **Price:** | **$$$$** | |

As evidenced by all those Teslas parked out front, this is a swanky spot for fine-dining in the Rosewood Sand Hill hotel. The grand open kitchen, roaring fireplace, and large outdoor patio complete with gorgeous views of the Santa Cruz mountains draw a moneyed crowd of local techies.

While its location inside a hotel may mean it is open for three meals a day, come for dinner to taste this kitchen's ambition and pure talent. The cuisine is contemporary, thoughtfully composed with seasonal ingredients, and even surprising at times. An excellent risotto sings with the flavors of roasted butternut squash, Perigord black truffles, airy Lacinato kale chips, and the unexpected, wondrous touch of finger lime. The kitchen also flaunts its dexterity in three preparations of guinea hen, including tender breast meat with crackling-crisp skin, sliced thigh, and excellent springy sausages accompanied by charred peaches bursting with sweetness, pickled chanterelles, toasted pecans, and smooth green onion soubise.

Desserts are fun, delicious, and do not hold back, especially the insanely rich peanut butter and black sesame parfait, layered as fudgy brownie, ganache, mousse, and brittle in a glass goblet.

# Mama Coco

F4

**1081 El Camino Real (bet. Menlo & Santa Cruz Aves.), Menlo Park**

**Phone:** 650-272-6634

**Web:** www.mamacocinamexicana.com

**Price:** ⓔⓢ

Lunch & dinner Mon – Sat

 ♿  ☂️

If the quality of the recipes she handed down to her grandkids' family-run restaurant is any indication, Mama Coco was one heck of a cook. Made with top-notch ingredients and never heavy or oily, her chewy, caramelized *masa sopitos* and *huaraches* arrive stuffed with black beans, house-made salsa, shredded red chile chicken, and other goodies, while the smoky enchiladas spotlight salty jack cheese contrasted with crunchy cabbage.

Located in the heart of downtown Menlo Park, the welcoming spot boasts two big and colorful dining rooms, but its real star is the spacious back patio, strung with twinkling lights for a delightful alfresco experience. We may not all be lucky enough to have a Mama Coco in our lives, but at least we can enjoy her food.

# Mitsunobu

E4

**325 Sharon Park Dr., Ste. A-2 (at Sand Hill Rd.), Menlo Park**

**Phone:** 650-234-1084

**Web:** www.rmitsunobu.com

**Price:** $$$

Lunch Tue – Fri
Dinner Tue – Sun

 ♿

This tiny, nondescript spot may seem a bit plain amidst the ritzy shops and restaurants of Menlo Park, but it's well worth checking out for authentic Japanese fare. The top-notch nigiri selection includes sweet, creamy *ebi*, ultra-fresh uni, and buttery scallops, while a small offering of seasonal maki includes a "spring roll" packed with salmon, shrimp, squid, striped jack, and avocado, then topped with Japanese "Hollandaise."

Time-pressed lunchers should opt for the affordable prix-fixe sets with sashimi or *chirashi*, while a more luxurious experience can be had in the evening, when a seasonal kaiseki is offered alongside the à la carte menu. Sweet, professional service at all times only adds to Mitsunobu's hidden-gem vibe.

# New England Lobster Company

Seafood ✗

**C2**

824 Cowan Rd. (off Old Bayshore Hwy.), Burlingame

**Phone:** 650-443-1559        Lunch daily
**Web:** www.newenglandlobster.net      Dinner Tue – Sat
**Price:** $$

You'll know your meal is fresh at this Peninsula palace of seafood, where flat-screen TVs showcase the bevy of crustaceans in their huge seawater holding tanks. Set in an industrial warehouse, NELC is both a fish market and a counter-service restaurant—complete with a nautical theme, picnic tables indoors and out, and a happy crowd of young and old diners donning lobster bibs.

Kick things off with the justifiably beloved lobster-corn chowder, thick with sweet, succulent meat in a rich and creamy—but not overly heavy—stock. (For dedicated fans, frozen to-go quarts are offered.) Then go for broke with the outstanding lobster roll, lightly dressed with mayo on a fluffy, buttery roll and accompanied by excellent house-made potato chips.

# Pasta Moon

Italian ✗✗

**B4**

315 Main St. (bet. Mill St. & Stone Pine Rd.), Half Moon Bay

**Phone:** 650-726-5125        Lunch & dinner daily
**Web:** www.pastamoon.com
**Price:** $$

One of Half Moon Bay's most popular restaurants, Pasta Moon is always packed to the gills with locals and tourists filling up on massive portions of hearty Italian-American fare. With its vaulted ceilings, pops of bright red, and multiple intimate dining rooms, it's a hit with diners of all ages, especially those seated at tables with a view of the lovely side garden.

House-made pastas steal the show, with tempting options like the delicate 30-layer lasagna filled with ricotta, parmesan, and house Sicilian sausage. A grilled pork chop stuffed with peaches, pancetta, and caramelized onions arrives with mascarpone mashed potatoes. The butterscotch pudding (with shards of Ghirardelli chocolate, natch) is bound to send you over the moon.

# Pazzo

Pizza

1179 Laurel St. (bet. Brittan & Greenwood Aves.), San Carlos

**Phone:** 650-591-1075
**Web:** www.pazzosancarlos.com
**Price:** $$

Dinner Mon – Sat

New Haven transplants longing for the region's signature chewy, charred *apizza* will find a taste of home at this San Carlos jewel, which churns out authentically blistered pies. Keep it traditional with red sauce topped with house-made fennel sausage and crimini mushrooms. Or go slightly Californian with the garlicky asparagus pie, draped with creamy crescenza cheese.

*Pazzo* (Italian for "crazy") is anything but, thanks to a relaxed, family-friendly vibe. Kids of all ages will delight in the back counter, with a great view of the chef slipping pizzas into the cherry-red, wood-fired oven. And don't sleep through the house-made pastas: pillowy ricotta gnocchi, tucked into a lemony mascarpone and artichoke sauce, are good enough to steal the *apizzas'* show.

# Quattro

Italian

2050 University Ave. (at I-101), East Palo Alto

**Phone:** 650-470-2889
**Web:** www.quattrorestaurant.com
**Price:** $$$

Lunch & dinner daily

As is to be expected from a restaurant housed inside the Four Seasons, Quattro comes with a hefty price tag. But it's nothing that deal-doing tech moguls can't handle—even at lunchtime, when it's often bustling. With a sleek, airy atmosphere full of natural light (check out the impressive sculptures that line the stone walls), this is a swanky retreat worthy of its high-dollar clientele.

The Italian-influenced menu has something for everyone, from a light pea, zucchini, and watercress "garden bisque" to a hearty seafood salad full of octopus, grilled prawns, and squid. Drinks are also notable: whether you seek tasty "mocktails" for lunchtime teetotaling or a pricey dinnertime bottle from the fully stocked iPad wine list, you'll find your match.

# Ramen Dojo

Japanese ✗

**F1**

805 S. B St. (bet. 8th & 9th Aves.), San Mateo

**Phone:** 650-401-6568
**Web:** N/A
**Price:** 🍴

Lunch & dinner Wed – Mon

The two-hour lines may have died down, but a 40-minute wait on the sidewalk is still standard at this noodle hot spot. The interior, when you finally reach it, is utterly spare—the better to showcase steaming bowls of tasty and satisfying soup. Customize your broth (soy sauce, garlic pork, soybean), spiciness, and toppings (like spicy cod roe and kikurage mushrooms), then dive in.

The ramen arrives in minutes, loaded with the standard fried garlic cloves, hard-boiled quail egg, scallion, chili, and two slices of roast pork. Your job is to slurp the chewy, delicious noodles (and maybe some seaweed salad or edamame), then hit the road—the hyper-efficient staff needs to keep the line moving, after all. But for one of the best bowls in town, it's worth it.

# Rasoi

Indian ✗✗

**C2**

1425 Burlingame Ave. (bet. El Camino Real & Primrose Rd.), Burlingame

**Phone:** 650-579-5661
**Web:** www.rasoiburlingame.com
**Price:** $$

Dinner nightly

Mission District standby Aslam's Rasoi has expanded to the 'burbs with this sleek and contemporary outpost, featuring glimmering metallic floor tiles, tufted ottomans, and dark wood furnishings. Come early to enjoy a drink in the swank front lounge, which features a flickering gas fireplace.

While Rasoi looks ultra-modern, its cooking is blessedly traditional, with standards like samosas, tangy-tender lamb *rogan josh* and soft, fluffy garlic naan. Warm and welcoming servers bustle cheerfully among the tables, offering tips on their favorite dishes. One suggestion you should plan to take them up on is the chicken korma, loaded with super-smoky pieces of tender chicken in a creamy, well-spiced, buttery sauce. It may be the best rendition you'll ever taste.

# Rasa ❀

C2

**209 Park Rd. (bet. Burlingame & Howard Aves.), Burlingame**

**Phone:** 650-340-7272
**Web:** www.rasaindian.com
**Price:** $$

Lunch & dinner daily

Peninsula

In a bustling tech corridor that's also home to Indian expats with high culinary standards, Rasa has managed to find the perfect middle ground. No-joke dishes that aren't toned down for Western palates cater to the likes of software execs and area couples, and though the bi-level space boasts a gorgeous, minimalist-mod décor with bright splashes of orange, sleek pendant lights, and stylish dark wood fittings, the focus here is on food.

The kitchen excels in elevating the cuisine of South India with solid technique and superlative ingredients. Get the party started with *dahi vada* (crispy fried lentil fritters buried in smooth yogurt), before savoring a basil-chutney *dosa* starring a crisp rice-lentil crêpe stuffed with potato masala and served with chutney, as well as an ultra-spicy ghost chili version—to be risked by hardcore hotheads only.

Each plate is carefully composed, as shown in the complex Andhra chicken curry, enriched with coconut and bobbing with tender dark meat. Sop up the pungent sauce with a flaky Kerala *paratha*. Then cool down over a creamy and smooth *chikku* frappe, that blends the eponymous pear-like fruit with vanilla ice cream and candied rice puffs for a captivating finale.

# Romesco

**B4**

225 Cabrillo Hwy. (bet. Kelly Ave. & San Mateo Rd.), Half Moon Bay

**Phone:** 650-560-8174

**Web:** www.romescobistrotapas.com

**Price:** $$

Lunch Fri – Sun
Dinner Wed – Mon

The pace of life is slower in Half Moon Bay, and this Spanish hangout encourages the town's siesta vibes with its laid-back service and ultra-authentic tapas that come straight from a Spanish-born chef. The red-and-black dining room is an ideal place to gather with friends and sip sangria after a day at the beach, and the generous portions are perfect for sampling and sharing.

The menu covers all the beloved classics: *jamón serrano* croquettes are crisp and creamy, accompanied by a skewer of tart pickled vegetables, while the fluffy *tortilla Española* is stuffed with buttery potatoes and accompanied by creamy garlic aïoli. Lovers of seafood shouldn't miss the shrimp in garlic oil or the *bacalao* toasts with roasted red pepper—both are perfect.

# Sakae

**C2**

243 California Dr. (at Highland Ave.), Burlingame

**Phone:** 650-348-4064

**Web:** www.sakaesushi.com

**Price:** $$

Lunch Mon – Sat
Dinner nightly

Its glory days of crowds packed to the rafters have passed, but Sakae is still a solid option for elegant sushi and other Japanese specialties. Adjacent to downtown Burlingame and the Caltrain station, this is a sleek space clad in varying shades of wood, Japanese pottery, and fresh flowers. Local families enjoy sitting at the bar, where a friendly and engaging sushi chef is a hit with kids.

Skip the specialty rolls and stick to fresh and neat nigiri topped with the likes of albacore, yellowtail, crab, salmon, or daily featured fish. Otherwise, go for the whiteboard's changing specials like maitake mushroom tempura or grilled baby octopus.

Be sure to order a pot of *hoji cha,* a roasted green tea that nicely complements the impressive range of fish.

259

# Shalizaar

D3

Persian ** XX**

**300 El Camino Real (bet. Anita & Belmont Aves.), Belmont**

**Phone:** 650-596-9000
**Web:** www.shalizaar.com
**Price:** **$$**

Lunch & dinner daily

A perennial favorite for Persian flavors, Shalizaar is friendly, charming, and authentic. Lunchtime draws a large business crowd, while dinners cater to couples on dates. The upscale space features chandeliers, linen-topped tables, Persian carpets, and walls of framed windows that flood everything with light.

Meals here are always a pleasure, thanks to the high quality of every ingredient. Try the signature *koobideh*, smoky ground beef and chicken kebabs served with char-broiled whole tomatoes and rice. Or, tuck into *baghali polo*, a fork-tender lamb shank over bright green rice full of dill and young fava beans. For dessert, take the friendly servers' advice and order the *zoolbia barnieh*, sticky-crisp squiggles of fried cake soaked in rosewater syrup.

# Sichuan Chong Qing

E1

Chinese **X**

**211 S. San Mateo Dr. (bet. 2nd & 3rd Aves.), San Mateo**

**Phone:** 650-343-1144
**Web:** N/A
**Price:** **$$**

Lunch & dinner Tue – Sun

The medical staff at the Mills Health Center take plenty of heat in an average day, but that doesn't stop them from piling into this compact neighboring Sichuan restaurant for their fix of spicy chili oil and numbing peppercorns. Both ingredients are featured in the crispy Chong Qing chicken and shrimp, each laden with chili peppers (be sure to watch out for shards of bone in the cleaver-chopped chicken).

Skip the mild Mandarin dishes and stick to the house's fiery specialties, like the nutty, smoky cumin lamb with sliced onion and still more chilies and chili oil. Aside from a few contemporary touches, the décor isn't newsworthy and the staff is more efficient than engaging—but you'll likely be too busy enjoying the flavor-packed food to mind.

# The Striped Pig

**F2**

917 Main St. (bet. Middlefield Rd. & Stambaugh St.), Redwood City

**Phone:** 650-257-3710
**Web:** www.thestripedpig.com
**Price:** $$

Dinner Tue – Sat

Craft cocktails may be the focus at this trendy gastropub, but the food is far from an afterthought, with plenty of creative small plates to tempt drinkers into a snack or ten. Some are light and fresh—think chicories tossed in a tangy crème fraîche vinaigrette and topped with a crisped polenta cake—while others are rich and decadent, like a masa sope layered with duck confit in a spectacular *mole negro*. Attentive bartenders are happy to suggest pairings—try the Beldar, a light and floral blend of vodka, St. Germain, Aperol, and champagne.

Sleek and stylish, the compact space features a U-shaped bar at its center, where local professionals sip after-work libations and couples have a chat as they take in the action from the glassed-in kitchen.

# Sushi Sam's

**E1**

218 E. 3rd Ave. (bet. B St. & Ellsworth Ave.), San Mateo

**Phone:** 650-344-0888
**Web:** www.sushisams.com
**Price:** $$

Lunch Thu – Sat
Dinner Tue – Sat

San Mateo's sushi connoisseurs know that some of the region's best can be found at this tiny, no-frills joint, where waits are all but inevitable. Formica tables and chipped plates are part of the package, but with sushi this exceptional at a price this reasonable, that won't keep you from getting hooked.

Skip the average teriyaki, tempura, and udon in favor of an all-sushi experience; you can't go wrong with the exquisite nigiri, from wild king salmon with a touch of lemon juice and wasabi to silky *medai* with spicy minced daikon. The unusual *battera* roll, combining rich, oily mackerel with sweet-salty poached kelp, is a surprise success, as is the decadent dragon roll, a blend of buttery avocado, smoky *unagi*, and sweet shrimp tempura.

# Sushi Yoshizumi ✤

**E1**

Japanese 🍴

### 325 E. 4th Ave. (bet. B St. & Railroad Ave.), San Mateo

**Phone:** 650-437-2282
**Web:** www.sushiyoshizumi.com
**Price:** $$$$

Dinner Wed – Sun

&

Plan ahead two months (to the day) before you'd like to dine here, then jump online for a reservation—Sushi Yoshizumi is worth the effort.

This is a place for Japanese expats yearning for a taste of home and sushi purists snapping iPhone shots faster than you can say "omakase." The setting is discreet in every way, with a tidy interior that consists of little more than eight seats, a cypress bar, as well as a chef's work station.

The menu is built around Edomae sushi, a style that Chef Akira Yoshizumi spent years perfecting in both Japan and New York. His training clearly pays off with food that is refined, delicate, and beautifully balanced. Employing wild seafood, mostly from Japan, to create an intimate omakase experience, Chef Yoshizumi offers detailed explanations and welcomes questions with his warm and open demeanor.

Clean flavors shine in each course; garnishes and sauces are kept to a minimum. A slice of wonderfully firm and surprisingly mild geoduck sashimi arrives with nothing more than fresh wasabi and a sprinkle of black sea salt. Still, the height of any meal here is the nigiri, with flavorful rice seasoned with red akazu vinegar, and fish so fresh that its taste seems to name its species.

# Sweet Basil

Thai ✗✗

E2

1473 Beach Park Blvd. (at Marlin Ave.), Foster City

**Phone:** 650-212-5738
**Web:** www.sweetbasilthai.net
**Price:** $$

Lunch & dinner daily

Set near a charming bayside walking and biking trail on Foster City's perimeter, Sweet Basil makes for a great meal after a leisurely stroll or strenuous ride. The space is snazzy and contemporary-looking with bamboo floors and rustic tables, but the vibe is casual with the waitstaff hustling to serve the daytime rush of office workers as well as families (at night).

Though you may have to wait for a table, their signature kabocha pumpkin and beef in a flavorful red curry will merit patience. Other delights include moist and well-marinated chicken *satay*; tofu stir-fried with bell peppers and basil; or sticky rice topped with mango. You can choose your own spice level here, but watch out: when this kitchen says hot, they're not kidding around.

# Taqueria El Metate

Mexican ✗

D3

120 Harbor Blvd. (at Hwy. 101), Belmont

**Phone:** 650-595-1110
**Web:** N/A
**Price:** ⊛

Lunch & dinner daily

Industrial and no-frills, El Metate isn't a looker—but taqueria connoisseurs know it's the place to go for a great meal. Sidle up to the counter and order a round of street-style tacos, topped with well-seasoned carne asada or piquant shredded chicken, then crowned with onions and cilantro. Or go big with an enormous super burrito, stuffed with caramelized, pineapple-studded *al pastor*, fluffy rice, pinto beans, avocado, cheese, sour cream, and *pico de gallo*.

Located right off the 101, the restaurant's minimal room has lines of both white- and blue-collar lunchtime workers streaming out the door, and crowds of Mexican families on weekends (kids adore it). A well-stocked salsa bar, crisp chips, and a refreshing melon *agua fresca* help ease the wait.

# Taqueria San Bruno

**C2**

**1045 San Mateo Ave. (bet. Hermosa & Scott Sts.), San Bruno**

**Phone:** 650-873-1752
**Web:** N/A
**Price:** 💰

Lunch & dinner daily

If you're willing to forgive its divey, industrial location in San Bruno's auto-repair corridor, this taqueria will reward you with flavor-packed food that's worthy of the largely Mexican clientele that congregates here at lunchtime. Expect to sit elbow-to-elbow at communal tables, where options range from authentically Mexican to delightfully Americanized (hello, hefty super burritos).

Every type of taco served here is perfection—from fresh, plump marinated shrimp to sweet, caramelized *al pastor*. The superior chicken enchiladas sub smoky grilled chicken for the traditional boiled variety, then get added zest from a garlicky red chile sauce. Throw in warm, well-salted tortilla chips and piquant salsa, and you'll be a happy camper.

# Taste In Mediterranean Food

**C2**

**1199 Broadway, Ste. 1 (bet. Chula Vista & Laguna Aves.), Burlingame**

**Phone:** 650-348-3097
**Web:** www.tasteinbroadway.com
**Price:** 💰

Lunch & dinner Mon – Sat

Taste In Mediterranean Food could easily get lost along Broadway's blocks of cafés and boutiques, but this tiny restaurant is truly not to be missed. Beyond the deli cases of baklava and salads, find the open kitchen, where rotating lamb, chicken, and beef slowly turn and roast to become gyros, shawarma platters, and wraps.

About half of the guests grab takeout; the others sit in the small dining room to enjoy the likes of combo platters spanning the Mediterranean from Greece to Lebanon. Chewy pita bread scoops up nutty hummus, smoky-garlicky baba ghanoush, and herbaceous Moroccan eggplant salad. Or try thin slices of lamb shawarma in a pita wrap with homemade garlic sauce, cabbage, and fried potatoes. Don't forget the baklava from the counter.

# Vespucci

Italian ✕✕

**E1**

### 147 E. 3rd Ave. (bet. Ellsworth Ave. & San Mateo Dr.), San Mateo

**Phone:** 650-685-6151
**Web:** www.vespucciristorante.com
**Price:** $$

Lunch Fri – Sat
Dinner Tue – Sun

Though this charming Italian standby was recently acquired by its former manager and his wife, its flavorful, hearty food hasn't changed a bit: envision delicate *mezzaluna* ravioli, stuffed with ricotta and spinach, arriving in a luscious sauce rich with parmesan and sage; while the nicely charred, juicy lamb chops are tender and well-seasoned. Even a simple tiramisu, with velvety mascarpone and not-too-sweet espresso-soaked sponge, is perfectly executed.

Thanks to its long standing in the community, Vespucci has a family feel; the staff knows regulars by name, and eagerly welcomes newcomers. The owners have also spruced up the quaint dining room, adding a fresh look to the decorative pillars, wine displays, and burgundy-clothed tables.

# Vesta 😊

Pizza ✕✕

**F2**

### 2022 Broadway St. (bet. Jefferson Ave. & Main St.), Redwood City

**Phone:** 650-362-5052
**Web:** www.vestarwc.com
**Price:** $$

Lunch & dinner Tue – Sat

Whether they're rolling in from their offices at lunch or their condos at dinner, Redwood City locals are always up for a wood-fired pie at this stylish downtown pizzeria. With an airy, mosaic-filled dining room extending into a large front patio, it's a relaxed, roomy space perfect for groups and families.

The menu is divided into red and white pies, and they're equally delicious: zesty tomato sauce enlivens a combo of peppery *soppressata*, smoked mozzarella, and spinach, while a white version with crumbled French feta, fresh slices of garlic, cherry tomatoes, and chopped applewood-smoked bacon is irresistible. Get your greens in with the arugula salad, tossed with shaved *Parmigiano Reggiano*, toasted hazelnuts, and a delicious apricot vinaigrette.

# The Village Pub ✿

E4

Gastropub ✗✗✗

**2967 Woodside Rd. (off Whiskey Hill Rd.), Woodside**

**Phone:** 650-851-9888
**Web:** www.thevillagepub.net
**Price:** $$$

Lunch Sun – Fri
Dinner nightly

Though it has the feel of a chichi private club, this attractive New American restaurant is open to all—provided they can live up to the style standards set by its fan base of tech tycoons and ladies-who-lunch. Draw your eyes away from those Teslas in the lot and head inside for fine-dining that exceeds this sophisticated restaurant's humble name.

That said, the cuisine is surprisingly approachable, with offerings like house charcuterie and a superb Pub burger available in the lounge and main dining areas. A crisp, lunchtime flatbread is loaded with flavor and all too easy to devour. The kitchen shines its brightest at dinner, with starters like octopus carpaccio adorned with shaved radish, tomato confit, cucumber brunoise, and a drizzle of paprika oil.

Service is a priority, and this staff readily attends to every need—even grinding coffee to order as an accompaniment for warm, fluffy, sugar-dusted beignets served with creamy almond anglaise and tangy cranberry compote. The wine list is similarly designed to court the deepest of pockets, with an outstanding selection of French vintages and aged Bordeaux. On a budget? Aim for lunch, which is lighter not only in approach, but also on the wallet.

# Viognier

Contemporary    XXX

**E1**

### 222 E. 4th Ave. (at B St.), San Mateo

| | | |
|---|---|---|
| **Phone:** | 650-685-3727 | Dinner Mon – Sat |
| **Web:** | www.viognierrestaurant.com | |
| **Price:** | **$$$** | |

One of the few remaining special-occasion spots in an increasingly casual dining landscape, this refined restaurant is full of guests dressed in their best; and the charming dining room with its roaring central fireplace is their equal. Service is attentive, and the semi-open exhibition kitchen is perpetually abuzz.

Sip on a glass of Viognier's namesake wine before embarking on their multi-course tasting menu, full of beautifully plated fare like a pungent spiced carrot soup with smoked *ricotta salata*; delicate winter squash tortellini in a brown butter-sage emulsion; as well as meaty 72-hour braised short ribs. Desserts are particularly exquisite—the white chocolate cheesecake, accented by tangy citrus curd and mandarin sorbet, is quite divine.

# wonderful 😊

Chinese    X

**C2**

### 270 Broadway (bet. La Cruz & Victoria Aves.), Millbrae

| | | |
|---|---|---|
| **Phone:** | 650-692-2829 | Lunch & dinner daily |
| **Web:** | www.wonderful.restaurant | |
| **Price:** | **$$** | |

Hunanese cuisine often takes a backseat to the Bay Area's bumper crop of Cantonese and Sichuanese restaurants, so this hot spot is a welcome addition to the Chinese-food landscape. It's already caught on with the area's Chinese transplants, so you can expect a wait at peak meal hours—especially for large parties, as the dining room is compact.

The boldly flavored dishes incorporate oodles of smoked, cured, and fermented ingredients—from the bacon-like pork wok-tossed with leeks, garlic, and soy, to the pungent pork, black bean, and pickled chili mixture that tops those spicy, chewy, hand-cut Godfather's noodles. The whole chili-braised fish, fresh and flaky in its bath of bright red mild chili sauce flecked with scallions and garlic, is an absolute must.

# Wakuriya ✿

**D3**

### 115 De Anza Blvd. (at Parrott Dr.), San Mateo

**Phone:** 650-286-0410
**Web:** www.wakuriya.com
**Price:** $$$$

Dinner Wed – Sun

Innovative, serious, and very well-established, Wakuriya successfully combines a deep respect for kaiseki tradition with a contemporary touch. This is largely thanks to the lone chef behind the counter, Katsuhiro Yamasaki; his wife is the one so deftly managing and serving the dining room. The location is charmless, but there is a sober elegance here that is enhanced by the kitchen's quiet confidence. The room books a month in advance—set your alarm for midnight, phone them exactly 30 days ahead, and pray for a callback.

Each month brings a new, refined menu that combines the chef's personal style with superlative Japanese and Californian ingredients. Course after course arrives uniquely presented, perhaps on handcrafted ceramics or even a silver spoon, cradling chunks of poached lobster with intensely smoky dashi gelée, soft-boiled Jidori egg, crisp asparagus and fried kombu.

This may not be a *sushi-ya*, but the sashimi course is nonetheless excellent. Find that same level of talent in the *yamaimo* gratin with silky morsels of black cod and tender Brussels sprouts that are crisp, yet light as air and so delicious. The *shirako* tofu topped with Kabocha pumpkin tempura is beyond luxurious.

# Yi Yuan

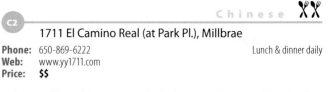

Chinese ✗✗

**C2**

**1711 El Camino Real (at Park Pl.), Millbrae**

**Phone:** 650-869-6222          Lunch & dinner daily
**Web:** www.yy1711.com
**Price:** $$

Millbrae boasts no end of Chinese restaurants, but this fire-hot spot stands out for its tasty Sichuan-style dishes laden with chilies, peppercorns, and chili oil, as well as its attempts to bring some decorative polish to the oft-dumpy area landscape. Sure, the faux-pagoda ceilings and strings of red lanterns are a bit kitschy, but the food is worth it.

Try to score a table near the glass-enclosed kitchen, where you can watch a cook expertly hand-pull the chewy, thick noodles in your *dan dan mien*, a spicy blend of ground pork and chili paste. Fatty, rich smoked pork is sautéed with leeks, garlic, and plenty of spice, just as crispy, tongue-numbing Chongqing chicken arrives under a pile of still more peppers. If you like your food fiery, look no further.

# Yummy Szechuan

Chinese ✗

**C2**

**1661 El Camino Real (bet. Park Blvd. & Park Pl.), Millbrae**

**Phone:** 650-615-9648          Lunch & dinner daily
**Web:** www.yummyszechuan.com
**Price:** $$

Long waits for a great Chinese meal are common on the Peninsula, which makes this as yet line-free favorite doubly special. The space is no-frills, but the kitchen is all-thrills, knocking out classic dish after classic dish: crisp Chongqing-style fried chicken buried under a mound of dried chilies and numbing peppercorns, tender pork wontons swimming in gloriously mouth-searing chili oil, and chewy *dan dan* noodles tossed with ground pork, peanuts, and plenty of chili oil.

As with all Sichuan restaurants, those who can't stand the heat will have a hard go of it, but non-fiery options include a flaky rolled beef pancake and garlicky pea shoots. The moral of this story: while Yummy may not be anyone's idea of high style, the food assuredly lives up to its name.

# South Bay

# South Bay

## SILICON VALLEY

Silicon Valley has for long been revered as the tech capital of the world, but it's really so much more. Combine all that tech money with a diverse, international population and get a very dynamic culinary scene. If that doesn't sound like an outrageously successful formula on its own, think of the area's rich wine culture descending from the Santa Cruz Mountains, where a burgeoning vintner community takes great pride in its work, and realize that the South Bay may as well be sitting on a gold mine. Visitors should be sure to see everything the area has to offer, with a sojourn at **The Mountain Winery** in Saratoga—part-outdoor concert venue, part-event space, and part-winery—that offers stunning views of the vineyards and valley below.

## FESTIVALS GALORE

The Valley is proud of its tech-minded reputation, but don't judge this book by its cover as South Bay locals definitely know how to party. In San Jose, celebrations kick off in May at the wildly popular **South Bay Greek Festival** featuring music, eats, drinks and dance. With little time to recover, buckets of cornhusks wait to be stuffed and sold at the **Story Road Tamale Festival**, held every summer within the gorgeous grounds of Emma Prusch Farm Park. In July, **Japantown** breathes new life for the two-day **Obon/ Bazaar**, and come August, the Italian-American Heritage Foundation celebrates its annual **Family Festa**. It's a year-round shindig, and **Santana Row** (a sleek shopping village housing numerous upscale restaurants and a fantastic farmer's market) plays a pivotal role in these festivities. One of San Jose's most notable destinations is **San Pedro Square Market**, whose four walls harbor a spectrum of artisanal merchants at historic Peralta Adobe downtown.

Farmers and specialty markets are a way of life for South Bay residents and these locals cannot imagine living elsewhere.

## CULTURAL DYNASTY

As further testimony to its international repute, the capital of Silicon Valley is also a melting pot of global culinary influences. Neighborhood *pho* shops and *bánh mì* hangouts like **Huong Lan**, gratify the growing Vietnamese community. They can also be found gracing the intersection of King and Tully streets (home to some of the city's finest Vietnamese flavors) sampling decadent cream puffs at **Hong-Van Bakery** or crispy green waffles flavored with *pandan* paste at **Century Bakery** just a few blocks away. **Lion Plaza** is yet another hub for bakeries, markets, and canteens paying homage to this eighth most populated Asian country. Neighboring Cambodia makes an appearance through delicious noodle soups like **Nam Vang Restaurant** or **F&D Yummy**. And Chinese food makes its formidable presence known at lofty **Dynasty Chinese Seafood Restaurant**. Located on Story Road, this is a popular arena for big parties and favored

destination for dim sum. **Nijiya Market**, for instance, is a jewel with several locations, all of which sparkle with specialty goods, top ingredients, and all things Far East. Long before it was cool to be organic in America, Nijiya was focused on bringing the taste of Japan by way of high-quality, seasonal, and local ingredients to the California coast. Today, it continues to tantalize with some of the area's most pristine seafood and meat, as well as an array of tasty sushi and bento boxes. Also available via their website are sumptuous, homespun recipes for a variety of noodle dishes, fried rice signatures, and other regional specialties. Encompassing the globe and travelling from this Eastern tip to South America, Mexican food enthusiasts in San Jose seem eternally smitten by the still-warm tortillas at **Tropicana**, as well as the surprisingly delish tacos from one of the area's many **Mi Pueblo Food Centers**.

## A STUDENT'S DREAM

And yet there is more to the South Bay than just San Jose. Los Gatos is home to prized patisseries like **Fleur de Cocoa** and such historic, continually operating, and specialized wineries like **Testarossa**. Meanwhile, cool and casual Palo Alto is home base for celebrated Stanford University, its countless students, and impressive faculty. Find locals lining up for homemade fresh and frozen yogurt at **Fraîche**. Others fulfill a Korean fantasy in Santa Clara, where these same settlers enjoy a range of authentic nibbles and tasty spreads at food court favorite— **Lawrence Plaza**. Just as foodies favor the *soondubu jjigae* at **SGD Tofu House**, more conservative palates have a field day over caramelized sweet potatoes at **Sweet Potato Stall**, just outside the Galleria. Fill a belly with impeccable produce along El Camino Real near the Lawrence Expressway intersection. Then treat your senses to a feast at Mountain View's **Milk Pail Market**, showcasing over 300 varieties of cheese. Have your pick among such splendid choices as Camembert, Bleu d'Auvergne, Morbier, and Cabriquet, as well as imported Mamie Nova Yogurt. Despite the fast pace of technology in Silicon Valley, **Slow Food**—the grassroots movement dedicated to local food traditions—has a thriving South Bay chapter. Even Google in Mountain View feeds its large staff three organic, square meals a day. For a wider range of delicacies, they may frequent surrounding eateries or stores selling ethnic eats.

Residents of Los Altos also have their German food cravings covered between **Esther's German Bakery** and **Dittmer's Gourmet Meats & Wurst-Haus**. In fact, Dittmer's sausages are made extra special when served on a salted pretzel roll from Esther's. **Los Gatos Meats & Smokehouse** is another stalwart serving these meat-loving mortals an embarrassment of riches. Think poultry, fish and freshly butchered meat sandwiches served alongside savory beef jerky, prime rib roasts, pork loin, corned beef, and of course, bacon. But wait… did you want it regular, pepper, country-style or Canadian? Pair all these salt licks with a sip from Mountain View's **Savvy Cellar Wine Bar & Wine Shop** only to discover that it's a picnic in the making. Smokers looking to wind down in luxury may head to the handsome, upscale and members-only Los Gatos Cigar Club, where the choices are exceptional and conversation intriguing.

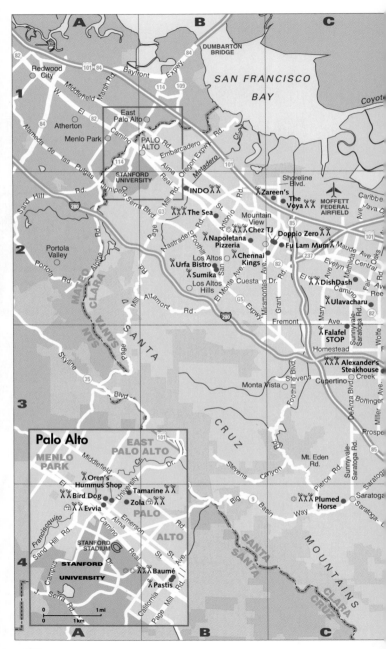

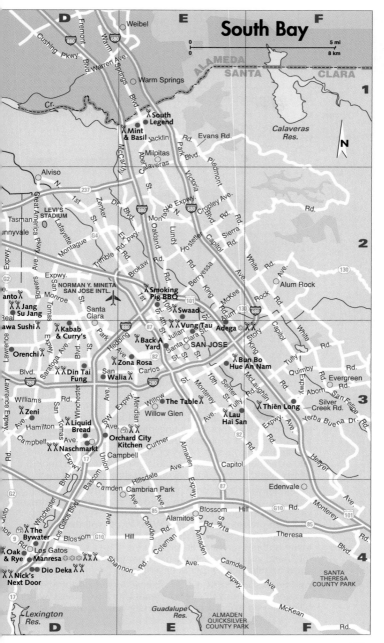

# South Bay

Weibel

Fremont

Cushing Pkwy.

Warren Ave.

Warm Springs

ALAMEDA
SANTA CLARA

Calaveras Res.

0 — 5 mi
0 — 8 km

N

South Legend

Mint & Basil

Jacklin

Milpitas

Evans Rd.

Calaveras

McCarthy Blvd.

Abel St.

Piedmont Rd.

Alviso

1st St.

Tasman

LEVI'S STADIUM

Zenker Rd.

Montague Expwy.

Oakland Rd.

Cropley Ave.

Sierra Rd.

Rd.

Sunnyvale

Great America Pkwy.

Lafayette St.

Trimble Rd.

Brokaw Rd.

Berryessa Rd.

Hostetter Rd.

Capitol Ave.

White Rd.

Alum Rock

130

Expwy.

NORMAN Y. MINETA SAN JOSE INTL.

anto

Jang Su Jang

Monroe

San Tomas Expwy.

Santa Clara

Smoking Pig BBQ

4th St.

Swaad

King Rd.

McKee Rd.

Rock Rd.

awa Sushi

Kabab & Curry's

Saratoga Ave.

Hedding Ave.

Vung Tau

Adega

White

Orenchi

Park Ave.

Back Yard

Julian St.

Santa Clara St.

SAN JOSE

Story Rd.

Capitol Expwy.

Rd.

Zeni

Zona Rosa

San Carlos St.

Monterey

Bun Bo Hue An Nam

McLaughlin Ave.

Quimby Rd.

Evergreen

San Felipe Rd.

Din Tai Fung

Walia

10th St.

7th St.

Tully Rd.

Abom

Real

Lawrence Expwy.

Williams Rd.

Winchester Blvd.

Meridian Ave.

The Table

Willow Glen

Lau Hai San

Thiên Long

Silver Creek Rd.

Yerba Buena Dr.

Hamilton Ave.

Campbell Ave.

Liquid Bread

Willow St.

Almaden Expwy.

Hillsdale Ave.

Capitol

Edenvale

Monterey

101

Campbell

Orchard City Kitchen

Naschmarkt

Curtner Ave.

Bascom Ave.

Union Ave.

Camden Ave.

Cambrian Park

Blossom Hill Rd.

G10

85

SANTA THERESA COUNTY PARK

Los Gatos Blvd.

The Bywater

Oak & Rye

Los Gatos

Manresa

Dio Deka

Nick's Next Door

Blossom Hill Rd.

Alamitos

Coleman Rd.

Santa Theresa Blvd.

Camden Ave.

McKean Rd.

Lexington Res.

Guadalupe Res.

ALMADEN QUICKSILVER COUNTY PARK

# Adega ✿

Portuguese 🍴🍴

### 1614 Alum Rock Ave. (bet. 33rd & 34th Sts.), San Jose

| | | |
|---|---|---|
| **Phone:** | 408-926-9075 | Lunch & dinner Wed — Sun |
| **Web:** | www.adegarest.com | |
| **Price:** | $$$ | |

San Jose's "Little Portugal" may not be as thoroughly Portuguese as it once was, but this retreat has kept local tradition alive with its playful, contemporary riffs on the classics of this nation's cuisine. From rabbit terrine studded with pine nuts and drizzled with a luscious port reduction to tender roasted octopus atop fingerling potatoes and spinach, a meal here will win over both longtime fans of Portuguese fare and new converts. Many of them likely made after one bite of the delicious *arroz de pato*, rice cooked with a smoky, savory blend of *chouriço*, bacon, and shredded roast duck.

Adega's environs are on the gritty side, but the space itself is lovely, with wood beams, brown leather banquettes, vintage winemaking tools on the walls, and a stunning glass-enclosed private dining room. Wine lovers will thrill to the stellar selection of more than 200 vintages from Portugal, many of them rarely or never found in the U.S. Of course, the friendly staff who largely hail from the same nation, are eager to help pick the perfect glass.

And finally, don't miss out on creative desserts like the *"ovo de ovos,"* a whimsical "egg" of cream with a sweetened yolk filling, nested in cinnamon-dusted egg yolk threads.

# Alexander's Steakhouse

Steakhouse XXX

**C3**

10330 N. Wolfe Rd. (at I-280), Cupertino

**Phone:** 408-446-2222
**Web:** www.alexanderssteakhouse.com
**Price:** $$$$

Lunch Tue – Fri
Dinner nightly

Wealthy techies set down their smartphones and plug in face-to-face at this swank steakhouse, where a double-wide dining room, fireside lounge, and duo of exhibition kitchens aim to sate executives doing deals on the company tab. Pricey steaks emerge from the glass-enclosed aging room, while the bar is the place to go for high-dollar Napa cabernets and rare whiskeys.

The flash at Alexander's extends to the more-is-more menu, which often piles on overpowering ingredients to diminishing returns—and those with sensitive palates should order carefully. If you're not dining with a group, opt for the more sedate bar, which boasts friendlier, less-scripted service (you can skip the upsold hamachi shots) and a cast of interesting Silicon Valley characters.

# Back A Yard

Caribbean X

**E3**

80 N. Market St. (bet. Santa Clara & St. John Sts.), San Jose

**Phone:** 408-294-8626
**Web:** www.backayard.net
**Price:** ⊜

Lunch & dinner Mon – Sat

Though this Caribbean spot is located in the heart of downtown San Jose, dining here feels like a vacation thanks to cheerful murals, a lively soundtrack, and hospitable servers. Unlike its Menlo Park predecessor, which mainly does to-go orders, this location boasts a capacious brick dining room.

Back A Yard is a Jamaican term meaning "the way things are done back home," and the food doesn't disappoint on that count. Specialties include smoky, spicy, and tender jerk chicken, flavorful curry goat, and vinegar-marinated *escovitch* fish fillets, all accompanied by coconut rice and red beans, a side salad, and caramelized fried plantains. Cool off your palate with a glass of coconut water, then order a slice of dense, flan-like sweet potato pudding.

# Baumé ✿ ✿

Contemporary  🍴🍴🍴

### 201 S. California Ave. (at Park Blvd.), Palo Alto

**Phone:** 650-328-8899
**Web:** www.maisonbaume.com
**Price:** $$$$

Lunch Fri – Sat
Dinner Wed – Sat

A bold orange door in an otherwise nondescript single-story building along Palo Alto's main thoroughfare marks the entrance to the mystical Baumé. Inside, find an exquisite dining room with a modernist sensibility that carries through orange-hued walls and fabric room dividers. The kitchen may do only one dinner seating a night, but tables are spaced widely for privacy and never rushed. The service staff adds to the luxury with their warmth, knowledge, and clear enthusiasm for Chef Bruno Chemel's progressive cuisine.

Each contemporary dish is refined, balanced, and demonstrates an enormous attention to detail.

The kitchen focuses on sublime seasonal ingredients and coaxing flavor to profound levels. Sweet morsels of Brittany blue lobster are poached in butter, then topped with a creamy quenelle of cauliflower mousse, garnished with a Lilliputian bouquet of broccoli. Meals may reach their height of decadence with a gently warmed Jidori egg yolk set between a tuile of crisped Ibérico ham and velvety potato purée over wilted kale, aptly adorned with a gold leaf.

Exquisite desserts include pear mousse sandwiched between very fine sables with an artfully formed "blossom" of ginger ice cream.

# Bird Dog

Contemporary ✕✕

**A4**

420 Ramona St. (bet. Lytton & University Aves.), Palo Alto

**Phone:** 650-656-8180
**Web:** www.birddogpa.com
**Price:** $$

Dinner nightly

Anyone on the hunt for a happening scene in Palo Alto should follow the scent to Bird Dog, where the décor is sleek, the cocktails flow freely, and the diners sport head-to-toe designer duds. Boisterous and social, this is the kind of place where air kisses fly easily from the lips of Silicon Valley types who've scored must-have reservations. If you're hoping for a quiet meal, this is not your spot.

The food is as ambitious as the yuppie crowd, and while it may misstep here and there, it gets points for a modern approach. Delicious options include an exquisitely conceived *tai* crudo with chopped pecans and *aji amarillo*; green curry-breaded chicken thighs served over uni mousse; and finally, a chocolate crémeux enriched by ginger and white ale ice cream.

# Bun Bo Hue An Nam

Vietnamese ✕

**E3**

740 Story Rd., Ste. 3 (bet. Lucretia & Roberts Aves.), San Jose

**Phone:** 408-993-1755
**Web:** N/A
**Price:** ⊜☜

Lunch & dinner Wed – Mon

Amid a sea of small Vietnamese spots, this one stands out for its condensed but excellent menu of noodle soups, which have made it a favorite among the expat crowd. The original location has a more traditional rosewood aspect, while its equally popular sequel, on Tully Road, is quite contemporary. As the name suggests, *bun bo hue* is the specialty, though it may be a pleasure limited to intrepid diners. The spicy beef noodle soup blazes with chili oil, lemongrass, scallions, and cilantro, yet remains slightly gamey and rich with ample portions of tripe, tendon, and congealed pork blood. An array of *pho* is also a popular choice: try the *pho dac biet*, a fragrant star anise and lemongrass broth overflowing with meat and served with lime, basil, and chilies.

# The Bywater 😊

Southern ✗

**D4**

532 N. Santa Cruz Ave. (bet. Andrews St. & Roberts Rd.), Los Gatos

**Phone:** 408-560-9639
**Web:** www.thebywaterca.com
**Price:** $$

Lunch & dinner Tue – Sun

If dining at Manresa is like a weeklong stay at a luxury resort, this New Orleans-inspired little sib from Chef/owner David Kinch is more like a weekend of partying in the Big Easy. With its zinc bar, pressed ceilings, and open kitchen stacked with bottles of Crystal hot sauce, it might just fool you into thinking you're in Louisiana—right down to the zydeco and jazz playing on the stereo.

Reservations aren't accepted, so locals (some with kids in tow) line up early to get a taste of spicy, Andouille-flecked gumbo *z'herbes*, golden-brown hushpuppies, oyster po'boys, and other Cajun and Creole classics. For the finale, a luscious butterscotch *pot de crème* may sound less traditional, but rest assured that it tastes like heaven.

# Chennai Kings

Indian ✗

**C2**

856 El Camino Real (bet. Castro & Oak Sts.), Mountain View

**Phone:** 650-938-1333
**Web:** www.chennaikings.us
**Price:** $$

Lunch & dinner daily

The rank-and-file of Silicon Valley may never be royals, but they can still eat like them at this Mountain View gem, which specializes in the regional cuisine of Chennai. Throngs of Indian immigrants speaking their native tongues gather here at lunchtime, catching live cricket matches on the television as they scoop up boldly spiced curries from colorful plastic plates.

Expect to see some new-to-you dishes: the *urandai kofta* curry, made with *paneer* and lotus-root balls in a creamy, aromatic sauce, is revelatory, as is the stir-fried green chili chicken with *thokku*—a vibrant paste of ground cashews, spices, and tomato. The friendly manager is happy to suggest something novel to try, or to recommend familiar but delicious items like the excellent *masala dosa*.

# Chez TJ

**C2**

Contemporary ✗✗✗

938 Villa St. (bet. Bryant & Franklin Sts.), Mountain View

**Phone:** 650-964-7466
**Web:** www.cheztj.com
**Price:** $$$$

Dinner Tue – Sat

Set in a quaint Victorian, Chez TJ has launched the careers of innumerable culinary talents—and the latest chef at the helm, Jarad Gallagher, is more than worthy of its legacy. Though it may seem old-fashioned for its Mountain View zip code, this former home decked with flowers and Tiffany lamps, has a throwback appeal with a hint of romance that's perfect for escaping the demands of technology. Attentive, polished servers add to the pleasure.

The dining room offers two menus: either a seven-course exploration into seasonal cooking sourced from within 100 miles; or a more lengthy chef's tasting resplendent with luxurious global ingredients. Both exhibit thoughtful technique with Mediterranean dishes that play with Spanish and Japanese flavors. Opah crudo arrives as a unique and very beautiful arrangement beneath micro herbs, trout roe, pomegranate arils, shaved persimmon, toasted rice and beads of quince jam.

To the contrary, the straightforward appearance of dry-aged beef almost undermines this beguiling and complex array of mineral-rich, perfectly cooked tenderloin and ribeye. It is served on a creamy pool of buttermilk potato purée with caramelized roasted carrot and pleasantly bitter kale and cress coulis.

# Din Tai Fung

Chinese ✕✕

2855 Stevens Creek Blvd. (bet. Monroe St. & Winchester Blvd.), Santa Clara

**Phone:** 408-248-1688
**Web:** www.dintaifungusa.com
**Price:** $$

Lunch & dinner daily

You'll need to wait (and wait, and wait) to get a taste of the much-coveted dumplings at the first Bay Area outpost of this acclaimed international chain, which has drawn crazy crowds to the Westfield Valley Fair mall since day one.

With only a handful of reservations taken a month in advance, expect to cool your heels for anywhere from 45 minutes to two hours. Is the wait worth it? Depends on how much you love *xiao long bao*, the Shanghai-style soup dumplings that are offered here in outstanding pork-crab and utterly decadent black truffle variations. Bring a crew so you can sample the non-dumpling offerings as well: delectably spicy wontons, top-flight barbecue pork buns, springy house-made noodles, and lightly sweetened black sesame buns for dessert.

# Dio Deka

Greek ✕✕

210 E. Main St. (bet. Jackson St. & Villa Ave.), Los Gatos

**Phone:** 408-354-7700
**Web:** www.diodeka.com
**Price:** $$$

Dinner nightly

Dio Deka may specialize in Greek food, but this is no typical taverna, as the stylish dining room (complete with a roaring fireplace) ably demonstrates. A wealthy, well-dressed Los Gatos crowd flocks to the front patio on warm evenings, dining and people-watching within the vine-covered walls of the Hotel Los Gatos. The bar also draws a brace of cheery regulars.

Skip the dull mesquite-grilled steaks and keep your order Greek: think stuffed grape leaves with tender braised beef cheek, or a bright pan-seared local salmon with roasted yellow peppers, potatoes, and artichokes. The adventurous shouldn't miss out on the fun offering of Greek wines, and sweet buffs should allow space for the *crema me meli*, a fantastic burnt-honey mousse with almond and lemon.

# DishDash

C2

Middle Eastern

**190 S. Murphy Ave. (bet. Evelyn & Washington Aves.), Sunnyvale**

**Phone:** 408-774-1889
**Web:** www.dishdash.com
**Price:** $$

Lunch & dinner Mon – Sat

Dining on the run is certainly possible at this Middle Eastern favorite on historic Murphy Avenue—just ask the tech types flooding the to-go counter to bring food back to their desks. Families and small groups congregate in the colorful dining room. But you might want to linger on the front sidewalk patio, all the better to people-watch while savoring a bright, tangy, and healthy tabbouleh salad, or indulging in the tender-crisp falafel, redolent of spices, topped with whipped tahini. Served on griddled bread and topped with garlicky yogurt-parsley sauce, wraps like the incredibly tender, smoky, and juicy lamb shawarma are full-flavored and downright memorable. For dessert, try the *m'halabieh*, a floral rosewater and creamy pistachio pudding.

# Doppio Zero

Italian

C2

**160 Castro St. (bet. Evelyn Ave. & Villa St.), Mountain View**

**Phone:** 650-938-4147
**Web:** www.dzpizzeria.com
**Price:** $$

Lunch & dinner daily

True pizza lovers know that the best flour is 00 and that some of the best pies can be found at this Mountain View smash-hit, which draws big crowds for its hearty and authentic offerings. Set right on Castro Street's restaurant row, this is a casual spot with a jolly and boisterous Italian staff, but the crown jewel is their authentic wood-burning oven.

The calzone-like fried pizza may seem like a diet-buster, but it's light and crisp, not oily, with a peppery and cheesy filling of smoked mozzarella, ricotta, salami, and tomato sauce. Other highlights include the namesake pie, a white variety with prosciutto, arugula, and shaved *parmigiano*. Pastas, salads, and a few larger plates are equally strong—and equally enormous, so expect leftovers.

South Bay

# Evvia 😳

Greek ✗✗

**A4**

### 420 Emerson St. (bet. Lytton & University Aves.), Palo Alto

**Phone:** 650-326-0983
**Web:** www.evvia.net
**Price:** $$

Lunch Mon – Fri Dinner nightly

You'll feel like Adonis after ascending to the heights of this culinary Olympus, which serves some of the best Hellenic fare in the entire Bay Area. Inviting and cozy with its rustic wood beams, hanging copper pots, and roaring wood-burning fireplace, this Greek God's central Palo Alto location is a draw for local techies and VCs by day, and couples or families in the evening.

Much of the menu emerges from the wood-fired grill, including smoky, tender artichoke and eggplant skewers drizzled in olive oil and paired with garlicky Greek yogurt. The rustic, impossibly moist lamb souvlaki is nicely contrasted by a refreshing tomato, cucumber, and red onion salad. For dessert, pumpkin cheesecake is subtle, sweet, and accented with syrup-poached chunks of pumpkin.

# Falafel STOP

Israeli ✗

**C3**

### 1325 Sunnyvale Saratoga Rd. (at Fremont Ave.), Sunnyvale

**Phone:** 408-735-7182
**Web:** www.falafelstop.biz
**Price:**

Lunch & dinner daily

It's little more than a bungalow with some picnic tables out front, but true falafel aficionados know that looks can be deceiving—and that Falafel STOP serves the most appetizing made-to-order falafel in town. It doesn't hurt that the accompaniments are also stellar: the hummus is insanely creamy and supremely smooth, with a hefty dose of nutty tahini, and the rounds of fresh-baked pita, served warm, are as fluffy as clouds. As an added bonus, prices and portions are both generous.

You'll want to choose your line before you order (those seeking a shawarma plate should get into the designated Grill STOP line). Then grab your food, seat yourself at a picnic table—they're tented in the winter months—and enjoy a transportive taste of the Middle East.

# Fu Lam Mum

**C2**

Chinese ✗

**153 Castro St. (bet. W. Evelyn Ave. & Villa St.), Mountain View**

Phone: 650-967-1688
Web: n/a
Price: ⊜⊜

Lunch & dinner daily

Dim sum aficionados seeking a tasty and affordable Chinese lunch arrive en masse at midday to dine at this bustling hot spot, where numerous delicious options cruise by on carts. You'll find all the standards, from steamy dumplings to pork buns to shrimp rice noodle rolls, as well as larger plates of creamy, nutty walnut shrimp and delicately flavored roast duck, accompanied by tender-crisp Chinese broccoli. For dessert, egg custard tarts and mango jelly rule the day.

Fu Lam Mum's space is cavernous, with high ceilings and a big mezzanine, which is perfect for hosting parties and large groups. Things can get a little noisy, but the workaday crowd appreciates the speedy service and always-on-the-go vibe. For a quieter meal, try visiting at dinnertime.

# INDO

**B2**

Indonesian ✗✗

**3295 El Camino Real (at Lambert Ave.), Palo Alto**

Phone: 650-494-7168
Web: www.indorestaurant.com
Price: $$

Lunch Mon – Fri
Dinner nightly

The elite meet to eat at this smart, stylish Indonesian restaurant in the heart of Palo Alto, where deals are done over lunch and tech tycoons (including a big name or two) slip in unnoticed for a quiet, pretension-free family meal. At early-evening happy hours, single minglers hit the sizable bar and lounge for cocktails and industry gossip.

This kitchen's fare is best described as boldly flavored comfort food, whether that includes crunchy calamari with Makrut lime aïoli and galangal cocktail sauce, or sticky-sweet Indonesian-style ribs so tender, they're practically falling off the bone. Be sure to request a seat on the airy brick patio, where a trickling fountain, trellis, and heat lamps create a relaxing space to savor coconut fried rice or green vegetable curry.

# Jang Su Jang

**D2**

3561 El Camino Real, Ste. 10 (bet. Flora Vista Ave. & Lawrence Expwy.), Santa Clara

**Phone:** 408-246-1212
**Web:** www.jangsujang.com
**Price:** $$

Lunch & dinner daily

Smoky Korean barbecue, luscious soft tofu stews, and enormous seafood pancakes are among the standards at this Santa Clara classic and Koreatown star. Its strip-mall façade may not seem enticing, but the interior is classier than expected, thanks to granite tables equipped with grill tops and ventilation hoods, and a glass-enclosed exhibition kitchen located in the back.

This is fiery-flavored cuisine for gourmands who can stand the heat. A heavy-handed dose of kimchi flavors soft beef and pork dumplings, while the fierce red chili paste that slicks garlicky slices of marinated pork may actually cook the meat in *daeji bulgogi*. Cool down with *mul naeng myun*, a cold beef broth with tender, nutty buckwheat noodles, and a pot of *bori cha*.

# Kabab & Curry's

**D3**

1498 Isabella St. (at Clay St.), Santa Clara

**Phone:** 408-247-0745
**Web:** www.kababandcurrys.com
**Price:** ㄸ

Lunch & dinner Tue – Sun

The appeal is in the name at Kabab & Curry's, which has become a dining destination among Indian and Pakistani expats missing the comforts of home. On lunch breaks from the local tech giants, they pack the all-you-can-eat buffet, filling up their plates with fragrant chicken *boti kababs*, coupled with creamy *dal makhani* and slabs of charred naan for soaking up those savory sauces.

Set in a white house with simple tile floors and orange walls, Kabab & Curry's is more about food than service. But that doesn't deter the crowd of local families from gushing in for dinner or to pick up take-out. With to-go bags laden with rich chicken *tikka masala* and pungent lamb *kadahi*, it's clear that everybody loves this *desi* diner's bold and authentic flavors.

# Lau Hai San

**E3**

2597 Senter Rd. (bet. Feldspar Dr. & Umbarger Rd.), San Jose

**Phone:** 408-938-0650
**Web:** N/A
**Price:** $$

Lunch & dinner Thu – Tue

Most Westerners don't think of hot pot when they're craving Vietnamese food, but it's actually a traditional favorite well worth sampling—and the proof is in this sunny spot. The overstuffed menu boasts 20 different variations on the theme, including a spicy seafood version with shrimp, mussels, squid, fish balls stuffed with salmon roe, and other aquatic delights. Dip them into the sour, tangy broth; twirl them with noodles; garnish with herbs—the choice is yours.

If hot pot isn't adventurous enough, bring a group to sample delicacies like chewy, flavorful curried coconut snails and crispy fried pork intestine. The diner-like space and strip-mall setting are nothing special, but the hot pot is so outstanding that lines are to be expected.

# Liquid Bread

**D3**

379 E. Campbell Ave. (bet. Central Ave. & Civic Center Dr.), Campbell

**Phone:** 408-370-3400
**Web:** www.liquidbreadcampbell.com
**Price:** $$

Dinner Tue – Sun

Beer is serious business at this Campbell Avenue hot spot, which boasts a sizable menu of drafts and bottles. But the food is a step up from the typical brewpub, with dishes like an asparagus salad topped with shaved sunchokes, black garlic, and balsamic dressing; or roasted chicken breast over maple syrup-soaked waffles and garlicky escarole. Brews even show up on the food menu from time to time, as in the stout cream that crowns a fudgy chocolate brownie.

While it's far from a dive bar, Liquid Bread can get loud, making it better for sharing pints with friends than an intimate date-night. If the communal high-top tables, large front patio, and copious brews add up to a little too much fun, do as the regulars do and have Uber handle the drive home.

# Manresa ✿ ✿ ✿

Contemporary XXX

**D4**

320 Village Ln. (bet. Santa Cruz & University Aves.), Los Gatos

| | | |
|---|---|---|
| **Phone:** | 408-354-4330 | Dinner Wed – Sun |
| **Web:** | www.manresarestaurant.com | |
| **Price:** | $$$$ | |

Despite its reputation for being one of the Bay Area's more intense restaurants, Manresa is welcoming, distinctively stylish, and extraordinarily hospitable for a fine-dining establishment operating at this level. Sure, you might be seated next to a tech billionaire or celebrity chef, but there is little fuss as everyone relaxes into a superb meal.

Chef David Kinch's nightly menu is unknown until it arrives on the table as a parchment listing alphabetized ingredients. The food is at once cerebral and luxurious, yet grounded and thoroughly delicious. Each course is likely to represent a moment within a season, beginning with a selection of savory petit fours that are an illusory play on the palate. Sample red-pepper pâtes de fruits, black olive madeleines, or green-garlic panisse with Meyer lemon curd and tahini. Black cod is a surprising, clever, and cohesive dish, featuring an exemplary fillet with crisped Brussels sprout leaves, tart vinegar reduction, and root purée served alongside a chestnut "truffle" rolled in truffle dust.

Memorable desserts flaunt pumpkin purée with chocolate crémeux as well as sherry vinegar. Finally, don't miss those excellent sea salt-caramels offered on your way out.

# Mint & Basil

**E1**

1741 N. Milpitas Blvd. (bet. Dixon Landing Rd. & Sunnyhills Ct.), Milpitas

**Phone:** 669-235-5285
**Web:** www.mintnbasil.com
**Price:** ⊗⊗

Lunch & dinner daily

Set in a light and bright outpost in a strip mall, this casual meat-free Vietnamese restaurant draws big crowds of vegetarians, vegans, and carnivores alike, resulting in waits that can run up to an hour.

Don't be shocked by mentions of "sausage" or "fish sauce": everything on the menu is faux, and—surprise!—much of it will satisfy even the pickiest meat eaters. (To that end, be sure to try the soy-marinated seitan "pork," served atop a heaping bowl of vermicelli with crisp shredded vegetables.) Fresh rolls are yet another menu highlight—a combo platter allows diners to taste all four "seasons," including a spicy autumn roll with vegan sausage, greens, and crunchy apple—and the citrusy, spicy lemongrass variation is a must for tofu lovers.

# Napoletana Pizzeria

**B2**

1910 El Camino Real (bet. Escuela & Rengstorff Aves.), Mountain View

**Phone:** 650-969-4884
**Web:** www.napoletanapizzeria.com
**Price:** $$

Lunch Fri – Sun
Dinner nightly

For a taste of old Napoli, it's hard to beat this unassuming little strip-mall pizzeria, which relies on a bevy of house-made and imported ingredients (including coveted "00" flour) to turn out its beautifully blistered wood-fired pies. Topping combos like rapini, sausage, and smoked mozzarella, are very authentic, and the pizzas are chewy, never overladen. A few antipasti and main courses, including a tasty Caesar with homemade dressing, round out the menu.

Napoletana is petite, with wood floors, black granite tabletops, and a colorful cityscape mural, but the *pizzaiolo* offers plenty of entertainment, busily cramming pies into the 900-degree oven. After you've savored yours, indulge in the chocolate mousse with mascarpone cream for dessert.

# Naschmarkt

**D3**

384 E. Campbell Ave. (bet. Central & Railway Aves.), Campbell

**Phone:** 408-378-0335      Dinner Tue – Sun
**Web:** www.naschmarkt-restaurant.com
**Price:** $$

A slice of Vienna in downtown Campbell, Naschmarkt scores high marks for its authentic flavors, inviting space, and friendly service. The cozy, brick-walled dining room is a favorite among couples, and solo diners will have a ball at the wraparound counter, which has a great view of the busy open kitchen.

Most of the menu is traditional: think bratwurst, kraut rouladen, and weiner schnitzel. The pan-roasted chicken breast, moist and juicy with a golden-brown seared crust, is served over a "napkin dumpling" made with compressed bread, tomato, and herbs. But, rest easy as there are a few items that have lighter Californian twists, like spätzle made with quark (a fresh white cheese) and tossed with smoked chicken, yellow corn, English peas, and wild mushrooms.

# Nick's Next Door

**D4**

11 College Ave. (at Main St.), Los Gatos

**Phone:** 408-402-5053      Lunch & dinner Tue – Sat
**Web:** www.nicksnextdoor.com
**Price:** $$

Though it originally opened as the sibling to Chef Difu's Nick's on Main, Nick's Next Door is now his sole restaurant—even more confusing given that it's actually across the street from his original spot and hidden behind a patio, in the shadow of a towering redwood tree. One fact is evident, though: the crowd here has ritzy tastes, often flocking in from the high-end cigar shop located merely steps away.

Upscale American bistro cooking is the focus, with such first-rate specialties as pan-fried abalone served with soft risotto and crispy Brussels sprouts, as well as meatloaf with potatoes and wild mushroom gravy. Whether you dine in the cozy and elegant dining room with its black-and-gray motif or outdoors, you'll receive a warm welcome—often from Nick himself.

# Oak & Rye

✗✗

**D4**

303 N. Santa Cruz Ave. (bet. Almendra & Bachman Aves.), Los Gatos

**Phone:** 408-395-4441
**Web:** www.oakandryepizza.com
**Price:** $$

Lunch & dinner daily

A longtime *pizzaiolo* from Brooklyn's acclaimed Roberta's is behind the pies at this South Bay jewel, where a coppery wood-fired oven produces chewy, blistered crusts. The pies' toppings are as quirky and delightful as their monikers, like the Scottie 2 Hottie (*soppressata*, *pepperoncini* oil, tomatoes, mozzarella, honey) and the Truffle Shuffle (Gruyère, green onion, truffle oil, cornichon).

The menu is rounded out by a handful of small plates like a shaved Brussels sprout, lemon, and pecorino salad, but the real focus is the pizza, for which Oak & Rye has quickly become Los Gatos' go-to. Friendly and casual, with gregarious servers, its only drawback is the need to arrive early—reservations for parties fewer than 10 aren't accepted, and waits can get long.

# Orchard City Kitchen

✗✗

**D3**

1875 S Bascom Ave., Ste. 190 (off Campisi Way), Campbell

**Phone:** 408-340-5285
**Web:** www.orchardcitykitchen.com
**Price:** $$

Lunch & dinner daily

Jeffrey Stout is at the helm of this international small-plates spot, which has been getting a level of buzz that radiates far beyond its humble shopping-center environs. Polished yet casual with a big front bar and patio, a meal here is best enjoyed with a group—so come prepared to max out the menu.

Kick things off with a cocktail, then get ready to savor a dizzying array of great dishes, including grilled artisanal bread spread with ricotta cheese and a mélange of wild mushrooms beneath a silky slow-poached egg. Then, slices of firm and fresh hamachi sashimi are arranged with shaved radishes and fuyu persimmon, finely diced avocado and a truffled ponzu sauce. Finally, toasted coconut takes rich butterscotch *pot de crème* to new heights.

# Orenchi

**D3**

Japanese ✗

**3540 Homestead Rd. (near Lawrence Expy.), Santa Clara**

**Phone:** 408-246-2955
**Web:** www.orenchi-ramen.com
**Price:** ⬬

Lunch & dinner Tue – Sun

Whether at lunch or dinner, this ramen specialist is known for its lines of waiting diners that curl like noodles outside its door. Even those who arrive before they open may face a long wait, so don't come if you're in a rush. Once inside, you'll be seated at a simple wood table or at the bar, collaged with Polaroid portraits of guests savoring their ramen.

The reason for the wait becomes clear when you're presented with a rich and utterly delicious bowl of *tonkotsu* ramen full of chewy noodles, roasted pork, and scallions. S*hoyu* ramen is equally delish, but make a point to show up early for spicy miso *tsukemen* or miso ramen as they're limited to only 15 and 20 servings, respectively, at lunch and dinner.

Orenchi Beyond is an equally busy younger sib in SF.

# Oren's Hummus Shop

**A4**

Israeli ✗

**261 University Ave. (bet. Bryant & Ramona Sts.), Palo Alto**

**Phone:** 650-752-6492
**Web:** www.orenshummus.com
**Price:** ⬬

Lunch & dinner daily

An authentic taste of the Holy Land in Silicon Valley, Oren's tiny space is as crowded as the Wailing Wall. At prime hours, expect to see diners spilling out onto the sidewalk and lining up for takeout at the back counter. The staff can seem overwhelmed at times, but it's an experience worth the wait, whether in Palo Alto or Mountain View.

You'll understand the lines after your first bite of the incredible hummus, drizzled with olive oil, and the crisp falafel with its moist, well-seasoned interior. Tender, spice-rubbed chicken breast in a fluffy pita, topped with a refreshing Israeli salad of chopped cucumber, tomato, onion, and parsley, as well as a spoonful of green harissa, is a satisfying lunch. Wash it all down with a dark Israeli beer.

# Pastis

South Bay

French ✗

**B4**

**447 S. California Ave. (bet. Ash St. & El Camino Real), Palo Alto**

**Phone:** 650-324-1355
**Web:** www.pastispaloalto.com
**Price:** $$

Lunch Tue – Sun
Dinner Tue – Sat

Parisian charm flowers in the heart of Silicon Valley at Pastis, a delightful Palo Alto French bistro. Compact and cheery with yellow walls, a sprinkling of tables, and specials on the chalkboard, it's every inch the European experience (just don't bring along a big group). You'll hear a lot of French spoken by both the staff and guests as it's a favorite with the expats—always a good sign for American gastronomes.

The low-key, laid-back menu is heavy on Gallic classics like fluffy, buttery quiche Lorraine; a grilled merguez sandwich with roasted bell peppers and *harissa* mayonnaise; as well as a simple but perfect crème brûlée. *Le Benedict* and *les omelettes* are big draws for brunch, particularly when enjoyed on the lovely front patio.

# Sawa Sushi

Japanese ✗

**D3**

**1042 E. El Camino Real (at Henderson Ave.), Sunnyvale**

**Phone:** 408-241-7292
**Web:** www.sawasushi.net
**Price:** $$$$

Dinner Mon – Sat

Strict rules and big rewards unite at this zany, unusual and randomly located (in a mall) dive, where Chef Steve Sawa rules the roost. After going through the rigmarole of landing a reservation for his omakase-only affair, throw all caution to the wind and just go with the flow. Yes, the décor is nothing special; however, the food is anything but so-so, and the ad hoc prices are quite high.

So what draws such a host of regulars? Their pristine and very sublime fish, of course—from creamy Hokkaido sea scallops to delicious toro ribbons. Sawa is also an expert on sauces: imagine the likes of *yuzu kosho* topping kanpachi, or a sweet-spicy tamarind glaze on ocean trout. Accompany these with a top sake or cold beer and feel the joy seep in.

# Plumed Horse ⁕

Contemporary 𝄪𝄪𝄪

**C4**

## 14555 Big Basin Way (bet. 4th & 5th Sts.), Saratoga

| | | |
|---|---|---|
| **Phone:** | 408-867-4711 | Dinner Mon – Sat |
| **Web:** | www.plumedhorse.com | |
| **Price:** | $$$$ | |

This cozy bungalow's small-town setting almost seems at odds with the luxury cars regularly parked out front. Tech money infuses the well-to-do suburb, making this a fine-dining favorite among locals. The surprisingly large interior features some specialized touches, like an iPad wine list and fiber-optic chandeliers, as a nod to the clientele. The vibe generally tilts towards classic luxury, thanks to the attentive staff and contemporary space with its enormous glass wine cellar and arched barrel ceiling.

The chef's table facing the kitchen has the best seats in the house—for those who reserve well in advance.

The fact that this kitchen showcases its own home-grown seasonal ingredients may not be entirely unique, but in the hands of such skilled cooks it translates into a noteworthy vegetarian tasting menu. More impressive is that they are equally adept with game meats, such as the supremely tender antelope loin served over farro and drizzled with tangy huckleberry sauce. Squab, with its beautifully lacquered skin and medium-rare meat, arrives with chive-flecked potato gnocchi and lightly fermented Brussels sprouts. For dessert, there may be no purer taste of chocolate than the Valrhona ganache.

# The Sea

Seafood XxX

4269 El Camino Real (at Dinah's Ct.), Palo Alto

**Phone:** 650-213-1111                                    Dinner nightly
**Web:** www.theseausa.com
**Price:** $$$$

Wealthy venture capitalists come ashore in waves to blow their expense accounts at this seafood-centric sister to Alexander's Steakhouse, where the central Palo Alto location is prime, the wine list is strewn with expensive bottles, and the menu brims with top-dollar delicacies. The white-tablecloth vibe is appropriately corporate and formal, so be sure to don your best.

The stratospherically priced selection ranges from Maine lobster to Hokkaido scallops to landlubber-friendly Australian Wagyu. But, for those seeking a closer shore, the Quinault River king salmon, served in a creamy, bacon-accented sauce over maitake mushrooms and haricots verts, is worthy. Don't skip dessert, either: the yuzu mousse with kumquats and avocado cream is quite simply fabulous.

# Smoking Pig BBQ

Barbecue X

1144 N. 4th St. (bet. Commercial St. & Younger Ave.), San Jose

**Phone:** 408-380-4784                                Lunch & dinner daily
**Web:** www.smokingpigbbq.net
**Price:** 

Identifiable by the aroma of wood smoke that surrounds it for a block in every direction, this barbecue-slinging dive is wildly popular. Read: plan on a wait in the smoker-ringed parking lot if you want to dine at prime meal times. Accommodations are beyond basic, with tattered booths and disposable servingware, but service is friendly, and something about the lack of ambience amplifies the gustatory pleasure.

Indeed, there is plenty of pleasure to be found on the combination plates, especially the signature pork ribs—smoky and well-seasoned, they fall off the bone. Order them in a combination plate of peppery brisket or juicy pulled pork, along with a cornbread muffin and tasty, smoky beans with burnt ends. This is pigging out at its finest.

# South Legend

Chinese ✗

**E1**

1720 N. Milpitas Blvd. (bet. Dixon Landing Rd. & Sunnyhills Ct.), Milpitas

**Phone:** 408-400-7040                                      Lunch & dinner daily
**Web:** www.southlegends.com
**Price:** $$

In the Sunnyhills strip mall, packed with Chinese restaurants and Asian markets, South Legend stands out for its fiery and lip-numbing interpretations of classic Sichuan cooking. Though Chengdu-style dim sum provides a brief respite on weekend mornings, it's all about the heat for the rest of the week—as seen in their Chongqing chicken topped with dried chilies.

Large and no-frills, this hot spot is usually crammed with locals looking for an authentic taste of their Chinese childhoods—the well-worn dining room and dated décor be damned. They're too busy sweating it out after the likes of spicy pickled vegetables and braised whole fish covered in—you guessed it—chilies, before cooling off over milder *dan dan* noodles and a pot of black tea.

# Sumika

Japanese ✗

**B2**

236 Plaza Central (bet. 2nd & 3rd Sts.), Los Altos

**Phone:** 650-917-1822                                          Lunch Tue – Sat
**Web:** www.sumikagrill.com                                  Dinner Tue – Sun
**Price:** $$

Yak it up at this local hot spot for Japanese-style skewers, where every part of the chicken (from thighs to liver to skin) is grilled over charcoal to smoky deliciousness. Sumika's atmosphere may be no-frills, but the food is solid and its beloved sister ramen shop, Orenchi, gives it an enormous pedigree (which makes snagging a seat or two in the tiny space a real challenge).

If you're willing to sacrifice *yakitori*, crowds die down considerably during skewer-free lunches, when moist chicken *karaage* with a crisp, golden-brown exterior and the signature Sumika salad (featuring cabbage, chicken, and wonton strips) take center stage. Udon in an umami-rich dashi broth with fish cake, kombu, and a carrot-daikon *kakiage* fritter is always a solid bet.

# Swaad

Indian ✗

**E2**

498 N. 13th St. (at Empire St.), San Jose

**Phone:** 408-947-2030
**Web:** www.swaadindiancuisine.com
**Price:** $$

Lunch Mon – Sat
Dinner nightly

Indian transplants have quickly cottoned to this ultra-authentic spot, whose dishes are jam-packed with flavor and liberally seasoned with herbs and spices that aren't toned down for Western palates. The space is simple and nondescript with yellow walls and stark furnishings, but no one seems to mind: they're just here for the food.

On that point, the kitchen delivers, with perfectly crispy vegetable samosas loaded with potatoes and green peas, creamy chicken korma full of tender vegetables and pungent spices, and massive rounds of naan stuffed with shredded cauliflower. Don't miss their flavorful, spicy *seekh* kebabs, featuring ground lamb and presented on a smoking-hot iron skillet with tomatoes, peppers, and onion for terrific a contrast in texture.

# The Table

American ✗

**E3**

1110 Willow St. (at Lincoln Ave.), San Jose

**Phone:** 408-638-7911
**Web:** www.thetablesj.com
**Price:** $$

Lunch Wed– Sun
Dinner nightly

The casual, farm-to-table food that's standard fare in SF is harder to come by in San Jose, which explains why this ingredient-centric gathering place is always packed with diners. With long wood tables, large windows, a busy back bar, and lots of hard, modern surfaces—not to mention a bevy of craft cocktails fueling the crowds—it can get noisy. Read: don't plan an intimate evening here.

Instead, make The Table your spot to share bites and drinks with friends, like caramelized sourdough spaetzle with smoked butternut squash and pea tendrils, or sugar-dusted ricotta beignets with lemon curd. Brunch is so popular that it's offered Wednesday through Sunday, but you should expect a wait to enjoy your omelette, hash browns, and more of those beignets.

# Tamarine

South Bay

**A4**

Vietnamese ✗✗

546 University Ave. (bet. Cowper & Webster Sts.), Palo Alto

**Phone:** 650-325-8500
**Web:** www.tamarinerestaurant.com
**Price:** $$$

Lunch Mon – Fri
Dinner nightly

Tamarine has long been a Palo Alto standby for its refined take on Vietnamese food that doesn't sacrifice authentic flavor. There's nearly always a corporate lunch happening in the private dining room, and techies, families and couples alike fill the rest of its linen-topped tables.

Family-style sharing of dishes is encouraged, which is good because deciding on just one entrée is nearly impossible. To start, make like the regulars and order one of the "Tamarine Taste" appetizer platters with a round of tropical fruit-infused cocktails. Then move on to the fresh shrimp spring rolls, full of bean sprouts and mint; the springy ginger-chili seitan with steamed coconut rice; and curried long beans, sautéed with fragrant Makrut lime leaves and chili.

# Tanto

**D2**

Japanese ✗

1063 E. El Camino Real (bet. Helen & Henderson Aves.), Sunnyvale

**Phone:** 408-244-7311
**Web:** N/A
**Price:** $$

Lunch Tue – Fri
Dinner Tue – Sun

Lone rangers on tech-office lunch breaks pack this strip-mall Japanese spot, whose crowded parking lot belies its unimpressive façade. Waits are inevitable, but it's worth it to sit down to a steaming bowl of simple and flavorful udon. Indeed, all the standards are rendered beautifully here, from crisp vegetable tempura to tender, flaky grilled *unagi* set atop freshly steamed rice.

Tanto's menu expands a bit at dinner, bringing more grilled items and *izakaya*-style small plates. Pristine sushi and sashimi like albacore with ponzu are also a strong pick. You'll likely be seated at one of the closely spaced dining room tables, but the occasional stroke of luck might land you in one of the curtained, semi-private alcoves popular with business diners.

# Thiên Long

Vietnamese 🍴

3005 Silver Creek Rd., Ste. 138 (bet. Aborn Rd. & Lexann Ave.), San Jose

**Phone:** 408-223-6188
**Web:** www.thienlongrestaurant.com
**Price:** 💰

Lunch & dinner daily

There are plenty of Vietnamese restaurants catering to the local expats in San Jose, but Thiên Long stands out for its pleasant dining room presenting delicious cooking—as the numerous families filling the large space will attest. Tile floors and rosewood-tinted chairs decorate the space, while walls hung with photos of Vietnamese dishes keep the focus on food.

Begin with sweet-salty barbecued prawns paired with smoky grilled pork and served atop rice noodles. But, it is really the *pho* with a broth of star anise, clove, and ginger, topped with perfectly rare beef that is a true gem—even the regular-sized portion is enormous. English is a challenge among the staff, but they are very friendly; plus the authentic flavors make up for any inadequacies.

# Ulavacharu

Indian 🍴

685 E. El Camino Real (bet. Fair Oaks Ave. & Maria Ln.), Sunnyvale

**Phone:** 408-310-3111
**Web:** N/A
**Price:** 💰

Lunch & dinner daily

Silicon Valley's expat community can't get enough of this South Indian-style spot, which draws tech workers for its weekday thali lunch combos, before catering to local families in the evening. There's even a party room for special events. Though the lunchtime throng can make it a bit of a free-for-all, the bungalow space is a pretty mix of serene aqua walls and vaulted ceilings.

The kitchen excels with traditional dishes: smoky, well-spiced *baingan bharta* (eggplant), fork-tender chicken biryani that nearly melts off the bone into its confines of fluffy basmati rice, as well as aromatic lamb Chettinad, served in a spicy chili- tomato- and caramelized onion gravy. Be sure to order some fluffy naan to soak up every last bit of their outstanding sauces.

South Bay

# Urfa Bistro

Mediterranean ✗

**B2**

### 233 State St. (bet. 2nd & 3rd Sts.), Los Altos

**Phone:** 650-397-5614
**Web:** www.urfabistrolosaltos.com
**Price:** ෨෨

Lunch & dinner daily

Despite its affluence, Los Altos isn't heavy on good restaurant options, which has made this Mediterranean spot a welcome addition to the scene. Set in a strip mall, Urfa's simple space boasts a small back patio for sunny days, with warm and welcoming service to boot.

Homey and well-seasoned, the dishes here span the Mediterranean and Middle East, with a particular focus on Turkey (*urfa* is, after all, a type of Turkish chili pepper). The crowd of local families is always up for a round of the smoky chicken shish kabobs, piled on buttery white rice with chargrilled tomatoes and peppers; or the crisp, herbaceous falafel. For dessert, try something new: *künefe*, a Turkish sweet of melted, soft white cheese covered in crisp pastry threads and sweet syrup.

# The Voya

Latin American ✗✗

**C2**

### 1390 Pear Ave. (at Shoreline Blvd.), Mountain View

**Phone:** 650-386-6471
**Web:** www.thevoyarestaurant.com
**Price:** $$

Lunch daily
Dinner Mon – Sat

Yes, it's located in a strip-mall, but this Latin-American spot doesn't hesitate to pile on the glitz and glam: crystal chandeliers float above banquettes piled with velour pillows, and a long, 20-seat marble counter faces the open kitchen. Though it's a bit far from downtown Mountain View, it's a popular haunt for the techies from nearby offices, who link up to power-lunch.

Skillfully prepared dishes, however, prove that The Voya isn't just for show. Tender *cochinita pibil* tacos, drizzled with habanero sauce, arrive with a pile of tasty cilantro-infused rice, and the sweet and crunchy coconut shrimp with herb aïoli are full of flavor. For dessert, a molten chocolate cake may be a '90s throwback, but it's a gooey, rich and captivating one.

# Vung Tau

**E3**

Vietnamese ✕✕

**535 E. Santa Clara St. (at 12th St.), San Jose**

**Phone:** 408-288-9055
**Web:** www.vungtaurestaurant.com
**Price:** ⊖⊖

Lunch & dinner daily

It's easy to see why Vung Tau is a longtime love and go-to favorite among South Bay locals: picture an elegant décor, hospitable service, massive menu, and tasty food. Inside, the large space combines several dining areas styled with soft beiges, wood accents, and pendant lights. Lunchtime draws in business crowds while dinner brings families, many of whom are of Vietnamese heritage.

Authenticity is paramount in such offerings as hearty *bun bo hue*—ask for Vietnamese not American style—which comes with sliced flank steak, beef tendons, and pork blood in a spicy, earthy broth, served with a side of fresh herbs, lime, onions, and bean sprouts. Delicately sweet and creamy pleasures abound in *bánh khot*, delightful coconut-prawn cups served with chili-fish sauce.

# Walia

**D3**

Ethiopian ✕

**2208 Business Cir. (at Bascom Ave.), San Jose**

**Phone:** 408-645-5001
**Web:** www.waliaethiopian.com
**Price:** ⊖⊖

Lunch & dinner Wed – Mon

Authentic Ethiopian flavors are delivered without pretense at this easygoing, affordable restaurant, housed in a strip mall just off Bascom Avenue. Though the space is basic, the service is friendly and it's casual enough for kids in tow.

Start things off with an order of *sambussas*, fried dough triangles filled with lentil, onion, and chilies. Then choose from an all-meat, all-veggie, or mixed selection of tasty Ethiopian stews, like *tibs firfir*, featuring lamb in a garlicky berbere sauce dolloped on spongy, flaky *injera*. Vegetarians will particularly love dining here, as all of the plant-based options including *alicha wot* or split peas in turmeric sauce, *shiro* (spiced chickpeas), and *gomen* (wilted collard greens with onion and spices), are big winners.

# Zareen's

South Bay

**C2**

Indian

**1477 Plymouth St. (off Shoreline Blvd.), Mountain View**

**Phone:** 650-641-0335
**Web:** www.zareensrestaurant.com
**Price:** ⊜⊜

Lunch & dinner daily

Taking up residence just steps from the Googleplex, it's no surprise that this wholesome little Pakistani-cum-Indian restaurant is absolutely packed with tech employees seeking a taste of their homelands. But local families love Zareen's as well, perusing books from the lending library or doodling their heartfelt thanks on the wall. An added bonus: the space is set in a small shopping plaza with a big lot out front, making parking a non-issue.

The chicken Memoni samosas, supposedly made from a recipe known to only 23 grandmothers worldwide, are a must-order: crispy, well-spiced and flavorful, they're so good they don't need chutney. Follow these with the outstanding chicken *shami kababs*, juicy and caramelized in their bed of fluffy basmati rice.

# Zeni

**D3**

Ethiopian

**1320 Saratoga Ave. (at Payne Ave.), San Jose**

**Phone:** 408-615-8282
**Web:** N/A
**Price:** ⊜⊜

Lunch & dinner Tue – Sun

From its home at the end of a shopping plaza, Zeni caters to expats, tech types, and families alike. The interior has a standard dining area decorated with colorful portraits and tapestries as well as traditional seating on low stools at woven tables. Either way, group dining is encouraged.

Relish the spongy, enticingly sour *injera* used to scoop up delicious *yemisir wot* (red lentils with spicy *berbere*); *kik alitcha* (yellow peas tinged with garlic and ginger); or beef *kitfo* (available raw or cooked) tossed with that aromatic spice blend, *mitmita*, and crowned by crumbled *ayib* cheese. Here, *injera* is your only utensil, but be assured as there's a sink in the back to tidy up. Balance the fiery food with cool honey wine, or opt for an after-dinner Ethiopian coffee.

# Zola 😊

French  🍴🍴

**A4**

### 565 Bryant St. (bet. Hamilton & University Aves.), Palo Alto

**Phone:** 650-521-0651
**Web:** www.zolapaloalto.com
**Price:** $$

Dinner Tue – Sat

&

A Palo Alto sparkler, Zola charms its way into diners' hearts via a seductive French bistro menu with Californian flair. Whether you're spreading smoky salmon rillettes on toasted artisan levain, twirling pillowy caramelized ricotta gnocchi into the yolk of a soft-cooked egg in brown butter, or tucking into exquisite roasted pork loin and belly over Brussels sprouts and apple, you're sure to fall hard for the food.

The stylish space updates a few classics (wood tables, bistro chairs, pressed ceilings) with a dark teal color scheme and enticingly low lighting, and the well-chosen wine list is equal parts Gallic and Golden State. Crème caramel for dessert may be traditional, but it's also perfectly golden-brown and decadently creamy.

# Zona Rosa

Mexican  🍴

**E3**

### 1411 The Alameda (bet. Hester & Shasta Aves.), San Jose

**Phone:** 408-275-1411
**Web:** www.zonarosasj.com
**Price:** $$

Lunch & dinner Tue – Sun

For food just like *abuela's* (but somehow even better), make a beeline to this soul-warming cantina, which makes its salsas, blue and white corn tortillas, and other timeless dishes by hand. Start with an *antojito* like *albondigas fundido,* then proceed to tacos filled with *guajillo*-braised pork ribs and tomatillo-avocado salsa or pan-seared skirt steak with vibrant and garlicky *chimichurri*. Another star: a roasted *chile relleno*, which is smoky, spicy, sweet, and earthy in equal measure.

What the space lacks in square footage, it more than makes up for in down-home appeal. But this isn't a great choice for those in a rush, as the homespun service can get easily overwhelmed.

Check out the second location on Main Street in Los Gatos as well.

# Wine Country

## GRAPES GALORE

Revered as one of the most exalted wine growing regions in the world, Napa Valley is a 35 mile-long and luscious basin where wine is king. Given its grape-friendly climate and prime location (north from San Pablo Bay to Mount St. Helena, between the Mayacama and Vaca mountains), Napa ranks with California's most prestigious wineries. Here, powerfully hot summer days and cool nights provide the perfect environment for cabernet sauvignon grapes, a varietal for which the county is justifiably famous. But, it's not all about just *vino* here. Top chefs also have a buffet of exceptional ingredients to choose from, including locally grown and pressed extra virgin olive oils from the **Tasting Room**. **The Brasswood Bakery**, a deli and culinary emporium housed within the Cairdean Estate compound—is primo for excursion essentials like market-driven salads, hearty sandwiches, flaky pastries, and so much more. Moving on to other savory spreads, foodies, cooks, and scientists make their annual expedition to the **Napa Truffle Festival**, a veritable shindig of all things earthy. Also on offer here are cooking demos, seminars, and foraging. Among the region's many winemakers are names like **Robert Mondavi**, **Francis Ford Coppola**, and **Miljenko "Mike" Grgich**. Originally from Croatia, Grgich rose to fame as the winemaker at **Chateau Montelena** when his 1973 chardonnay took the top prize at the Judgment of Paris in 1976, outshining France's best white Burgundies. This triumph

turned the wine world on its ear, and put California on the map as a bona fide producer. Since then, Napa's indisputable success with premium wines has fostered endless pride, country-wide. American Viticultural Areas (AVAs) currently regulate the boundaries for districts such as Calistoga, Stags Leap, Rutherford, and Los Carneros.

## SPECIALTY FINDS

The Valley's wine-rich culture coupled with its illustrious restaurants that are destinations in themselves, make this region one of the world's most popular tourist attractions. Reclaimed 19th century stone wineries and gorgeous Victorian homes punctuate the rolling landscape and serve as a constant reminder that there were some 140 wineries here prior to 1890. Up from a Prohibition-era low of perhaps a dozen, the area today boasts over 400 growers and producers. However, this is not to say that there aren't stellar alfresco dining spots and specialty stores situated along its picturesque streets. Gourmands never fail to make the trek to **Rancho Gordo**, headquartered here, for heirloom beans of the highest quality. Serving as the main supplier to area chefs, it is also open to the public—who seem smitten by their divine selection. Looking for some inspiration? They can also instruct you on how best to cook them! Picnic supplies are the main draw at **Oakville Grocery**, the oldest operating store in town on Route 29; while **Model Bakery** in St. Helena or **Bouchon Bakery** in Yountville are wildly popular for fresh-baked breads and finger-licking pastries.

Napa's continued growth in wine production has spawned a special kind of food and wine tourism in this county, and tasting rooms, tours, as well as farm-fresh cuisine are de rigueur here. **Olivier Napa Valley** is a quaint and historic retail shop in St. Helena that proffers oils, vinegars, and other local food products alongside beautiful handcrafted tableware and ceramics from Provence. Residents who aren't rejoicing over their wares may be found scouring the vendibles at **NapaStyle**, a lifestyle store from local celebrity chef Michael Chiarello, purveying everything from furniture and tabletop items, to kitchenware and pantry staples. Other megawatt personalities like Thomas Keller, Richard Reddington, Cindy Pawlsyn, and Philippe Jeanty also hail from around the way, and may be found rubbing elbows at the flagship location of gourmet grocer, **Dean & Deluca**.

## SHOPPING TREATS

Visitors touring the Valley will spot fields of wild fennel, silvery olive trees, and rows of wild mustard that bloom between the grapevines in February and March. Mustard season kicks off each year with the **Napa Valley Mustard Festival** paying homage to the food, wine, art, and agricultural bounty of this region. Likewise, several towns host seasonal farmer's markets from May through October, including one in Napa (held near the **Oxbow Public Market** on Tuesdays and Saturdays); St. Helena (Fridays in Crane Park); and Calistoga (on Saturdays at Sharpsteen Museum plaza on Washington Street). Launched in early 2008, the **Oxbow Public Market** is a block-long, 40,000-square-foot facility that is meant to rival the **Ferry Building Marketplace** that is housed across the Bay. Packed to the rafters with food artisans and wine vendors from within a 100-mile radius of the market, and cradled inside a barn-like building, Oxbow keeps fans returning for everything under the sun. Think cheese, charcuterie, and spices; or olive oils, organic ice cream, and specialty teas. Shoppers who work up an appetite while perusing these shelves can rest assured as there are numerous snacks available to take-away.

## SIGHTS TO BEHOLD

Regional products such as **St. Helena Olive Oil** and **Woodhouse Chocolates** on Main Street, also in St. Helena, have similarly gained a large-scale nation-wide following. Three generations of one family run the latter, very charming chocolatier, which is most cherished for its handmade toffees. Just north of downtown St. Helena, the massive stone building that was erected in 1889 as Greystone Cellars, now inhabits the West Coast campus of the renowned **Culinary Institute of America (CIA)**. Their intensive training and syllabus ensures a striking lineup of hot chefs in the making.

With all this going for the wine-rich valley, one thing is for certain—from the city of Napa (the county's largest population center) north to the town of Calistoga known for its mineral mud baths and clean, spa cuisine, this narrow yet noteworthy region is nothing less than pure nirvana for lovers of great food and fine wine.

Toffee
Milk
Chocolate
$2⁰⁰

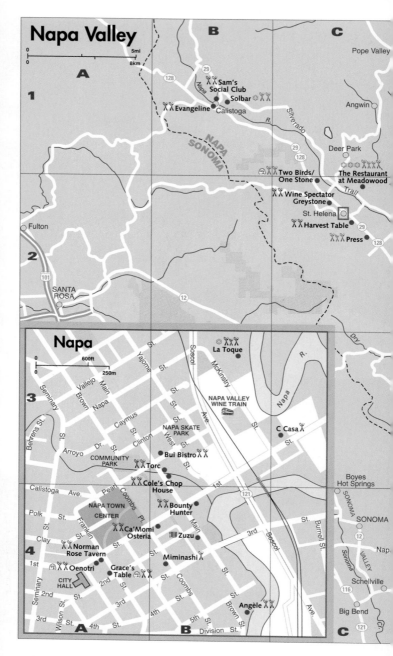

# Napa Valley

0 — 5mi
0 — 8km

**A**

**B**

**C**

Pope Valley

128
29
Napa R.

✂✂ **Sam's Social Club**
Calistoga
✿ **Solbar** ✂✂

✂✂ **Evangeline**

Angwin

**NAPA SONOMA**

Silverado Trail

29
128

Deer Park

✂ ✿✂ **Two Birds/One Stone**

✿✿✿ ✂✂✂✂ **The Restaurant at Meadowood**

✂✂ **Wine Spectator Greystone**

St. Helena

✂✂ **Harvest Table**

29
128

✂✂✂ **Press**

**1**

Fulton

101

**SANTA ROSA**

12

**2**

Dry Creek

# Napa

0 — 600ft
0 — 250m

Seminary St.
Vallejo St.
Brown St.
Napa St.
Yajome St.
Main St.
Caymus St.
Clinton St.
West St.
Soscol St.
McKinstry St.
Napa R.

✿ ✂✂✂ **La Toque**

**NAPA VALLEY WINE TRAIN**

**3**

Belvens St.
Arroyo Dr.

**COMMUNITY PARK**

**NAPA SKATE PARK**

● **Bui Bistro** ✂✂
✂✂ **Torc** ●
✂✂ **Cole's Chop House** ●

1st St.

● **C Casa** ✂

Boyes Hot Springs

**SONOMA VALLEY**

Calistoga Ave.

Pearl St.
Coombs St.
Franklin St.

**NAPA TOWN CENTER**

✂✂ **Bounty Hunter**

121

Soscol St.
Burnell St.

**SONOMA**

12

Nap

Polk St.
Clay St.

✂✂ **Ca'Momi Osteria**

🍴 **Zuzu**

3rd St.

✂✂ **Norman Rose Tavern**

✿ ✂✂✂ **Oenotri**

**Miminashi** ✂

Main St.

Schellville

116

**CITY HALL**

1st St.
2nd St.
3rd St.
Wilson St.
Seminary St.

**Grace's Table** ✿✂✂

2nd St.
3rd St.
4th St.
Coombs St.
5th St.
Brown St.

● **Angèle** ✂✂

Big Bend

121

**4**

4th St.
Division St.

**A**

**B**

**C**

312

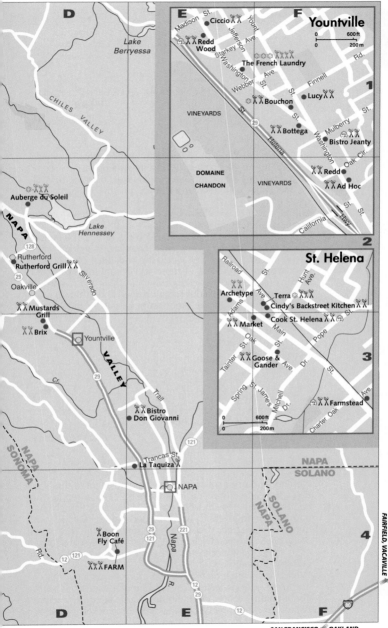

# Yountville

Madison St.
Ciccio
Redd Wood
Jefferson St.
Starkey
Yount Ave.
The French Laundry
Washington St.
Webber St.
Finnell Rd.
Bouchon
Lucy
VINEYARDS
Bottega
Mulberry St.
Washington
Bistro Jeanty
Oak Cir.
DOMAINE
CHANDON
VINEYARDS
Redd
Ad Hoc
Hwy.
California

0  600ft
0  200m

D
E
F
1
2

Lake
Berryessa

CHILES VALLEY

NAPA

Auberge du Soleil

Lake
Hennessey

Rutherford
Rutherford Grill
Oakville
Silverado
Mustards Grill
Brix
Yountville

VALLEY

Cr.
Trail

Bistro
Don Giovanni

## St. Helena

Railroad
Hunt Ave.
Archetype
Adams St.
Terra
Cindy's Backstreet Kitchen
Cook St. Helena
Market
Oak Ave.
Main St.
Pope St.
Goose & Gander
Tainter St.
Spring St.
Mitchell Dr.
James
St. James
Charter Oak
Dr.
Farmstead
Ave.

0  600ft
0  200m

3

Trancas St.
La Taquiza

NAPA
SONOMA

NAPA
NAPA

NAPA
NAPA
SOLANO

NAPA

Boon Fly Café
FARM

Napa R.

SOLANO
NAPA

4

# Ad Hoc

American ✖✖

**F2**

6476 Washington St. (bet. California Dr. & Oak Circle), Yountville

**Phone:** 707-944-2487
**Web:** www.adhocrestaurant.com
**Price:** $$$

Lunch Sun
Dinner Thu – Mon

By far the most casual of Thomas Keller's three Yountville restaurants, Ad Hoc offers accessible American fare served family-style in a bright and inviting wood-paneled room. Waits are inevitable without a reservation, but the engaging staff keeps things hopping.

Ad Hoc's breezy prix-fixe menu boasts four delicious courses (three at brunch), kicking off with a salad like the luscious heirloom tomato, arugula, and pickled red onion. The famous fried chicken, served every other Monday, is tender, spicy, deeply flavorful—and well worth the additional cost. Be sure to save room for dessert, because you'll want to linger over a wedge of the decadent peanut butter pie. Silky and custardy, it comes complete with a dollop of whipped chocolate Chantilly on top. In the back garden, Addendum sells boxed lunches and that famous fried chicken to go

# Angèle

French ✖✖

**B4**

540 Main St. (at 5th St.), Napa

**Phone:** 707-252-8115
**Web:** www.angelerestaurant.com
**Price:** $$

Lunch & dinner daily

Nestled into a sun-splashed river bend adjacent to the Napa River Inn, attractively rustic Angèle is set in a repurposed boathouse replete with wood panels and beams, French blue-framed windows, and linen-dressed tables topped with miniature olive trees. Not only is the setting of this downtown Napa *bijou* completely charming, but the impressive pedigree of its father-daughter team includes experience at key wine country destinations.

While the menu at dinner may be more expanded, both day and night options feature classical French specialties with a contemporary touch. From nibbles like steak tartare and pork rillettes, to more hearty offerings (maybe chicken *pot au feu* or veal sweetbreads?), this is well-prepared bistro food in all its glory.

# Archetype

**E2**

1429 Main St. (bet. Adams & Pine Sts.), St. Helena

**Phone:** 707-968-9200
**Web:** www.archetypenapa.com
**Price:** $$

Lunch & dinner Wed – Sun

Simple, sophisticated, and stylish, Archetype—designed by legendary local architect Howard Backen—is "archetypally" wine country-chic. The former retail store still displays a few local goods, from pottery to small-batch spirits, but the array of regulars are really here to enjoy either lunch or dinner in its beautiful dining room, full of lush bamboo and rattan chairs. Ryder Zetts, formerly of Solbar, runs the kitchen, riffing on American classics for a moneyed, stylish crowd. Wood-oven-grilled duck breast arrives over a delicate white miso and black tea jus, while thick buckwheat blinis are topped with creamy burrata and sweet huckleberry compote. And for a non-barbecue restaurant, the baby back ribs are surprisingly outstanding.

# Bistro Don Giovanni

**E3**

4110 Howard Ln. (at Hwy. 29), Napa

**Phone:** 707-224-3300
**Web:** www.bistrodongiovanni.com
**Price:** $$

Lunch & dinner daily

Located just off Highway 29, Bistro Don Giovanni can be easy to pass, but driving by would mean forgoing incredible Napa people-watching and superbly consistent Italian food. Park among the olive trees and grapevines, then take a seat in the airy, flower-decked dining room. If it's sunny, choose one of the rattan chairs on the peerless, postcard-perfect garden terrace.

A *pizzaiolo* mans the wood-burning oven in the front, firing up a selection of seasonal pies that are popular with families. Meanwhile, the adult set opts for fried olives with warm Marcona almonds, *garganelli* with duck ragù, and seared salmon with tomato-chive butter, all washed down with local wines. Already conquered a number of wineries? Switch to a cocktail at the busy front bar.

# Auberge du Soleil ✧

**D2**

180 Rutherford Hill Rd. (off the Silverado Trail), Rutherford

**Phone:** 707-963-1211  
**Web:** www.aubergedusoleil.com  
**Price:** $$$$

Lunch & dinner daily

This is one of the first restaurants to elevate the Napa Valley to greatness. For the past decade, Chef Robert Curry has been ensuring its legacy with cooking that is the very definition of California cuisine: global flavors expressed through local, seasonal, and fresh ingredients. The kitchen's work is as impressive as the setting. Everything seems just a bit more beautiful from this extraordinary perch, overlooking the vineyards, mountains, and gardens. Those terrace tables have some of the best views in northern California.

Meals may be inspired by the comforting fall flavors of rosemary-enriched chicken jus, root vegetable purée, and intensely salty-sweet pancetta to complement a fillet of red snapper. Medallions of bacon-wrapped veal are cooked to a uniform blush, served alongside gnocchi interspersed with pearl onions and balsamic-braised radicchio for refreshing bitterness. For dessert, a buttery lemon cake is topped with faintly pine-scented ice cream, deep purple huckleberries, and lemon meringue.

Service is stylish, polite, and manages to refill your glass after each sip, without seeming intrusive.

Their wine list is one of the most notable in the valley and proudly showcases local growers.

# Bistro Jeanty

F1

**French** ✗✗

6510 Washington St. (at Mulberry St.), Yountville

**Phone:** 707-944-0103          Lunch & dinner daily
**Web:** www.bistrojeanty.com
**Price:** $$

Napa transforms into the French countryside via a meal at Jeanty, which serves rib-sticking favorites like coq au vin, boeuf Bourguignon, and a sinfully rich milk-fed veal chop with chanterelle mushrooms and Camembert sauce. But California's lighter side is here, too: a salad of silken smoked trout and frisée is garden-fresh, and daily specials highlight the best in local produce.

The classic bistro accoutrements (yellow walls, wooden tables, framed retro posters) are present and accounted for, but there's an element of quirky fun here as well—from the flower-bedecked bicycle out front to the porcelain hens and hogs that dot the dining room. Like the flaky, caramelized, and unmissable tarte Tatin, this is a gorgeous update on a classic.

# Boon Fly Café

D4

**American** ✗

4048 Sonoma Hwy. (at Los Carneros Ave.), Napa

**Phone:** 707-299-4870          Lunch & dinner daily
**Web:** www.thecarnerosinn.com
**Price:** $$

Set amid the verdant pastures of the chic Carneros Inn, this rustic red barn is a friendly and unpretentious modern roadhouse, complete with a gracious staff. Fresh and well-made American standards include a classic Caesar with toasted onion, shaved parmesan, and anchovy vinaigrette; or a generous Margherita flatbread pizza layered with mozzarella, tomatoes, and Italian sausage. Quesadillas and burritos are good, too. Be sure to check the blackboard for daily specials.

Though it's open from breakfast to dinner, Boon Fly Café's most popular meal is brunch, when parties wait on porch swings for eggs Benedict with jalapeño hollandaise. Whether they're locals in the know about its relaxed charm or travelers seeking a break, everybody leaves with a smile.

# Bottega

**F1**

Italian

6525 Washington St. (near Yount St.), Yountville

**Phone:** 707-945-1050  
**Web:** www.botteganapavalley.com  
**Price:** $$

Lunch Tue – Sun  
Dinner nightly

Michael Chiarello is one of the original celebrity chefs, and his higher-end Napa outpost draws fans from around the globe seeking a glimpse of the *NapaStyle* star. Hopefuls are indeed likely to see him in the kitchen, drizzling olive oil on plates of creamy, almost liquid fresh burrata and marinated mushrooms; or pouring persimmon purée across thick slices of yellowfin tuna crudo. Even the wine list features his house blends, which pair nicely with pastas like whole-wheat *tagliarini* tossed in a pitch-perfect Bolognese.

Large and boisterous, Bottega's autumn-hued dining room welcomes crowds with comfy banquettes; find lovely outdoor seating by the firepit. A well-made tiramisu and espresso offer a fine *Italiano* end to the festivities.

# Bounty Hunter

**B4**

American

975 First St. (at Main St.), Napa

**Phone:** 707-226-3976  
**Web:** www.bountyhunterwinebar.com  
**Price:** $$

Lunch & dinner daily

California cowboys will want to post up at downtown Napa's fun fusion of a barbecue joint and wine bar. Large and well-lit, with taxidermy hung from the brick walls, country music on the playlist, and a striking saloon-like façade, this is a cool and unpretentious hangout.

If you're not all tasted out, Bounty Hunter's "wine slingers" will be happy to recommend something from the list of wines by the glass—there are forty!—available as two ounce pours, a flight, or for purchase. As for the food, wildly flavorful dry-rubbed St. Louis-style ribs practically fall off the bone, and three house-made sauces provide plenty of pep. Delicious shrimp and scallop ceviche tostadas are a fun south-of-the-border option with zippy acidity and creamy avocado.

# Bouchon ❀

**F1**

### 6534 Washington St. (at Yount St.), Yountville

**Phone:** 707-944-8037
**Web:** www.bouchonbistro.com
**Price:** $$$

Lunch & dinner daily

Timeless French food is re-created with great regard for quality and technique at Thomas Keller's exuberant brasserie, set down the street from his iconic French Laundry. Complete with lush potted palms, shimmering brass accents, and enormous mirrors, this chic dining room is the spitting image of a Parisian bistro. A theatrical crowd uplifts the space with conviviality, and every lavish banquette or stool at the bustling bar is full. Always.

Thanks to the house bakery next door, the bread here is ace, so grab an extra hunk of the supremely fresh and crusty epi baguette to slather with butter. The menu lists well-executed bistro classics, including a rosy foie gras torchon with seasonal orange preserves and golden-brown toasted brioche. And, thanks to the attentive staff, you may even get a second slice. Then, braised lamb demonstrates the power of rustic French cooking, set over polenta with grilled young leeks and carrots.

Desserts are quite literally the icing on the cake and often the very definition of decadence. Even the humble pie is elevated here to be served as an almond-spiced pear, glazed with juice and set over a tiny round of puff pastry matched with rich vanilla ice cream.

319

# Brix

Californian XX

**D3**

Californian XX

**7377 St. Helena Hwy. (at Washington St.), Napa**

**Phone:** 707-944-2749
**Web:** www.brix.com
**Price:** $$$

Lunch & dinner daily

This roadside treat overlooking the Mayacamas Mountains is almost as lauded for its 16-acre produce garden (which also provides many of the ingredients seen on your plate) and vineyard, as it is for its ultra-seasonal and eclectic-Californian cuisine. Dishes are wide-ranging and often refined as verified in ricotta gnocchi cooked to a gentle gold in rosemary-browned butter with creamy squash, plump Medjool dates, and almonds; or saffron and orange salmon that arrives firm and pink with quail eggs, dill aïoli, and potato salad. An extensive Sunday brunch buffet highlights offerings from the wood-fired oven and charcoal grill.

The interior feels like a mountain ranch with its stone walls, fireplaces, and chandeliers cleverly crafted from cutlery. Service is exceptional.

# Bui Bistro

**B3**

Vietnamese XX

**976 Pearl St. (bet. Main & West Sts.), Napa**

**Phone:** 707-255-5417
**Web:** www.buibistro.com
**Price:** ⊖

Lunch & dinner Mon – Sat

Large and airy, Bui looks and feels like an upscale French bistro, rife with an Asian pantry serving Vietnamese cuisine—and so the fun begins! Clean-lined but not stark, the space contrasts olive-green walls with bright red booths and tall paper lanterns. Solo diners hit the bar for a chardonnay and plate of fried rice with well-seasoned tofu. Dishes like earthy banana flower with strips of tender chicken and cubes of juicy Bosc pear aren't Hanoi-authentic, but are tasty all the same. Purists might prefer the mild yet fragrant chicken curry, studded with lemongrass and ginger.

Delicious sautéed pea sprouts with olive oil and garlic are a favorite among vegetarians. For dessert, a Makrut lime crème brulée underscores the fusion of the menu.

# Ca'Momi Osteria

B4

Italian 🍴🍴

**1141 1st St. (bet. Coombs & Main Sts.), Napa**

**Phone:** 707-224-6664          Lunch & dinner daily
**Web:** www.camomiosteria.com
**Price:** $$

A spinoff of the beloved Ca'Momi Enoteca kiosk in the nearby Oxbow Public Market, this stand-alone spot aims to promote *buon gusto* with its "heartcrafted" food (as indicated in a sign above the bar). Big and airy, with exposed brick and wooden beams, it is abuzz with *pizzaiolos* turning out Neapolitan pies from the wood-burning oven (note that the counter opposite the fire is the best seat in the house).

The massive menu is inspired by every region of Italy featuring crispy Piemontese sunchoke chips dusted with salt and fried parsley as well as Tuscan spinach-ricotta *gnudi* in creamy butter-and-sage sauce. There are also a variety of outstanding pizzas and the Campanian *angioletti* or fried pizza dough with hazelnut and chocolate makes for a sinfully delicious finish.

# C Casa

Mexican 🍴

C3

**610 1st St. (at McKinstry St.), Napa**

**Phone:** 707-226-7700          Lunch & dinner daily
**Web:** www.myccasa.com
**Price:** ⊜⊜

Even in the foodie paradise of Napa's Oxbow Public Market, this little taqueria stands out for both its sustainable ethos and its creative, flavor-packed food.

Tortillas are pressed by hand for each taco, with innovative fillings like cumin-spiced rotisserie duck with spinach, goat cheese, and orange segments, and citrusy prawns with roasted corn, cabbage, and cilantro *crema*. But while C Casa's take on tacos is high-end, its surroundings are relaxed: you'll order at the counter and receive a buzzer. Peruse the full array of Oxbow vendors (think oysters, coffee, and everything in between) while you wait, then head for the communal seating area to nosh. Bonus: the entire menu is gluten-free, including a tempting selection of baked goods.

# Ciccio

Italian ✗✗

**E1**

**6770 Washington St. (bet. Madison & Pedroni Sts.), Yountville**

**Phone:** 707-945-1000        Dinner Wed – Sun
**Web:** www.ciccionapavalley.com
**Price:** $$

A pleasant contrast to the sleek new spots around town, Ciccio's country-style curtains and slatted front porch are a ticket to another era. Its location (a wood-framed 1916-era grocery) could pass as some John Wayne film set, but Ciccio is more of a spaghetti Western, thanks to the focused Italian-influenced menu featuring a mega-rich pasta accented with fresh uni, crisp breadcrumbs, and a generous dose of cream. Segue from carbs to the bone-in pork chop with fennel gratin, but don't miss the remarkable signature Ciccio sponge cake, soaked in citrus liqueur and topped with grapefruit and orange.

With turn-of-the-century square footage, tables are a hot ticket here. Expect a wait for even a lowly bar stool, happily passed with a glass of local pinot.

# Cindy's Backstreet Kitchen

American ✗✗

**F2**

**1327 Railroad Ave. (bet. Adams St & Hunt Ave), St. Helena**

**Phone:** 707-963-1200        Lunch & dinner daily
**Web:** www.cindysbackstreetkitchen.com
**Price:** $$

Owner Cindy Pawlcyn may be a nationally renowned chef, but a meal at Backstreet feels like dining in a friend's home—albeit a well-appointed one with great food. From a blossoming garden retreat to the capacious dining area, this space is warm and comfortable. If there's a wait, be sure to perch at the bar, where genial regulars are happy to welcome new diners to the fold.

The cooking is eclectic and ingredient-driven, from the pristine tomatoes in a "Vietnamese vinaigrette" with fish paste, lemongrass, and Thai basil, to the radishes, crisp arugula, and tender chicken in a creamy curried salad. Enjoy it all with an excellent glass of local Chardonnay, and save room for the tart lemon buttermilk pudding cake with raspberries and crème fraîche.

# Cole's Chop House

B3

Steakhouse ✖✖

**1122 Main St. (bet. 1st & Pearl Sts.), Napa**

**Phone:** 707-224-6328                                      Dinner nightly
**Web:** www.coleschophouse.com
**Price:** $$$$

Prime meat at prime prices is the modus operandi at Cole's, which gives diners their pick of deeply flavorful cuts like dry-aged California rib-eye or 21-day Chicago dry-aged New York strip. Faithful accompaniments like roasted Brussels sprouts with bacon, baked potatoes, creamed spinach, and asparagus with Hollandaise round out the menu. While traditional desserts like Bourbon bread pudding or a flourless chocolate cake dusted with powdered sugar make for a satisfying end to any meal. A selection of gutsy red wines, Bourbons and single-malt Scotches stand up to the steak.

In place of the clubby atmosphere of traditional steakhouses, this Napa retreat is more refined, with a barn-like stone interior and choice of cozy booths or mezzanine tables.

# Cook St. Helena

Italian ✖✖

F3

**1310 Main St. (bet. Adams St. & Hunt Ave.), St. Helena**

**Phone:** 707-963-7088                                      Lunch Mon – Sat
**Web:** www.cooksthelena.com                                Dinner nightly
**Price:** $$

An artistically lit antelope head hangs in this Italian haven on St. Helena's main drag. Random? Not really, when one considers how rare solid cooking and sane prices can be in this tony burg. The cozy space has two seating options: a gleaming marble counter as well as tables that stretch from front to back (the ones up front are lighter, airier, and more preferable).

The food is thoughtful and refined with a daily rotating risotto, house-stretched mozzarella and burrata, and glorious pastas like ricotta *fazoletti* with a deeply flavored Bolognese. Grilled octopus salad with potatoes, olives, and tomato dressing is boosted by prime ingredients and careful seasoning. The wine list tempts at dinner, but bloody Marys are all the rage at brunch, served at sister restaurant Cook Tavern next door.

Wine Country ▲ Napa Valley

# Evangeline

American ✕✕

**1226 Washington St. (bet. 1st St. & Lincoln Ave.), Calistoga**

**Phone:** 707-341-3131                 Lunch Sat – Sun
**Web:** www.evangelinenapa.com          Dinner nightly
**Price:** $$

Jazzy New Orleans flair infuses every inch of this Southern charmer, which adds just a hint of spice to the easy Californian charm of quaint Calistoga. A trellised garden patio (a must-visit on a warm day) blooms with fragrant jasmine, while the cozy indoor dining room provides an intimate retreat complete with midnight-blue banquettes.

A collection of French bistro- Californian- and Cajun-inspired dishes abound on the approachable menu. Rich, creamy duck rillettes arrive with toasted baguette and red pepper jelly; shrimp etouffee is spicy and complex, its thick, dark roux coating a heap of fluffy white rice; and melt-in-your-mouth tarte Tatin slathered with locally made Three Twins vanilla ice cream is as good as any beignet.

# FARM

Californian ✕✕✕

**4048 Sonoma Hwy. (at Old Sonoma Rd.), Napa**

**Phone:** 707-299-4880                 Dinner nightly
**Web:** www.thecarnerosinn.com
**Price:** $$$

In the compound of the Carneros Inn, FARM welcomes diners with a spacious outdoor lounge area complete with glowing fire pits. Inside, canoodling couples fill the cavernous and dimly lit dining room, which features soaring farmhouse ceilings, cozy banquettes, and a soundtrack of sultry lounge beats.

The restaurant sources many ingredients from its own half-acre garden, which shine in dishes like a bean soup bursting with heirloom specimens from Rancho Gordo and accompanied by a DIY topping bar of fried garlic, spiced croutons, and smoked almonds. A flaky salmon fillet is crowned with crushed mustard seeds and set atop creamy parsnip purée. For dessert, delicate peanut butter panna cotta has a fun twist—a sprinkling of deep-fried jelly cubes.

# Farmstead

Californian ✗✗

**F3**

738 Main St. (at Charter Oak Ave.), St. Helena

**Phone:** 707-963-9181      Lunch & dinner daily
**Web:** www.longmeadowranch.com
**Price:** $$

For a down-home (but still Napa-chic) alternative to the Cal-Ital wine country grind, follow your nose to this Long Meadow Ranch-owned farmhouse, whose intoxicating smoker is parked right in the front yard. The cathedral ceiling, old-school country music, and boisterous locals give Farmstead a permanent buzz; for quieter dining, hit the front terrace.
Dishes are laden with ranch-grown products (from veggies to olive oil), utilized in outstanding preparations like a wood-grilled artichoke with sauce *gribiche*, meatballs with caramelized onions and tomato marmalade, or a smoked chicken sandwich with avocado, sweet onion rings, and a side of herb-fried potatoes. Try the ranch's own wine, or splurge on a fancy bottle at a shockingly reasonable markup.

# Goose & Gander

American ✗✗

**F3**

1245 Spring St. (at Oak Ave.), St. Helena

**Phone:** 707-967-8779      Lunch & dinner daily
**Web:** www.goosegander.com
**Price:** $$

This Napa Valley gastropub continues to up the ambition level without sacrificing the fun. The much-praised burger remains a juicy knockout (complete with duck-fat fries!), but other dishes like grilled asparagus with a *brandade* fritter, poached egg, and smoked trout roe are worthy of equal attention.
Housed in a cottage-like structure just off the St. Helena highway, the Goose has a dark, gentleman's club-like feel with leather chairs, tufted banquettes, and an intimate downstairs bar that serves the full menu. Drinks are a big deal here (the booze list is referred to as a "bible"), so be sure to peruse the wide selection of cocktails—or sip a local vintage.

# The French Laundry ✿ ✿ ✿

Contemporary 𝗫𝗫𝗫𝗫

E1

**6640 Washington St. (at Creek St.), Yountville**

**Phone:** 707-944-2380
**Web:** www.frenchlaundry.com
**Price:** $$$$

Lunch Fri – Sun
Dinner nightly

After more than 20 years of topping every foodie's bucket list, Thomas Keller's legendary destination still doesn't miss a beat, despite behind-the-scenes changes. The cuisine and service remain at their height, but a temporary kitchen has been in use for some time as a shiny new one is finished. This new kitchen may be known as the greatest cooking space in America, not even counting the talent who run it. One thing that will not escape attention however, is that after a last meal on New Year's Eve, The French Laundry will shutter for a period of time as it transitions to its new, knockout kitchen.

Chef Keller continues to pair incredibly technical cooking with wildly fresh ingredients in a setting that is a perfect storm of restaurant greatness—we should all be so lucky to score a reservation here in our lifetime. Choose from two seasonal tasting menus or a vegetarian option. Dinners may highlight signature oysters paired with white sturgeon caviar in a warm sabayon studded with tapioca pearls, followed by golden striped bass with deconstructed deviled eggs.

Located along a shady and winding road, it is the picture of bucolic charm, with ivy creeping up its stone exterior and a homey dining room with elegant everything.

# Grace's Table

International ✗✗

**A4**

1400 2nd St. (at Franklin St.), Napa

**Phone:** 707-226-6200  
**Web:** www.gracestable.net  
**Price:** $$

Lunch & dinner daily

Around the world in four courses without leaving wine country? It's possible at this bright, contemporary downtown Napa space that balances fun with excellence. Only here can a top-notch tamale filled with chipotle pulled pork, green chile, and black beans be followed by cassoulet that would do any Frenchman proud—thanks to its decadent mélange of butter beans, duck confit, and two kinds of sausage.

With Italian and American staples in the mix as well, it might sound too eclectic for one meal, but Grace's Table earns its name with charming service and a thoughtful, well-priced wine list to bridge any gaps between cuisines. Don't miss the satiny, ganache-layered devil's food chocolate cake—a slice is big enough to split, and a winner in any tongue.

# Harvest Table

Californian ✗✗

**C2**

1 Main St. (bet. Lewelling Ln. & Sulphur Springs Ave.), St. Helena

**Phone:** 707-967-4695  
**Web:** www.harvesttablenapa.com  
**Price:** $$$

Lunch Wed – Sun  
Dinner Tue – Sun

Charlie Palmer's Harvest Inn is now also a culinary destination with the arrival of Harvest Table. Its Californian menu relies on local purveyors and the Inn's own gardens for ingredients, and guests are encouraged to tour these grounds before or after meals. The space is simple and appealingly rustic thanks in part to the large brick fireplace. Two covered patios offer a comfy perch to enjoy the natural beauty of the inn.

Smooth dark wood tables can be seen groaning under the weight of such enjoyable items as crunchy pig's head fritters coupled with a light frisée salad and creamy *gribiche*. Batons of yellowfin are then crowned with shaved fennel for balance in texture as well as pickled Fresno chilies for that bit of heat. A sweet-salty peanut butter bar topped with a thin layer of chocolate should be saved (read: savored) for the end.

# La Taquiza

E3

Mexican ✗

**2007 Redwood Rd., Ste. 104 (at Solano Ave.), Napa**

**Phone:** 707-224-2320                              Lunch & dinner Mon – Sat
**Web:** www.lataquizanapa.com
**Price:** ∞

For sustainable *sabor* that doubles as a budget-saver in pricey Napa, La Taquiza's upscale take on Mexican fast food is well worth a visit. Whether you prefer your fish California-style (flame-grilled) or Baja-style (battered and fried), you'll find no end to spicy, tangy, and savory options, available in heat levels from mild to spicy and in configurations from tacos to burritos to rice bowls.

However, the adventurous shouldn't stop at crisp corn tortillas—there's also a fine selection of snappy ceviches, grilled octopus, beer-battered oysters, and other delights from the sea. Counter service is friendly and prompt, and massive, colorful paintings from a local artist give the room a vibe almost as bright as their delicious strawberry *agua fresca*.

# Lucy

F1

Californian ✗✗

**6526 Yount St. (bet. Finnell Rd. & Mulberry St.), Yountville**

**Phone:** 707-204-6030                              Lunch & dinner daily
**Web:** www.lucyrestaurantandbar.com
**Price:** $$$

If you're not staying at the posh Bardessono hotel, come early for a glass of chardonnay and a stroll through the lovely gardens, which provide much of the food for this chic on-site restaurant. Savvy diners can keep the outdoorsy vibe going with a seat on the fountain-accented front terrace, where an afternoon can be happily spent exploring the wine list, heavy on local producers.

Lucy's food is refreshing and casual, with a few fun touches. First, a creamy chilled pea soup is amped up with the addition of yuzu crème fraîche and chunks of meaty lobster, while a spicy rhubarb-and-pineapple chutney electrifies the perfectly seared diver scallops, accompanied by peppery watercress and caramelized fennel. A rich, buttery, and delicious pound cake paired with grapefruit sorbet is a fresh finish worth savoring.

# La Toque

Contemporary 🗙🗙🗙

**B3**

**1314 McKinstry St. (at Soscol Ave.), Napa**

Phone: 707-257-5157     Dinner nightly
Web: www.latoque.com
Price: $$$$

You'll want to tip your own toque in appreciation after a meal at this downtown fine-dining palace in the Westin Verasa Napa, which blends a serious approach to cuisine and service that has just enough cheek to keep things lively.

La Toque may display an oversized inflatable chef's hat hanging above its walkway, but the interior is the soul of modern sophistication, with leather-topped tables, a fireplace, and an extensive wine list—proffered on an iPad. The cadre of staff is notable, and the well-trained, knowledgeable waiters move in synchronicity within the celebratory crowd.

Choose from a four- or five-course à la carte, beginning with exquisite canapés like perfectly seasoned tuna tartare, clams with apple vinaigrette, or crostini with a terrine of foie gras. Thin slices of beef loin carpaccio are lightly smoked, then artfully presented to resemble a flower, topped with creamy tuna sauce, sautéed wild mushroom, and dried tomato. Intense Lebanese spices come to life in wonderfully tender braised squid with dates, almond, cauliflower and a spoonful of Greek yogurt. Desserts like the triple-baked, butter-crunch cake with apple underscore the homey, glamorous, delicious character of the restaurant itself.

# Market

F3

American  ✕✕

**1347 Main St. (bet. Adams St. & Hunt Ave.), St. Helena**

**Phone:** 707-963-3799                                      Lunch & dinner daily
**Web:** www.marketsthelena.com
**Price:** $$

St. Helena's scenic main drag is a trip back to the '50s, complete with quaint shops and an old-school movie theater. But the food at this legendary downtown fixture is happily modern. Lobster rolls forgo buttered buns for Vietnamese-inspired rice paper with avocado and mango (all dipped in a delicious cilantro-basil-lime sauce); while a seared steak sandwich, loaded with onion and jack cheese, gets a spark from pickled jalapeño. Childhood-inspired s'mores for dessert end the meal on a nostalgic and graceful note.

The massive mahogany bar (a magnificent eBay find) is the heart of the pleasant space, which boasts stone-covered walls and big, open windows for prime people-watching. Service is friendly and fuss-free, not unlike its picturesque surrounds.

# Miminashi

B4

Japanese  ✕

**821 Coombs St. (bet. 2nd & 3rd Sts.), Napa**

**Phone:** 707-254-9464                                      Lunch Mon– Fri
**Web:** www.miminashi.com                                  Dinner nightly
**Price:** $$

*Izakaya* fare gets Californian flair at this downtown Napa site, which has a distinctive and minimalist look inspired by several trips to Japan. A buzzy crowd of locals fills the wooden booths and tables, while an arrow-shaped bar is a major draw for solo diners.

A variety of skewered chicken parts grilled over the white-hot *binchotan* are the highlight of the menu—imagine the likes of succulent and smoky chicken thighs, or springy *tsukune* in an umami-rich *tare* glaze. A handful of seats at the narrow counter allow guests to chat with the grill cook. The rest of the menu emphasizes local produce, including rice and noodle bowls stuffed with seasonal vegetables; crunchy sweet corn fritters with Kewpie mayo; as well as gingery pan-fried chicken *gyoza*.

# Mustards Grill

American ✗✗

**D3**

**7399 St. Helena Hwy. (at Hwy. 29), Yountville**

| | |
|---|---|
| **Phone:** | 707-944-2424 |
| **Web:** | www.mustardsgrill.com |
| **Price:** | **$$** |

Lunch & dinner daily

At Cindy Pawlcyn's iconic roadhouse, it's a joy to eat your greens. Lettuces are freshly plucked from the restaurant's bountiful garden boxes and tossed with tasty dressings including a shallot- and Dijon mustard-spiked Banyuls vinaigrette. Fish of the day may unveil grilled halibut sauced with oxtail reduction and plated with silken leeks, fingerling potatoes, and baby carrots. But, save room as this is not the place to skip dessert, and the lemon-lime tart capped with brown sugar meringue that is fittingly described on the menu as "ridiculously tall," doesn't disappoint.

It should come as no surprise that there's usually a wait for a table here. But no matter; use the time to take a stroll on the grounds for a preview of what the kitchen has in store.

# Norman Rose Tavern

American ✗✗

**A4**

**1401 1st St. (at Franklin St.), Napa**

| | |
|---|---|
| **Phone:** | 707-258-1516 |
| **Web:** | www.normanrosenapa.com |
| **Price:** | **$$** |

Lunch & dinner daily

Right in the heart of downtown Napa, this appealing gastropub offers something for everyone, from hearty bacon-wrapped meatloaf with a smoky coffee-barbecue glaze, to satisfying and soul-warming vegetable soup. Burgers, salads, and even a menu of dressed-up fries (from chili-cheese, truffle-parmesan and sausage gravy to cheddar "disco" fries) are both appealing and affordable.

The open, wood-beamed space with its rich leather banquettes and soft lighting, is ideal for both a beer-soaked game at the bar or group dinners in the bustling dining room. Solo diners will enjoy well-lit perches that peer into the kitchen, and charming servers are more than adept at keeping the party going until the last wedge of decadent, triple-layered carrot cake is devoured.

# Oenotri

Italian ✗✗

**A4**

### 1425 1st St. (bet. Franklin & School Sts.), Napa

**Phone:** 707-252-1022
**Web:** www.oenotri.com
**Price:** $$

Lunch Sat – Sun
Dinner nightly

There's no sweeter greeting than the aroma of wood smoke that beckons diners into this downtown standout. And with its Neapolitan pizza oven, sunny textiles, and exposed brick, Oenotri—from an ancient Italian word for "wine cultivator"—looks as good as it smells.

Chef/owner Tyler Rodde imbues the cooking of Southern Italy with a dash of Californian spirit and the resulting cuisine is nothing short of enticing. Options change with the season, but true fans know that pizza is a must. Mixed chicory salad with *mozzarella di bufala*, pickled red chilies, and house-cured *salametto* is also a crowd-pleaser. Not far behind is the *torchio*, or corkscrew pasta, presented with diced roasted winter squash, toasted pine nuts, fried sage, and a drizzle of brown butter.

# Press

Steakhouse ✗✗✗

**C2**

### 587 St. Helena Hwy. (near Inglewood Ave.), St. Helena

**Phone:** 707-967-0550
**Web:** www.presssthelena.com
**Price:** $$$$

Dinner Wed – Mon

It's hard to get more wine country-chic than this gorgeous farmhouse-inspired restaurant, perfectly situated along the St. Helena highway, for wrapping up a day of wine tasting. With a wood-burning fireplace, soaring ceilings, and rich leather chairs, it's a genuine looker, drawing an affluent crowd of tourists to relax and savor some great *vino*.

The casual yet sleek vibe extends to the steakhouse menu, where gorgeous grass-fed bavettes and buttery filet mignons can be seen on nearly every table. You'll definitely want to order some of the generously portioned sides, like earthy brown butter mushrooms or caramelized Brussels sprouts with bacon, which can easily feed four. Velvety sunchoke soup with walnut yogurt is yet another exquisite addition.

# Redd

Contemporary ✗✗

**F2**

### 6480 Washington St. (at Oak Circle), Yountville

**Phone:** 707-944-2222        Lunch Fri – Sun
**Web:** www.reddnapavalley.com        Dinner nightly
**Price:** $$$$

In this quaint hamlet, Redd stands out both for its modern look and contemporary approach to cuisine, with flavors from around the globe. A meal here might begin with Chinese-style lettuce cups filled with succulent chicken, stir-fried eggplant, and fresh herbs; then veer into India and Spain simultaneously via a Petrale sole fillet with coconut-jasmine rice, curry-saffron broth, and salty-spicy chorizo. And any Londoner would be proud of the buttery sticky toffee pudding, with tart crème fraîche ice cream and huckleberries.

The sleek, modernist décor attracts a sedate crowd, attended to by professional servers.

On nice days, be sure not to miss the serene outdoor patio, which begs to be savored with a glass of Joseph George sauvignon blanc from Yountville.

# Redd Wood 😳

Italian ✗✗

**E1**

### 6755 Washington St. (bet. Madison & Pedroni Sts.), Yountville

**Phone:** 707-299-5030        Lunch & dinner daily
**Web:** www.redd-wood.com
**Price:** $$

Napa's answer to the hip Cal-Ital hot spots of San Francisco, Redd Wood boasts an edgy indie soundtrack and a parade of bearded, tattooed waiters. But unlike some cityside establishments, the staff here is personable and enthusiastic, and there's plenty of breathing room (including a private area that's popular for events).

Artisan pizzas are the main draw, like a sassy spin on "eggplant parm" with *coppa*, basil, crispy breadcrumbs, and fried garlic. But don't let that limit your choices, as the house-cured *salumi*, fresh pastas, and alluring antipasti (think chilled corn soup with house bacon and pickled chanterelles) are also winners. Just be sure to save some room for the outstanding toffee cannoli, as they are some of the best you'll ever have.

# The Restaurant at Meadowood ✿ ✿ ✿

Contemporary ✕✕✕✕

**C2**

**900 Meadowood Ln. (off Silverado Trail), St. Helena**

Phone: 707-967-1205     Dinner Tue – Sat
Web: www.therestaurantatmeadowood.com
Price: **$$$$**

Located in a sprawling resort amid mountains and vineyards, The Restaurant at Meadowood is the peak of wine country-chic, and the kind of place that leaves you speechless. The bar and lounge resemble a plush mountain lodge by way of fireplaces, vintage books, and soft leather seating. Beyond this, the extraordinary dining room boasts a vaulted ceiling over tables made from granite and columns of Canadian redwood. Every detail conveys American beauty and grace; service is usually faultless, anticipatory and adept.

Chef Christopher Kostow's cuisine is not only as beautiful as the surrounds but thoroughly delicious and so creative that it can seem like California's avant-garde kitchen. Each course seems to outdo the previous, beginning with delicately smoked eel fillet wrapped in black nori with beef tongue. Lobster is grilled and then served chilled with cold-braised sunchokes, two types of seaweed, and portions of caviar that boost the dish with enormous flavors. Black cod is cooked with fragrant spices, sliced, and served with matching sections of root vegetables cooked al dente for a trompe l'oeil that must be experienced.

Little pastry cups of chocolate babka are melt-in-your-mouth spectacular.

# Rutherford Grill

American ✗✗

**D2**

**1180 Rutherford Rd. (at Hwy. 29), Rutherford**

**Phone:** 707-963-1792                                       Lunch & dinner daily
**Web:** www.hillstone.com
**Price:** $$

As the crowds filter out of neighboring Beaulieu Vineyards and other Highway 29 wineries, they head straight to this upscale chain, which boasts long lines at even the earliest hours. Kudos to the amiable host staff for handling them smoothly. The dark wood interior is clubby yet accommodating, and a large patio offers drinks for waiting diners.

Every portion here can easily serve two, beginning with a seasonal vegetable platter boasting buttery Brussels sprouts, a wild rice salad, and braised red cabbage. For those looking to stave off tasting-induced hangovers, the steak and enchilada platter is *the* ticket with plenty of juicy tri-tip, yellow and red *escabeche* sauce, and a poached egg. A wedge of classic banana cream pie delivers the knockout punch.

# Sam's Social Club

American ✗✗

**B1**

**1712 Lincoln Ave. (at Indian Springs Resort), Calistoga**

**Phone:** 707-942-4913                                       Lunch & dinner daily
**Web:** www.samssocialclub.com
**Price:** $$

Despite its historic Spanish colonial look, this easygoing restaurant at Calistoga's Indian Springs Resort is actually a newcomer. Named for resort founder Samuel Brannan, it boasts a sizable lounge full of comfortable couches and bright murals, a Mission Revival dining room with a stylish country-Western vibe, and a big patio, complete with a geyser-fed water feature.

The unpretentious atmosphere extends to the plates, from a lively gazpacho made from fresh local tomatoes and endowed with plenty of jalapeño bite to a delectable seared chicken paillard with rosemary Hollandaise as well as a potato-and-green bean salad. Napa tourists have already caught on: you'll find them happily sharing bottles of wine and digging into plates of strawberry-rhubarb crisp.

# Solbar &#10047;

B1

**755 Silverado Trail (at Rosedale Rd.), Calistoga**

**Phone:** 707-226-0850
**Web:** www.solagecalistoga.com
**Price:** $$$

Lunch & dinner daily

It may take a few twists and turns around the palatial Solage Calistoga property to locate Solbar, but once inside, you'll find that a recent décor overhaul has it looking fresher and more sophisticated than ever. The dining room now features high-backed gray banquettes perfect for romance-seeking couples, and a contemporary fireplace still adds flickering warmth.

Well-heeled wine country tourists flock to the beautiful outdoor patio to dine under a canopy of palms and twinkling lights, while larger groups should consider another of Solbar's new additions: the glassed-in Chef's Atrium, which offers a private seven-course chef's menu for parties of up to ten.

While its look is updated, Solbar's culinary focus hasn't changed: it still offers Californian cuisine at its finest, with ultra-local produce accented by globe-trotting influences, like an inspired Mexican appetizer of grilled gulf prawns, pickled nopales, fork-tender carnitas, and yellow *mole*. The lightly crusted red snapper comes bathed in a saffron soubise, with heavenly Yukon gold gnocchi and roasted red kale sprouts beneath. And the rum and butterscotch pudding, topped with amaretti cookies, is a buttery delight of a dessert.

# Terra

Contemporary XXX

F2

**1345 Railroad Ave. (bet. Adams St. & Hunt Ave.), St. Helena**

Phone: 707-963-8931  Dinner Thu – Mon
Web: www.terrarestaurant.com
Price: **$$$$**

Serious and mature yet understated, Terra is quaintly tucked into a 19th century building known as The Hatchery (because it really was a chicken hatchery). The décor embraces its rustic past with an eye on luxury, through floor-to-ceiling wine racks, exposed stone and chunky wood beams. The result looks decidedly more old-world European than 21st century wine country—nothing here changes and that is a nice thing.

The kitchen's distinct personality is evident in each seasonally driven menu, ranging from four to six courses of Japanese and Mediterranean-influenced cuisine. Begin with broiled and marinated black cod served in a clear shellfish broth floating a dumpling stuffed with minced shrimp. A fine, delicate hand is clear in the light and airy *chawan mushi* filled with remarkably tender lobster meat finished with a few snips of chives. Rosy duck breast is served atop creamy polenta scattered with chanterelles and foie gras duck jus.

Classic desserts promise wonderful balance of flavors. Find evidence of this in the tartlet filled with huckleberries that are none too sweet, deliciously tart, and a perfect contrast to the crispy oatmeal crumble on top, as well as the crème fraîche ice cream on the side.

# Torc

American ✗✗

**B3**

### 1140 Main St. (bet. 1st & Pearl Sts.), Napa

**Phone:** 707-252-3293        Dinner Wed – Mon
**Web:** www.torcnapa.com
**Price:** $$

Torc may be Gaelic for "boar," but the food from Chef Sean O'Toole (who boasts the aforementioned boar on his family crest) is definitely not Irish. The large menu offers dishes with globe-trotting influences: Italian-leaning gnocchi with peas and favas; swordfish with artichokes and calamari; as well as a free-range roast chicken for two are some of his signatures. Classic desserts include a highly refined milk-chocolate caramel bar, and the wines are great too—look to the warm and genuine staff to recommend a well-priced bottle from the moderately-sized list.

As for the ambience, the former Ubuntu space remains quite the looker with its exposed brick walls, highly coveted banquettes (complete with views of the open kitchen), and industrial-barn vibe.

# Two Birds/One Stone

Fusion ✗✗

**C2**

### 3020 St. Helena Hwy. (bet. Ehlers & Lodi Lns.), St. Helena

**Phone:** 707-302-3777        Dinner Thu – Mon
**Web:** www.twobirdsonestonenapa.com
**Price:** $$

Acclaimed Chefs Douglas Keane and Sang Yoon joined forces for this hip St. Helena aviary, located within the recently renovated Freemark Abbey Winery. The space blends the original stone walls with steel trusses, overhead skylights, as well as a spacious patio—reflecting the menu's Californian take on traditional Japanese *kushiyaki.*

Meals start with seasonal small plates like *hirame* sashimi with compressed melon and cucumber or duck egg custard with lemon verbena, crab, and uni. Then shift into the big selection of grilled skewers, from chicken thighs with Thai basil vinaigrette to silky yuzu-glazed pork belly with kimchi and grilled scallions. They pair nicely with one of the exclusive wines produced just for the restaurant—or a splash of Japanese whisky.

# Wine Spectator Greystone

Californian XX

C2

**2555 Main St. (at Deer Park Rd.), St. Helena**

**Phone:** 707-967-1010                     Lunch & dinner Tue – Sat
**Web:** www.ciarestaurants.com
**Price:** $$$

The kitchen is the classroom at the Culinary Institute of America's West Coast training restaurant, housed (with the school) in the former Christian Brothers château. The big, visually impressive room—with stone walls, copper lighting, and display of oversized spoons and whisks—is a comfortable perch in which to watch students at work in the open kitchen. Dishes showcase seasonal ingredients that are sure to highlight the talents of these chefs in training. And though the menu may change daily, the diverse offerings may reveal an autumnal plate of tender butternut squash gnocchi sautéed in a light shallot cream sauce. Other items guaranteed to please include a crisp-skinned fillet of Artic char set over celery root purée with dots of garlicky saffron aïoli.

# Zuzu

Spanish

B4

**829 Main St. (bet. 2nd & 3rd Sts.), Napa**

**Phone:** 707-224-8555                     Lunch Mon – Fri
**Web:** www.zuzunapa.com                    Dinner nightly
**Price:** $$

This Mediterranean-inspired cutie was dishing out small plates long before it was cool, and its rustic bi-level space still draws a steady crowd of local regulars. Spanish-style tile floors, a pressed-tin ceiling, and honey-colored walls give Zuzu an enchanting old-world vibe, setting the scene for sharing the more than two dozen tapas, both *frio* and *caliente*. They include the popular *boquerónes*, grilled bread heaped with aïoli, hard-boiled eggs, and cured anchovies, as well as the outstanding pork cheek—its rich, caramelized flavor balanced by a tart sherry gastrique. In the evening, killer wood-fired paellas are worth saving a slot for.

For similar cuisine in a more modern atmosphere, sister restaurant La Taberna is also worth a visit.

# Sonoma County

## WINE & DINE

Bordering the North Bay, Sonoma County boasts around 76 miles of Pacific coastline and over 250 wineries. Eclipsed as a wine region by neighboring Napa Valley, this county's wineries know how to take full advantage of some of California's best grape-growing conditions. Today, thirteen distinct wine appellations (AVAs) have been assigned in this area, which is slightly larger than the state of Rhode Island itself, and produce a groundbreaking range of fine varietals. But, this county is also cherished for its culinary destinations starting with **The Naked Pig**, an amazing pit-stop for brunch or lunch. Reinforcing the wine country's ethos of farm-to-table dining, the items on offer here ooze with all things local and sustainable—maybe savory leek waffles with SCMC bacon and Point Reyes blue cheese? But, there are plenty of big and bold bites to be had in town. **Bar-B-Que Smokehouse** in Sebastopol is quite literally award-winning, when their 'cue took home the crown at the **Sonoma County Harvest Fair** in 2010. Other premium pleasures include **Screamin' Mimi's**, a local but nationally known ice cream shop that has been preparing its 300-plus recipes since 1995, as well as **Moustache Baked Goods**, a boutique operation churning out exceptional, all-American baked goods with

quirky names. In fact, cupcakes (like The Outlaw or even The Vitner) have been known to cultivate a sizable following. The North American headquarters of the South American energy-boosting beverage line, **Guayaki Yerba Mate Cafe**, is also settled here as a café-cum-community center, while **The National Heirloom Exposition** is commended among epicureans for its sustainable farming and healthy food practices. Along Highway 12 heading north, byroads lead to isolated wineries, each of which puts its own unique stamp on the business of winemaking. Named after the river that enabled Russian trading outposts along the coast, **The Russian River Valley** is one of the coolest growing regions in Sonoma, largely due to the river basin that acts as a conduit for coastal climates. At the upper end of the Russian River, **Dry Creek Valley** yields excellent sauvignon blanc, chardonnay, and pinot noir. This region is also justifiably famous for zinfandel—a grape that does especially well in the valley's rock-strewn soil. And for snacks to go with these notable sips, the town's eight-acre plaza is occupied by restaurants, shops, and other such stops. Of epicurean note is building contractor Chuck Williams who bought a hardware store here in 1956. He gradually converted its stock to unique French cookware and kitchen tools, and today, **Williams-Sonoma** has over 200 stores nationwide. Following in his footsteps, **Bram** is beloved for handmade earthenware inspired by the Egyptian clay pots of yore. Located on the same square, **Sign of the Bear** is yet another specialty shop and essential stop for all types of table- and kitchen-ware.

## BEST IN LIFE

Throughout scenic and bucolic Sonoma County (also known locally as SoCo), vineyards rub shoulders with orchards and farms. The words "sustainable" and "organic" headline these local farmer's markets, where one may find every item imaginable—from just-picked heirloom vegetables to uni so fresh that it still appears to be moving. Of course, freshness comes first at **Amy's Drive Thru**, where organic veggie burgers and the plant-covered "living rooftop" are well-worth a visit. In business since 2010, **Petaluma Pie Co.** keeps picky palates sated and happy with both sweet and savory pies crafted from organic ingredients. And over on Petaluma Blvd., find a cult of carb fans at **Della Fattoria**—drooling over their lineup of just-baked bread.

This very fertile territory also has more than a just fair share of great seafood. In fact, some of the best oysters can be found off of the Sonoma coast and enthusiasts drive along Highway 1 to sample as many varieties as possible—from **Tomales Bay Oyster Company** and **The Marshall Store**, to **Hog Island Oyster Company**. Naturally there are much more than just

mollusks to be relished here. Start your day right with a serious breakfast at **The Fremont Diner** where the Bellweather Farms' ricotta pancakes are light, fluffy, and...you guessed it...regionally sourced. Devour these hearty eats at local sensation **Bear Republic Brewing Company Pub & Restaurant**—a family-owned Healdsburg hot spot favored for unique, award-winning brews and tours (by appointment only); or over a top-notch IPA, which are all the rage at **Lagunitas Brewing Co.**—a taproom for the Petaluma-based brewery. And what goes best with beer? Small bites of course, with an enticing lineup of authentically prepared, globally inspired fare at roadside stall extraordinaire—**The Secret Kitchen**. Meals here are composed of fresh herbs, spices, succulent grilled meats, and locally sourced fruits and vegetables. They're usually ready to go at a moment's notice, so study the menu beforehand and enjoy its benevolence later.

Numerous ethnic food stands bring global cuisines to this wine-centric community, with offerings that have their roots as close as Mexico and far off as India and Afghanistan. Thanks to Sonoma County's natural bounty, farm-to-table cuisine takes on new heights in many of its surrounding restaurants and some chefs need go no farther than their own on-site gardens for delicious fruits, vegetables, and aromatic herbs. With such easy access to local products like Dungeness crab from Bodega Bay, poultry from Petaluma, and cheeses from the **Sonoma Cheese Factory**, it's no wonder that the cooking in this town

has attracted such high-levels of national attention. Serious home gardeners should make sure to scour the shelves of **Petaluma Seed Bank**, located in the historic Sonoma County Bank Building, as it happily counts motivated farmers among its clientele. Find them along with a host of other visitors rejoicing at the Bank's selection of over 1500 heirloom seeds, after which a luscious scoop or slice from stylish **Noble Folk Ice Cream & Pie Bar** seems perfectly in order. Finally, both area residents as well as tourists in town can't seem to get enough of the local and hand-crafted bounty found inside the original **Powell's Sweet Shoppe** in Windsor. This old-fashioned candy store carries an impressive spectrum of old-world classics, modern (gluten-free) items, and "sweet gift boxes" that are big during the holidays. All you have to do is walk in, pick up a pail, and start filling up! If that doesn't result in a sugar rush, there's no going wrong with a scoop of creamy gelato.

# SHED

HealdsburgShed.com

**OPEN WED-MON: 8AM-7PM**

**=COFFEE BAR=**    **=CAFÉ**
Dine-In
Breakfast Pastries    ~Breakf
Cookies and Ice Cream    8-11

          ~Lunc
**=FERMENTATION BAR=**   1130AM
Local Wines, Beers,    changin
Kombuchas and other
Fermented Beverages,    ~Brun
Afternoon Savories,    Saturday
Flatbreads,Charcuterie
and Cheese Plates    8AM-

      **=LARDER & PANTR**
Farmhouse Cheeses, Charcuter
Vinegars, Freshly Milled Flours,
Breads,Local Produce,Prepared

      **HOUSEWARES**
Traditional Wares Focusing on
Cooking and Food Preservat

      **=FARM & GARD**

Quality Tools, Supplies a

   **=COMMUNITY & PRIVAT**
Workshops,Classes, Sund
Private Events & Tast

**=25 NORTH ST· 707·**

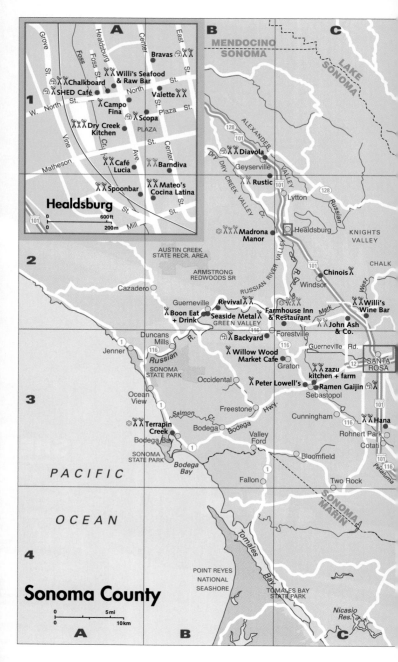

**Healdsburg**

| | |
|---|---|
| A | B | C |

Grove St.
Healdsburg Ave.
Foss St.
Foss St.
Center St.
East St.

**Bravas** XX

**Willi's Seafood & Raw Bar** XX

⊛ XX **Chalkboard**

⊛ X **SHED Café**

North St.

**Valette** XX

W. North St.

X **Campo Fina**

X **Scopa**

Plaza St.

Vine St.

XXX **Dry Creek Kitchen**

PLAZA

Matheson

XX **Café Lucia**

Center St.

Center Ave.

X **Barndiva**

X X **Spoonbar**

XX **Mateo's Cocina Latina**

St.

St.

Mill St.

0 — 600ft
0 — 200m

101

MENDOCINO
SONOMA

LAKE SONOMA

128

ALEXANDER VALLEY

101

DRY DRY CREEK VALLEY

XXX **Diavola**

Geyserville

XX **Rustic**

101

Lytton

128

Russian

KNIGHTS VALLEY

⊛ XXX **Madrona Manor**

Healdsburg

**2**

AUSTIN CREEK
STATE RECR. AREA

ARMSTRONG
REDWOODS SR

RUSSIAN RIVER VALLEY

R. R.

Mark West

CHALK

Cazadero ○

Guerneville

X **Revival** XX

X **Boon Eat + Drink**

**Seaside Metal** X

GREEN VALLEY

⊛XXX **Farmhouse Inn & Restaurant**

Chinois X

Windsor

101

West

XX **Willi's Wine Bar**

R.

116

XX **John Ash & Co.**

Duncans
Mills

Russian R.

116

Forestville

⊛ X **Backyard**

116

Guerneville Rd.

12

SANTA ROSA

Jenner ○

1

SONOMA
STATE PARK

X **Willow Wood Market Cafe**

Graton

XX **zazu kitchen + farm**

Occidental ○

X **Peter Lowell's**

**Ramen Gaijin** ⊛ X

101

**3**

Ocean
View

1

Salmon Cr.

Freestone ○

Sebastopol

Bohemian Hwy.

Cunningham

116

XX **Hana**

⊛ XX **Terrapin Creek**

Bodega ○

Bodega

Rohnert Park

Cotati

Bodega Bay

SONOMA
STATE PARK

Bodega
Bay

Valley
Ford

○ Bloomfield

116

Petaluma

101

**PACIFIC**

1

SONOMA
MARIN

Fallon ○

○ Two Rock

**OCEAN**

**4**

POINT REYES
NATIONAL
SEASHORE

TOMALES BAY
STATE PARK

Tomales Bay

Nicasio
Res.

**Sonoma County**

0 — 5mi
0 — 10km

A B C

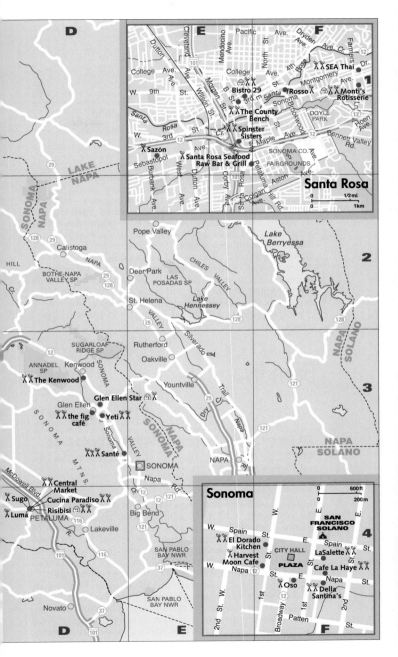

# Backyard

**B3**

### 6566 Front St. (bet. 1st & 2nd Sts.), Forestville

**Phone:** 707-820-8445  
**Web:** www.backyardforestville.com  
**Price:** $$

Lunch & dinner Thu – Mon

Savvy locals flock to this out-of-the-way charmer in Forestville, where reasonable prices, an inviting dining room, and an approachable menu draw a crowd of regulars—many of whom have standing dates for the famed fried-chicken Thursdays. Thanks to Backyard's attentive husband-and-wife team, you'll feel as though you're eating in a private home.

Dishes rotate with the seasons to showcase Mother Nature's finest ingredients. You might encounter tender grilled calamari salad with blood oranges and pickled sunchokes; or creamy house-made pasta *à la carbonara* complete with black trumpet mushrooms and smoky bacon. It would be amiss to not try one of their delectable desserts, like velvety chocolate pudding with salted caramel and sweet whipped cream.

# Barndiva

**B1**

### 231 Center St. (bet. Matheson & Mills Sts.), Healdsburg

**Phone:** 707-431-0100  
**Web:** www.barndiva.com  
**Price:** $$

Lunch & dinner Wed – Sun

Pristine ingredients are the real stars at this decidedly un-diva-like restaurant, which thoughtfully showcases California's bounty. Beautifully composed salads, like a combo of romaine, apples, avocado, blue cheese, and bacon, shine bright; while creative takes on croquettes (with goat cheese and tomato jam) and lobster rolls (a "club" with bacon, tomato, and arugula) don't sacrifice balance or technique.

With a thoughtfully constructed cocktail menu boasting an array of spirits, herbs, and infusions, Barndiva offers lots to explore off the plate. Witty decorative touches like two-story green velvet curtains and a wall-hanging made of wood shoe stretchers only add to the fun. And for post-meal perusing, there's even an art gallery located right next door.

# Bistro 29 😊

French ✗✗

E1

620 5th St. (bet. D St. & Mendocino Ave.), Santa Rosa

**Phone:** 707-546-2929
**Web:** www.bistro29.com
**Price:** $$

Dinner Tue – Sat

French pride oozes from every pore of this vibrant Breton charmer, where tiny French flags, a replica Eiffel Tower, and signs reading "I Love Paris" decorate *le petit* dining room. With its white tile floors and parchment-topped tables, it's every inch the classic bistro—and Santa Rosa locals wouldn't have it any other way.

Savory and sweet galettes (buckwheat crêpes) appear on the menu, their bubbly exteriors concealing a rich filling of tender duck confit, spinach, mushrooms, and Gruyère. The exquisite seafood cassoulet is satisfying yet light, nestling prawns, mussels, calamari, and crab around buttery flageolet beans in a bright tomato broth. For dessert, a moist sticky toffee pudding, accented with fresh figs and whipped cream, is sheer delight.

# Boon Eat + Drink

Californian ✗

B2

16248 Main St. (bet. Armstrong Woods Rd. & Church St.), Guerneville

**Phone:** 707-869-0780
**Web:** www.eatatboon.com
**Price:** $$

Lunch & dinner Thu – Tue

Its setting on cheerful Main Street may suggest small-town Americana, but Boon's fare is globally inflected. This is clear from the cool and refreshing toasted cumin yogurt that enlivens a tender Moroccan lamb stew, to the tang of buttermilk in an enticingly sour panna cotta with blueberry-thyme compote and plenty of vanilla. A large chalkboard offers numerous specials, tempting the crowds that flock here each evening.

The petite space is lovingly pitched between old-fashioned and modern, with extraordinary tables cut straight from large trees and aluminum bistro chairs. With lots of demand, even the outdoor seats are a hot ticket. French-press pots of locally roasted coffee and glasses of cabernet adorn each tabletop throughout the day.

347

# Bravas

**B1**

Spanish ✗✗

## 420 Center St. (bet. North & Piper Sts.), Healdsburg

**Phone:** 707-433-7700

Lunch & dinner daily

**Web:** www.starkrestaurants.com

**Price:** $$

"Jamón in" says the cheeky neon sign at this lively tapas bar, set in a former home full of sunny accents and '70s psychedelic posters. While there's a small bar inside, most visitors make a beeline to the huge backyard with its outdoor porch and garden. Thanks to a welcoming cocktail-party vibe, this is the kind of place where big groups of tourists and locals can be found in abundance.

Whether you like your tapas traditional or with a little added flair, there's plenty to sample and share, from *plancha*-seared sea scallops with creamy romesco to a classic tortilla Española. Lighter appetites will enjoy the chilled tuna belly salad packed with crisp fennel and buttery green olives—it's practically made for washing down with a glass of cava-spiked sangria.

# Cafe La Haye

**F4**

Californian ✗✗

## 140 E. Napa St. (bet. 1st & 2nd Sts.), Sonoma

**Phone:** 707-935-5994

Dinner Tue – Sat

**Web:** www.cafelahaye.com

**Price:** $$

For years, Cafe La Haye has been a standby off the square in downtown Sonoma. One bite of its luscious burrata, surrounded with Early Girl tomatoes and crispy squash blossoms in the summer, or vinaigrette-dressed pea shoots in spring, proves it hasn't aged a day. The small, modern space is still charming, with large windows and lots of mirrors. Stunning local artwork for sale decorates the walls.

The food spans cultural influences, including a delicate risotto with pine nuts in a cauliflower broth, or soy-sesame glazed halibut atop whipped potatoes and braised kale. A postage stamp-sized bar pours glasses of Sonoma chardonnay and cabernet, perfect with rich *strozzapreti* tossed with braised pork ragù, Grana Padano, and toasted breadcrumbs.

# Café Lucia

**A1**

Portuguese  XX

235 Healdsburg Ave., Ste. 105 (bet. Matheson & Mill Sts.), Healdsburg

**Phone:** 707-431-1113
**Web:** www.cafelucia.net
**Price:** $$

Lunch & dinner daily

Tucked just outside of Healdsburg's main plaza, this sibling to LaSalette shares its emphasis on authentic Portuguese ingredients, like seafood, stewed meats, tomatoes, garlic, and olive oil. Day boat scallops seared with a thin crust of *chouriço* sausage set over mashed Japanese sweet potatoes, and tender wood-oven roasted sea bass are among the delicious options. A serene, plant-lined interior courtyard leads to an airy dining room with a dark red horseshoe bar and prints of the owners' hometown, São Jorge, in the Azores. Settle into one of the espresso leather banquettes and be rewarded with cumin- and cinnamon-tinged dinner rolls, just like the chef's mother used to make—perfect for savoring over generous flights of Portuguese or Sonoma wine.

# Campo Fina

**A1**

Italian  X

330 Healdsburg Ave. (bet. North & Plaza Sts.), Healdsburg

**Phone:** 707-395-4640
**Web:** www.campo-fina.com
**Price:** ⬢⬢

Lunch & dinner daily

Just as card games inspire Scopa, this sister restaurant features a highly coveted patio for backyard bocce during the sunny months (expect a wait). The long, narrow dining room combines brick walls, Edison bulbs, and a wood-burning pizza oven, then gives way to the patio's arched twig roof for a lovely balance of sun and shade.

An antipasto like roasted and chilled spicy-sweet cherry peppers stuffed with tuna salad or burrata with grilled bread are great for savoring with a Negroni or black-walnut Manhattan. Sandwiches like *il nonno* with house-made *soppressata*, rapini, fried egg, salsa verde, and Calabrian chilies make for a hearty lunch. At dinner, the Neapolitan pies take center stage, while a rich *shakerato* iced coffee is perfect anytime.

# Central Market

Mediterranean ✗✗

**D4**

### 42 Petaluma Blvd. N. (at Western Ave.), Petaluma

**Phone:** 707-778-9900
**Web:** www.centralmarketpetaluma.com
**Price:** $$

Dinner nightly

Petaluma locals go gaga for this outstanding Mediterranean restaurant, which produces its own meats and vegetables, bakes delicious baguettes in-house, and serves as a community gathering place. The décor is equal parts French country farmhouse and art gallery, with colorful paintings on the walls, fresh flowers on the tables, and a wood-burning oven in the open kitchen.

The nightly prix-fixe offers a tour of the menu, from cabbage rolls stuffed with ground lamb and plump rice to perfectly seared diver scallops atop a silken potato purée, accented by chopped black olives and sweet roasted cherry tomatoes. The buttery, flaky strawberry galette, full of deep red candied berries and topped with excellent vanilla ice cream, is a draw in and of itself.

# Chalkboard

American ✗✗

**A1**

### 29 North St. (bet. Foss St. & Healdsburg Ave.), Healdsburg

**Phone:** 707-473-8030
**Web:** www.chalkboardhealdsburg.com
**Price:** $$

Lunch Fri –Sun
Dinner nightly

Located in the luxury boutique Hotel Les Mars, Chalkboard is a surprisingly laid-back boîte, with a casual vibe and a buzzing bar that offer a refreshing counterpoint to a day of wine tasting. The dining room's low vaulted ceilings and marble tables might feel a touch austere if not for the rustic wooden chairs, open kitchen, and warm, easygoing service.

The menu of small plates spans every cuisine and appetite— from whitefish crudo with blood orange and sesame seeds to fried chicken and sunchoke-black truffle soup.

Be sure to sample at least one of the homemade pastas, including tiny shells with SarVecchio cheese, spicy pork sausage, and braised greens. Of course, be sure to leave room for the sticky toffee cake, finished with tart green apple foam.

# Chinois

✗

**C2**

### 186 Windsor River Rd. (at Bell Rd.), Windsor

**Phone:** 707-838-4667
**Web:** www.chinoisbistro.com
**Price:** $$

Lunch Mon – Fri
Dinner Mon – Sat

Pan-Asian fare is given the fresh, seasonal California treatment at this Windsor bistro. The menu offers everything: plump, flavorful Filipino *lumpia*; Chinese dim sum; calamari and prawns in a peppy Cambodian garlic sauce. Thai curries, Taiwanese honey prawns, and even Indian *roti prata* are also represented, but the dance between cuisines is elegant and streamlined, not muddled.

The entry features a small wine bar that's great for solo dining, while the modern dining room is marked by red and white barrel light fixtures. The wine list is respectable (thanks to the surroundings); beer and sake or *sochu* cocktails are also strong. Happy hour, with $5 dishes and drinks, packs in crowds until 6:00 P.M. on the dot—get there early to savor it all.

# The County Bench

✗✗

**E1**

### 535 4th St. (bet. B St. & Santa Rosa Ave.), Santa Rosa

**Phone:** 707-535-0700
**Web:** www.thecountybench.com
**Price:** $$

Lunch Tue– Fri & Sun
Dinner nightly

A new kid on the block with lots of ambition, The County Bench has already brought a jolt of life to downtown Santa Rosa's dining scene. The difference is immediately visible in its stylish interior, which blends tile and wood accents with a pop of lime-green from modern sofas at the front tables. Yet service remains friendly and down-to-earth, with a neighborhood feel.

The menu extols "The County Bench Way," a simple approach to cooking highlighting top-quality ingredients like flaky, flavorful hamachi collar, accented by fava beans and grilled scallions; or sumptuous braised chicken thighs over a paprika-kissed chickpea and chorizo stew. And you'll have sweet dreams about the rich chocolate ganache bar, drizzled with sweet-salty *cajeta*.

# Cucina Paradiso

Italian XX

**D4**

### 114 Petaluma Blvd. N. (bet. Washington St. & Western Ave.), Petaluma

**Phone:** 707-782-1130  
**Web:** www.cucinaparadisopetaluma.com  
**Price:** $$

Lunch & dinner Mon — Sat

Set adjacent to the art galleries, boutiques, and theaters of Petaluma's delightful downtown, a meal at this farmhouse-style restaurant is like a jaunt to the Italian countryside. Deep yellow walls lined with wine bottles, embedded arches, and dark wood trestles set the rustic scene, while a large windowed façade gives diners a showcase view of the pedestrians strolling by.

Dinner always commences with fluffy house-made focaccia, a favorite among regulars. From there, choose from other delectable offerings like deliciously briny spaghetti with clams and mussels or tender, lightly crisped veal cutlets Saltimbocca, oozy with *Prosciutto di Parma* and provolone. Pair your meal with a bottle of great Italian wine, which the warm servers will happily recommend.

# Della Santina's

Italian XX

**F4**

### 133 E. Napa St. (bet. 1st & 2nd Sts.), Sonoma

**Phone:** 707-935-0576  
**Web:** www.dellasantinas.com  
**Price:** $$

Lunch & dinner daily

Diners at this homey trattoria off Sonoma's town square are treated like members of the Della Santina family, whose vintage photographs fill the walls and whose treasured family recipes pour out of the kitchen regularly. From the first welcome to the final goodbye, the namesake tribe is here to look after you, with warm smiles and friendly pats on the back.

The rustic food has its roots in Tuscany, with favorite dishes like pappardelle in a rich, hearty duck sugo with chunks of tender garlic and sweet tomato. A spatchcocked roast quail has juicy flesh and a beautifully browned, spice-coated exterior, alongside a heaping helping of nutty wild rice and meaty mushrooms. On the way out, grab a bottle of Italian wine from the *enoteca* next door.

# Diavola 😊

Italian ✗✗

**B1**

21021 Geyserville Ave. (at Hwy. 128), Geyserville

**Phone:** 707-814-0111               Lunch & dinner daily
**Web:** www.diavolapizzeria.com
**Price:** $$

Its home in downtown Geyserville may look like the Wild West, but this devilishly good Italian restaurant can hold its own with any city slicker. Festooned with statues of saints, boar tusks, and stacks of cookbooks, it has a playful yet smart vibe.

Excellent pizzas, like the signature combo of spicy meatballs, red peppers, provolone, pine nuts, and raisins, are the reason why crowds pack this spot. And top-notch house ingredients like *salumi*, *lardo*, and cured olives elevate each and every dish. But, that's not to count out their exquisite pastas, including linguine tossed with baby octopus, bone marrow, zucchini, and *bottarga*. Desserts, like the chocolate pistachio semifreddo paired with a perfectly pulled Blue Bottle espresso, are yet another delight.

# Dry Creek Kitchen

Californian ✗✗✗

**A1**

317 Healdsburg Ave. (bet. Matheson & Plaza Sts.), Healdsburg

**Phone:** 707-431-0330               Dinner nightly
**Web:** www.drycreekkitchen.com
**Price:** $$$

With its white tablecloths, plush cushioned banquettes, and formally attired waiters, this Charlie Palmer-owned restaurant is dressy enough for a special occasion. Yes, it's pricey, but the food is unpretentious, the servers are friendly, and there's more than enough wine-country charm to go around.

A cast-iron pan of fluffy focaccia precedes the no-fuss Californian food, like crisp Delta asparagus and salty *boquerones* with a tangy buttermilk-lemon vinaigrette. The pan-seared local halibut arrives atop a summery succotash of fava beans, sweet corn, and cherry tomatoes, and desserts include a quirky take on s'mores complete with Pop Rocks. To ease the sting on your wallet, the prix-fixe is a particularly good deal.

# El Dorado Kitchen

**F4**

Californian

**405 1st St. W. (at Spain St.), Sonoma**

**Phone:** 707-996-3030
**Web:** www.eldoradosonoma.com
**Price:** $$

Lunch & dinner daily

Bigger than the hotel of the same name that houses it, El Dorado Kitchen proves that dining is a big deal in Sonoma. With its long wood communal table, decorative succulents, and palette of warm earth tones, it's a comfy and minimalist space. When the weather is right, grab one of the outdoor tables, nestled poolside beneath fig trees.

The Cal-French menu gets some pop from Latin accents, like a fresh and flavorful pizza topped with *carne seca* (Brazilian salted dried beef), tomato salsa, cilantro, and jalapeños. A selection of charcuterie, from tart wine-cured salami to spicy chorizo, is made in house, as is the excellent country bread. Finally, it would be a sin to miss the rich and flaky fried fig pie, accented by tangy balsamic ice cream, for dessert.

# Glen Ellen Star 🐶

**D3**

Californian

**13648 Arnold Dr. (at Warm Springs Rd.), Glen Ellen**

**Phone:** 707-343-1384
**Web:** www.glenellenstar.com
**Price:** $$

Dinner nightly

The country charm of this quaint cottage belies the level of culinary chops that will impress even a hardened city slicker. With knotty pine tables, well-worn plank floors, and a wood-burning oven, the space is delightful. A perch at the chef's counter affords a great view of the action.

Here, Chef Ari Weiswasser showcases his signature style via the use of Mediterranean and Middle Eastern ingredients. Imagine wood-roasted asparagus with *lavash* crackers and shaved radish over a tangy hen egg emulsion; or chicken cooked under a brick with coconut curry and sticky rice. Daily pizzas like the tomato-cream pie with Turkish chilies are also a thrill. Save room for house-made ice cream in flavors like vanilla maple Bourbon, salted peanut butter, or peach verbena.

# Farmhouse Inn & Restaurant ✿

**C2**

### 7871 River Rd. (at Wohler Rd.), Forestville

**Phone:** 707-887-3300  
**Web:** www.farmhouseinn.com  
**Price:** $$$

Dinner Thu – Mon

Urbanites seeking an escape from the fray head to this charming inn, nestled in a quiet, woodsy corner of Sonoma, for fine cooking, upscale accommodations, or both. Dinner guests will find themselves charmed by the dining room's soothing colors, rustic-elegant décor, crackling fireplace, and numerous intimate nooks—including an enclosed patio.

The protein-centric menu reads like an ode to California's purveyors, and a focus on seasonality is in keeping with the area's ethos. Not surprisingly, the results are often rewarding: succulent, perfectly balanced heirloom tomatoes are twirled with crunchy seaweed, briny clams, and mirin dressing, while flaky halibut arrives atop a richly flavored fennel-tomato beurre blanc, dotted with corn and *huitlacoche* pudding. The signature "rabbit, rabbit, rabbit" showcases the kitchen's creativity, bringing together a confit rabbit leg, an applewood-smoked bacon-wrapped loin, and a minuscule rack of chops rounded out with Yukon potatoes and whole grain mustard-cream sauce.

Pair your meal with a bottle from the impressive list of local and European wines. Then complete the seduction with an airy soufflé concealing a treasure of Blenheim apricot preserves.

# Hana

C3

Japanese **XX**

### 101 Golf Course Dr. (at Roberts Lake Rd.), Rohnert Park

**Phone:** 707-586-0270
**Web:** www.hanajapanese.com
**Price:** $$

Lunch Mon – Sat
Dinner nightly

Rohnert Park denizens continue their love affair with this spacious gem featuring semi-private nooks and a lounge. Tucked in a hotel plaza next to the 101, Hana is run by affable Chef/owner Ken Tominaga, who sees to his guests' every whim. For the full experience, park it at the bar where the obliging chefs can steer you through the best offerings of the day. Top quality fish flown in from Tsukiji Market (ask for the daily specials), traditional sushi and small plates are the secret to their success, though mains like pan-seared pork loin with ginger-soy jus also hit the spot.

The omakase is a fine way to go—six pieces of nigiri which may include toro, hamachi belly, kampachi, *tai*, halibut with ponzu sauce, or sardine sprinkled with Hawaiian lava salt.

# Harvest Moon Cafe

F4

Californian **X**

### 487 1st St. W. (bet. Napa & Spain Sts.), Sonoma

**Phone:** 707-933-8160
**Web:** www.harvestmooncafesonoma.com
**Price:** $$

Dinner Wed – Sun

Local sourcing and sustainability are top-of-mind and top-of-menu at this small, unassuming restaurant from a husband-and-wife duo of CIA grads. The simple dining room and heated, covered outdoor patio are favorites among the Sonoma locals. They flood this café for the freshest ingredients from area producers, served at moderate prices by a welcoming, genuine waitstaff.

The menu keeps pace with the seasons, but might include a roasted pear topped with potent black truffle-goat cheese and crispy prosciutto, or juicy, perfectly cooked duck breast over crunchy green romanesco and golden-crusted sweet potatoes. For dessert, house-made peppermint ice cream—spiked with tiny bits of chewy candy—arrives atop a fudgy wedge of brownie.

# John Ash & Co.

Californian XX

**C2**

4330 Barnes Rd. (off River Rd.), Santa Rosa

**Phone:** 707-527-7687                      Dinner nightly
**Web:** www.vintnersinn.com
**Price:** $$$

A pioneer in farm-to-table dining, this stalwart in the Vintners Inn (owned by Ferrari-Carano) is 35 years strong and still serving the region's best, much of it grown in the on-site gardens. The rustic Front Room is a popular happy-hour spot with its menu of bar snacks, while the Tuscan-inspired dining room boasts plush booths, a stone fireplace, and Italian landscapes on the walls.

Chef Tom Schmidt has broadened the restaurant's focus, incorporating Latin touches like a halibut ceviche with *aji amarillo* and creamy sweet potato. But there are still indulgent classics aplenty, like the dry-aged beef filet, cooked to a buttery medium rare and accompanied by decadent Point Reyes blue cheese mashed potatoes, or the rich chocolate truffle cake for dessert.

# The Kenwood

Californian XX

**D3**

9900 Sonoma Hwy. (near Libby Ave.), Kenwood

**Phone:** 707-833-6326                Lunch & dinner Wed – Sun
**Web:** www.kenwoodrestaurant.com
**Price:** $$

Meals at The Kenwood are long and leisurely, with appropriately paced service to match. Nestled amid the sprawling vineyards along the Sonoma Highway, it's the kind of place made for lingering, either on the covered patio with its gurgling water fountain, or in the casual dining room or front bar.

The menu is simple but packed with pristine ingredients, like the juicy cherry tomatoes and perfectly ripe avocado that top slices of thick grilled toast. Moist, flaky king salmon boasting a nicely blackened skin and peppery seasoning is another winner, and its accompanying summer squash, white bean and corn succotash is full of flavor. Skip the forgettable desserts in favor of another glass of wine, perhaps from one of the neighboring vintners.

# LaSalette

Portuguese  ✗✗

### 452 1st St. E., Ste. H (bet. Napa & Spain Sts.), Sonoma

**Phone:** 707-938-1927                                      Lunch & dinner daily
**Web:** www.lasalette-restaurant.com
**Price:** $$

Portuguese fare with wine country flair is the name of the game at this stalwart off downtown Sonoma's central square, where gleaming azulejo tiles point the way into the dark wood dining room, adorned with hanging copper pots and pans.

Most diners begin with *tascas*, customizable appetizer tasting plates packed with delicacies like garlic-brined lupini beans, pig's feet terrine, and sardine pâté. Heirloom tomato salad arrives with chickpea purée, creamy fresh cheese, and toasted almonds, while chipotle-port barbecue pork and melted onions are stuffed into a traditional Portuguese roll and accompanied by crispy *piri piri* fries. For a sweet finish, try the creamy, cinnamon-infused rice pudding topped with Madeira-braised figs.

# Luma

Californian  ✗

### 500 1st St. (at G St.), Petaluma

**Phone:** 707-658-1940                                      Lunch & dinner Tue – Sun
**Web:** www.lumapetaluma.com
**Price:** $$

A glowing presence in its industrial neighborhood, Luma's attractive red-and-yellow neon sign (the handiwork of owner Tim Tatum) is immediately recognizable. The artsy atmosphere meshes well with sunny orange walls and deep chocolate booths, though it can get a bit noisy. For a quieter meal, request a table in the front corner nook. This is a friendly, crowd-pleasing, neighborhood destination drawing local families to dine on crispy build-your-own pizzas and other comforting delights.

Consider your pizza options while indulging in guilt-ridden starters like "friends of the devil," a duo of prosciutto-wrapped figs and bacon-wrapped dates filled with goat cheese. Follow your pizza with chocolate-raspberry crêpes and excellent French-press coffee.

# Madrona Manor ✿

Contemporary XXX

**B2**

1001 Westside Rd. (at W. Dry Creek Rd.), Healdsburg

**Phone:** 707-433-4231
**Web:** www.madronamanor.com
**Price:** $$$$

Dinner Wed – Sun

This romantic Victorian mansion is the unexpected home of a forward-looking kitchen. It's the kind of place that makes one want to dress up—at least a little bit—to fully engage in the art of dining. Arrive early to enjoy a sunset drink out on the terrace. You can either stay there to dine, or head inside to settle into one of several timelessly elegant dining rooms cloaked in sleek marble, plush silk and old-world grandeur.

The showmanship here extends to the artistic, often theatrical plates that make the most of fine herbs and flowers to create novel and very focused flavors throughout the seven- and nine-course fixed menus. Expect a separate amuse for each new dish to prepare the palate, so bread with mustard-*lardo* cream arrives as a prelude to kohlrabi cooked *al forno*, then topped with shallots and cress. The kitchen is also particularly adept with raw vegetables, as may be found in the roasted quail that is cut and served with raw and olive oil-fried chard with onion soubise.

A green profiterole stuffed with tart apple mousse leads to a "morning breakfast dessert" of Turkish figs, apple sorbet, thin and crunchy melba toast, as well as a host of garnishes like chocolate, jelly, raisins, and corn caramels.

359

# Mateo's Cocina Latina

Mexican

**B2**

**214 Healdsburg Ave. (bet. Matheson & Mill Sts.), Healdsburg**

**Phone:** 707-433-1520          Lunch & Dinner Wed - Mon
**Web:** www.mateoscocinalatina.com
**Price:** $$

On a warm Sonoma day, it's hard to beat the patio at Mateo's, unquestionably one of the area's most captivating. Surrounded by planter beds and protected by Sunbrellas, guests have a full view into the kitchen. And if the weather takes a turn, the interior, full of rustic wood furnishings and soft lighting, is just as beautiful as the outdoors.

Flavors of the Yucatán abound here, from a heap of succulent *cochinita pibil*, to *panucho* pockets filled with a delicious black bean purée and topped with chicken and avocado. For extra heat, add a drop or two of the house-made habanero sauces. If you love them, you can buy bottles to take home—and if you can't handle the heat, a tall glass of hibiscus-raspberry *agua fresca* will cool things down.

# Monti's Rotisserie

American **XX**

**F1**

**714 Village Court (at Sonoma Ave.), Santa Rosa**

**Phone:** 707-568-4404          Lunch & dinner daily
**Web:** www.starkrestaurants.com
**Price:** $$

With the scent of wood smoke hanging in the air, it seems impossible to resist ordering the day's offering hot off the rotisserie. Those smoked prime ribs or pomegranate-glazed pork ribs do not disappoint, either. But the oak-roasted chicken is a perennial favorite and deserves a visit on its own. Succulent auburn skin, seasoned flesh, heirloom carrots, smashed fingerling potatoes, and crisped pancetta, render this dish a thing of beauty. End your meal over baby lettuces with Point Reyes blue cheese and candied walnuts; or butterscotch pudding for lip-smacking comfort food—Monti's-style.

Set within Santa Rosa's Montgomery Village, this is your quintessential wine country hangout, dressed with rustic tables and centered around a roaring fireplace—natch.

# Oso

International ✗

**F4**

### 9 E. Napa St. (at Hwy. 12), Sonoma

| | | |
|---|---|---|
| **Phone:** | 707-931-6926 | Lunch Thu – Sun |
| **Web:** | www.ososonoma.com | Dinner nightly |
| **Price:** | **$$** | |

Though Oso means "bear" in Spanish, Sonoma locals are actually quite bullish about this good-natured little restaurant, where the "small" plates are generously portioned and the welcome is warm. The globe-trotting menu is ever-changing, and might include an ultra-fresh ahi tuna poke with cucumber, avocado, and sesame oil; charred asparagus in a Caesar dressing with buttery croutons; and flaky sea bass over light and tangy romesco sauce, with a hint of piquant olive tapenade.

The décor inside features an appealing mix of '80s rock and California rustic barnyard, with baseball-capped cooks—including owner David Bush—working furiously at the open kitchen counter. Night owls, rejoice: it's also open late, at least by the area's standards.

# Peter Lowell's

Californian ✗

**C3**

### 7385 Healdsburg Ave. (at Florence Ave.), Sebastopol

| | | |
|---|---|---|
| **Phone:** | 707-829-1077 | Lunch & dinner daily |
| **Web:** | www.peterlowells.com | |
| **Price:** | **$$** | |

With a devoted following in an artsy neighborhood, Peter Lowell's finely tuned design, staff, food, and philosophy are entirely in sync. The lofty, minimalistic space has a modern pantry-like vibe, with comfortable nooks for relishing the Italian-inspired Californian food.

Hyper-local, largely organic produce arrives in starters like caramelized acorn squash tossed with spiced chickpeas and chard from the restaurant's own farm. Then, move on to smoked-trout ravioli with apples, fennel, and whole-grain mustard. Or, feast on a carefully grilled swordfish steak basted with herb-infused olive oil over red quinoa, matsutake, and shiitake mushrooms.

Bring home some muffins with house Meyer lemon marmalade from the adjacent café for the morning after.

# Ramen Gaijin 😊

Japanese ✗

C3

6948 Sebastopol Ave. (bet. Main St. & Petaluma Ave.), Sebastopol

**Phone:** 707-827-3609  
**Web:** www.ramengaijin.com  
**Price:** $$

Lunch & dinner Tue – Sat

♿ 🏠

"Gaijin" is the none-too-polite Japanese term for a foreigner, but the American chefs of this clandestine noodle joint clearly take pride in their outsider status, fusing local ingredients with traditional technique. The restaurant is newly expanded, but retains its friendly and casual vibe.

The best seats are at the counter, where you can chat with the chef as he assembles bowls of light, fresh *shoyu* ramen filled with thick house-made rye noodles and caramelized pork belly *chashu*. Appetizers are also notable, like a surprisingly elegant salad of smoked cod and baby gem lettuces. Don't miss such creative and delicious desserts as black-sesame ice cream with miso caramel. After 3:30, the menu goes on to offer *izakaya* fare, like *gyoza* and *okonomiyaki*.

# Revival

Californian ✗✗

B2

13555 Hwy. 116 , Guerneville

**Phone:** 707-869-9093  
**Web:** www.eatatrevival.com  
**Price:** $$$

Dinner Thu – Mon

♿

The Applewood Inn's restaurant has indeed been revived under new management, with a contemporary farmhouse makeover that befits its boho Guerneville environs. Rough-hewn tables and spindle-back dining chairs echo the exposed wood beams and wrought-iron chandeliers overhead, but there's also plenty of warmth from a duo of fireplaces on either end of the room. It's a spot with more than a little romance, buzzing with a mature crowd of couples.

Revival's menu is tiny, but what it lacks in size, it makes up for in ambitious cooking and good looks. Local halibut crudo gets a boost from a *meuniére*-like caper and brown butter sauce and slightly smoky halibut gelée, while aged Liberty duck breast is a stunner over a bright red mélange of beets and berries.

# Risibisi

Italian ✗✗

**D4**

154 Petaluma Blvd. N. (bet. Washington St. & Western Ave.), Petaluma

**Phone:** 707-766-7600                                          Lunch & dinner daily
**Web:** www.risibisirestaurant.com
**Price:** $$

Though it's named for a comforting dish of rice and peas, Risibisi's seafood-heavy take on Italian cuisine is a bit more sophisticated. A meal at this Petaluma treasure might begin with a chilled slice of veal roast topped with creamy tuna sauce and dried capers. Also try the *pesce di giorno*, perhaps featuring beautifully grilled swordfish served alongside cheesy potatoes and green beans in olive-lemon sauce. End with their house-made tiramisu or cannoli with bits of candied fruit, caramel and strawberry sauce.

A makeshift picture gallery constructed out of salvaged Tuscan chestnut window frames, wine barrels, and wagon wheels bring character to this inviting brick-walled dining room. A back patio offers views of the river and old train tracks.

# Rosso

Pizza ✗

**F1**

53 Montgomery Dr. (at 3rd St.), Santa Rosa

**Phone:** 707-544-3221                                          Lunch & dinner daily
**Web:** www.rossopizzeria.com
**Price:** $$

Red wine, red sauce, and red meat are only the beginning at this pizzeria and wine bar. In fact, you're just as likely to go on to enjoy a fresh crab Louie, tender fried calamari and green beans with a green chili aïoli, or a Caesar salad with Gorgonzola Dolce. Crunchy, uniquely-topped pizzas fly out of the wood oven and may feature a braised short rib number topped with gooey cheddar and tomato marmalade.

Set in a small shopping mall, Rosso is identifiable by the locals dining on its terrace, many of whom sign on for the restaurant's regular schedule of cooking classes. Rely on the upbeat staff for friendly advice on the Californian/Italian wine selection, all of which is also available to-go—an ideal alternative given their strong takeout business.

# Rustic

Italian XX

B2

## 300 Via Archimedes (off Independence Ln.), Geyserville

**Phone:** 707-857-1485
**Web:** www.franciscoppolawinery.com
**Price:** $$

Lunch & dinner daily

Those Godfather Oscars certainly could have funded a posh restaurant for Francis Ford Coppola, but the director has kept it relatively simple at his enormous Geyserville eatery, offering Italian classics from his childhood. Savory *pettole* doughnuts in a paper bag kick off the meal, followed by crispy chicken *al mattone* sautéed in olive oil with strips of red pepper.

Coppola's personality is a big part of Rustic's appeal, and these walls are covered with his film memorabilia as well as his own wines. Although the real reason for the crowds is the Italian-American music, games, and nostalgia that define Coppola's past as well as those of his customers.

Come on Tuesdays to find a special prix fixe, as well as the sociable staff donning vintage garb.

# Santa Rosa Seafood Raw Bar & Grill

Seafood X

E1

## 958 Santa Rosa Ave. (at Petaluma Hill Rd.), Santa Rosa

**Phone:** 707-579-3474
**Web:** www.santarosaseafood.com
**Price:** $$

Lunch & dinner Wed – Sun

Locals have trusted Santa Rosa Seafood Market to buy their fresh fish for years, so the arrival of this adjoining restaurant was welcomed with open arms. Stroll past the intoxicatingly scented salmon smokers and pergola-covered patio, and you'll reach the petite, no-frills fish shack and its handful of tables.

The lineup of catches, listed on a TV screen for your perusal, includes flaky, tender grilled salmon, plump barbecue oysters bathed in garlic butter and tangy 'cue sauce, and a daily tuna poke preparation complete with rotating accents like roasted pineapple. Though the bustling diner kitchen may look a little worn, rest assured that the energetic young staff knows their fish—and everything from fried calamari to fish tacos comes out just right.

# Santé

D3

Californian ✗✗✗

### 100 Boyes Blvd. (at Hwy. 12), Sonoma

**Phone:** 707-939-2415                                    Dinner nightly
**Web:** www.santediningroom.com
**Price:** $$$

The tony Fairmont Sonoma Mission Inn provides the backdrop to this luxurious fine-dining restaurant, which draws a sophisticated crowd of wine country tourists for its refined cuisine. The carpeted room has a touch of rustic elegance, lending itself to quiet conversation, and the tightly orchestrated staff offers truly outstanding service that still retains a friendly air.

Though it bills itself as focused on Californian ingredients, Santé embraces classic French techniques—from a terrine of lobster with Alaskan halibut and tarragon mousseline to a lobster-pumpkin bisque that surrounds flaky Pacific cod and fried Yukon potatoes. The wine selection is substantial, and desserts like a crisply caramelized "apple tart" with cinnamon ice cream are divine.

# Sazón

E1

Peruvian ✗

### 1129 Sebastopol Rd. (at Roseland Ave.), Santa Rosa

**Phone:** 707-523-4346                                 Lunch & dinner daily
**Web:** sazonsr.com
**Price:** $$

Set just outside downtown Santa Rosa, this family-run favorite serves homestyle Peruvian dishes like *aji de gallina*, chicken stewed in a yellow pepper sauce with chopped walnuts and hard-boiled egg; as well as *papas rellenos*, deep-fried, panko-crusted potato croquettes stuffed with minced beef, onions, and olives. And, if that's not enough to tempt your palate, ceviche and a selection of Asian-influenced stir-fries are also on offer.

With its open kitchen displaying a full view of the chopping and sautéing, it's no wonder the small, yet lively space boasts a constant stream of locals. Daytime diners should be sure to check out the "executive lunch" special, a delicious steal of a deal that includes an entrée, salad, appetizer, and soft drink for under $20.

Wine Country ▶ Sonoma County

# Scopa 😋

Wine Country ▶ Sonoma County

Italian ✗

**109A Plaza St. (bet. Center St. & Healdsburg Ave.), Healdsburg**

Phone: 707-433-5282        Dinner Tue – Sat
Web: www.scopahealdsburg.com
Price: **$$**

♿

The house always wins at Scopa, which is named for a bluff-centric Italian card game. Patrons will happily concede victory after their first bite of the heady *spaghettini* with a deeply flavored, spicy Calabrese beef and pork rib sugo. Fans of rarely seen Italian treats like thick-skinned, munchable *lupini* beans or *ciambella*, a cornmeal cake studded with citrus and cranberries, have definitely met their match.

Loud and dimly lit, Scopa's cool, railroad-narrow space quickly fills with bar-goers looking to achieve the other sense of its name ("scoring"—and, ahem, we don't mean points in a card game). Glasses of local cabernet sauvignon fuel the meeting and eating, though perfectly pulled espressos are always available for a little sobering up.

# Seaside Metal

Seafood ✗

**16222 Main St. (bet. Armstrong Woods Rd. & Church St.), Guerneville**

Phone: 707-604-7250        Dinner Wed – Sun
Web: www.seasidemetal.com
Price: **$$**

♿

Quaint Guerneville has gotten an infusion of cityside-chic, thanks to this younger sibling of SF favorite Bar Crudo. Located in the heart of town, its relaxed vibe and kind service draw both tourists and locals. They perch at the white marble counter, where an extensive raw bar is displayed alongside jars of house-pickled vegetables and a sizable cookbook collection.

You'll definitely want at least one raw item to start, whether it's fresh, briny Walker Creek oysters from nearby Point Reyes, or a vibrant yellowtail crudo with lemon curd, crispy shallots, and basil. Move on to the outstanding smoked shellfish platter of Dungeness crab, shrimp, and scallops that arrives on a wood board with crostini, coarse mustard, and those tangy pickled veggies.

366

# SEA Thai

Thai **XX**

**F1**

### 2350 Midway Dr. (bet. Hahman Dr. & Hwy. 12), Santa Rosa

**Phone:** 707-528-8333        Lunch & dinner daily
**Web:** www.seathaibistro.com
**Price:** $$

This long-running Thai spot may have moved just a stone's throw from its original home, but it appears to have gotten a new lease on life in the process. The capacious space is lively and modern, complete with schools of eye-catching fish-shaped light fixtures hanging from the ceiling above stylish wooden tables and mid-century modern chairs. Chef Tony Ounpamornchai has created a menu that infuses traditional Thai fare with fresh California vibes, making for a combination that truly sparkles. The house-made pork cheek and jicama potstickers are divine, as is the springy Monterey squid, stir-fried with tender Japanese eggplant, lemongrass, and red chili.

For a more noodle- and bowl-centric menu, check out sister spot SEA Noodle Bar, in the Coddingtown Mall.

# SHED Café

Californian **X**

**A1**

### 25 North St. (at Foss St.), Healdsburg

**Phone:** 707-431-7433        Lunch & dinner Wed – Mon
**Web:** www.healdsburgshed.com
**Price:** $$

Thanks to its gourmet market and event space, this big, airy grange is already a Healdsburg destination. Now, it's aiming to offer a serious restaurant as well, though it's somewhat awkwardly wedged into an alcove at the market's center (you'll find the host stand between the kitchenware and gardening sections).

If you can overcome the lack of ambiance and equally shaky service, there's much to enjoy on the plate at SHED, where all ingredients are sourced from farms within a 10-mile radius. Sip a blood orange and Prosecco cocktail as you sample the gorgeous rainbow carrot salad, which expertly interplays tart yogurt, sugary dates and pecans, or the deliciously meaty black bass, served in a piping *cazuela* of artichoke, cream, and thyme broth.

# Spinster Sisters

American ✗✗

E1

**401 S. A St. (at Sebastopol Ave.), Santa Rosa**

**Phone:** 707-528-7100
**Web:** www.thespinstersisters.com
**Price:** $$

Lunch daily
Dinner Tue – Sun

This terra cotta-tinged bungalow is housed on a residential block off the city center and flaunts a hip, modern vibe, as evidenced in concrete walls and a large circular wood counter. With a rotating art show that changes bimonthly, this urban respite also reeks of good taste—not only in design, but also in its delicious range of food crafted from local produce. While it's open through dinner, Spinster Sisters draws its biggest crowds at brunch, lured by dishes like hearty granola-studded waffles topped with fresh fruit and agave syrup, or farm-fresh scrambled eggs mixed with delicata squash, onions, and mushrooms. At either meal, don't miss the spicy-salty kimchi and bacon deviled eggs, a cultural fusion that works surprisingly well.

# Spoonbar

Contemporary ✗✗

A2

**219 Healdsburg Ave. (bet. Matheson & Mill Sts.), Healdsburg**

**Phone:** 707-433-7222
**Web:** www.spoonbar.com
**Price:** $$

Dinner nightly

Seeking a modern departure from wine country's faux-rustic aesthetic? This restaurant in the eco-chic h2hotel will fit the bill with reclaimed-wood tables and 3-D artwork. Its bar is a local haunt, with wine-weary tasters arriving to palate-cleanse via an extensive list of cocktails.

In the kitchen, a husband-and-wife chef team successfully guides the menu in a sophisticated, vegetable-driven direction. Find such inventive dishes as Meyer lemon ricotta *gnudi* in a parmesan-mushroom broth; or seared scallops with roasted and pickled brassicas and black garlic purée. Should you order a dessert, like the honey crème fraîche-panna cotta, don't be surprised if a second arrives *gratis*—the chef likes to test out her latest experiments on an all-too-willing public.

# Sugo

Italian ✕

**D4**

### 5 Petaluma Blvd. S. (at B St.), Petaluma

**Phone:** 707-782-9298          Lunch & dinner daily
**Web:** www.sugotrattoria.com
**Price:** $$

A family-friendly, farm-to-table ethos is embodied in this cute Italian-American trattoria, brought to you by a husband-and-wife team. Housed in a petite, blink-and-you'll-miss-it strip mall, Sugo is decorated with vibrant photos including those of roosters (a tribute to Petaluma's agricultural past). The walls may be plain brick, but they are adorned with chalkboards that offer insight into the colorful display of wine bottles.

Straightforward dishes here include panzanella with chunks of grilled ciabatta, tomato, and fresh mozzarella; as well as a creamy fettuccine Alfredo intertwined with poached salmon, sweet cherry tomatoes, and wilted spinach. Finish with a lovely *affogato* (vanilla ice cream drowned with espresso), which hits the spot at all times.

# the fig café

Californian ✕✕

**D3**

### 13690 Arnold Dr. (at O'Donnell Ln.), Glen Ellen

**Phone:** 707-938-2130          Lunch Sat – Sun
**Web:** www.thefigcafe.com          Dinner nightly
**Price:** $$

Sondra Bernstein's Cal-Med café takes on a more modern look with communal tables, orange bar stools, and geometric lighting. But pilgrims to this sleepy address shouldn't fret: Rhone-style wines (a house specialty) remain on the shelves, and inviting horseshoe-shaped booths are still the best seats in the house. The nightly prix-fixe—displayed on butcher paper—is as great a deal as ever, and approachable faves like fried olives and a burger are out in force. Start with a salad like grill-charred romaine Caesar with anchovy-spiked dressing; then segue to a seasonal entrée like trout with wild rice, caramelized onions, and green beans.

For like-minded cuisine, visit the girl & the fig in Sonoma's main square.

# Terrapin Creek ❀

Californian XX

**B3**

### 1580 Eastshore Rd. (off Hwy. 1), Bodega Bay

**Phone:** 707-875-2700
**Web:** www.terrapincreekcafe.com
**Price:** $$

Lunch & dinner Thu – Sun

Terrapin Creek isn't easy to find, but those who persevere will be rewarded with a delightful little hideaway bearing delicious cuisine. Dramatically situated above picturesque Bodega Bay, this lovely retreat is just steps from the water. (During the January-March whale-watching season, you might even catch a glimpse of these gentle giants bobbing in the Pacific.)

The upbeat, sun-filled dining room, done in orange and yellow and filled with big, bold paintings, is clean and unfussy. The small-town staff are every bit as warm as the space, and treat everyone like a regular. A meal might begin with a mixed-green salad topped with goat cheese, persimmon, prosciutto, and a tart cherry vinaigrette. Then segue into three coins of ravioli filled with kabocha squash and floating in a fragrant black truffle-and-butter sauce. Tender duck breast with deliciously seasoned and crisped skin is then cooked to pink perfection and coupled with a sauté of cabbage, shiitakes and fingerling potatoes. Paired with a Napa red blend, it's equal parts modern and classic.

Desserts promise to please, but for a powerful—never heavy—finish, opt for the dark chocolate *pot de crème* topped with slices of sweet banana.

# Valette

Californian ✗✗

**B1**

### 344 Center St. (at North St.), Healdsburg

**Phone:** 707-473-0946                              Dinner nightly
**Web:** www.valettehealdsburg.com
**Price:** $$$

Housed in the former Zin space, this contemporary darling is actually a full-circle comeback for Chef Dustin Valette and his brother/General Manager Aaron Garzini, whose grandfather owned the building in the 1940s. Its current look, however, is as cutting-edge as ever thanks to dandelion-like light fixtures, concrete walls, and horseshoe-shaped banquettes. The bill of fare is modern American with a few French twists. Scallops arrive beneath squid ink puff pastry, into which a server pours caviar-flecked champagne-beurre blanc. Then, Peking-spiced duck breast set atop hearty forbidden rice is taken to the next level with a touch of tamarind sauce.

For a happy ending, dig into the smooth, creamy block of chocolate mousse with a luscious salted caramel center.

# Willi's Seafood & Raw Bar

Seafood ✗✗

**A1**

### 403 Healdsburg Ave. (at North St.), Healdsburg

**Phone:** 707-433-9191                              Lunch & dinner daily
**Web:** www.starkrestaurants.com
**Price:** $$

"Eat oysters, love longer," reads a cheeky neon sign above the raw bar at Willi's, and seafood fans certainly feel affection for local restaurant mavens Mark & Terri Stark's love boat. The eclectic seafood offerings are designed for smiles, as in the crisp-fried oyster over jicama kimchi and Key lime aïoli, or bamboo skewers of plump bacon-wrapped scallops with tamarind-barbecue glaze.

The quirky space is a fun blend of tropical and New England accents. This is a favorite for groups, trading sips of cocktails and tasty bites of grilled fish tacos topped with plenty of salsa and avocado. The diet-conscious and landlubbers will find enticing options, as will the environmentalists: all the fish and shellfish served here are Safe Harbor certified.

# Willi's Wine Bar

International **✕✕**

C2

**4404 Old Redwood Hwy. (at Ursuline Rd.), Santa Rosa**

| | |
|---|---|
| **Phone:** 707-526-3096 | Lunch Tue – Sat |
| **Web:** www.starkrestaurants.com | Dinner nightly |
| **Price:** **$$** | |

Don't be fooled by the roadhouse vibe at Mark and Terri Stark's flagship spot, which actually boasts an extremely well-traveled menu. The eclectic dishes are meant to be shared—and paired with local wine, naturally—and the clean, comfortable environs, rich with dark wood, create an ideal setting for a fun evening out with friends.

Willi's wide-ranging menu isn't afraid to take inspiration from wherever it comes—whether adding pancetta and sherry vinegar butter to scallop dumplings; or piling Dungeness crab, baby artichokes, and crescenza cheese on a puffy flatbread. To really indulge, opt for the warm spinach salad with goat cheese and dates, before digging into the Meyer lemon pudding cake, with its airy top and delightful lemon curd.

# Willow Wood Market Cafe

Californian **✕**

C3

**9020 Graton Rd. (at Edison St.), Graton**

| | |
|---|---|
| **Phone:** 707-823-0233 | Lunch daily |
| **Web:** www.willowwoodgraton.com | Dinner Mon – Sat |
| **Price:** **$$** | |

Whether they're fueling up for work or for wine tasting, a down-to-earth crowd can always be found at this friendly, casual neighborhood diner, full of quirky local art, shelves stocked with gag food gifts and local sundries. Then there's also that big wall of wines (this is Sonoma, after all). Waitresses shout orders, coffee comes from serve-yourself thermoses, and guests couldn't be happier.

Get your veggies with the generously portioned farmer's scramble, full of soft and spicy peppers and onions, not to mention plenty of creamy white cheddar and springy, meaty New Mexican chicken-turkey sausage. For a sweet tooth, the challah French toast, golden-brown and topped with a generous scoop of cinnamon butter and chopped pecans, is where it's at.

# Yeti

**D3**

14301 Arnold Dr., Ste. 19 (in Jack London Village), Glen Ellen

**Phone:** 707-996-9930                              Lunch & dinner daily
**Web:** www.yetirestaurant.com
**Price:** $$

Its sleepy location may be unusual, but with a creekside view and friendly service, Yeti makes for a pleasant getaway from the wine country grind. Inside the sunken dining room, soft folk music, Tibetan artwork, and a blisteringly hot tandoor set an authentic scene.

Though the fare is described as Nepalese-cum-Indian, most dishes are from both the north (think grilled meats and biryanis) as well as the coastal regions of the sub-continent (fish curries and coconut sauces). Try the lamb chops coated in *garam masala* and served over a bed of charred onion and bell pepper. Vegetable *momos* (steamed dumplings stuffed with cabbage, carrots, beans, and green onion) served with spicy *sambal*, cilantro, and sweet tamarind dipping sauces, are a party in your mouth.

# zazu kitchen + farm

**C3**

6770 McKinley St., Ste. 150 (bet. Brown & Morris Sts.), Sebastopol

**Phone:** 707-523-4814                              Lunch Thu – Sun
**Web:** www.zazukitchen.com                        Dinner Wed – Mon
**Price:** $$

A fun change from the rustic décor seen in much of wine country, this big and bright industrial space is practically translucent, thanks in large part to its garage-like doors and glossy cement floors. Natural wood tables and huge wild flower arrangements keep it from feeling chilly, as do surprisingly great acoustics—you won't struggle to be heard, even if the massive 20-seat family table is full.

Pork is the priority here, as evidenced by the sharp, spicy, and addictive Cuban sandwich with house-made mortadella. Vegetarians will delight in the tart tomato soup with an oozing Carmody grilled cheese, or the black beans with baked eggs. But the real key for carnivores is to bring home the bacon; it's a little bit pricey, but worth every penny.

# Where to **Eat**

Alphabetical List
of Restaurants_____376

Restaurants
by Cuisine_____384

Cuisines
by Neighborhood_____392

Starred Restaurants_____402

Bib Gourmand_____405

Under $25_____406

# Alphabetical List of Restaurants

## A

| | | | |
|---|---|---|---|
| Aatxe | | X | 18 |
| Absinthe | | XX | 26 |
| Acquerello | ✿✿ | XxX | 102 |
| Adega | ✿ | XX | 278 |
| Ad Hoc | | XX | 314 |
| 'āina | 🙂 | X | 78 |
| Akiko's | | X | 46 |
| alaMar | | X | 176 |
| Alexander's Steakhouse | | XxX | 279 |
| aliment | | X | 103 |
| All Spice | | XX | 238 |
| Al's Place | ✿ | XX | 79 |
| Alta CA | | XX | 26 |
| Anchor Oyster Bar | 🙂 | X | 18 |
| Angèle | | XX | 314 |
| An Japanese | | X | 61 |
| AQ | | XX | 150 |
| Archetype | | XX | 315 |
| Ark Grill | | XX | 238 |
| Arti | | X | 215 |
| Arun | | X | 215 |
| A16 | 🙂 | XX | 61 |
| Aster | ✿ | XX | 80 |
| Atelier Crenn | ✿✿ | XX | 62 |
| Auberge du Soleil | ✿ | XxX | 316 |
| Aziza | ✿ | XX | 134 |

## B

| | | | |
|---|---|---|---|
| Baan | | X | 216 |
| Babushka | | X | 176 |
| Back A Yard | | X | 279 |
| Backyard | 🙂 | X | 346 |
| Bar Agricole | | XX | 150 |
| Bar Bocce | | X | 216 |
| Barcha | | XX | 151 |
| Barcote | | X | 177 |
| Bar Crudo | | 🍲 | 27 |
| Barndiva | | XX | 346 |
| Barrel House Tavern | | XX | 217 |
| Bar Tartine | 🙂 | XX | 78 |
| Battambang | | X | 177 |
| Baumé | ✿✿ | XxX | 280 |
| Belcampo | | X | 103 |
| Belga | | XX | 63 |
| Bellanico | | XX | 178 |
| Bellota | | XX | 151 |
| Belotti Ristorante e Bottega | | X | 178 |
| Benu | ✿✿✿ | XxX | 152 |
| Beretta | | X | 81 |
| Bird Dog | | XX | 281 |
| Bistro Aix | 🙂 | XX | 63 |
| Bistro Don Giovanni | | XX | 315 |
| Bistro Jeanty | 🙂 | XX | 317 |
| Bistro 29 | 🙂 | XX | 347 |
| Blackwood | | XX | 64 |
| Blue Plate | | XX | 81 |
| Boiling Beijing | | XX | 239 |
| Boon Eat + Drink | | X | 347 |
| Boon Fly Café | | X | 317 |
| Boot and Shoe Service | | XX | 179 |
| Bottega | | XX | 318 |
| Bouchon | ✿ | XX | 319 |
| Boulevard | | XX | 153 |
| Bounty Hunter | | XX | 318 |
| Boxing Room | | XX | 27 |
| Bradley's Fine Diner | | XX | 239 |
| Bravas | 🙂 | XX | 348 |
| Brenda's | | X | 28 |
| Brix | | XX | 320 |
| Brown Sugar Kitchen | | X | 179 |

| | | | |
|---|---|---|---|
| Buckeye Roadhouse | | XX | 217 |
| Bui Bistro | | XX | 320 |
| Bun Bo Hue An Nam | | X | 281 |
| Bungalow 44 | | XX | 218 |
| Burma Superstar | | X | 135 |
| Burmatown | | X | 218 |
| Bywater (The) | 🍸 | X | 282 |

## C

| | | | |
|---|---|---|---|
| Café Capistrano | | X | 240 |
| Café Colucci | | X | 180 |
| Café Jacqueline | | X | 120 |
| Cafe La Haye | | XX | 348 |
| Café Lucia | | XX | 349 |
| Cafe Reyes | | X | 219 |
| Café Romanat | | X | 180 |
| Cala | | XX | 28 |
| Calavera | | XX | 181 |
| Californios | 🏵 | XX | 82 |
| Camino | | X | 181 |
| Ca'Momi Osteria | | XX | 321 |
| Campo Fina | | X | 349 |
| Campton Place | 🏵🏵 | XxX | 47 |
| Carmel Pizza Company | | X | 120 |
| Cavalier (The) | | XX | 153 |
| C Casa | | X | 321 |
| Central Kitchen | | XX | 83 |
| Central Market | | XX | 350 |
| Cetrella | | XxX | 240 |
| Chalkboard | 🍸 | XX | 350 |
| Chapeau! | 🍸 | X | 135 |
| Chennai Kings | | X | 282 |
| Chez Panisse | | XX | 182 |
| Chez TJ | 🏵 | XxX | 283 |
| Chiaroscuro | | XX | 46 |
| Chilli Padi | | XX | 182 |

| | | | |
|---|---|---|---|
| China Village | 🍸 | XX | 183 |
| Chinois | | X | 351 |
| Cholita Linda | | X | 183 |
| Ciccio | | XX | 322 |
| Cindy's Backstreet Kitchen | | XX | 322 |
| Cobani | | X | 241 |
| Cockscomb | | XX | 154 |
| Coi | 🏵🏵 | XxX | 122 |
| Cole's Chop House | | XX | 323 |
| Comal | 🍸 | XX | 184 |
| Commis | 🏵🏵 | XX | 185 |
| Commissary (The) | | XX | 64 |
| Commonwealth | 🏵 | XX | 84 |
| Contigo | | XX | 19 |
| Cooking Papa | | X | 241 |
| Cook St. Helena | 🍸 | XX | 323 |
| Copita | | XX | 219 |
| Coqueta | 🍸 | XX | 48 |
| Corso | 🍸 | X | 184 |
| Cosecha | | X | 186 |
| Cotogna | 🍸 | XX | 121 |
| County Bench (The) | | XX | 351 |
| Crouching Tiger | | XX | 242 |
| Cucina Paradiso | | XX | 352 |
| Cuisinett | | X | 242 |

## D

| | | | |
|---|---|---|---|
| Delage | | X | 186 |
| Delarosa | | X | 65 |
| Delfina | 🍸 | XX | 83 |
| Delizie | | XX | 243 |
| Della Santina's | | XX | 352 |
| Del Popolo | 🍸 | X | 48 |
| Diablo's JJ | | X | 243 |
| Diavola | 🍸 | XX | 353 |
| Din Tai Fung | | XX | 284 |

| | | | |
|---|---|---|---|
| Dio Deka | | XX | 284 |
| DishDash | | XX | 285 |
| Doc Ricketts | | X | 121 |
| Donato Enoteca | | XX | 244 |
| Doña Tomás | | X | 187 |
| Doppio Zero | | XX | 285 |
| Dosa | ☺ | XX | 65 |
| Dragon Beaux | | XX | 136 |
| Dragon Well | | X | 66 |
| Dry Creek Kitchen | | XxX | 353 |
| Duende | | XX | 187 |

**E**

| | | | |
|---|---|---|---|
| El Dorado Kitchen | | XX | 354 |
| El Huarache Loco | | X | 220 |
| El Paseo | | XX | 220 |
| Encuentro | | X | 188 |
| Esin | | XX | 188 |
| Evangeline | | XX | 324 |
| Evvia | ☺ | XX | 286 |

**F**

| | | | |
|---|---|---|---|
| Falafel STOP | | X | 286 |
| Farallon | | XxX | 49 |
| FARM | | XxX | 324 |
| Farmhouse Inn & Restaurant | ☼ | XxX | 355 |
| Farmhouse Kitchen Thai | ☺ | X | 85 |
| Farmstead | ☺ | XX | 325 |
| Fashion Wok | | X | 244 |
| Fey | | XX | 245 |
| 54 Mint | | XX | 154 |
| Fiorella | | X | 136 |
| Fish | | X | 221 |
| FIVE | ☺ | XX | 189 |
| Flavas Jamaican Grill | | X | 245 |
| Flea St. | | XX | 246 |
| Florio | | XX | 66 |
| flour + water | | X | 85 |
| 4505 Burgers & BBQ | | X | 29 |
| Frances | | XX | 19 |

| | | | |
|---|---|---|---|
| Frantoio | | XX | 221 |
| Frascati | | XX | 104 |
| French Laundry (The) | ☼☼☼ | XxxX | 326 |
| Fringale | | XX | 155 |
| Fu Lam Mum | | X | 287 |

**G**

| | | | |
|---|---|---|---|
| Gary Danko | ☼ | XxX | 123 |
| Gaspar | | XX | 49 |
| Gather | | X | 189 |
| Gintei | | XX | 246 |
| Gioia | | X | 104 |
| Glen Ellen Star | ☺ | X | 354 |
| Goose & Gander | | XX | 325 |
| Grace's Table | ☺ | XX | 327 |
| Grand Avenue Thai | | XX | 190 |
| Great China | ☺ | XX | 190 |
| Greens | | X | 67 |

**H**

| | | | |
|---|---|---|---|
| Hakkasan | | XxX | 50 |
| Hamro Aangan | | X | 191 |
| Hana | | XX | 356 |
| Happy Sichuan | | XX | 247 |
| Harvest Moon Cafe | | X | 356 |
| Harvest Table | | XX | 327 |
| Hashiri | ☼ | XxX | 156 |
| Haven | | XX | 191 |
| Hawker Fare | | X | 192 |
| Heirloom Café | | XX | 86 |
| Helmand Palace | | XX | 105 |
| High Peaks Kitchen | | X | 192 |
| Hina Yakitori | | X | 193 |
| Hog Island Oyster Co. | | X | 50 |
| Homage | | X | 51 |
| Homestead | | X | 193 |
| Hong Kong Flower Lounge | | XX | 247 |
| Hong Kong Lounge II | ☺ | XX | 67 |
| Hopscotch | | X | 194 |
| house (the) | | X | 124 |
| Huxley | | X | 105 |

## I

| | | | |
|---|---|---|---|
| Ichi Sushi + Ni Bar | | XX | 86 |
| Ijji | | X | 29 |
| Il Casaro | | X | 124 |
| Imm Thai Street Food | | X | 194 |
| INDO | | XX | 287 |
| Infinite Thai Eatery | | XX | 195 |
| Insalata's | ⊛ | XX | 222 |
| In Situ | | XX | 155 |
| Ippuku | ⊛ | X | 195 |
| Iyasare | | XX | 196 |
| Izakaya Rintaro | ⊛ | XX | 87 |
| Iza Ramen | | X | 30 |

## J

| | | | |
|---|---|---|---|
| Jang Su Jang | | XX | 288 |
| Jannah | | XX | 30 |
| Jardinière | | XxX | 31 |
| John Ash & Co. | | XX | 357 |
| John Bentley's | | XX | 248 |
| jū-ni | ✿ | XX | 32 |

## K

| | | | |
|---|---|---|---|
| Kabab & Curry's | | X | 288 |
| Kabul | | XX | 248 |
| Kamakshi's Kitchen | | X | 249 |
| Kamdesh | | X | 196 |
| Kappou Gomi | ⊛ | X | 137 |
| Keiko à Nob Hill | ✿ | XxX | 106 |
| Kemuri Japanese Barú | | X | 249 |
| Kenwood (The) | | XX | 357 |
| Khan Toke Thai House | | X | 137 |
| Kingston 11 | | X | 197 |
| Kin Khao | ✿ | X | 52 |
| Kiss | | X | 68 |
| Kitchen Istanbul | | X | 138 |
| Koi Palace | | XX | 250 |
| Kokkari Estiatorio | ⊛ | XX | 125 |
| Kusakabe | | XX | 51 |

## L

| | | | |
|---|---|---|---|
| La Ciccia | | XX | 87 |
| La Costanera | ⊛ | XX | 250 |
| La Folie | | XxX | 107 |
| Lai Hong Lounge | ⊛ | X | 125 |
| La Marcha | | X | 197 |
| L'Ardoise | | XX | 20 |
| LaSalette | | XX | 358 |
| La Taquiza | | X | 328 |
| La Toque | ✿ | XxX | 329 |
| La Torta Gorda | | X | 88 |
| Lau Hai San | | X | 289 |
| Lavash | | XX | 138 |
| La Viga | | X | 251 |
| Lazy Bear | ✿✿ | XX | 89 |
| Left Bank | | XX | 222 |
| Le Garage | ⊛ | X | 223 |
| Leopold's | | XX | 107 |
| Leo's Oyster Bar | | XX | 53 |
| Liholiho Yacht Club | | XX | 108 |
| Liquid Bread | | X | 289 |
| Locanda | | XX | 88 |
| Locanda Positano | | XX | 251 |
| Lolinda | | XX | 90 |
| Longbranch Saloon | | X | 198 |
| Lord Stanley | ✿ | XX | 109 |
| Los Cilantros | | X | 198 |
| Luce | ✿ | XxX | 157 |
| Lucy | | XX | 328 |
| Luma | | X | 358 |
| LV Mar | | XX | 252 |

## M

| | | | |
|---|---|---|---|
| Madera | ✿ | XxX | 253 |
| Madrona Manor | ✿ | XxX | 359 |
| Magda Luna | | X | 252 |
| Mamacita | ⊛ | XX | 68 |
| Mama Coco | | X | 254 |
| Mama Papa Lithuania | | X | 199 |
| Manresa | ✿✿✿ | XxX | 290 |

| | | |
|---|---|---|
| Marché aux Fleurs | XX | 223 |
| Marinitas | XX | 224 |
| Market | XX | 330 |
| Marlowe | XX | 158 |
| Mason Pacific | 🏠 XX | 108 |
| Matador | X | 53 |
| Mateo's Cocina Latina | XX | 360 |
| Mela Tandoori Kitchen | XX | 31 |
| Mensho | X | 110 |
| Michael Mina | ✿ XxX | 54 |
| Michel Bistro | 🏠 X | 199 |
| Millennium | 🏠 XX | 200 |
| Miminashi | X | 330 |
| Mint & Basil | X | 291 |
| Mission Street Oyster Bar | XX | 90 |
| Miss Ollie's | X | 200 |
| Mister Jiu's | ✿ XX | 111 |
| Mitsunobu | X | 254 |
| Modern Thai | X | 110 |
| Molina | XX | 224 |
| Monsieur Benjamin | XX | 33 |
| Montesacro Pinseria-Enoteca | X | 158 |
| Monti's Rotisserie | 🏠 XX | 360 |
| Mosu | ✿ XX | 34 |
| Mourad | ✿ XxX | 159 |
| Mustards Grill | XX | 331 |
| M. Y. China | 🏠 XX | 160 |
| Myriad | X | 91 |

## N

| | | |
|---|---|---|
| Napoletana Pizzeria | X | 291 |
| Naschmarkt | XX | 292 |
| New England Lobster Company | X | 255 |
| Nick's Cove | XX | 225 |
| Nick's Next Door | XX | 292 |
| Nico | ✿ XX | 69 |
| Nido | X | 201 |
| Nopa | XX | 33 |
| Nopalito | 🏠 X | 35 |
| Norman Rose Tavern | XX | 331 |

## O

| | | |
|---|---|---|
| Oak & Rye | XX | 293 |
| Octavia | ✿ XX | 70 |
| Oenotri | 🏠 XX | 332 |
| Ohgane | X | 201 |
| Okane | 🏠 X | 160 |
| Oliveto | XX | 202 |
| Omakase | ✿ X | 161 |
| One Market | XX | 162 |
| Orchard City Kitchen | 🏠 XX | 293 |
| Orenchi | X | 294 |
| Oren's Hummus Shop | X | 294 |
| Orexi | XX | 139 |
| Oriental Pearl | XX | 112 |
| Oso | X | 361 |
| Osteria Stellina | XX | 225 |
| Outerlands | X | 139 |

## P

| | | |
|---|---|---|
| Pabu | XX | 55 |
| Padrecito | XX | 20 |
| Pancho Villa Taqueria | X | 91 |
| Papalote | X | 92 |
| Papito | X | 92 |
| Paprika | X | 93 |
| Parallel 37 | XxX | 112 |
| Park Chow | X | 140 |
| Park Tavern | XX | 126 |
| Pasta Moon | XX | 255 |
| Pastis | X | 295 |
| Pathos | XX | 202 |
| Pazzo | XX | 256 |
| Perbacco | XX | 55 |
| Per Diem | XX | 56 |
| Perennial (The) | XX | 162 |
| Peter Lowell's | X | 361 |
| Petit Crenn | XX | 35 |
| Piccino | XX | 93 |
| Picco | XX | 226 |
| Piperade | XX | 126 |

Indexes ▶ Alphabetical List of Restaurants

| | | | |
|---|---|---|---|
| Piqueo's | | XX | 94 |
| PizzaHacker | | X | 94 |
| Pizzaiolo | | X | 203 |
| Pizzetta 211 | | X | 140 |
| Pläj | | XX | 36 |
| Plumed Horse | ✿ | XxX | 296 |
| Poggio | ☺ | XX | 226 |
| Prabh | | XX | 227 |
| Press | | XxX | 332 |
| Progress (The) | ✿ | XX | 37 |
| Prospect | | XxX | 163 |
| Prubechu | | X | 95 |

### Q

| | | | |
|---|---|---|---|
| Quattro | | XX | 256 |
| Quince | ✿✿✿ | XxxX | 127 |

### R

| | | | |
|---|---|---|---|
| Ramen Dojo | | X | 257 |
| Ramen Gaijin | ☺ | X | 362 |
| Ramen Shop | | X | 203 |
| Rasa | ✿ | XX | 258 |
| Rasoi | | XX | 257 |
| Redd | | XX | 333 |
| Redd Wood | ☺ | XX | 333 |
| Regalito | | X | 95 |
| Restaurant at Meadowood (The) | ✿✿✿ | XxxX | 334 |
| Revival | | XX | 362 |
| Rich Table | ☺ | XX | 36 |
| Risibisi | ☺ | XX | 363 |
| Riva Cucina | | X | 204 |
| Rivoli | | XX | 204 |
| R'Noh Thai | | XX | 227 |
| RN74 | | XX | 163 |
| Romesco | | X | 259 |
| Rosso | | X | 363 |
| Royal Indian Grill | | X | 205 |
| Rustic | | XX | 364 |
| Rusty's Southern | | X | 38 |
| Rutherford Grill | | XX | 335 |

### S

| | | | |
|---|---|---|---|
| Saap Ver | | X | 164 |
| Sahn Maru | | X | 205 |
| Saison | ✿✿✿ | XxX | 165 |
| Sakae | | X | 259 |
| Sam's Social Club | | XX | 335 |
| Santa Rosa Seafood Raw Bar & Grill | | X | 364 |
| Santé | | XxX | 365 |
| San Tung | | X | 141 |
| Saru | | X | 21 |
| Sawa Sushi | | X | 295 |
| Sazón | | X | 365 |
| Scopa | ☺ | X | 366 |
| Sea (The) | | XxX | 297 |
| Seaside Metal | | X | 366 |
| SEA Thai | | XX | 367 |
| Seven Hills | | XX | 113 |
| 1760 | | XX | 113 |
| Shakewell | | XX | 206 |
| Shalizaar | | XX | 260 |
| SHED Café | ☺ | X | 367 |
| Shizen | | XX | 96 |
| Sichuan Chong Qing | | X | 260 |
| Sichuan Home | ☺ | X | 141 |
| Sidebar | | X | 206 |
| Sir and Star | ☺ | XX | 228 |
| 1601 Bar & Kitchen | ☺ | XX | 164 |
| Slanted Door (The) | | XX | 56 |
| Smoking Pig BBQ | | X | 297 |
| Sociale | ☺ | XX | 71 |
| Solbar | ✿ | XX | 336 |
| Sol Food | | X | 228 |
| Sons & Daughters | ✿ | XX | 114 |
| South Legend | | X | 298 |
| Spinster Sisters | | XX | 368 |
| Spoonbar | | XX | 368 |
| SPQR | ✿ | XX | 72 |
| Spruce | ✿ | XX | 73 |
| Starbelly | ☺ | XX | 21 |

Indexes ▶ Alphabetical List of Restaurants

| | | | |
|---|---|---|---|
| State Bird Provisions | ❀ | ✕✕ | 39 |
| STEM Kitchen & Garden | | ✕✕ | 96 |
| Stones Throw | | ✕ | 115 |
| Striped Pig (The) | | ✕ | 261 |
| Sugo | | ✕ | 369 |
| Sumika | | ✕ | 298 |
| Sushi Ran | ❀ | ✕✕ | 229 |
| Sushi Sam's | | ✕ | 261 |
| Sushi Yoshizumi | ❀ | ✕ | 262 |
| Sutro's | | ✕✕ | 142 |
| Swaad | | ✕ | 299 |
| Sweet Basil | | ✕✕ | 263 |

**T**

| | | | |
|---|---|---|---|
| Table (The) | | ✕ | 299 |
| Tacos Sinaloa | ❀ | ✕ | 207 |
| Tacubaya | | ✕ | 207 |
| Tadu | | ✕ | 38 |
| Tamarind Hall | | ✕ | 128 |
| Tamarine | | ✕✕ | 300 |
| Tanto | | ✕ | 300 |
| Taqueria El Metate | | ✕ | 263 |
| Taqueria San Bruno | | ✕ | 264 |
| Taste In Mediterranean Food | | ✕ | 264 |
| Terra | ❀ | ✕✕✕ | 337 |
| Terrapin Creek | ❀ | ✕✕ | 370 |
| Thai Aroi-Dee | | ✕ | 229 |
| Thai House | ❀ | ✕✕ | 208 |
| the fig café | | ✕✕ | 369 |
| Thep Phanom | | ✕ | 40 |
| The Western Room | | ✕✕ | 230 |
| Thiên Long | | ✕ | 301 |
| Tin Vietnamese | | ✕ | 166 |
| Tony's Pizza Napoletana | | ✕ | 128 |
| Torc | | ✕✕ | 338 |
| Tosca Café | | ✕✕ | 129 |
| Trabocco | | ✕✕ | 208 |
| Trattoria da Vittorio | | ✕✕ | 142 |
| Trestle | ❀ | ✕✕ | 57 |
| Trou Normand | | 🍴 | 166 |
| Tsubasa | ❀ | ✕ | 40 |

| | | | |
|---|---|---|---|
| Tuba | | ✕✕ | 97 |
| Twenty Five Lusk | | ✕✕✕ | 167 |
| Two Birds/One Stone | ❀ | ✕✕ | 338 |
| Tycoon | | ✕ | 41 |

**U**

| | | | |
|---|---|---|---|
| Ulavacharu | | ✕ | 301 |
| Una Pizza Napoletana | | ✕ | 167 |
| Urfa Bistro | | ✕ | 302 |

**V**

| | | | |
|---|---|---|---|
| Va de Vi | | ✕✕ | 209 |
| Valenti & Co. | | ✕✕ | 230 |
| Valette | | ✕✕ | 371 |
| Vespucci | | ✕✕ | 265 |
| Vesta | ❀ | ✕✕ | 265 |
| Village Pub (The) | ❀ | ✕✕✕ | 266 |
| Village Sake | ❀ | ✕ | 231 |
| Viognier | | ✕✕✕ | 267 |
| Viva Goa | | ✕ | 71 |
| Volta | | ✕✕✕ | 168 |
| Voya (The) | | ✕✕ | 302 |
| Vung Tau | | ✕✕ | 303 |

**W**

| | | | |
|---|---|---|---|
| Wako | ❀ | ✕ | 143 |
| Wakuriya | ❀ | ✕ | 268 |
| Walia | | ✕ | 303 |
| Waterbar | | ✕✕ | 168 |
| Waxman's | | ✕✕ | 129 |
| Wayfare Tavern | | ✕✕ | 57 |
| Willi's Seafood & Raw Bar | | ✕✕ | 371 |
| Willi's Wine Bar | | ✕✕ | 372 |
| Willow Wood Market Cafe | | ✕ | 372 |
| Wine Spectator Greystone | | ✕✕ | 339 |
| wonderful | ❀ | ✕ | 267 |
| Wood Tavern | ❀ | ✕✕ | 209 |

**Y**

| | | | |
|---|---|---|---|
| Yank Sing | ❀ | ✕✕ | 169 |
| Yeti | | ✕✕ | 373 |

| Yi Yuan | | XX | 269 |
| Yummy Szechuan | | X | 269 |
| Yuzuki | ⊛ | X | 97 |

### Z

| Zareen's | | X | 304 |
| zazu kitchen + farm | | XX | 373 |

| Zeni | | X | 304 |
| Zero Zero | ⊛ | XX | 169 |
| Zola | ⊛ | XX | 305 |
| Zona Rosa | | X | 305 |
| Zuni Café | | XX | 41 |
| Zuzu | | ▤ | 339 |
| Z & Y | ⊛ | X | 115 |

# Restaurants by Cuisine

## Afghan

| | | |
|---|---|---|
| Helmand Palace | XX | 105 |
| Kabul | XX | 248 |
| Kamdesh | X | 196 |

## American

| | | | |
|---|---|---|---|
| Ad Hoc | | XX | 314 |
| aliment | | X | 103 |
| Belcampo | | X | 103 |
| Blue Plate | | XX | 81 |
| Boon Fly Café | | X | 317 |
| Bounty Hunter | | XX | 318 |
| Bradley's Fine Diner | | XX | 239 |
| Brown Sugar Kitchen | | X | 179 |
| Buckeye Roadhouse | | XX | 217 |
| Bungalow 44 | | XX | 218 |
| Chalkboard | ⊛ | XX | 350 |
| Cindy's Backstreet Kitchen | | XX | 322 |
| Cockscomb | | XX | 154 |
| County Bench (The) | | XX | 351 |
| Doc Ricketts | | X | 121 |
| El Paseo | | XX | 220 |
| Evangeline | | XX | 324 |
| FIVE | ⊛ | XX | 189 |
| Goose & Gander | | XX | 325 |
| Homestead | | X | 193 |
| Hopscotch | | X | 194 |
| Huxley | | X | 105 |
| Market | | XX | 330 |
| Marlowe | | XX | 158 |
| Monti's Rotisserie | ⊛ | XX | 360 |
| Mustards Grill | | XX | 331 |
| Nick's Cove | | XX | 225 |
| Nick's Next Door | | XX | 292 |
| Norman Rose Tavern | | XX | 331 |
| Outerlands | | X | 139 |
| Park Chow | | X | 140 |
| Park Tavern | | XX | 126 |
| Per Diem | | XX | 56 |
| Prospect | | XxX | 163 |
| Rutherford Grill | | XX | 335 |
| Sam's Social Club | | XX | 335 |
| Spinster Sisters | | XX | 368 |
| State Bird Provisions | ✿ | XX | 39 |
| Table (The) | | X | 299 |
| Torc | | XX | 338 |
| Trestle | ⊛ | XX | 57 |
| Twenty Five Lusk | | XxX | 167 |
| Waxman's | | XX | 129 |
| Wood Tavern | ⊛ | XX | 209 |
| zazu kitchen + farm | | XX | 373 |

## Argentinian

| | | |
|---|---|---|
| Lolinda | XX | 90 |

## Asian

| | | | |
|---|---|---|---|
| Benu | ✿✿✿ | XxX | 152 |
| Chinois | | X | 351 |
| Hawker Fare | | X | 192 |
| Kemuri Japanese Barú | | X | 249 |
| Mosu | ✿ | XX | 34 |
| house (the) | | X | 124 |

## Austrian

| | | |
|---|---|---|
| Leopold's | XX | 107 |
| Naschmarkt | XX | 292 |

## Barbecue

| | | |
|---|---|---|
| 4505 Burgers & BBQ | X | 29 |

| Smoking Pig BBQ | | X | 297 |
|---|---|---|---|

## Basque

| Piperade | | XX | 126 |
|---|---|---|---|

## Belgian

| Belga | | XX | 63 |
|---|---|---|---|

## Burmese

| Burma Superstar | | X | 135 |
|---|---|---|---|
| Burmatown | | X | 218 |

## Californian

| Al's Place | ❀ | XX | 79 |
|---|---|---|---|
| Alta CA | | XX | 26 |
| Archetype | | XX | 315 |
| Aster | ❀ | XX | 80 |
| Auberge du Soleil | ❀ | XxX | 316 |
| Backyard | ❀ | X | 346 |
| Bar Agricole | | XX | 150 |
| Barndiva | | XX | 346 |
| Barrel House Tavern | | XX | 217 |
| Boon Eat + Drink | | X | 347 |
| Boulevard | | XX | 153 |
| Brix | | XX | 320 |
| Cafe La Haye | | XX | 348 |
| Camino | | X | 181 |
| Central Kitchen | | XX | 83 |
| Chez Panisse | | XX | 182 |
| Dry Creek Kitchen | | XxX | 353 |
| El Dorado Kitchen | | XX | 354 |
| FARM | | XxX | 324 |
| Farmhouse Inn & Restaurant | ❀ | XxX | 355 |
| Farmstead | ❀ | XX | 325 |
| Flea St. | | XX | 246 |
| Frances | | XX | 19 |
| Gather | | X | 189 |
| Glen Ellen Star | ❀ | X | 354 |
| Harvest Moon Cafe | | X | 356 |
| Harvest Table | | XX | 327 |
| Heirloom Café | | XX | 86 |
| Homage | | X | 51 |
| Jardinière | | XxX | 31 |
| John Ash & Co. | | XX | 357 |
| Lord Stanley | ❀ | XX | 109 |
| Lucy | | XX | 328 |
| Luma | | X | 358 |
| Molina | | XX | 224 |
| Nopa | | XX | 33 |
| Octavia | ❀ | XX | 70 |
| One Market | | XX | 162 |
| Peter Lowell's | | X | 361 |
| Revival | | XX | 362 |
| Rivoli | | XX | 204 |
| RN74 | | XX | 163 |
| Saison | ❀❀❀ | XxX | 165 |
| Santé | | XxX | 365 |
| SHED Café | ❀ | X | 367 |
| Sir and Star | ❀ | XX | 228 |
| Solbar | ❀ | XX | 336 |
| Spruce | ❀ | XX | 73 |
| Starbelly | ❀ | XX | 21 |
| Sutro's | | XX | 142 |
| Terrapin Creek | ❀ | XX | 370 |
| Commissary (The) | | XX | 64 |
| the fig café | | XX | 369 |
| Kenwood (The) | | XX | 357 |
| Progress (The) | ❀ | XX | 37 |
| The Western Room | | XX | 230 |
| Valette | | XX | 371 |

| | | |
|---|---|---|
| Willow Wood Market Cafe | X | 372 |
| Wine Spectator Greystone | XX | 339 |

## Cambodian

| | | |
|---|---|---|
| Battambang | X | 177 |

## Caribbean

| | | |
|---|---|---|
| Back A Yard | X | 279 |
| Kingston 11 | X | 197 |
| Miss Ollie's | X | 200 |

## Chamorro

| | | |
|---|---|---|
| Prubechu | X | 95 |

## Chinese

| | | | |
|---|---|---|---|
| Boiling Beijing | | XX | 239 |
| China Village | 🍴 | XX | 183 |
| Cooking Papa | | X | 241 |
| Crouching Tiger | | XX | 242 |
| Din Tai Fung | | XX | 284 |
| Dragon Beaux | | XX | 136 |
| Dragon Well | | X | 66 |
| Fashion Wok | | X | 244 |
| Fey | | XX | 245 |
| Fu Lam Mum | | X | 287 |
| Great China | 🍴 | XX | 190 |
| Hakkasan | | XxX | 50 |
| Happy Sichuan | | XX | 247 |
| Hong Kong Flower Lounge | | XX | 247 |
| Hong Kong Lounge II | 🍴 | XX | 67 |
| Koi Palace | | XX | 250 |
| Lai Hong Lounge | 🍴 | X | 125 |
| M. Y. China | 🍴 | XX | 160 |
| Mister Jiu's | 🕸 | XX | 111 |
| Oriental Pearl | | XX | 112 |
| San Tung | | X | 141 |
| Sichuan Chong Qing | | X | 260 |
| Sichuan Home | 🍴 | X | 141 |
| South Legend | | X | 298 |
| wonderful | 🍴 | X | 267 |
| Yank Sing | 🍴 | XX | 169 |

| | | | |
|---|---|---|---|
| Yi Yuan | | XX | 269 |
| Yummy Szechuan | | X | 269 |
| Z & Y | 🍴 | X | 115 |

## Contemporary

| | | | |
|---|---|---|---|
| AQ | | XX | 150 |
| Atelier Crenn | 🕸🕸 | XX | 62 |
| Baumé | 🕸🕸 | XxX | 280 |
| Bird Dog | | XX | 281 |
| Chez TJ | 🕸 | XxX | 283 |
| Coi | 🕸🕸 | XxX | 122 |
| Commis | 🕸🕸 | XX | 185 |
| Commonwealth | 🕸 | XX | 84 |
| Gary Danko | 🕸 | XxX | 123 |
| Haven | | XX | 191 |
| John Bentley's | | XX | 248 |
| La Toque | 🕸 | XxX | 329 |
| Lazy Bear | 🕸🕸 | XX | 89 |
| Luce | 🕸 | XxX | 157 |
| Madera | 🕸 | XxX | 253 |
| Madrona Manor | 🕸 | XxX | 359 |
| Manresa | 🕸🕸🕸 | XxX | 290 |
| Mason Pacific | 🍴 | XX | 108 |
| Michael Mina | 🕸 | XxX | 54 |
| Nico | 🕸 | XX | 69 |
| Parallel 37 | | XxX | 112 |
| Plumed Horse | 🕸 | XxX | 296 |
| Redd | | XX | 333 |
| Rich Table | 🍴 | XX | 36 |
| 1760 | | XX | 113 |
| Sons & Daughters | 🕸 | XX | 114 |
| Spoonbar | | XX | 368 |
| Stones Throw | | X | 115 |
| Terra | 🕸 | XxX | 337 |
| French Laundry (The) | 🕸🕸🕸 | XxxX | 326 |
| Perennial (The) | | XX | 162 |
| Restaurant at Meadowood (The) | 🕸🕸🕸 | XxxX | 334 |
| Viognier | | XxX | 267 |

# Eastern European

| | | |
|---|---|---|
| Babushka | X | 176 |
| Bar Tartine | 🐝 XX | 78 |
| Mama Papa Lithuania | X | 199 |
| Paprika | X | 93 |

# Ethiopian

| | | |
|---|---|---|
| Barcote | X | 177 |
| Café Colucci | X | 180 |
| Café Romanat | X | 180 |
| Tadu | X | 38 |
| Walia | X | 303 |
| Zeni | X | 304 |

# European

| | | |
|---|---|---|
| Volta | XxX | 168 |

# French

| | | |
|---|---|---|
| Angèle | XX | 314 |
| Bistro 29 | 🐝 XX | 347 |
| Bistro Jeanty | 🐝 XX | 317 |
| Bouchon | 🏵 XX | 319 |
| Café Jacqueline | X | 120 |
| Chapeau! | 🐝 X | 135 |
| Cuisinett | X | 242 |
| Fringale | XX | 155 |
| Gaspar | XX | 49 |
| L'Ardoise | XX | 20 |
| La Folie | XxX | 107 |
| Le Garage | 🐝 X | 223 |
| Left Bank | XX | 222 |
| Michel Bistro | 🐝 X | 199 |
| Monsieur Benjamin | XX | 33 |
| Pastis | X | 295 |
| Petit Crenn | XX | 35 |
| Zola | 🐝 XX | 305 |

# Fusion

| | | |
|---|---|---|
| Blackwood | XX | 64 |
| Californios | 🏵 XX | 82 |
| Keiko à Nob Hill | 🏵 XxX | 106 |
| Two Birds/One Stone | 🐝 XX | 338 |

# Gastropub

| | | |
|---|---|---|
| Liquid Bread | X | 289 |
| Longbranch Saloon | X | 198 |
| Sidebar | X | 206 |
| Cavalier (The) | XX | 153 |
| Striped Pig (The) | X | 261 |
| Village Pub (The) | 🏵 XxX | 266 |
| Wayfare Tavern | XX | 57 |

# Greek

| | | |
|---|---|---|
| Dio Deka | XX | 284 |
| Evvia | 🐝 XX | 286 |
| Kokkari Estiatorio | 🐝 XX | 125 |
| Orexi | XX | 139 |
| Pathos | XX | 202 |

# Hawaiian

| | | |
|---|---|---|
| Liholiho Yacht Club | XX | 108 |
| 'āina | 🐝 X | 78 |

# Indian

| | | |
|---|---|---|
| Ark Grill | XX | 238 |
| Arti | X | 215 |
| Campton Place | 🏵🏵 XxX | 47 |
| Chennai Kings | X | 282 |
| Dosa | 🐝 XX | 65 |
| High Peaks Kitchen | X | 192 |
| Kabab & Curry's | X | 288 |
| Kamakshi's Kitchen | X | 249 |
| Mela Tandoori Kitchen | XX | 31 |
| Prabh | XX | 227 |
| Rasa | 🏵 XX | 258 |
| Rasoi | XX | 257 |
| Royal Indian Grill | X | 205 |
| Swaad | X | 299 |
| Ulavacharu | X | 301 |
| Viva Goa | X | 71 |
| Zareen's | X | 304 |

Indexes ▶ Restaurants by Cuisine

## Indonesian

| | | | |
|---|---|---|---|
| INDO | | XX | 287 |

## International

| | | | |
|---|---|---|---|
| All Spice | | XX | 238 |
| Grace's Table | ☺ | XX | 327 |
| In Situ | | XX | 155 |
| Myriad | | X | 91 |
| Orchard City Kitchen | ☺ | XX | 293 |
| Oso | | X | 361 |
| Va de Vi | | XX | 209 |
| Willi's Wine Bar | | XX | 372 |

## Israeli

| | | | |
|---|---|---|---|
| Falafel STOP | | X | 286 |
| Oren's Hummus Shop | | X | 294 |

## Italian

| | | | |
|---|---|---|---|
| A16 | ☺ | XX | 61 |
| Acquerello | ✿✿ | XxX | 102 |
| Bellanico | | XX | 178 |
| Belotti Ristorante e Bottega | | X | 178 |
| Beretta | | X | 81 |
| Bistro Don Giovanni | | XX | 315 |
| Bottega | | XX | 318 |
| Ca'Momi Osteria | | XX | 321 |
| Campo Fina | | X | 349 |
| Chiaroscuro | | XX | 46 |
| Ciccio | | XX | 322 |
| Cook St. Helena | ☺ | XX | 323 |
| Corso | ☺ | X | 184 |
| Cotogna | ☺ | XX | 121 |
| Cucina Paradiso | | XX | 352 |
| Delarosa | | X | 65 |
| Delfina | ☺ | XX | 83 |
| Delizie | | XX | 243 |
| Della Santina's | | XX | 352 |
| Diavola | ☺ | XX | 353 |
| Donato Enoteca | | XX | 244 |
| Doppio Zero | | XX | 285 |
| 54 Mint | | XX | 154 |
| Fiorella | | X | 136 |
| Florio | | XX | 66 |
| flour + water | | X | 85 |
| Frantoio | | XX | 221 |
| La Ciccia | | XX | 87 |
| Locanda | | XX | 88 |
| Locanda Positano | | XX | 251 |
| Oenotri | ☺ | XX | 332 |
| Oliveto | | XX | 202 |
| Osteria Stellina | | XX | 225 |
| Pasta Moon | | XX | 255 |
| Perbacco | | XX | 55 |
| Piccino | | XX | 93 |
| Picco | | XX | 226 |
| Poggio | ☺ | XX | 226 |
| Quattro | | XX | 256 |
| Quince | ✿✿✿ | XxXX | 127 |
| Redd Wood | ☺ | XX | 333 |
| Risibisi | ☺ | XX | 363 |
| Riva Cucina | | X | 204 |
| Rustic | | XX | 364 |
| Scopa | ☺ | X | 366 |
| Seven Hills | | XX | 113 |
| Sociale | ☺ | XX | 71 |
| SPQR | ✿ | XX | 72 |
| Sugo | | X | 369 |
| Tosca Café | | XX | 129 |
| Trabocco | | XX | 208 |
| Trattoria da Vittorio | | XX | 142 |
| Valenti & Co. | | XX | 230 |
| Vespucci | | XX | 265 |

## Jamaican

| | | | |
|---|---|---|---|
| Flavas Jamaican Grill | | X | 245 |

## Japanese

| | | | |
|---|---|---|---|
| Akiko's | | X | 46 |
| An Japanese | | X | 61 |
| Delage | | X | 186 |
| Gintei | | XX | 246 |

| | | |
|---|---|---|
| Hana | ✗✗ | 356 |
| Hashiri | ✿ ✗✗✗ | 156 |
| Hina Yakitori | ✗ | 193 |
| Ichi Sushi + Ni Bar | ✗✗ | 86 |
| Ijji | ✗ | 29 |
| Ippuku | ⊕ ✗ | 195 |
| Iyasare | ✗✗ | 196 |
| Iza Ramen | ✗ | 30 |
| Izakaya Rintaro | ⊕ ✗✗ | 87 |
| jū-ni | ✿ ✗✗ | 32 |
| Kappou Gomi | ⊕ ✗ | 137 |
| Kiss | ✗ | 68 |
| Kusakabe | ✗✗ | 51 |
| Mensho | ✗ | 110 |
| Miminashi | ✗ | 330 |
| Mitsunobu | ✗ | 254 |
| Okane | ⊕ ✗ | 160 |
| Omakase | ✿ ✗ | 161 |
| Orenchi | ✗ | 294 |
| Pabu | ✗✗ | 55 |
| Ramen Dojo | ✗ | 257 |
| Ramen Gaijin | ⊕ ✗ | 362 |
| Ramen Shop | ✗ | 203 |
| Sakae | ✗ | 259 |
| Saru | ✗ | 21 |
| Sawa Sushi | ✗ | 295 |
| Sumika | ✗ | 298 |
| Sushi Ran | ⊕ ✗✗ | 229 |
| Sushi Sam's | ✗ | 261 |
| Sushi Yoshizumi | ✿ ✗ | 262 |
| Tanto | ✗ | 300 |
| Tsubasa | ⊕ ✗ | 40 |
| Village Sake | ⊕ ✗ | 231 |
| Wako | ✿ ✗ | 143 |
| Wakuriya | ✿ ✗ | 268 |
| Yuzuki | ⊕ ✗ | 97 |

## Korean

| | | |
|---|---|---|
| Jang Su Jang | ✗✗ | 288 |
| Ohgane | ✗ | 201 |
| Sahn Maru | ✗ | 205 |

## Latin American

| | | |
|---|---|---|
| Cholita Linda | ✗ | 183 |
| LV Mar | ✗✗ | 252 |
| Marinitas | ✗✗ | 224 |
| Voya (The) | ✗✗ | 302 |

## Malaysian

| | | |
|---|---|---|
| Chilli Padi | ✗✗ | 182 |

## Mediterranean

| | | |
|---|---|---|
| Absinthe | ✗✗ | 26 |
| Barcha | ✗✗ | 151 |
| Bistro Aix | ⊕ ✗✗ | 63 |
| Central Market | ✗✗ | 350 |
| Cetrella | ✗✗✗ | 240 |
| Cobani | ✗ | 241 |
| Esin | ✗✗ | 188 |
| Frascati | ✗✗ | 104 |
| Insalata's | ⊕ ✗✗ | 222 |
| Marché aux Fleurs | ✗✗ | 223 |
| Shakewell | ✗✗ | 206 |
| STEM Kitchen & Garden | ✗✗ | 96 |
| Taste In Mediterranean Food | ✗ | 264 |
| Trou Normand | 🎴 | 166 |
| Urfa Bistro | ✗ | 302 |
| Zuni Café | ✗✗ | 41 |

## Mexican

| | | |
|---|---|---|
| C Casa | ✗ | 321 |
| Café Capistrano | ✗ | 240 |
| Cala | ✗✗ | 28 |
| Calavera | ✗✗ | 181 |
| Comal | ⊕ ✗✗ | 184 |
| Copita | ✗✗ | 219 |
| Cosecha | ✗ | 186 |
| Diablo's JJ | ✗ | 243 |
| Doña Tomás | ✗ | 187 |
| El Huarache Loco | ✗ | 220 |
| La Taquiza | ✗ | 328 |
| La Torta Gorda | ✗ | 88 |

Indexes ► Restaurants by Cuisine

| La Viga | | ✗ | 251 |
| Los Cilantros | | ✗ | 198 |
| Magda Luna | | ✗ | 252 |
| Mama Coco | | ✗ | 254 |
| Mamacita | ☺ | ✗✗ | 68 |
| Matador | | ✗ | 53 |
| Mateo's Cocina Latina | | ✗✗ | 360 |
| Nido | | ✗ | 201 |
| Nopalito | ☺ | ✗ | 35 |
| Padrecito | | ✗✗ | 20 |
| Pancho Villa Taqueria | | ✗ | 91 |
| Papalote | | ✗ | 92 |
| Papito | | ✗ | 92 |
| Regalito | | ✗ | 95 |
| Tacos Sinaloa | ☺ | ✗ | 207 |
| Tacubaya | | ✗ | 207 |
| Taqueria El Metate | | ✗ | 263 |
| Taqueria San Bruno | | ✗ | 264 |
| Zona Rosa | | ✗ | 305 |

## Middle Eastern

| DishDash | | ✗✗ | 285 |
| Jannah | | ✗✗ | 30 |

## Moroccan

| Aziza | ✿ | ✗✗ | 134 |
| Mourad | ✿ | ✗✗✗ | 159 |

## Nepali

| Hamro Aangan | | ✗ | 191 |
| Yeti | | ✗✗ | 373 |

## Persian

| Lavash | | ✗✗ | 138 |
| Shalizaar | | ✗✗ | 260 |

## Peruvian

| La Costanera | ☺ | ✗✗ | 250 |
| Piqueo's | | ✗✗ | 94 |
| Sazón | | ✗ | 365 |

## Pizza

| Bar Bocce | | ✗ | 216 |
| Boot and Shoe Service | | ✗✗ | 179 |
| Cafe Reyes | | ✗ | 219 |
| Carmel Pizza Company | | ✗ | 120 |
| Del Popolo | ☺ | ✗ | 48 |
| Gioia | | ✗ | 104 |
| Il Casaro | | ✗ | 124 |
| Montesacro Pinseria e Enoteca | | ✗ | 158 |
| Napoletana Pizzeria | | ✗ | 291 |
| Oak & Rye | | ✗✗ | 293 |
| Pazzo | | ✗✗ | 256 |
| PizzaHacker | | ✗ | 94 |
| Pizzaiolo | | ✗ | 203 |
| Pizzetta 211 | | ✗ | 140 |
| Rosso | | ✗ | 363 |
| Tony's Pizza Napoletana | | ✗ | 128 |
| Una Pizza Napoletana | | ✗ | 167 |
| Vesta | ☺ | ✗✗ | 265 |
| Zero Zero | ☺ | ✗✗ | 169 |

## Portuguese

| Adega | ✿ | ✗✗ | 278 |
| Café Lucia | | ✗✗ | 349 |
| LaSalette | | ✗✗ | 358 |

## Puerto Rican

| Sol Food | | ✗ | 228 |

## Scandinavian

| Pläj | | ✗✗ | 36 |

## Seafood

| alaMar | | ✗ | 176 |
| Anchor Oyster Bar | ☺ | ✗ | 18 |
| Bar Crudo | | 🍴 | 27 |
| Farallon | | ✗✗✗ | 49 |
| Fish | | ✗ | 221 |
| Hog Island Oyster Co. | | ✗ | 50 |
| Leo's Oyster Bar | | ✗✗ | 53 |

| | | |
|---|---|---|
| Mission Street Oyster Bar | XX | 90 |
| New England Lobster Company | X | 255 |
| Santa Rosa Seafood Raw Bar & Grill | X | 364 |
| Seaside Metal | X | 366 |
| Sea (The) | XxX | 297 |
| Waterbar | XX | 168 |
| Willi's Seafood & Raw Bar | XX | 371 |

## Southern

| | | |
|---|---|---|
| Boxing Room | XX | 27 |
| Brenda's | X | 28 |
| Rusty's Southern | X | 38 |
| Bywater (The) | ⊛ X | 282 |

## Spanish

| | | |
|---|---|---|
| Aatxe | X | 18 |
| Bellota | XX | 151 |
| Bravas | ⊛ XX | 348 |
| Contigo | XX | 19 |
| Coqueta | ⊛ XX | 48 |
| Duende | XX | 187 |
| La Marcha | X | 197 |
| Romesco | X | 259 |
| Zuzu | ▤ | 339 |

## Sri Lankan

| | | |
|---|---|---|
| 1601 Bar & Kitchen | ⊛ XX | 164 |

## Steakhouse

| | | |
|---|---|---|
| Alexander's Steakhouse | XxX | 279 |
| Cole's Chop House | XX | 323 |
| Press | XxX | 332 |

## Thai

| | | |
|---|---|---|
| Arun | X | 215 |
| Baan | X | 216 |
| Farmhouse Kitchen Thai | ⊛ X | 85 |
| Grand Avenue Thai | XX | 190 |
| Imm Thai Street Food | X | 194 |
| Infinite Thai Eatery | XX | 195 |
| Khan Toke Thai House | X | 137 |
| Kin Khao | ✿ X | 52 |
| Modern Thai | X | 110 |
| R'Noh Thai | XX | 227 |
| Saap Ver | X | 164 |
| SEA Thai | XX | 367 |
| Sweet Basil | XX | 263 |
| Tamarind Hall | X | 128 |
| Thai Aroi-Dee | X | 229 |
| Thai House | ⊛ XX | 208 |
| Thep Phanom | X | 40 |
| Tycoon | X | 41 |

## Turkish

| | | |
|---|---|---|
| Kitchen Istanbul | X | 138 |
| Tuba | XX | 97 |

## Vegan

| | | |
|---|---|---|
| Millennium | ⊛ XX | 200 |
| Shizen | XX | 96 |

## Vegetarian

| | | |
|---|---|---|
| Encuentro | X | 188 |
| Greens | X | 67 |
| Mint & Basil | X | 291 |

## Vietnamese

| | | |
|---|---|---|
| Bui Bistro | XX | 320 |
| Bun Bo Hue An Nam | X | 281 |
| Lau Hai San | X | 289 |
| Tamarine | XX | 300 |
| Slanted Door (The) | XX | 56 |
| Thiên Long | X | 301 |
| Tin Vietnamese | X | 166 |
| Vung Tau | XX | 303 |

Indexes ▶ Restaurants by Cuisine

# Cuisines by Neighborhood

## Castro

### Californian
| | | |
|---|---|---|
| Frances | XX | 19 |
| Starbelly | ⊛ XX | 21 |

### French
| | | |
|---|---|---|
| L'Ardoise | XX | 20 |

### Japanese
| | | |
|---|---|---|
| Saru | X | 21 |

### Mexican
| | | |
|---|---|---|
| Padrecito | XX | 20 |

### Seafood
| | | |
|---|---|---|
| Anchor Oyster Bar | ⊛ X | 18 |

### Spanish
| | | |
|---|---|---|
| Aatxe | X | 18 |
| Contigo | XX | 19 |

## Civic Center

### American
| | | |
|---|---|---|
| State Bird Provisions | ✿ XX | 39 |

### Asian
| | | |
|---|---|---|
| Mosu | ✿ XX | 34 |

### Barbecue
| | | |
|---|---|---|
| 4505 Burgers & BBQ | X | 29 |

### Californian
| | | |
|---|---|---|
| Alta CA | XX | 26 |
| Jardinière | XxX | 31 |
| Nopa | XX | 33 |
| Progress (The) | ✿ XX | 37 |

### Contemporary
| | | |
|---|---|---|
| Rich Table | ⊛ XX | 36 |

### Ethiopian
| | | |
|---|---|---|
| Tadu | X | 38 |

### French
| | | |
|---|---|---|
| Monsieur Benjamin | XX | 33 |

| Petit Crenn | XX | 35 |
|---|---|---|

### Indian
| | | |
|---|---|---|
| Mela Tandoori Kitchen | XX | 31 |

### Japanese
| | | |
|---|---|---|
| Ijji | X | 29 |
| Iza Ramen | X | 30 |
| jū-ni | ✿ XX | 32 |
| Tsubasa | ⊛ X | 40 |

### Mediterranean
| | | |
|---|---|---|
| Absinthe | XX | 26 |
| Zuni Café | XX | 41 |

### Mexican
| | | |
|---|---|---|
| Cala | XX | 28 |
| Nopalito | ⊛ X | 35 |

### Middle Eastern
| | | |
|---|---|---|
| Jannah | XX | 30 |

### Scandinavian
| | | |
|---|---|---|
| Pläj | XX | 36 |

### Seafood
| | | |
|---|---|---|
| Bar Crudo | 📋 | 27 |

### Southern
| | | |
|---|---|---|
| Boxing Room | XX | 27 |
| Brenda's | X | 28 |
| Rusty's Southern | X | 38 |

### Thai
| | | |
|---|---|---|
| Thep Phanom | X | 40 |
| Tycoon | X | 41 |

## Financial District

### American
| | | |
|---|---|---|
| Per Diem | XX | 56 |
| Trestle | ⊛ XX | 57 |

### Californian
| | | |
|---|---|---|
| Homage | X | 51 |

### Chinese
| | | |
|---|---|---|
| Hakkasan | XxX | 50 |

### Contemporary
Michael Mina    ❀ XxX   54

### French
Gaspar    XX   49

### Gastropub
Wayfare Tavern    XX   57

### Indian
Campton Place    ❀❀ XxX   47

### Italian
Chiaroscuro    XX   46
Perbacco    XX   55

### Japanese
Akiko's    X   46
Kusakabe    XX   51
Pabu    XX   55

### Mexican
Matador    X   53

### Pizza
Del Popolo    ☺ X   48

### Seafood
Farallon    XxX   49
Hog Island Oyster Co.    X   50
Leo's Oyster Bar    XX   53

### Spanish
Coqueta    ☺ XX   48

### Thai
Kin Khao    ❀ X   52

### Vietnamese
Slanted Door (The)    XX   56

## Marina

### Belgian
Belga    XX   63

### Californian
Commissary (The)    XX   64
Octavia    ❀ XX   70
Spruce    ❀ XX   73

### Chinese
Dragon Well    X   66
Hong Kong Lounge II    ☺ XX   67

### Contemporary
Atelier Crenn    ❀❀ XX   62
Nico    ❀ XX   69

### Fusion
Blackwood    XX   64

### Indian
Dosa    ☺ XX   65
Viva Goa    X   71

### Italian
A16    ☺ XX   61
Delarosa    X   65
Florio    XX   66
Sociale    ☺ XX   71
SPQR    ❀ XX   72

### Japanese
An Japanese    X   61
Kiss    X   68

### Mediterranean
Bistro Aix    ☺ XX   63

### Mexican
Mamacita    ☺ XX   68

### Vegetarian
Greens    X   67

## Mission

### American
Blue Plate    XX   81

### Argentinian
Lolinda    XX   90

### Californian
Al's Place    ❀ XX   79
Aster    ❀ XX   80
Central Kitchen    XX   83
Heirloom Café    XX   86

Indexes ▶ Cuisines by Neighborhood

**Chamorro**
Prubechu ... X ... 95

**Contemporary**
Commonwealth ... ✿ XX ... 84
Lazy Bear ... ✿✿ XX ... 89

**Eastern European**
Bar Tartine ... ☺ XX ... 78
Paprika ... X ... 93

**Fusion**
Californios ... ✿ XX ... 82

**Hawaiian**
'āina ... ☺ X ... 78

**International**
Myriad ... X ... 91

**Italian**
Beretta ... X ... 81
Delfina ... ☺ XX ... 83
flour + water ... X ... 85
La Ciccia ... XX ... 87
Locanda ... XX ... 88
Piccino ... XX ... 93

**Japanese**
Ichi Sushi + Ni Bar ... XX ... 86
Izakaya Rintaro ... ☺ XX ... 87
Yuzuki ... ☺ X ... 97

**Mediterranean**
STEM Kitchen & Garden ... XX ... 96

**Mexican**
La Torta Gorda ... X ... 88
Pancho Villa Taqueria ... X ... 91
Papalote ... X ... 92
Papito ... X ... 92
Regalito ... X ... 95

**Peruvian**
Piqueo's ... XX ... 94

**Pizza**
PizzaHacker ... X ... 94

**Seafood**
Mission Street Oyster Bar ... XX ... 90

**Thai**
Farmhouse Kitchen Thai ☺ X ... 85

**Turkish**
Tuba ... XX ... 97

**Vegan**
Shizen ... XX ... 96

## Nob Hill

**Afghan**
Helmand Palace ... XX ... 105

**American**
aliment ... X ... 103
Belcampo ... X ... 103
Huxley ... X ... 105

**Austrian**
Leopold's ... XX ... 107

**Californian**
Lord Stanley ... ✿ XX ... 109

**Chinese**
Mister Jiu's ... ✿ XX ... 111
Oriental Pearl ... XX ... 112
Z & Y ... ☺ X ... 115

**Contemporary**
Mason Pacific ... ☺ XX ... 108
Parallel 37 ... XxX ... 112
1760 ... XX ... 113
Sons & Daughters ... ✿ XX ... 114
Stones Throw ... X ... 115

**French**
La Folie ... XxX ... 107

**Fusion**
Keiko à Nob Hill ... ✿ XxX ... 106

**Hawaiian**
Liholiho Yacht Club ... XX ... 108

**Italian**
Acquerello ... ✿✿ XxX ... 102
Seven Hills ... XX ... 113

**Japanese**
Mensho ... X ... 110

**Mediterranean**
Frascati ... XX ... 104

**Pizza**
Gioia ... X ... 104

**Thai**
Modern Thai ... X ... 110

## North Beach

### American
| | | |
|---|---|---|
| Doc Ricketts | X | 121 |
| Park Tavern | XX | 126 |
| Waxman's | XX | 129 |

### Asian
| | | |
|---|---|---|
| house (the) | X | 124 |

### Basque
| | | |
|---|---|---|
| Piperade | XX | 126 |

### Chinese
| | | |
|---|---|---|
| Lai Hong Lounge | ⊛ X | 125 |

### Contemporary
| | | |
|---|---|---|
| Coi | ❀❀ XxX | 122 |
| Gary Danko | ❀ XxX | 123 |

### French
| | | |
|---|---|---|
| Café Jacqueline | X | 120 |

### Greek
| | | |
|---|---|---|
| Kokkari Estiatorio | ⊛ XX | 125 |

### Italian
| | | |
|---|---|---|
| Cotogna | ⊛ XX | 121 |
| Quince | ❀❀❀ XxxX | 127 |
| Tosca Café | XX | 129 |

### Pizza
| | | |
|---|---|---|
| Carmel Pizza Company | X | 120 |
| Il Casaro | X | 124 |
| Tony's Pizza Napoletana | X | 128 |

### Thai
| | | |
|---|---|---|
| Tamarind Hall | X | 128 |

## Richmond & Sunset

### American
| | | |
|---|---|---|
| Outerlands | X | 139 |
| Park Chow | X | 140 |

### Burmese
| | | |
|---|---|---|
| Burma Superstar | X | 135 |

### Californian
| | | |
|---|---|---|
| Sutro's | XX | 142 |

### Chinese
| | | |
|---|---|---|
| Dragon Beaux | XX | 136 |
| San Tung | X | 141 |
| Sichuan Home | ⊛ X | 141 |

### French
| | | |
|---|---|---|
| Chapeau! | ⊛ X | 135 |

### Greek
| | | |
|---|---|---|
| Orexi | XX | 139 |

### Italian
| | | |
|---|---|---|
| Fiorella | X | 136 |
| Trattoria da Vittorio | XX | 142 |

### Japanese
| | | |
|---|---|---|
| Kappou Gomi | ⊛ X | 137 |
| Wako | ❀ X | 143 |

### Moroccan
| | | |
|---|---|---|
| Aziza | ❀ XX | 134 |

### Persian
| | | |
|---|---|---|
| Lavash | XX | 138 |

### Pizza
| | | |
|---|---|---|
| Pizzetta 211 | X | 140 |

### Thai
| | | |
|---|---|---|
| Khan Toke Thai House | X | 137 |

### Turkish
| | | |
|---|---|---|
| Kitchen Istanbul | X | 138 |

## SoMa

### American
| | | |
|---|---|---|
| Cockscomb | XX | 154 |
| Marlowe | XX | 158 |
| Prospect | XxX | 163 |
| Twenty Five Lusk | XxX | 167 |

### Asian
| | | |
|---|---|---|
| Benu | ❀❀❀ XxX | 152 |

### Californian
| | | |
|---|---|---|
| Bar Agricole | XX | 150 |
| Boulevard | XX | 153 |
| One Market | XX | 162 |
| RN74 | XX | 163 |
| Saison | ❀❀❀ XxX | 165 |

### Chinese
| | | |
|---|---|---|
| M. Y. China | ⊛ XX | 160 |
| Yank Sing | ⊛ XX | 169 |

### Contemporary
| | | |
|---|---|---|
| AQ | XX | 150 |
| Luce | ❀ XxX | 157 |
| Perennial (The) | XX | 162 |

## Indexes ▸ Cuisines by Neighborhood

### European
Volta  XxX  168

### French
Fringale  XX  155

### Gastropub
Cavalier (The)  XX  153

### International
In Situ  XX  155

### Italian
54 Mint  XX  154

### Japanese
Hashiri  ❀ XxX  156
Okane  ⊛ X  160
Omakase  ❀ X  161

### Mediterranean
Barcha  XX  151
Trou Normand  ▤  166

### Moroccan
Mourad  ❀ XxX  159

### Pizza
Montesacro Pinseria -Enoteca  X  158
Una Pizza Napoletana  X  167
Zero Zero  ⊛ XX  169

### Seafood
Waterbar  XX  168

### Spanish
Bellota  XX  151

### Sri Lankan
1601 Bar & Kitchen  ⊛ XX  164

### Thai
Saap Ver  X  164

### Vietnamese
Tin Vietnamese  X  166

## EAST BAY

### Afghan
Kamdesh (Oakland)  X  196

### American
Brown Sugar Kitchen (Oakland)  X  179
FIVE (Berkeley)  ⊛ XX  189
Homestead (Oakland)  X  193
Hopscotch (Oakland)  X  194

Wood Tavern (Oakland)  ⊛ XX  209

### Asian
Hawker Fare (Oakland)  X  192

### Californian
Camino (Oakland)  X  181
Chez Panisse (Berkeley)  XX  182
Gather (Berkeley)  X  189
Rivoli (Berkeley)  XX  204

### Cambodian
Battambang (Oakland)  X  177

### Caribbean
Kingston 11 (Oakland)  X  197
Miss Ollie's (Oakland)  X  200

### Chinese
China Village (Albany)  ⊛ XX  183
Great China (Berkeley)  ⊛ XX  190

### Contemporary
Commis (Oakland)  ❀❀ XX  185
Haven (Oakland)  XX  191

### Eastern European
Babushka (Walnut Creek)  X  176
Mama Papa Lithuania
  (Alameda)  X  199

### Ethiopian
Barcote (Oakland)  X  177
Café Colucci (Oakland)  X  180
Café Romanat (Oakland)  X  180

### French
Michel Bistro (Oakland)  ⊛ X  199

### Gastropub
Longbranch Saloon (Berkeley)  X  198
Sidebar (Oakland)  X  206

### Greek
Pathos (Berkeley)  XX  202

### Indian
High Peaks Kitchen (Oakland)  X  192
Royal Indian Grill (Danville)  X  205

### International
Va de Vi (Walnut Creek)  XX  209

### Italian
Bellanico (Oakland)  XX  178
Belotti Ristorante e Bottega
  (Oakland)  X  178

| Corso *(Berkeley)* | ⊛ | X | 184 |
| Oliveto *(Oakland)* | | XX | 202 |
| Riva Cucina *(Berkeley)* | | X | 204 |
| Trabocco *(Alameda)* | | XX | 208 |

## Japanese
| | | | |
|---|---|---|---|
| Delage *(Oakland)* | | X | 186 |
| Hina Yakitori *(Oakland)* | | X | 193 |
| Ippuku *(Berkeley)* | ⊛ | X | 195 |
| Iyasare *(Berkeley)* | | XX | 196 |
| Ramen Shop *(Oakland)* | | X | 203 |

## Korean
| | | | |
|---|---|---|---|
| Ohgane *(Oakland)* | | X | 201 |
| Sahn Maru *(Oakland)* | | X | 205 |

## Latin American
| | | |
|---|---|---|
| Cholita Linda *(Oakland)* | X | 183 |

## Malaysian
| | | |
|---|---|---|
| Chilli Padi *(Oakland)* | XX | 182 |

## Mediterranean
| | | |
|---|---|---|
| Esin *(Danville)* | XX | 188 |
| Shakewell *(Oakland)* | XX | 206 |

## Mexican
| | | | |
|---|---|---|---|
| Calavera *(Oakland)* | | XX | 181 |
| Comal *(Berkeley)* | ⊛ | XX | 184 |
| Cosecha *(Oakland)* | | X | 186 |
| Doña Tomás *(Oakland)* | | X | 187 |
| Los Cilantros *(Berkeley)* | | X | 198 |
| Nido *(Oakland)* | | X | 201 |
| Tacos Sinaloa *(Berkeley)* | ⊛ | X | 207 |
| Tacubaya *(Berkeley)* | | X | 207 |

## Nepali
| | | |
|---|---|---|
| Hamro Aangan *(Albany)* | X | 191 |

## Pizza
| | | |
|---|---|---|
| Boot and Shoe Service *(Oakland)* | XX | 179 |
| Pizzaiolo *(Oakland)* | X | 203 |

## Seafood
| | | |
|---|---|---|
| alaMar *(Oakland)* | X | 176 |

## Spanish
| | | |
|---|---|---|
| Duende *(Oakland)* | XX | 187 |
| La Marcha *(Berkeley)* | X | 197 |

## Thai
| | | | |
|---|---|---|---|
| Grand Avenue Thai *(Oakland)* | | XX | 190 |
| Imm Thai Street Food *(Berkeley)* | | X | 194 |
| Infinite Thai Eatery *(Oakland)* | | XX | 195 |
| Thai House *(Danville)* | ⊛ | XX | 208 |

## Vegan
| | | | |
|---|---|---|---|
| Millennium *(Oakland)* | ⊛ | XX | 200 |

## Vegetarian
| | | |
|---|---|---|
| Encuentro *(Oakland)* | X | 188 |

# MARIN

## American
| | | |
|---|---|---|
| Buckeye Roadhouse *(Mill Valley)* | XX | 217 |
| Bungalow 44 *(Mill Valley)* | XX | 218 |
| El Paseo *(Mill Valley)* | XX | 220 |
| Nick's Cove *(Marshall)* | XX | 225 |

## Burmese
| | | |
|---|---|---|
| Burmatown *(Corte Madera)* | X | 218 |

## Californian
| | | | |
|---|---|---|---|
| Barrel House Tavern *(Sausalito)* | | XX | 217 |
| Molina *(Mill Valley)* | | XX | 224 |
| Sir and Star *(Olema)* | ⊛ | XX | 228 |
| The Western Room *(Nicasio)* | | XX | 230 |

## French
| | | | |
|---|---|---|---|
| Left Bank *(Larkspur)* | | XX | 222 |
| Le Garage *(Sausalito)* | ⊛ | X | 223 |

## Indian
| | | |
|---|---|---|
| Arti *(Lagunitas)* | X | 215 |
| Prabh *(Mill Valley)* | XX | 227 |

## Italian
| | | | |
|---|---|---|---|
| Frantoio *(Mill Valley)* | | XX | 221 |
| Osteria Stellina *(Point Reyes Station)* | | XX | 225 |
| Picco *(Larkspur)* | | XX | 226 |
| Poggio *(Sausalito)* | ⊛ | XX | 226 |
| Valenti & Co. *(San Anselmo)* | | XX | 230 |

## Japanese
| | | | |
|---|---|---|---|
| Sushi Ran *(Sausalito)* | ⊛ | XX | 229 |
| Village Sake *(Fairfax)* | ⊛ | X | 231 |

## Latin American
| | | |
|---|---|---|
| Marinitas *(San Anselmo)* | XX | 224 |

## Mediterranean
| | | | |
|---|---|---|---|
| Insalata's *(San Anselmo)* | ⊛ | XX | 222 |
| Marché aux Fleurs *(Ross)* | | XX | 223 |

## Mexican
| | | |
|---|---|---|
| Copita *(Sausalito)* | XX | 219 |
| El Huarache Loco *(Larkspur)* | X | 220 |

### Pizza
Bar Bocce *(Sausalito)* 𝕏 216
Cafe Reyes *(Point Reyes Station)* 𝕏 219

### Puerto Rican
Sol Food *(San Rafael)* 𝕏 228

### Seafood
Fish *(Sausalito)* 𝕏 221

### Thai
Arun *(Novato)* 𝕏 215
Baan *(San Anselmo)* 𝕏 216
R'Noh Thai *(Larkspur)* 𝕏𝕏 227
Thai Aroi-Dee *(San Rafael)* 𝕏 229

# PENINSULA

### Afghan
Kabul *(San Carlos)* 𝕏𝕏 248

### American
Bradley's Fine Diner
  *(Menlo Park)* 𝕏𝕏 239

### Asian
Kemuri Japanese Barú
  *(Redwood City)* 𝕏 249

### Californian
Flea St. *(Menlo Park)* 𝕏𝕏 246

### Chinese
Boiling Beijing *(San Bruno)* 𝕏𝕏 239
Cooking Papa *(Foster City)* 𝕏 241
Crouching Tiger *(Redwood City)* 𝕏𝕏 242
Fashion Wok *(Foster City)* 𝕏 244
Fey *(Menlo Park)* 𝕏𝕏 245
Happy Sichuan *(Millbrae)* 𝕏𝕏 247
Hong Kong Flower Lounge
  *(Millbrae)* 𝕏𝕏 247
Koi Palace *(Daly City)* 𝕏𝕏 250
Sichuan Chong Qing
  *(San Mateo)* 𝕏 260
wonderful *(Millbrae)* 😊 𝕏 267
Yi Yuan *(Millbrae)* 𝕏𝕏 269
Yummy Szechuan *(Millbrae)* 𝕏 269

### Contemporary
John Bentley's *(Redwood City)* 𝕏𝕏 248
Madera *(Menlo Park)* 🌸 𝕏𝕏𝕏 253
Viognier *(San Mateo)* 𝕏𝕏𝕏 267

### French
Cuisinett *(San Carlos)* 𝕏 242

### Gastropub
Striped Pig (The) *(Redwood City)* 𝕏 261
Village Pub (The) *(Woodside)* 🌸 𝕏𝕏𝕏 266

### Indian
Ark Grill *(Half Moon Bay)* 𝕏𝕏 238
Kamakshi's Kitchen *(San Carlos)* 𝕏 249
Rasa *(Burlingame)* 🌸 𝕏𝕏 258
Rasoi *(Burlingame)* 𝕏𝕏 257

### International
All Spice *(San Mateo)* 𝕏𝕏 238

### Italian
Delizie *(San Carlos)* 𝕏𝕏 243
Donato Enoteca *(Redwood City)* 𝕏𝕏 244
Locanda Positano *(San Carlos)* 𝕏𝕏 251
Pasta Moon *(Half Moon Bay)* 𝕏𝕏 255
Quattro *(East Palo Alto)* 𝕏𝕏 256
Vespucci *(San Mateo)* 𝕏𝕏 265

### Jamaican
Flavas Jamaican
  Grill *(South San Francisco)* 𝕏 245

### Japanese
Gintei *(San Bruno)* 𝕏𝕏 246
Mitsunobu *(Menlo Park)* 𝕏 254
Ramen Dojo *(San Mateo)* 𝕏 257
Sakae *(Burlingame)* 𝕏 259
Sushi Sam's *(San Mateo)* 𝕏 261
Sushi Yoshizumi *(San Mateo)* 🌸 𝕏 262
Wakuriya *(San Mateo)* 🌸 𝕏 268

### Latin American
LV Mar *(Redwood City)* 𝕏𝕏 252

### Mediterranean
Cetrella *(Half Moon Bay)* 𝕏𝕏𝕏 240
Cobani *(San Mateo)* 𝕏 241
Taste In Mediterranean
  Food *(Burlingame)* 𝕏 264

### Mexican
Café Capistrano
  *(Half Moon Bay)* 𝕏 240
Diablo's JJ *(Burlingame)* 𝕏 243
La Viga *(Redwood City)* 𝕏 251
Magda Luna *(Burlingame)* 𝕏 252
Mama Coco *(Menlo Park)* 𝕏 254
Taqueria El Metate *(Belmont)* 𝕏 263

Taqueria San Bruno *(San Bruno)*  X  264

## Persian
Shalizaar *(Belmont)*  XX  260

## Peruvian
La Costanera *(Montara)*  ⊛  XX  250

## Pizza
Pazzo *(San Carlos)*  XX  256
Vesta *(Redwood City)*  ⊛  XX  265

## Seafood
New England Lobster Company
    *(Burlingame)*  X  255

## Spanish
Romesco *(Half Moon Bay)*  X  259

## Thai
Sweet Basil *(Foster City)*  XX  263

# SOUTH BAY

## American
Nick's Next Door *(Los Gatos)*  XX  292
Table (The) *(San Jose)*  X  299

## Austrian
Naschmarkt *(Campbell)*  XX  292

## Barbecue
Smoking Pig BBQ *(San Jose)*  X  297

## Caribbean
Back A Yard *(San Jose)*  X  279

## Chinese
Din Tai Fung *(Santa Clara)*  XX  284
Fu Lam Mum *(Mountain View)*  X  287
South Legend *(Milpitas)*  X  298

## Contemporary
Baumé *(Palo Alto)*  ❀❀  XxX  280
Bird Dog *(Palo Alto)*  XX  281
Chez TJ *(Mountain View)*  ❀  XxX  283
Manresa *(Los Gatos)*  ❀❀❀  XxX  290
Plumed Horse *(Saratoga)*  ❀  XxX  296

## Ethiopian
Walia *(San Jose)*  X  303
Zeni *(San Jose)*  X  304

## French
Pastis *(Palo Alto)*  X  295
Zola *(Palo Alto)*  ⊛  XX  305

## Gastropub
Liquid Bread *(Campbell)*  X  289

## Greek
Dio Deka *(Los Gatos)*  XX  284
Evvia *(Palo Alto)*  ⊛  XX  286

## Indian
Chennai Kings
    *(Mountain View)*  X  282
Kabab & Curry's *(Santa Clara)*  X  288
Swaad *(San Jose)*  X  299
Ulavacharu *(Sunnyvale)*  X  301
Zareen's *(Mountain View)*  X  304

## Indonesian
INDO *(Palo Alto)*  XX  287

## International
Orchard City Kitchen
    *(Campbell)*  ⊛  XX  293

## Israeli
Falafel STOP *(Sunnyvale)*  X  286
Oren's Hummus Shop
    *(Palo Alto)*  X  294

## Italian
Doppio Zero *(Mountain View)*  XX  285

## Japanese
Orenchi *(Santa Clara)*  X  294
Sawa Sushi *(Sunnyvale)*  X  295
Sumika *(Los Altos)*  X  298
Tanto *(Sunnyvale)*  X  300

## Korean
Jang Su Jang *(Santa Clara)*  XX  288

## Latin American
Voya (The) *(Mountain View)*  XX  302

## Mediterranean
Urfa Bistro *(Los Altos)*  X  302

## Mexican
Zona Rosa *(San Jose)*  X  305

## Middle Eastern
DishDash *(Sunnyvale)*  XX  285

## Pizza
Napoletana Pizzeria
    *(Mountain View)*  X  291
Oak & Rye *(Los Gatos)*  XX  293

Indexes ▶ Cuisines by Neighborhood

### Portuguese
Adega *(San Jose)* ❀ XX 278

### Seafood
Sea (The) *(Palo Alto)* XxX 297

### Southern
Bywater (The) *(Los Gatos)* ⊜ X 282

### Steakhouse
Alexander's Steakhouse
  *(Cupertino)* XxX 279

### Vegetarian
Mint & Basil *(Milpitas)* X 291

### Vietnamese
Bun Bo Hue An Nam *(San Jose)* X 281
Lau Hai San *(San Jose)* X 289
Tamarine *(Palo Alto)* XX 300
Thiên Long *(San Jose)* X 301
Vung Tau *(San Jose)* XX 303

## WINE COUNTRY

### Napa Valley

### American
Ad Hoc *(Yountville)* XX 314
Boon Fly Café *(Napa)* X 317
Bounty Hunter *(Napa)* XX 318
Cindy's Backstreet Kitchen
  *(St. Helena)* XX 322
Evangeline *(Calistoga)* XX 324
Goose & Gander *(St. Helena)* XX 325
Market *(St. Helena)* XX 330
Mustards Grill *(Yountville)* XX 331
Norman Rose Tavern *(Napa)* XX 331
Rutherford Grill *(Rutherford)* XX 335
Sam's Social Club *(Calistoga)* XX 335
Torc *(Napa)* XX 338

### Californian
Archetype *(St. Helena)* XX 315
Auberge du Soleil
  *(Rutherford)* ❀ XxX 316
Brix *(Napa)* XX 320
FARM *(Napa)* XxX 324
Farmstead *(St. Helena)* ⊜ XX 325
Harvest Table *(St. Helena)* XX 327
Lucy *(Yountville)* XX 328
Solbar *(Calistoga)* ❀ XX 336

### Contemporary
French Laundry (The)
  *(Yountville)* ❀❀❀ XxxX 326
La Toque *(Napa)* ❀ XxX 329
Redd *(Yountville)* XX 333
Restaurant at Meadowood (The)
  *(St. Helena)* ❀❀❀ XxxX 334
Terra *(St. Helena)* ❀ XxX 337

### French
Angèle *(Napa)* XX 314
Bistro Jeanty *(Yountville)* ⊜ XX 317
Bouchon *(Yountville)* ❀ XX 319

### Fusion
Two Birds/One Stone
  *(St. Helena)* ⊜ XX 338

### International
Grace's Table *(Napa)* ⊜ XX 327

### Italian
Bistro Don Giovanni *(Napa)* XX 315
Bottega *(Yountville)* XX 318
Ca'Momi Osteria *(Napa)* XX 321
Ciccio *(Yountville)* XX 322
Cook St. Helena
  *(St. Helena)* ⊜ XX 323
Oenotri *(Napa)* ⊜ XX 332
Redd Wood *(Yountville)* ⊜ XX 333

### Japanese
Miminashi *(Napa)* X 330

### Mexican
C Casa *(Napa)* X 321
La Taquiza *(Napa)* X 328

### Spanish
Zuzu *(Napa)* 🍴 339

### Steakhouse
Cole's Chop House *(Napa)* XX 323
Press *(St. Helena)* XxX 332

### Vietnamese
Bui Bistro *(Napa)* XX 320

### Sonoma County

### American
Chalkboard *(Healdsburg)* ⊜ XX 350

400

County Bench (The)
*(Santa Rosa)* XX 351
Monti's Rotisserie
*(Santa Rosa)* ⊕ XX 360
Spinster Sisters *(Santa Rosa)* XX 368
zazu kitchen + farm
*(Sebastopol)* XX 373

## Asian
Chinois *(Windsor)* X 351

## Californian
Backyard *(Forestville)* ⊕ X 346
Barndiva *(Healdsburg)* XX 346
Boon Eat + Drink
*(Guerneville)* X 347
Cafe La Haye *(Sonoma)* XX 348
Dry Creek Kitchen
*(Healdsburg)* XxX 353
El Dorado Kitchen *(Sonoma)* XX 354
Farmhouse Inn & Restaurant
*(Forestville)* ⊛ XxX 355
Glen Ellen Star *(Glen Ellen)* ⊕ X 354
Harvest Moon Cafe *(Sonoma)* X 356
John Ash & Co. *(Santa Rosa)* XX 357
Kenwood (The) *(Kenwood)* XX 357
Luma *(Petaluma)* X 358
Peter Lowell's *(Sebastopol)* X 361
Revival *(Guerneville)* XX 362
Santé *(Sonoma)* XxX 365
SHED Café *(Healdsburg)* ⊕ X 367
Terrapin Creek
*(Bodega Bay)* ⊛ XX 370
the fig café *(Glen Ellen)* XX 369
Valette *(Healdsburg)* XX 371
Willow Wood Market Cafe
*(Graton)* X 372

## Contemporary
Madrona Manor
*(Healdsburg)* ⊛ XxX 359
Spoonbar *(Healdsburg)* XX 368

## French
Bistro 29 *(Santa Rosa)* ⊕ XX 347

## International
Oso *(Sonoma)* X 361
Willi's Wine Bar *(Santa Rosa)* XX 372

## Italian
Campo Fina *(Healdsburg)* X 349
Cucina Paradiso *(Petaluma)* XX 352
Della Santina's *(Sonoma)* XX 352
Diavola *(Geyserville)* ⊕ XX 353
Risibisi *(Petaluma)* ⊕ XX 363
Rustic *(Geyserville)* XX 364
Scopa *(Healdsburg)* ⊕ X 366
Sugo *(Petaluma)* X 369

## Japanese
Hana *(Rohnert Park)* XX 356
Ramen Gaijin *(Sebastopol)* ⊕ X 362

## Mediterranean
Central Market *(Petaluma)* XX 350

## Mexican
Mateo's Cocina Latina
*(Healdsburg)* XX 360

## Nepali
Yeti *(Glen Ellen)* XX 373

## Peruvian
Sazón *(Santa Rosa)* X 365

## Pizza
Rosso *(Santa Rosa)* X 363

## Portuguese
Café Lucia *(Healdsburg)* XX 349
LaSalette *(Sonoma)* XX 358

## Seafood
Santa Rosa Seafood Raw Bar &
Grill *(Santa Rosa)* X 364
Seaside Metal *(Guerneville)* X 366
Willi's Seafood & Raw Bar
*(Healdsburg)* XX 371

## Spanish
Bravas *(Healdsburg)* ⊕ XX 348

## Thai
SEA Thai *(Santa Rosa)* XX 367

Indexes ▶ Cuisines by Neighborhood

# Starred Restaurants

**W**ithin the selection we offer you, some restaurants deserve to be highlighted for their particularly good cuisine. When giving one, two, or three Michelin stars, there are a number of elements that we consider including the quality of the ingredients, the technical skill and flair that goes into their preparation, the blend and clarity of flavours, and the balance of the menu. Just as important is the ability to produce excellent cooking time and again. We make as many visits as we need, so that our readers may be assured of quality and consistency.

A two or three-star restaurant has to offer something very special in its cuisine; a real element of creativity, originality, or "personality" that sets it apart from the rest. Three stars – our highest award – are given to the choicest restaurants, where the whole dining experience is superb.

Cuisine in any style, modern or traditional, may be eligible for a star. Due to the fact we apply the same independent standards everywhere, the awards have become benchmarks of reliability and excellence in over 20 countries in Europe and Asia, particularly in France, where we have awarded stars for 100 years, and where the phrase "Now that's real three-star quality!" has entered into the language.

The awarding of a star is based solely on the quality of the cuisine.

❀ ❀ ❀

## Exceptional cuisine, worth a special journey

One always eats here extremely well, sometimes superbly. Distinctive dishes are precisely executed, using superlative ingredients.

| | | |
|---|---|---|
| Benu | XxX | 152 |
| Manresa | XxX | 290 |
| Quince | XxxX | 127 |
| Saison | XxX | 165 |
| French Laundry (The) | XxxX | 326 |
| Restaurant at Meadowood (The) | XxxX | 334 |

❀ ❀

## Excellent cuisine, worth a detour

Skillfully and carefully crafted dishes of outstanding quality.

| | | |
|---|---|---|
| Acquerello | XxX | 102 |
| Atelier Crenn | XX | 62 |
| Baumé | XxX | 280 |
| Campton Place | XxX | 47 |
| Coi | XxX | 122 |
| Commis | XX | 185 |
| Lazy Bear | XX | 89 |

❀

## A very good restaurant in its category

A place offering cuisine prepared to a consistently high standard.

| | | |
|---|---|---|
| Adega | XX | 278 |
| Al's Place | XX | 79 |
| Aster | XX | 80 |
| Auberge du Soleil | XxX | 316 |
| Aziza | XX | 134 |
| Bouchon | XX | 319 |
| Californios | XX | 82 |
| Chez TJ | XxX | 283 |
| Commonwealth | XX | 84 |
| Farmhouse Inn & Restaurant | XxX | 355 |
| Gary Danko | XxX | 123 |
| Hashiri | XxX | 156 |

| | | |
|---|---|---|
| jū-ni | XX | 32 |
| Keiko à Nob Hill | XxX | 106 |
| Kin Khao | X | 52 |
| La Toque | XxX | 329 |
| Lord Stanley | XX | 109 |
| Luce | XxX | 157 |
| Madera | XxX | 253 |
| Madrona Manor | XxX | 359 |
| Michael Mina | XxX | 54 |
| Mister Jiu's | XX | 111 |
| Mosu | XX | 34 |
| Mourad | XxX | 159 |
| Nico | XX | 69 |
| Octavia | XX | 70 |
| Omakase | X | 161 |
| Plumed Horse | XxX | 296 |
| Rasa | XX | 258 |
| Solbar | XX | 336 |
| Sons & Daughters | XX | 114 |
| SPQR | XX | 72 |
| Spruce | XX | 73 |
| State Bird Provisions | XX | 39 |
| Sushi Yoshizumi | X | 262 |
| Terra | XxX | 337 |
| Terrapin Creek | XX | 370 |
| Progress (The) | XX | 37 |
| Village Pub (The) | XxX | 266 |
| Wako | X | 143 |
| Wakuriya | X | 268 |

# Bib Gourmand

This symbol indicates our inspectors' favorites for good value. For $40 or less, you can enjoy two courses and a glass of wine or a dessert (not including tax or gratuity).

| | | | | | | |
|---|---|---|---|---|---|---|
| 'āina | ☺ | ✗ | 78 | Mamacita | ✗✗ | 68 |
| Anchor Oyster Bar | | ✗ | 18 | Mason Pacific | ✗✗ | 108 |
| A16 | | ✗✗ | 61 | Michel Bistro | ✗ | 199 |
| Backyard | | ✗ | 346 | Millennium | ✗✗ | 200 |
| Bar Tartine | | ✗✗ | 78 | Monti's Rotisserie | ✗✗ | 360 |
| Bistro Aix | | ✗✗ | 63 | M. Y. China | ✗✗ | 160 |
| Bistro Jeanty | | ✗✗ | 317 | Nopalito | ✗ | 35 |
| Bistro 29 | | ✗✗ | 347 | Oenotri | ✗✗ | 332 |
| Bravas | | ✗✗ | 348 | Okane | ✗ | 160 |
| Bywater (The) | | ✗ | 282 | Orchard City Kitchen | ✗✗ | 293 |
| Chalkboard | | ✗✗ | 350 | Poggio | ✗✗ | 226 |
| Chapeau! | | ✗ | 135 | Ramen Gaijin | ✗ | 362 |
| China Village | | ✗✗ | 183 | Redd Wood | ✗✗ | 333 |
| Comal | | ✗✗ | 184 | Rich Table | ✗✗ | 36 |
| Cook St. Helena | | ✗✗ | 323 | Risibisi | ✗✗ | 363 |
| Coqueta | | ✗✗ | 48 | Scopa | ✗ | 366 |
| Corso | | ✗ | 184 | SHED Café | ✗ | 367 |
| Cotogna | | ✗✗ | 121 | Sichuan Home | ✗ | 141 |
| Delfina | | ✗✗ | 83 | Sir and Star | ✗✗ | 228 |
| Del Popolo | | ✗ | 48 | 1601 Bar & Kitchen | ✗✗ | 164 |
| Diavola | | ✗✗ | 353 | Sociale | ✗✗ | 71 |
| Dosa | | ✗✗ | 65 | Starbelly | ✗✗ | 21 |
| Evvia | | ✗✗ | 286 | Sushi Ran | ✗✗ | 229 |
| Farmhouse Kitchen Thai | | ✗ | 85 | Tacos Sinaloa | ✗ | 207 |
| Farmstead | | ✗✗ | 325 | Thai House | ✗✗ | 208 |
| FIVE | | ✗✗ | 189 | Trestle | ✗✗ | 57 |
| Glen Ellen Star | | ✗ | 354 | Tsubasa | ✗ | 40 |
| Grace's Table | | ✗✗ | 327 | Two Birds/One Stone | ✗✗ | 338 |
| Great China | | ✗✗ | 190 | Vesta | ✗✗ | 265 |
| Hong Kong Lounge II | | ✗✗ | 67 | Village Sake | ✗ | 231 |
| Insalata's | | ✗✗ | 222 | wonderful | ✗ | 267 |
| Ippuku | | ✗ | 195 | Wood Tavern | ✗✗ | 209 |
| Izakaya Rintaro | | ✗✗ | 87 | Yank Sing | ✗✗ | 169 |
| Kappou Gomi | | ✗ | 137 | Yuzuki | ✗ | 97 |
| Kokkari Estiatorio | | ✗✗ | 125 | Zero Zero | ✗✗ | 169 |
| La Costanera | | ✗✗ | 250 | Zola | ✗✗ | 305 |
| Lai Hong Lounge | | ✗ | 125 | Z & Y | ✗ | 115 |
| Le Garage | | ✗ | 223 | | | |

# Under $25

| | | |
|---|---|---|
| Arti | X | 215 |
| Arun | X | 215 |
| Back A Yard | X | 279 |
| Barcote | X | 177 |
| Battambang | X | 177 |
| Brown Sugar Kitchen | X | 179 |
| Bui Bistro | XX | 320 |
| Bun Bo Hue An Nam | X | 281 |
| Café Capistrano | X | 240 |
| Café Colucci | X | 180 |
| Café Romanat | X | 180 |
| Campo Fina | X | 349 |
| Carmel Pizza Company | X | 120 |
| C Casa | X | 321 |
| China Village | 😊 XX | 183 |
| Cholita Linda | X | 183 |
| Cobani | X | 241 |
| Cooking Papa | X | 241 |
| Cosecha | X | 186 |
| Crouching Tiger | XX | 242 |
| Diablo's JJ | X | 243 |
| Dragon Well | X | 66 |
| El Huarache Loco | X | 220 |
| Falafel STOP | X | 286 |
| Fashion Wok | X | 244 |
| Flavas Jamaican Grill | X | 245 |
| 4505 Burgers & BBQ | X | 29 |
| Fu Lam Mum | X | 287 |
| Grand Avenue Thai | XX | 190 |
| Hamro Aangan | X | 191 |
| Hawker Fare | X | 192 |
| Homage | X | 51 |
| Imm Thai Street Food | X | 194 |
| Infinite Thai Eatery | XX | 195 |
| Iza Ramen | X | 30 |
| Kabab & Curry's | X | 288 |
| Kamakshi's Kitchen | X | 249 |
| Kamdesh | X | 196 |
| Khan Toke Thai House | X | 137 |
| La Taquiza | X | 328 |
| La Torta Gorda | X | 88 |
| La Viga | X | 251 |
| Los Cilantros | X | 198 |
| Magda Luna | X | 252 |
| Mama Coco | X | 254 |
| Mensho | X | 110 |
| Mint & Basil | X | 291 |
| Modern Thai | X | 110 |
| Montesacro Pinseria-Enoteca | X | 158 |
| Orenchi | X | 294 |
| Oren's Hummus Shop | X | 294 |
| Pancho Villa Taqueria | X | 91 |
| Papalote | X | 92 |
| Papito | X | 92 |
| Paprika | X | 93 |
| Ramen Dojo | X | 257 |
| R'Noh Thai | XX | 227 |
| Smoking Pig BBQ | X | 297 |
| Tacos Sinaloa | 😊 X | 207 |
| Tacubaya | X | 207 |
| Tadu | X | 38 |
| Taqueria El Metate | X | 263 |
| Taqueria San Bruno | X | 264 |
| Taste In Mediterranean Food | X | 264 |
| Thiên Long | X | 301 |
| Tycoon | X | 41 |
| Ulavacharu | X | 301 |
| Urfa Bistro | X | 302 |
| Viva Goa | X | 71 |
| Vung Tau | XX | 303 |
| Walia | X | 303 |
| Zareen's | X | 304 |
| Zeni | X | 304 |

# Credits

MICHELIN
IS CONTINUALLY
INNOVATING
FOR SAFER, CLEANER,
MORE ECONOMICAL,
MORE CONNECTED
AND BETTER ALL
AROUND MOBILITY.

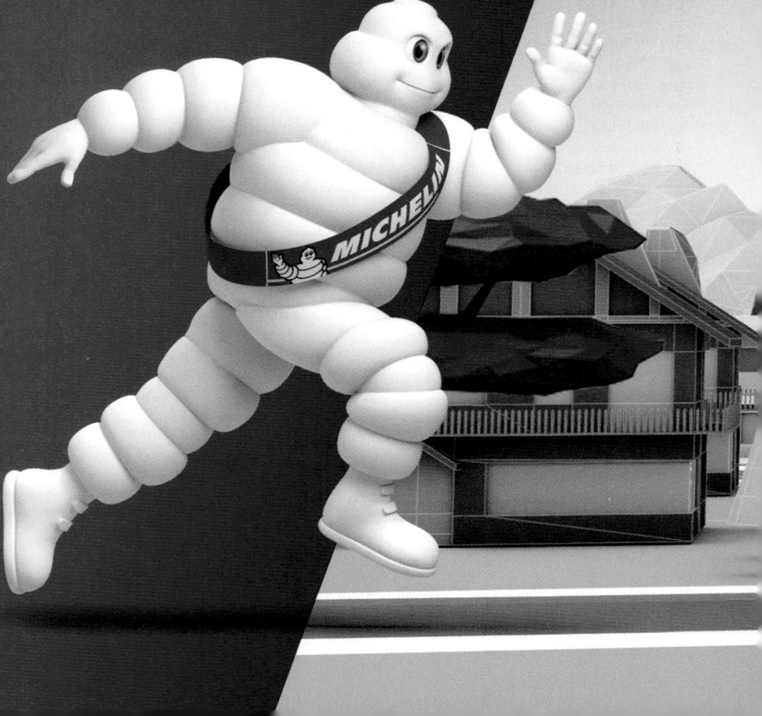

Tires wear more quickly on short urban journeys.

**?**

**TRUE!**

You tend to accelerate and brake more often when driving around town so your tires work harder!
If you are stuck in traffic, keep calm and drive slowly.

Tire pressure only affects your car's safety.

**?**

**FALSE!**

Driving with underinflated tires (0.5 below recommended pressure) doesn't just impact handling and fuel consumption, it will take 8,000 km off tire lifespan.
Make sure you check tire pressure about once a month and before you go on vacation or a long journey.

*If you only encounter* ***winter weather from time to time*** *- sudden showers, snowfall or black ice -* ***one type of tire*** *will do the job.*
?
**TRUE!**
The revolutionary ***MICHELIN CrossClimate*** - the very first summer tire with winter certification - is a practical solution to keep you on the road whatever the weather.

Fitting **2 winter tires** on my car guarantees maximum safety.

**?**

# FALSE!

In the winter, especially when temperatures drop below 44.5°F, to ensure better road grip, all four tires should be identical and fitted at the same time.

**2 WINTER TIRES ONLY =**
risk of compromised road grip.

**4 WINTER TIRES =**
**safer handling** when cornering, driving downhill and braking.

If you regularly encounter rain, snow or black ice, choose a **MICHELIN Alpin tire**. This range offers you sharp handling plus a comfortable ride to safely face the challenge of winter driving.

MICHELIN

# MICHELIN IS COMMITTED

▶ MICHELIN IS THE **GLOBAL LEADER IN FUEL-EFFICIENT TIRES** FOR LIGHT VEHICLES.

▶ *EDUCATING YOUNGSTERS ON ROAD SAFETY FOR BIKES,* NOT FORGETTING TWO-WHEELERS. LOCAL ROAD SAFETY CAMPAIGNS WERE RUN IN **16 COUNTRIES** IN 2015.

# QUIZ

**1** ## TIRES ARE BLACK SO WHY IS THE MICHELIN MAN WHITE?

Back in 1898 when the Michelin Man was first created from a stack of tires, they were made of natural rubber, cotton and sulphur and were therefore light-colored. The composition of tires did not change until after the First World War when carbon black was introduced. But the Michelin Man kept his color!

**2** ## HOW LONG HAS MICHELIN BEEN GUIDING TRAVELERS?

Since 1900. When the MICHELIN guide was published at the turn of the century, it was claimed that it would last for a hundred years. It's still around today and remains a reference with new editions and online restaurant listings in a number of countries.

**3** ## WHEN WAS THE "BIB GOURMAND" INTRODUCED IN THE MICHELIN GUIDE?

The symbol was created in 1997 but as early as 1954 the MICHELIN guide was recommending "exceptional good food at moderate prices." Today, it features on the MICHELIN Restaurants website and app.

If you want to enjoy a fun day out and find out more about Michelin, why not visit the l'Aventure Michelin museum and shop in Clermont-Ferrand, France:

**www.laventuremichelin.com**

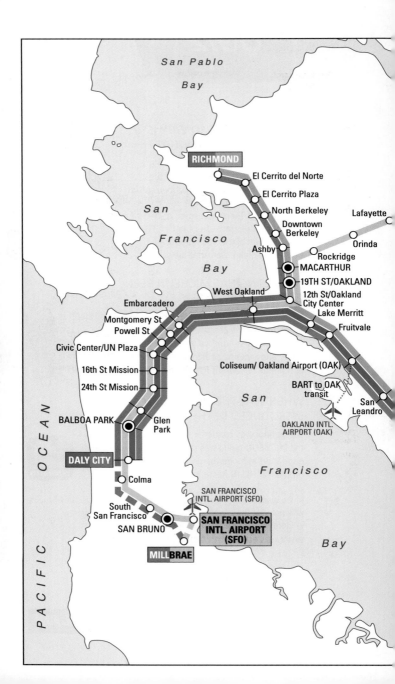

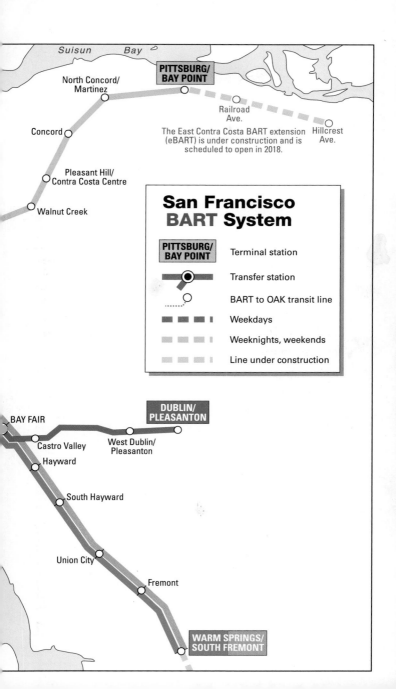

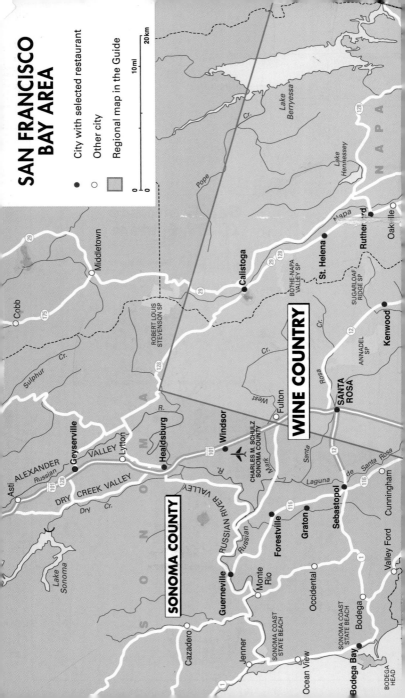